A VICTORIAN SUBURB

Workmen emerging from the United Flexible, probably on a Saturday at dinner time, before the First World War, another week's work done and heading homeward or to the pub.

A HISTORY OF ENFIELD

Volume Two - 1837 to 1914

A VICTORIAN SUBURB

BY

David Pam

Enfield Preservation Society

1992

For the next generation
Tom, Sarah, David and Stephen

A human life, I think, should be well rooted in some spot of a native land, where it may get the love of tender kinship for the face of earth, for the labours men go forth to, for the sounds and actions that haunt it, for whatever will give that early home a familiar unmistakable difference admidst the future widening of knowledge, a spot where the definiteness of early memories may be inwrought with affection.

George Eliot *Daniel Deronda*

© Copyright Enfield Preservation Society 1992

ISBN 0 907318 10 X

Published by Enfield Preservation Society Ltd, 107 Parsonage Lane, Enfield, Middlesex EN2 0AB

Registered Charity No 276451

Designed, typeset and produced by Moorland Publishing Co Ltd, Ashbourne, Derbyshire

Printed in the UK by
The Cromwell Press Ltd
Broughton Gifford, Wiltshire

Contents

ILLUSTRATIONS   vii
MAPS, PLANS AND GRAPHS   xi
NOTES ON SOURCES   xii
ACKNOWLEDGEMENTS   xiii
PREFACE   xv

I VICTORIAN DEVELOPMENTS
   1 Introduction: a Summary   1
   2 Road and Rail   2
   3 Land Companies, Builders and Building Societies   11
   4 The Bush Hill Park Estate   15
   5 The Bycullah and Ridgeway Estates and the Middle Classes   22
   6 Artisans' Dwellings: Chase Side, Lancaster Road and Eastern
      Enfield   30
   7 Enfield Town and Market   38
   8 Banks, Post Office, Police and Telephones   43
   9 Outlying Estates and Great Houses   47
  10 Land Sales and House Building 1897-1903   52

II EDWARDIAN DEVELOPMENTS
   1 Introduction   59
   2 The Great Northern Extension   63
   3 The Grange Park Estate   67
   4 Electric Trams   69
   5 Bush Hill Park and Winchmore Hill   76
   6 The Servant Problem   79
   7 Working-Class Housing   80
   8 Edwardian Changes   81

III EMPLOYMENT
   1 Introduction   94
   2 The Crape Factory   95
   3 The Royal Small Arms Factory   104
   4 The Gas Company   128
   5 The Jute Works and the Cortecine   131
   6 Edison and Swan   133
   7 Strikes and the Unions   137

   8 The Smaller Firms   140
   9 The Power Station   143
 10 Market Gardens and Other Farms   146
 11 Brickmakers   154

IV POVERTY
   1 Introduction   158
   2 The New Poor Law   159
   3 Enfield Workhouse School   161
   4 The House in Chase Side and the Workhouse Infirmary 168
   5 Stoneyard and Charity   171
   6 Poverty in the Nineties   174
   7 Edwardian Poverty   176

V THE ENVIRONMENT AND THE RATEPAYERS
   1 Introduction   184
   2 A Rural Slum   185
   3 Enfield Local Board of Health   187
   4 Penny-Pinching Policies   191
   5 Progress and the Ratepayers   202
   6 Progress Resumed   220
   7 The Urban District Council   231

VI SCHOOLS
   1 Introduction   242
   2 Secondary Education up to the First World War 243
   3 Private and Technical Education   255
   4 Vicar Hodson and the Voluntary Schools 259
   5 The School Board   273
   6 Edwardian Elementary Education   278

VII OUT-AND-OUT CHRISTIANS
   1 Introduction: Churches and Chapels   283
   2 The Vicar Against the Parish   285
   3 God's Church and the Devil's Chapel   294
   4 Late Victorian Respectability and its Decline 303

VIII LEISURE, PLEASURE AND POLITICS
   1 Introduction   309
   2 Culture Mostly Middle-Class   311
   3 The Pleasures of the People   316
   4 Sport   336
   5 Politics   343

Subscribers' List   350
Index   356

Illustrations

Frontispiece	United Flexible Metallic Tubing factory, South Street	
1	GER station Enfield Town, former Cowden Clarke school-house	4
2	GNR Enfield branch under construction 1870	5
3	GNR Enfield terminus	6
4	GNR Enfield terminus, island platform	6
5	Steam trams, New Road Edmonton	8
6	Horse trams, Tramway Avenue	9
7	Horse tram, Edmonton to Finsbury Park	10
8	GER Forty Hill (now Turkey Street) station	11
9	White House, London Road	14
10	Allen Fairhead and Son, Sydney Road	14
11	Bush Hill Park, the stables	16
12	Raleigh Road, Alice Cottage	17
13	Villas at Bush Hill Park	20
14	Bycullah Park estate	23
15	House in Bycullah Road	23
16	Chase Green Avenue	24
17	St Mary Magdalene and the windmill	25
18	Bycullah Athenaeum, Windmill Hill	26
19	Church Street, south side	29
20	Raleigh's House, Chase Side, front	32
21	Raleigh's House, Chase Side, rear	32
22	Primrose Avenue	35
23	Burlington Road	36
24	The Town, drinking fountain with fire escape	39
25	Market Place with Palace and cedar	41
26	The Town, east side	44
27	Vestry House as police station	45
28	Police Station, London Road	46
29	Trent Park	48
30	Old Park	50
31	Hertford Road, junction with Green Street	56
32	Edwardian Enfield Town, the east side	60, 61
33	Edwardian Enfield Town, looking west	60, 61
34	Ellis, tailor, advertisement	62
35	Chase Lodge, Holtwhites Hill	64
36	Chase Park, Windmill Hill	64

37	Steam navvy on GNR extension to Cuffley	65
38	Rendlesham viaduct	66
39	Grange Park station	68
40	Enfield Town before the trams	70
41	High Street, Ponders End before the trams	72
42	White Hart, Ponders End before the trams	72
43	Electric tram outside the White Hart, High Street	73
44	Electric tram outside the Two Brewers, High Street	73
45	London Road before the trams	74
46	Electric tram in London Road	74
47	Enfield Town, work on the tram terminus	75
48	Church Street, decorations for the trams 1909	75
49	Harman Road, junction with John Street	77
50	Halliwick, formerly Bush Hill House	78
51	The Ridgeway about 1910	80
52	Church Street, looking west	82
53	Church Street, Palace Parade	82
54	Town Park, aviary	83
55	Park Farm	84
56	Church Street, the post office	85
57	Post office staff 1906	85
58	Grout's shop, Southbury Road	87
59	The Hop Poles, Lancaster Road	88
60	Chase Side, junction with Parsonage Lane	89
61	Margetsons pond, Chase Side	90
62	Fox Hall, Baker Street	90
63	Shoreditch workhouse, 164 Baker Street	91
64	Baker Street chapel in Meeting House Yard	91
65	Eagle House, High Street, Ponders End	92
66	The crape factory in South Street	97
67	South Square off South Street	99
68	Government Row	105
69	Ferry at Enfield lock	105
70	Royal Small Arms Factory, Enfield	111
71	RSAF — testing swords and bayonets	117
72	Ordnance Road, approach to RSAF	119
73	RSAF Mafeking celebrations	123
74	David Weston	125
75	Funeral of David Weston	126
76	Enfield Wash, demonstration 1910	127
77	Ponders End gas works	129
78	Ediswan's, floods	134
79	Ediswan's, workers coming out	135
80	Ediswan's, cabinet shop	136
81	Sidney Graham and his 'Sociable'	141
82	Enfield Electricity Works, Ladysmith Road	144
83	Cosmos Imperial Works, Brimsdown	145
84	John Gibbons in his orchards	149
85	Cracknell's farmhouse Baker Street	150
86	Edmonton Union workhouse, the gates	159

87	Edmonton Union workhouse	161
88	Enfield parish workhouse, now St Michael's	162
89	Chase Farm School, now the hospital	165
90	Chase Farm School holiday	167
91	The Spotted Cow, Bulls Cross	177
92	King George V reservoir, labourers	180
93	Dr J.J. Ridge	180
94	High Street, Ponders End, Dr Agar's surgery	196
95	The Cottage Hospital, Chase Side	199
96	The Cottage Hospital and Primitive Methodist chapel	199
97	Silver Street, fire 1868	200
98	Sir Roland M. Stephenson	202
99	Hill Lodge, Clay Hill	203
100	Silverton in Silver Street	204
101	The New River, Enfield loop	206
102	The Crown and Horseshoes	206
103	Meeting House Yard, Baker Street	208
104	The Barracks, Clay Hill	211
105	Highlands Hospital, administration block	215
106	Daniel Gilsenan, the road surveyor	216
107	Silver Street, east side and the Nags Head	218
108	Water-tower, Holtwhites Hill	220
109	Pepper's stables, Silver Street	224
110	Southbury Road, fire station and post office	225
111	Fire station, Gentleman's Row and steam pump	225
112	Fairhead's yard, Sydney Road, fire 1885	227
113	The Town, north side, Barclay's Bank	229
114	James Meyer	230
115	Waterworks in Alma Road	232
116	Pumping station in Hadley Road	233
117	Isolation Hospital, Worlds End, administration block	236
118	Isolation Hospital, Worlds End, a pavilion	236
119	Milkman's barrow	238
120	Grammar School boys and staff 1883	251
121	County School site Holly Walk	253
122	Edith Clutten	254
123	North Middlesex High School for Girls	256
124	Percy House, Church Street	256
125	Shirley Lodge, Windmill Hill	257
126	Girls' School of Industry, former Assembly Rooms	260
127	The British School, Chase Side as a milk depot	261
128	The British School, Chase Side as the Moon Under Water	261
129	The National School, London Road	262
130	The Protestant School, Flash Lane	262
131	Prebendary George Hodson	264
132	St Michael's Church and School, Chase Side	266
133	The National School, Sydney Road	267
134	St Michael's School orchestra 1904	268
135	Ordnance Road, floods	269

136	Bush Hill Park School	274
137	Bush Hill Park School, class 1909	274
138	Dunraven, The Ridgeway	276
139	The Spicer family	276
140	Alma Road School, class 1907/8	277
141	Southbury School infants, about 1906	280
142	Wesleyan wooden chapel with children	284
143	John Moore Heath	286
144	Chase Hill House, Chase Green	287
145	Claysmore, Clay Hill	289
146	Admiral Bosanquet's drawing room	289
147	St John's Church, Clay Hill	291
148	John Riley Rignall	292
149	Baptist tabernacle, London Road	297
150	Baptist, later Methodist, church, South Street	297
151	Roman Catholic church, London Road	298
152	The Jute estate off South Street	299
153	Congregational chapel, Ponders End High Street	300
154	Christ Church and Chase Side Chapel	301
155	Henry Storer Toms	301
156	Church School of Industry, Silver Street	304
157	St Paul's Presbyterian Church, Church Street	307
158	The Town, south and east sides	312
159	Halcyon House, Private Road	314
160	Brooklyn, Private Road	315
161	Eeles's Forge, Ponders End High Street	317
162	The Rising Sun, Church Street	318
163	Quoits team, Wheatsheaf, Baker Street	319
164	Enfield Fair	320
165	Enfield Bonfire Boys	322
166	Ponders End station, excursion 1905	323
167	Enfield Tradesmen's Association at Rye Park	324
168	W.G. Wood, baker's cart	325
169	Chase Side Gardens	326
170	The Holly Bush, Lancaster Road	326
171	Enfield Volunteers' band 1865	328
172	Bandstand, Chase Green	329
173	Ponders End Temperance Mission band	330
174	Manor House, Bulls Cross	331
175	Sir Henry Bowles	332
176	PSA meeting 1911	333
177	Sutton's warehouse, Chase Side	334
178	Queens Hall, London Road	334
179	Ponders End Electric Theatre	335
180	Cricketers' Arms, Chase Side	337
181	Enfield Tradesmen's Cycling Club	338
182	Garrud's shop, Hertford Road, Ponders End	339
183	Hertford Road, Enfield Wash	340
184	Baker Street	341
185	Bathing lake in the Town Park	342

Maps and Plans

I	Railways 1840-1910	3
II	Enfield New Town estate	18, 19
III	Bush Hill Park estate 1882-6	21
IV	Gordon House estate	31
V	New Enfield estate, Birkbeck Freehold Land Soc.	34
VI	Putney Lodge estate	37
VII	South Street 1867	96
VIII	Royal Small Arms Factory 1851	108
IX	Enfield 1850	188/9
X	New River Enfield loop	205
XI	Chase Side and Lancaster Road	213

Graphs

I	Infant mortality 1892-1915	175
II	Population 1801-1911	186

Explanatory Notes on Sources

Board of Guardians, Edmonton Union minutes at the Greater London Record Office.

ED, Department of Education and Science records at PRO Kew.

EHHS, Edmonton Hundred Historical Society.

Enfield, material in the local history collection, Enfield Libraries.

Gazette, see also Observer.

H and TP, minutes of the Housing and Town Planning committee at Enfield.

HLG, Ministry of Housing and Local Government records at PRO Kew.

HO, Home Office records at PRO Kew.

LBH, Enfield Local Board of Health minutes at Enfield.

LQ, local queries file at Enfield.

MH, Ministry of Health records at PRO Kew.

MEPO, Metropolitan Police Office records at PRO Kew.

Meyers's Observer, see also Observer.

MOH, Enfield medical officer of health reports at Enfield.

MUN, Ministry of Munitions records at PRO Kew.

Observer, ie Meyers's Observer 1859- became Enfield Gazette and Observer in April 1913.

PP, Parliamentary Papers available in State Papers department, British Library.

PRO, Public Record Office at Kew and Chancery Lane.

RCRP, Royal Commission on the Prevention of Pollution of Rivers.

SUPP, Ministry of Supply records at PRO Kew.

Surveyors' reports at Enfield.

Vestry minute books, list in vol 1 p.xv.

VCH, Victoria County History of Middlesex, vol. 5 covers Edmonton Hundred.

WO, War Office records at PRO Kew.

X in references means October

Acknowledgements

My thanks are again due to my brother Charles for reading much of the text, for proposing improvements in style and punctuation and for drawing my attention to inconclusive arguments and false conclusions. Fortunately I have again been able to rely throughout upon the encyclopaedic knowledge which Graham Dalling, our local history librarian, brings to bear in answering my most obscure and unlikely questions; he never ceases to amaze me. Brian Warren and Terence Goulding have again made themselves responsible for the maps which so enhance and explain the text. Andrew Combe has devised the graphs. Valerie Carter has undertaken the final reading of the text and the eradication, we all hope, of whatever errors remain, to her above all are my thanks due for bringing this book into a fit state for publication.

I owe a debt of gratitude to those who have made available to me their written memoirs, particularly to Sid Robinson (his autobiography is now published) and Doris Shuttlewood. Sid Beadle, my late and much missed friend, generously helped me with his specialised knowledge of the local brickfields. I have met with unfailing consideration from Keri Davies and his staff at Enfield reference library despite the heavy demands which I have imposed upon them. I have received so much help and encouragement from Stanley and Irene Smith, that I doubt whether the work would ever have been published without them. The vast labour of typing and re-typing the text has fallen to my wife Maisie.

The debts which I have accumulated over many years in putting together this volume are so heavy and multifarious that it is inevitable that the names of some who have helped have been omitted here. I must however name Alan Jacques, Christopher Simons, John Letchford, Freda Farrant, K.F. Baker, Kate Godfrey, John Cutten, A.S. Keers and Mr Hussey. I can only beg that those not named will forgive me.

I have listed below those to whom my thanks are due for the illustrations they have so generously provided. Many have been copied from the postcard collection belonging to Peter Lister to whom I am particularly grateful. The numbers refer to plate numbers.

Enfield Libraries: frontispiece, 1, 2, 3, 5, 6, 8, 9, 11, 13, 16, 19, 20, 26, 27, 28, 29, 31, 35, 36, 37, 39, 43, 44, 45, 46, 47, 50, 56, 57, 59, 60, 61, 62, 63, 64, 65, 66, 67, 68, 70, 71, 73, 74, 75, 76, 77, 78, 79, 80, 81, 84, 85, 86, 87, 89, 90, 91, 92, 94, 95, 96, 97, 98, 99, 101, 102, 104, 106, 107, 108, 109, 110, 112, 113, 114, 115, 116, 117, 120, 124, 125, 126, 127, 129, 130, 131, 133, 135, 136, 137, 138, 139, 140, 141, 144, 145, 147, 148, 149, 150, 152, 153, 154, 156, 157, 158, 161, 162, 163, 166, 168, 169, 170, 171, 174, 175, 176, 178, 179, 182, 183, 184

Enfield Preservation Society: 4, 7, 10, 14, 17, 21, 24, 25, 32, 33, 34, 40, 41, 42, 48, 52, 53, 54, 55, 69, 72, 83, 103, 111, 121, 123, 132, 134, 142, 151, 164, 165, 172, 173, 185
David Pam: 12, 15, 23, 49, 82, 88, 105, 118
Enfield Gazette 18, 22, 30, 167
Norah Read 58
Stanley Smith 38, 128
Reg Williams 160, 177
John Letchford 51, 155
Dr Tim Ridge 93
Freda Farrant 122
Joan Heath 143
Ashmolean Museum Oxford 146
Denis Bowyer 134
Greater London Photographic Library 159
W. Larman 119
F. Adams 100
Enfield Advertiser portrait of author on dust jacket.
Many of the Enfield Preservation Society's photographs come from the Reg Williams bequest, or have been copied from the collection of glass slides generously donated by the Enfield Gazette.

Preface

Historians sometimes create dividing lines in history in an arbitrary manner. The year 1837 however seems almost to have been pre-selected for this history, for it marks the moment of transition in Enfield from village to suburb. The year 1837, moreover, is habitually used by national historians to begin a new chapter or a new book, for the remainder of the century carries the convenient and widely recognised label 'Victorian'. The year 1837 also saw the commencement of a series of changes which culminated in the supersession in Enfield of parish government by a variety of ad hoc bodies each covering a different area both of concern and territory. In that year the Edmonton Union took over from the parish its main function, the care of the poor. Another important change had begun in 1833 when Parliament first authorised grants in aid of elementary education; within a few years National and British schools had opened in the parish. A new transfer of power came in 1840 when the Metropolitan Police extended its jurisdiction into Enfield. Perhaps the most radical change came in 1850 with the establishment of a local board of health created to stem the rising tides of pollution and infection.

The decade 1830 to 1840 had also seen the beginnings of a democratisation which was to result, a hundred years later, in one man (even one woman) one vote; it was a change which affected local government no less than parliamentary government. This same decade also marked the beginning of an era in which man found himself able to travel and move his merchandise at speeds faster than the galloping of a horse.

Industry in Enfield began well before 1837 but its expansion occurred after the mid-century when mass production methods were introduced at the Royal Small Arms Factory. Other factories were built from 1860 onwards and the number increased more rapidly with each decade until, upon the outbreak of the First World War, eastern Enfield had become so highly industrialised that it could be transformed within a year, by government finance, into an important centre for war production.

The first of the many housing estates, which were ultimately to cover so much of Enfield, was set out in the 1850s. The growth of these estates was undertaken in intermittent bursts of frantic building followed by periods of complete stoppage.

Since volume two must end somewhere, there is a strong case for choosing the year 1914, for the First World War engendered many changes, and the way of life in the years which followed was seen, even by those who lived through them, to have become radically different from the lives of their families before the war.

Thus the years 1837 to 1914 saw the transformation of a parish near London into a suburb of London. The author had intended to complete this History of Enfield in two volumes but so much material of interest presented itself and so many fascinating photographs were offered, each demanding inclusion, that a third and final volume became essential. It will cover the years 1914 to 1939. The author apologises for stealing Professor Dyos's title, he in no way claims to have improved on that very fine work.

Chapter One
Victorian Developments

1. Introduction: A Summary

Over the years 1840 to 1850 the population of Enfield scarcely grew. It began to expand after the mid-century and during the following thirty years it more than doubled from 9,453 (1851) to 19,104 (1881). House builders could only respond to local demand when capital was available; house building was not a particularly profitable investment and at times, when better prospects were offered to investors, building came virtually to a standstill. Local demand for houses was dependent both on employment and good public transport and even when these were provided the demand could only be satisfied if land was available for building. Land near Enfield Town became available for middle-class commuter housing in 1852 with the beginning of the break-up of the Bush Hill Park estate. The rate of building however, remained low. Public transport from Enfield was certainly not good enough to attract middle-class commuters in any great numbers. The expansion of the Royal Small Arms Factory at the time of the Crimean War brought an influx of artisans and their families into the eastern side of the parish. The population of eastern Enfield trebled in the ten years 1851 to 1861, while that of the parish as a whole increased by less than thirty per cent. Building, however, did not accelerate until the 1870s; in 1869 land for house building found few buyers. New industry was introduced in the 1860s, including a jute works and a gas works and in the 1870s there was rapid extension of labour-intensive market gardening.

Population growth in the parish slowed to nineteen per cent during the period 1871 to 1881 despite an improvement of the railway service in the early 1870s and the new availability, from 1872, of cheap workmen's returns to Bishopsgate (after 1874 to Liverpool Street) from Enfield Town. This comparatively slow expansion may have been due to the high price of land for house building in the vicinity of the station at Enfield Town, but it also coincided with a declining level of house building nationally, which reached its lowest point in 1871-2. There was a housing shortage in Enfield by 1880 and that year saw a revival of the building industry nationally. Land became available locally and three hundred acres, enough to build 4,000 houses, were offered for development. The year 1880 saw a station opened at Bush Hill Park where land was cheap. Houses were at once begun there on the east side of the line and they found a ready market among working-class commuters anxious to take advantage of the cheap workmen's returns. More land, much of it market gardens, was taken for building in eastern Enfield. In the west, Bycullah Park, close to the Great Northern terminus on Windmill Hill, was offered for upper middle-class development at about the same time. The building of artisan houses now proceeded more rapidly on the Gordon estate on Chase Side and on the estates north and south of Lancaster Road. Over the following six years (1880-1886) there was a building boom which added twenty-three hundred dwellings to the housing stock in the parish, raising it from 3,569 to 5,868, an increase of sixty-three per cent. Entrepreneurs set up land companies which purchased the land, laid out the roads and divided the frontages into plots, each for one dwelling; they then disposed of the plots for house building. In the early stage of development the plots were sold in small groups of up to five, later in strips long enough for the erection of terraces. The year 1880 saw the foundation of two local building societies which could advance money to builders or to prospective landlords wishing to purchase houses.

There was a surfeit of houses by 1887, as H.J. Dyos points out (*Victorian Suburb* p.82) the nature of the building industry, with its vast number of small builders, readily available capital and a rising market for houses, led almost automatically to overbuilding. The year 1887 was followed in Enfield by a ten-year lull, again coinciding with a national trend; depression in the building industry reached its lowest point in 1891. The Boer War in 1897 brought enormous prosperity into the parish and an influx of new workers to the Royal Small Arms Factory. This created a shortage of houses, which forced up rents. Land sales and house building followed on a vast scale between 1897 and 1904. Many small houses were built to let at low rents around Alma Road and Scotland Green Road, and at Bush Hill Park. Others were built under the Small Dwellings Acquisitions Act which encouraged workmen to become owner-occupiers. Large numbers of artisans' dwellings were being built in the area of Lancaster Road, and between Southbury Road and Lincoln Road eastward from Enfield Town station; many more houses were built on the Gordon estate. By 1904 however, the war prosperity was over and there was again a surfeit of houses.

2. Road and Rail

Travelling to London before the railway was by the four-horse coach driven by William Glover, which started at the Kings Head in the Market Place at nine o'clock every morning. It went via Edmonton to the Flower Pot at Bishopsgate. Some City men rode horseback, others drove up in their own vehicles. There was a two-horse coach, up and down, in the afternoon. Many people walked to Edmonton and got one of the coaches which started there, and which cost only a shilling.

The year 1826 had seen the end of the Stamford Hill Green Lanes Turnpike Trust which had maintained the main roads in this area for over a hundred years. That year all the turnpike trusts north of the Thames were amalgamated under Commissioners for the Metropolitan Turnpike Roads. This body, which lasted until 1864, charged a uniform toll of 3d a horse. In 1864 an act assigned all the turnpike roads within the metropolitan area to the care of the local boards of health, operative from 1 July 1872, on which day the turnpikes on all these roads were removed. It was arranged that the county would henceforth contribute half the cost of maintaining the former metropolitan turnpike roads, provided that the county surveyor could certify their satisfactory condi-

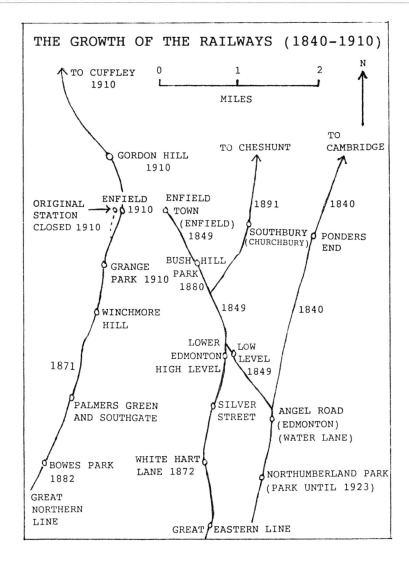

THE GROWTH OF THE RAILWAYS (1840-1910)

tion. The sixty miles of lesser roads in Enfield were placed under the supervision of the Local Board of Health which employed a road surveyor who also served as inspector of nuisances.

No roads running west to east into Essex existed for seven miles between Waltham Abbey in the north and Water Lane (now Angel Road) in the south and, even at these places, a heavy toll was levied. Certain public-spirited men joined together in September 1869 to build a new road from Ponders End to Chingford which, it was promised, would increase trade and open up for the people of Enfield the beautiful drives and walks of Epping Forest. The group secured financial support, purchased land and began construction. They had expended £500 by March 1872 and a meeting was called at the Railway Tavern in Ponders End to raise £700 needed to complete the work. The road was

1. The first station at Enfield Town was the former Cowden Clarke school house where John Keats had been educated. It was demolished in 1872, the new station being erected behind the old house.

opened in 1873. Before that time only a rough track had existed and traffic had crossed the Marditch and the River Lea by fords, although there had been a narrow footbridge over the Lea.

The Northern and Eastern Railway Company had been incorporated in 1836 to build a line to Cambridge along the Lea valley as the first stage of a trunk line to York. Financial problems, however, obliged the company to divert the London end of the line to join the Eastern Counties railway at Stratford. The arrangement did not work well and in January 1844 the Lea Valley line was leased to the Eastern Counties Railway Company. The circuitous route into London was to prove a serious disadvantage. The line from Stratford to Broxbourne was opened 15 September 1840 and reached Cambridge by 1845. There were stations at Angel Road in Edmonton and at Ponders End, but neither did much to serve the centres of population at Edmonton and at Enfield Town. To reach these places a single track branch was authorised in 1846 and opened 1 March 1849, from Angel Road to Enfield Town, with a station (the old low-level station) at Edmonton Green. It was projected, recalled the *Enfield Observer* (13 May 1898) by a few public-spirited men and, after the bill was passed, the railway company became the proprietors and constructed the line under the chairmanship of David Waddington.[1]

The day the line opened people came from miles around to watch. A splendid little steam rail-motor appeared during those early weeks. It had a thirty-six seat, four-compartment coach and could cover the $10^3/_4$ miles, Edmonton to Bishops-gate, in twenty-seven minutes, reaching fifty miles an hour and using only twelve pounds of coke a mile. Passengers had to change at the Angel Road junction, except those travelling by the 'swell', the 9.20am from Enfield which was a real express and made only two stops. The train had first and second class compart-

2.   *The Great Northern extension to Enfield under construction in 1870 with a party of Victorian navigators at work. The Congregational minister at Chase Side invited them to a 'substantial meat tea'.*

ments; smoking was allowed only in the first class. The 'swell' left Bishopsgate on its return journey at 4.40pm.

Enfield remained sparsely populated in 1860, its development retarded by the lack of adequate public transport. The train service to London was poor and expensive. Ten trains a day left Enfield Town on the Eastern Counties railway, the first at three minutes past eight in the morning, the last at ten minutes past eight in the evening. The last train to arrive reached Enfield at five minutes past ten. Glover's omnibus continued to run four journeys a day, and Charles Case's four-horse omnibus also ran until August 1865, leaving the Kings Head in the Market Place for Westminster Abbey via Winchmore Hill, Palmers Green, Wood Green and Manor House, twice a day at 8.45am and 2.15pm. The fare, Enfield to Islington, was one shilling, Islington to Westminster 3d, and it cost an extra 3d to ride inside.[2]

The railway service was much improved by the construction of a double track from Bishopsgate (later from Liverpool Street) which joined the line of the old single track branch at Edmonton junction and reached Enfield Town in August 1872. The new line provided a thirty-minute service to Bishopsgate, augmented at peak periods. Twopenny return workmen's trains stimulated the migration of the working classes from the East End, first to Tottenham, then to Edmonton and finally to Bush Hill Park after the opening of the station there in 1880. Enfield Town, because of the high price of land, continued for a time to house mostly middle-class and professional commuters, but the new service gave some impetus to the development of the Gordon estate of artisan houses.

The extension of the Great Northern railway in the 1870s was a major factor in promoting an increase in high-cost house building in western Enfield. It was

3.   *Enfield station was opened in April 1871. About sixteen trains arrived and departed daily, mostly for Moorgate. It was closed to passenger traffic in 1910 and replaced by a new station further down Windmill Hill. Both stations bore the name Enfield. The new station became Enfield Chase in 1924 to distinguish it from the former G.E.R. station at Enfield Town.*

4.   *Enfield station was the terminus on the Great Northern, its island platform had a wide canopy over much of its length.*

in November 1869 that a writer in the *Observer* commented, 'I see the railway to join the Great Northern at Wood Green is begun and is being carried on with great vigour'. Later that month the Reverend Storer Toms entertained the construction workers to 'a substantial meat tea' at the schoolroom in Chase Side (now the Moon under Water). A four-mile branch to Enfield (known from 1924 as Enfield Chase), with a terminus on Windmill Hill on the western edge of the Town, was opened in April 1871. The service was aimed at a potential middle-class clientele. The station was a two-storey, twin-gable house, similar in style to the single-storey stations at Palmers Green and Winchmore Hill. It was placed firmly across the end of the tracks, 'as if to emphasise, that all thought of further extension had been abandoned'. The island platform had a wide canopy over much of its length. About sixteen trains arrived and departed daily, mostly to Moorgate.[3]

The Great Northern made no attempt to compete with the Great Eastern for working-class custom. A correspondent in the *Observer* in 1885, writing with tongue in cheek, expressed his 'delight on reading a notice at Enfield station announcing that the Great Northern Railway Company issued workmen's returns to London from Enfield, (among other stations) on all trains reaching London before 8am. I could scarcely refrain from tossing my hat with joy' he goes on 'that this sleepy-headed railway was beginning to wake up from its profound stupor. And what a jolly time the landlords would have of it...' His 'joy', alas, was short-lived for, upon his consulting a timetable, it became evident that there was no train from Enfield on that line which reached London before 8am.[4]

An attempt was made in August 1897 by W. Welch to run an omnibus service from Forty Hill to the two railway stations, but the public made little use of it. The proprietor reduced his fares and made modifications to his timetable, but the service failed to pay and in January it was announced that it would be discontinued at the end of March.[5]

The North London and Suburban Tram Company began the work of constructing a tramway from Stamford Hill through Tottenham with a great display of energy in May 1880. Thirty-two gangs of men were labouring between Stamford Hill and Seven Sisters Road. 'Workmen', it was announced, 'will be employed day and night to complete the work by 24 June', but July came and found the work at a standstill. The rails, dispatched from Germany, had been delayed *en route* and the Tottenham Local Board of Health threatened to sue. The contractor had been replaced by October and hopes had risen that the High Road, within a few weeks, would be 'clear of the invading army of navigators'. The extension through Ponders End was being laid by November 1881. It was inspected by Major-General Hutchinson and formally opened in January 1882. A special car was chartered, drawn by a couple of gaily caparisoned horses, which left the Golden Lion on Edmonton Green at noon for Tramway Avenue. Its important passengers alighted there and an inspection of the newly built section, which terminated at a point two hundred yards north of Southbury Road, was made on foot. Afterwards the gentlemen re-entered the car where Mr Kitteringham, the Enfield surveyor, expressed his approbation. 'The work was done exceedingly well', he declared, and the party returned to the Golden Lion for a 'recherché luncheon'. The new cars, which were licensed to carry twenty, were comfortably fitted out and provided with timepieces.[6]

It was intended that the tramway would be continued northward through Enfield to Cheshunt, and that it would engender more houses and shops through the eastern side of the parish, but this was not to be, for the Great Eastern had made an application to construct a railway from Edmonton to Cheshunt. The Tram Company got cold feet and sought power in Parliament,

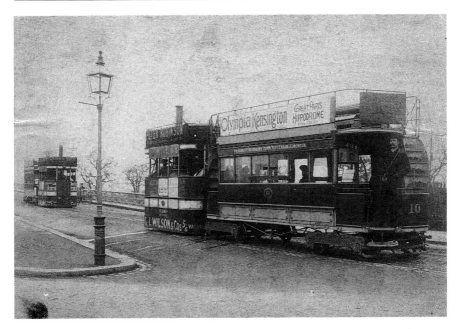

5. *The North London Tramways Company in 1884 placed an order for fifteen Merryweather steam locomotives. This one is at New Road, the bridge which carried the former turnpike road over the low-level railway near Edmonton Green.*

in June 1882, to abandon its plans for a line from Southbury Road to Cheshunt. The road from Southbury Road to Waltham Cross was henceforth served by an omnibus, but it ran only once an hour.[7]

The North London Tramways Company in 1884 placed an order for fifteen steep gradient Merryweather steam locomotives but, because of opposition from the Metropolitan Board of Works, they were granted permission to run them only north of Stamford Hill. Great play was made of the relief steam would afford to the unfortunate horses, previously condemned to 'the great cruelty of drawing cars sixteen miles a day whereby,' it was said, 'they were worn out in four years'. The steam trams were certainly popular at first. 'On one day alone' wrote a correspondent (*Observer* 25 April 1885) 'receipts from the steam cars doubled those of the horse cars running on the same line'.[8]

During the first half of the year 1889 the receipts of the tramway amounted to £8,668, costs to £7,787, which left a half-year profit of £880; this poor performance was attributed to bad weather. The company now owned twenty-five engines, the fifteen originally purchased at nearly £800 each and ten acquired between 1886 and 1889 at £940 each. In making an application to the Board of Trade in 1890 for renewal of powers to use steam for a further seven years, the company asserted that horses could not be worked at a profit. The local authorities all opposed the application, claiming that the engines frightened horses and led to accidents and that the vibration damaged property. The company had never paid any dividend on its ordinary share capital of £73,000, though six per cent had been paid on its preference shares in 1887. That year, 1,975,000 passengers had been carried; in 1888 there were 2,415,000 passengers

6. *The North London Metropolitan Tramways Co. had stables and a depot at the end of Tramway Avenue. The building on the corner had been the headquarters of the former North London Tramways Co.*

and in 1889 (due to a stoppage on the Wood Green and Hornsey branch) 2,268,000. The company was granted an extension of its licence only until the last Saturday in June 1891. On the following Monday there were no trams, but on the Tuesday when they resumed, every engine carried a flag. The company had been put into the hands of the receiver who was attempting to arrange a sale of the assets to the North Metropolitan Tramways Company which operated in the area adjoining to the south. That company took over on 1 August using horses; it paid only £20,000 for the purchase. The machinery, engines, stock and lines were valued at £3,000, but it was expected that the North Metropolitan would have to spend £50,000 on repairs and renewals over a period of a few years. Blue coloured tramcars drawn by two horses were introduced; each could carry forty-six passengers. One correspondent dwelt contentedly on the merry jingling of the bells on the horses, a merriment unlikely to have been shared by these poor animals, and he contrasted that sound jubilantly with the noise and stench of the steam cars. 'To ride on top of the old trams', he said, 'was to have one's eyes filled with grit and one's olefactory organs vexed with sulphurous effluvia'.[9]

Power was granted to the Great Eastern Railway Company to construct a loop line from Edmonton to Cheshunt and it was announced, in June 1884, that work would soon begin. A station at Southbury Road was promised and the company also announced that in the near future it would build a station on the Lea Valley line at Green Street.

The *Observer*, in September 1889, reported that work on the construction of the new GER Cheshunt loop line was in full progress. Five hundred men were employed and, though these included some who were already living in the area, there was a large influx of strangers who needed accommodation and feeding.

7.   *Blue coloured tramcars drawn by two horses replaced the steam trams on the Finsbury Park to Tramway Avenue route in 1891. Each could carry 46 passengers.*

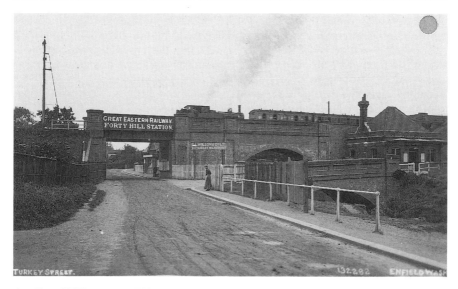

8. *Forty Hill Station in 1909, shortly before withdrawal of the passenger service. On reopening in 1960 the station was renamed Turkey Street.*

The Navvy Mission Society had appealed to local clergy for help in meeting their spiritual needs. One correspondent, writing in March 1890, having walked by way of the fields from the Town to the Highway, was impressed by the work in progress. A steam navvy had been used to make a cutting through the orchards and the construction of a number of bridges had caused chaos to road traffic. The line opened at the end of September 1891 with three stations: Churchbury (Southbury Road), Forty Hill (Turkey Street) and Theobalds Grove. It was intended to run twenty-four trains daily on weekdays and five on Sundays. But eastern Enfield was not commuter territory, most of its people being employed locally. Moreover no workmen's fares were offered which might have induced East End workers to seek houses in the district.[10]

3. Land Companies, Builders and Building Societies

Bylaws of 1865 (re-issued in 1875) were formulated to control the increasing volume of new building in Enfield. Every new street had to be at least thirty-six feet wide including the footways. No new building was to exceed in height the distance from the front to the front of the houses opposite. All outside walls were to be of brick or stone. Every dwelling was to have 150 square feet of open space. Every habitable room was to be at least eight feet high and to have at least one window. Drains were to be of glazed earthenware or fireclay pipes and should be approved by the surveyor. No cesspool was to be allowed except where no main drains had been laid. No new house was to be occupied until inspected by the local board.[11]

The process of building in the early stages of urbanisation was always the same.

The land was purchased by a land company, roads were set out and the estate was divided up into plots; these were sold by auction to small builders who built groups of houses, anything up to five or so, so that each road displayed a variety of dwellings. It gives this earlier development an attractive appearance, especially where the houses have remained externally unchanged. In 1870 for instance, plans were submitted and passed for five houses to be built by Mr Almond in South Street and five by Messrs Patman in Gordon Road. Single houses were built by Patman in Baker Street and by W. Murch in Totteridge Road. Building was as yet slow, an odd house or two in Mandeville, Totteridge, Halifax or Putney Roads. A new street was laid out called Raynton Road in 1871. Four new houses were built by Patman in Chase Side, another one in Sydney Road, two in Alma Road, two in Eastfield Road, three in Bell Road and four new houses in Riley Road. It was not until the late seventies that rows of uniform cottages began to be developed. Plans were submitted for new roads at Jammet's farm at Freezywater, and for eighteen houses in Gilbert Road in 1879. In 1880-81 plans were submitted for twenty-five cottages in Ordnance Road, thirty-five cottages in Canton Road (Primrose Avenue) fifty cottages on the Jute estate (Alma Road), fifty-one cottages in Fifth Avenue, forty-five on the Woodlands estate and twenty on the Cedars estate.[12]

Land for building was finding its way on to the market at an increasing pace. On the Bush Hill Park estate sixty acres were available within the parish of Enfield suitable for the erection of three distinct classes of residence, in all about five hundred houses. The Bycullah estate offered fifty-seven acres, providing room for 200 commodious family residences. The Conservative Land Society estate of three acres, in Southbury Road, would accommodate sixty or seventy houses. The New River Company had fifteen acres available for building, fronting London Road on which might be built two hundred respectable dwellings. In all, it was claimed in October 1880 that nearly three hundred acres were ripe for building in Enfield, room for up to four thousand houses.[13]

The system by which this land was to be developed was full of pitfalls and control by the local authority was incomplete. A writer in the *Enfield Observer*, in February 1886, explained how it worked, though he obviously took a somewhat critical view. The owner puts his estate up for sale, he wrote.

> 'Among the bidders are a clique of speculators including a financier, a lawyer and an agent. The agent is commissioned to bid up to a given price. The financier finds the money to pay the deposit and the lawyer looks to title and conveyance, finally the purchase is complete. The estate is staked out in plots, for some of these speculative builders are found who take them on lease and to mortgage. The lawyer keeps himself going by making conveyances and arranging mortgages. The financier advances the money at every stage and takes the interest. The agent, who is ostensibly the owner, looks after his commission. The roads are set out, but not properly made, the drainage is just as complete as the surveyor may have control over. House after house is built and promises are made that the roads will be made up after the building is completed. Later, however, it is discovered that the original owners of the building estate have parted with their interest. Plot after plot had changed hands till at length, what with bankrupt builders, mortgagees, and others, it is difficult to determine who are the real owners. When the estate is pretty fully developed, occupiers begin to grumble that the roads are unmade and the footpaths not distinguishable from the roads.'

An appeal might then be made to the local board. One such submission was from Mr Bullock who complained of the awful state of Glebe Avenue, a new road and on a middle-class estate. The road was so bad, he said, that the residents had to pay more than the normal fare for cab hire. The board would do nothing while the road was private, moreover it felt reluctant to force householders to pay additional money for roads after they had invested everything in the acquisition of their property. The roads thus remained private and unmade. In similar circumstances the clerk to the board had to write to the Metropolitan Freehold Land Company, early in December 1885, about the way their roads had been made on the Laurel Bank estate.[14]

This vast increase in house building throughout the parish was the incentive for the formation of building societies. There were three operating in Enfield by October 1881. The first had been set up in 1841 by Richard Brailsford, one of the clerks in the office of John Sawyer, solicitor in Silver Street. It became the Enfield Permanent Building Society, but it played no very active role in house sales; in 1875 for instance, it made loans amounting to only £330. The Enfield Independent Building Society was founded in 1880, as was the Royal Chase which advanced more than £6,000 during the first year of operation upon a share capital of £4,682. It paid five per cent to its investors. Compared to the land companies, which purchased the land and laid out the estates, the building societies were small, but they provided an opportunity for people to save, and they enabled would-be purchasers to borrow money without paying excessive interest. Each applicant for a loan was advised to take a number of shares according to the price he was paying for the property, and an advance was made at once. The property was mortgaged to the society, and the borrower repaid the principle and interest monthly. Most houses were purchased by landlords as a safe investment ('as safe as houses') and then rented to occupants in both working-class and middle-class areas. For example, in the *Observer* (3 January 1896) there is an entry 'Freehold, a block of twelve small houses, each producing 8s 6d a week, £265 each'. That same week six houses, each let at £26 per annum, were offered for £300 each. Rents had not risen rapidly, six- and seven-roomed houses were offered in January 1882 at £22 and £26 a year, and cottages at 6s 6d a week.[15]

Speculative builders put up most of the new houses in Enfield, financing the operation by mortgages arranged through the land companies. Once completed, the builder would aim to sell the house, assigning the lease at a price which he hoped would both cover the cost of building and provide him with a profit. Thus he would pay off his mortgage and sever any connection with whatever he had built. The term 'speculative builder' has acquired almost a pejorative connotation, but it merely meant 'those who built in anticipation of demand.' They were frequently condemned at the time for faults which more justly should have been attributed to the land companies, especially those companies which evaporated, leaving tenants loudly complaining about sewerage, water supply, street lighting, bad roads and no pavements.

Some small builders prospered and grew. Allen Fairhead came to Enfield from Tunstall in Suffolk in 1857 to build a house for his uncle Dr Fairhead, it was known as the White House in London Road. His first premises were in Cecil Road near the site later occupied by St Andrews National School. He lived then in Church Street, next to the 'Palace'. He built many of the houses in Enfield New Town estate. Later he moved, both house and yard, to a site at the junction

9.   Allen Fairhead the builder came to Enfield in 1857 to build this fine house, known as the White House in London Road, for his uncle Dr Fairhead. It was destroyed by bombs in November 1940.

10.   Allen Fairhead's premises were in Sydney Road. He died in 1901 but the firm continued to build in Enfield until 1965.

of Sydney Road and Cecil Road, and lived there until 1885 when a great fire destroyed both his residence and premises. He died in December 1901. The firm continued in Enfield and built Barclays Bank on the corner of the Market Place, the Presbyterian church, the council houses at Lavender Hill, and many of the schools in Enfield: it went bankrupt in 1965. C.J. Boswell junior, an enterprising young Enfield builder, had premises in Baker Street and Gordon Hill and called himself a builder and general contractor; in August 1882 he took his workmen on an excursion to St Albans. Other building tradesmen operating in Enfield were Joseph Boultwood, plumber and painter in the Town, J. Garrard plumber and gasfitter in Church Street, and Burman and Sons plumbers and decorators in Silver Street. H. Sawyer was a builder, undertaker and wheelwright. John Uff, of Bush Hill Park and Pimlico, built many of the houses on the east side of the railway at Bush Hill Park. He established there a working men's institute with a library and reading room. He was another who adopted the idea of a firm's outing, he and his men went to Brighton in August 1882 and took a trip on the Brighton 'steamer'.[16]

Some started building with so little capital that their existence remained always precarious. C.H. Jacobsen, who built thirty-one houses and two shops in Gordon Road, commenced trade in Enfield in 1899 with a capital of £50. Before that he had been a jobbing builder for nine years. He ran into some bad debts and went bankrupt four years later (*Observer* 31 July 1903). A similar reason caused the failure of Edward Woolven of The Lees, 8, First Avenue Bush Hill Park. He had gone into business with a capital of £100 which he secured by a second mortgage on his house at Hove. He began and completed four houses in First Avenue and in September 1903 he entered a contract to build eight houses in Edenbridge Road, but through want of capital he was unable to finish the work and Mr Rafferty, the contracting owner, took possession. Woolven was subsequently employed by Mr Rafferty to complete the properties. He had kept no books and attributed his bankruptcy to the high price of building materials.[17]

4. The Bush Hill Park Estate

The first housing developments in Enfield resulted from the breakup of Bush Hill Park, one of the finest and most magnificently timbered estates in Middlesex. The house, a large brick mansion on the south-east side of Bush Hill, had fine lawns sloping down to the New River which had been widened there to present the appearance of a lake. One entered the mansion up a flight of stone steps. There was stabling for fifteen horses, an ice-house and pleasure gardens. Sir Jeremy Sambrooke, a director of the East India Company, had lived there in the time of Queen Anne. He was succeeded by Sir Jeremy Vanacker Sambrooke, who also owned Gobions at North Mimms; it was he who had commissioned the still existent gateway known as Gobions Folly, probably by Gibbs. The second Sir Jeremy let Bush Hill Park to his sister Hannah. A fine old sundial supported by a leaden figure of a negro (later at Old Park) carried the arms of John Gore, her husband. Hannah subsequently inherited the estate and from her it passed to Ann Gore, who became the second wife of William Mellish in 1762. It was his younger brother Joseph who lived at Bush Hill Park and Joseph's second son William inherited the property. William was a director of the Bank of England

11.   The first of the great estates in Enfield to fall to the builder was Bush Hill Park. The large brick mansion of that name, sometimes known as the Clock House, was finally demolished in 1927. The illustration shows the stable block from the bridge over the New River.

and member of Parliament for Grimsby, later for Middlesex. Following his death in 1838 his fine art collection, which included the Grinling Gibbons wood carving known as the *Stoning of Stephen*, was sold at Christie's in March 1839. The property, over seven hundred acres, was put up for sale at the same time; the mansion, with 320 acres, was purchased by Lewis Raphael the famous Paris banker.[18]

Another area of the estate, on the west side of the London Road near to the Town, being sold, came in 1852 into the hands of the National Freehold Land Society. Here had been sited the local sports ground formerly used for archery and cricket, the entrance had been from Gashouse Lane (Sydney Road). The land, known then as Kaye's pightle, was farmed as a market garden by Mr Winterburn who lived in an ancient farmhouse entered down two or three steps. The house occupied the site (now, 1991, a car park) where the Roman Catholic chapel was built in 1863. The National Freehold Land Society laid out roads and divided the area into 462 plots, some of which were suitable for villa residences. Prices ranged from £400 for detached house plots in London Road to £100 for terrace cottage plots in Raleigh Road. The first house built there was erected in Raleigh Road by Mr Wood, a coachman. He called it Broomfield Cottage. Few sales were effected at first despite an offer, to purchasers of 'first- and second-rate houses', of free season tickets to London on the new railway.[19]

The estate was eventually transferred to the British Land Company and became known as Enfield New Town. A sale catalogue of 1861 shows that three detached and two semi-detached houses had been built in London Road, a

12.   The National Freehold Land Society in 1825 purchased Kaye's pightle, laid out roads and divided the area into 462 plots of varying sizes in London, Sydney, Raleigh and Essex Roads. The illustration shows Alice Cottage, Raleigh Road.

number of houses on both sides of Raleigh Road and a couple in Cecil Road. Forty-eight lots were at this time offered for sale, £275 was bid for one lot in London Road with a ninety-foot frontage and 275 feet in depth. Buying however did not become brisk until given impetus by the railway improvements in 1871. The New Town estate was covered with houses over the following few years. Those built by Allen Fairhead can be taken as typical. They were described in an advertisement (*Observer* July 1870) as:

> 'Enfield Villas: two very handsome detached villa residences situated near the Enfield turnpike in London Road, only four minutes from the railway station and the parish church ... front and kitchen gardens enclosed with iron pallisading'.

The bays and the first floor windows were 'enriched with handsomely carved stone'. On the ground floor was a spacious hall, a drawing room, a dining room, a kitchen, china pantry, scullery and a WC. The first floor had a large clothes and linen closet, a second WC and four lofty well-aired bedrooms. There were well-lit cellars with compartments for a larder and storage space for wine and beer, and for coal. Gas was laid to all principal parts of the house, seven burners being

Plan
of
FREEHOLD LAND & COTTAGES
AT
ENFIELD,
MIDDLESEX

To be Sold by Auction by
MR WHITTINGHAM.
AT THE KINGS HEAD, ENFIELD TOWN.
On Thursday 17th Octr 1861,
AT 6 FOR 7 O'CLOCK
IN 36 LOTS.

ENFIEI
NEW
TOWN
ESTAT

Stipulations

FOR LOTS 5, 27, 28, and 35.

1. Nothing shall be erected nearer to the roads than the building lines shown on the Plan, excepting fences, and those not more than 5 feet high.
2. The Purchaser of Lot 28 is forthwith to erect, and afterwards to maintain, the fence on the east side of his Lot of a height not exceeding 6 feet.
3. Nothing except fences is to be erected on any Lot until after a house or other building of the value specified below shall have been built on that Lot.

On Lot 5—£300.   On Lot 27—£350.   On Lots 28 and 35—£250.

 The value of a house or other building is the amount of its net first cost in materials and labour of construction only, estimated at the lowest current prices.
4. No building more than 45 feet from the front building line shall be erected or used as a dwelling house, and no building within 18 feet of the back boundary of Lots 27, 28, and 35, or within a like distance of the back boundary of the part tinted yellow on Lot 5, shall be more than 20 feet high, and no building between those spaces shall be more than 12 feet high.
5. No building is to be erected as a shop, warehouse, or factory, and no trade or manufacture is to be carried on, and and no operative machinery is to be fixed or placed on any Lot excepting on Lot 28.
6. The Purchaser of each of the above Lots shall in his conveyance covenant with the owners of all the other Lots on the Estate to observe the first, third, and fifth stipulations, and with the Vendors to observe the fourth stipulation.

STIPULATIONS FOR ALL THE LOTS.

The trade of an inn-keeper, victualler, or seller of wine, spirits, or beer, is not to be carried on upon any Lot, and the Purchaser of each Lot shall in his conveyance covenant with the owners of all the other Lots on the Estate to observe this stipulation.

No Purchaser shall be entitled to see to the execution of any such covenant by any other Purchaser, nor to delay the completion of his purchase in respect thereof, nor to require the production, or any abstract, or copy of, or extract from, the conveyance to any other Purchaser.

The Land coloured blue is reserved.

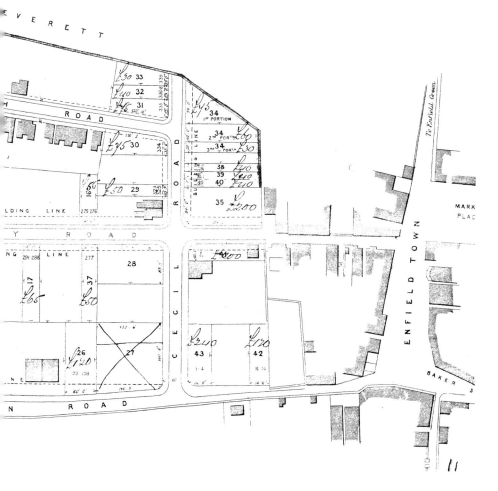

13.   Rustic bijou villas, Bush Hill Park, Enfield

fitted in each dwelling. An excellent supply of water could be had from a spring and soft water wells. A first-class season ticket on the railway was thrown in free. London Road, wrote an enthusiastic correspondent in the *Observer* in September 1875, 'now presents a boulevarde appearance'. He found it comparable with the glories of Eastbourne. He compared it also with its former state. Great progress had been made, he thought; before 1852 London Road had been nothing but a narrow lane with a high hedge separating it from the fields and the only pathway had been inside the hedge.[20]

The residue of the Bush Hill Park estate passed from Lewis Raphael to his nephew John Moorat, who in 1851 left it to his sons on condition that it should not be sold. But the sons quarrelled and the property was put into Chancery and finally the house and about five acres were sold to a Mr Bennett. The remainder, 373 acres, stretching from Bury Street to Lincoln Road, was purchased in 1875 by the North London Estates Company. By the time the Great Eastern Railway Company had opened its station at Bush Hill Park in 1880, sixty or seventy houses had been erected on the western side of the railway line. These were elegant villas, gabled and tile-hung, with large gardens, and situated along wide tree-lined roads. The company had spent a great deal of money; it had cost £36,000 to divide the land for building, to lay out the roads and to provide drains and sewers. The company sank a well at Quakers Walk, constructed a reservoir, erected a water-tower (now tastefully converted to a residence) and installed pumping plant, all at a cost of £11,000.

On the area now covered by Bagshot and Amberley Roads they found a deposit of brick-earth five feet in depth, sufficient it was thought to manufacture three hundred million stock and red bricks of the best quality. A brickyard of about nine acres was laid out there with kilns and sheds; it was served by a railway siding. The North London Estates Company went bankrupt in 1886 and the waterworks was taken over by the New River Company in 1887. The estate then came into the hands of the Bush Hill Park Company which prospered better. More than 320 houses had been built by August 1891; 238 acres still remained available for development.

The working-class housing on the east side of the line was begun immediately following the opening of Bush Hill Park station in 1880. Building was greatly

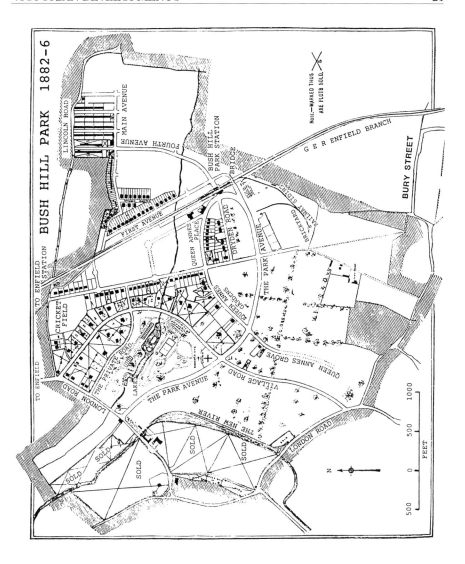

encouraged by the availability of twopenny workmen's return tickets to Liverpool Street, and the trains were heavily used. A correspondent in March 1883 describes a workmen's train with twenty-two passengers crowded into a compartment made to hold ten. It was reported in October 1892 that six hundred inhabitants from Bush Hill Park travelled daily on the line, excluding season ticket holders; two-thirds of them used the workmen's trains. Between 4.40am and 7.50am, thirteen trains left either Enfield or Lower Edmonton for Liverpool Street; there were eight twopenny workmen's returns and five half-fare trains. The population east of the railway at Bush Hill Park was now large enough to warrant a church and St Mark's was consecrated in 1893.[21]

There was an intense campaign, especially in Edmonton, in the nineties to secure more workmen's trains and to induce the company to run them later.

The last workmen's left Enfield at 6.11am but, from 1 March 1897, the time was changed to 6.06am. Many of the passengers, and a large proportion of them were young women and girls, did not start work until 8.30 or even 9 o'clock. The last twopenny workmen's which started from Edmonton left at 6.21am. It was always packed, with twenty people in each compartment. Those who were left behind to await the next train had to pay $4^1/_2$d each way. One Monday morning in January 1899 railway officials gave the order for the gates to be closed at Lower Edmonton, there being too many passengers already on the platform. Large numbers found themselves left outside. On the following day 1,500 men were waiting for the last workmen's, once again many were locked out. The workmen were angry; as the gates were about to close the crowd surged forward past the barriers and jumped on the train without tickets. At Liverpool Street the men refused to pay and thrust the ticket collectors aside. The GER was forced to make concessions; three additional twopenny workmen's trains were provided from October, one each from Enfield, Walthamstow and Stratford, scheduled to arrive at Liverpool Street between 6.47 and 7am. The company also agreed to make trials of two threepenny trains from Edmonton, to arrive between 7.30 and 8am. It was claimed that the workmen's trains were a direct loss to the shareholders, for it was only the last one that was crowded, the earlier ones leaving half empty.[22]

5. The Bycullah and Ridgeway Estates and the Middle Classes

The Bycullah estate of fifty-four acres was Enfield's most high-class development. It took its name from a district in Bombay for H.J. Riddell, the owner of Bycullah Park, had married an Indian princess. During their ownership Bycullah Park became popular for steeplechase meetings. In later years the Riddells spent much of their time abroad and the house was occupied by Mrs Leslie, the widow of an army officer. Culloden Rowan purchased the estate in 1879 for £24,000 and began to develop the property that same year. He later married Mrs Leslie. The land was offered for sale in plots of not less than a quarter of an acre, 'for the erection of villas of a character to suit professional and business men'. The dwellings put up were imposing; each stood within its own grounds:

> 'One of the prettiest estates in the vicinity of the metropolis', wrote the *Observer* (4 October 1879), 'is that now being laid out by Messrs Rowan and Brighten. At either end of the main carriage drive (Bycullah Road) large artificial circular mounds have been formed for the erection of ornamental fountains. The roads are being lined with limes and poplars. Near the Ridgeway men are engaged sinking an artesian well which has already reached 250 feet, at which depth a solid bed of chalk is reached. Water will be found at between 375 and 400 feet. When the water tower is erected at the upper part of the estate ... sanitary provisions could not be more perfect'.

One magnificent fountain of bronze and cement was erected but, despite the fact that a contemporary photograph shows it, even before the houses had been begun, in full working splendour, the water seems never to have been laid on. The houses were to have breakfast, dining and drawing rooms on the ground

14.   Bycullah estate, plots for sale 1879. Gas lamps were set on the gate pillars at the entrance on Windmill Hill.

15.   The Bycullah estate was Enfield's most high-class development. The land was offered for sale in plots of not less than a quarter of an acre 'for the erection of villas of a character to suit professional and business men.'

16.   Chase Green Avenue in 1907, near the crossroads with Bycullah Road, looking east towards Chase Side.

floor, six large sleeping apartments with a bathroom on the first floor and, on the top floor, a room suitable for a billiard room or nursery. Gates were set at the estate entrance on Windmill Hill with gas lamps (Argand burners) mounted on the gate pillars. A cottage was built there as an entrance lodge for a porter. Protection of the privileged was not entirely unnecessary. Windmill Hill was the place where the 'yobs' congregated on Sunday afternoons and amused themselves by abusing any respectable person who happened to pass that way. Why should 'inoffensive passengers be subjected to unprovoked insult', demanded a correspondent in a letter written in November 1885. He proposed that the attention of the police be given to this matter. Sixty houses had been built on the estate by 8 July 1882 and another forty were being erected to be let at rents of £70 a year and upward. The middle class would usually allocate around ten per cent of income for rent. Alas, the gates and fountains have long since gone and the white brick villas have been demolished, one by one, since the Second World War and replaced by late twentieth century town houses, blocks of flats and bungalows. Circumstances have obliged builders in this area to return to the earlier system of constructing small groups of dwellings to fill the spaces left by the demolition of single large mansions. Thus the streets retain a certain interest that is lacking on many large uniform estates put up in the nineteen thirties. Mr Rowan, in 1880, was allowed to construct a road across Chase Green; that road, Chase Green Avenue, was subsequently spanned by the fine red brick bridge which carries the railway towards Hertford.[23]

The following year the Ridgeway Park estate came into the hands of the builders. None but detached residences to the value of £1,000 and upward were to be built along the Ridgeway. Rowan, in March 1883, purchased the Springcroft estate, thirty-six acres facing the Ridgeway. On this he proposed to build several

17. St Mary Magdalene, standing proudly on the summit of Windmill Hill, was built in 1883. The architect was William Butterfield. The mill was not used after 1887, it lost two of its sails in 1901.

18.   The social requirements of the residents of Bycullah Park were largely met by the Bycullah Athenaeum which was completed in 1883. It was destroyed by fire in 1931.

large residences each in grounds of two acres. He sought permission to supply water from his artesian well on the Bycullah Park estate, only a quarter of a mile away, but the Local Board refused and Mr Rowan was much aggrieved. Some years later (8 September 1893) the Local Board took over the well on the estate despite the strongly expressed wishes of the residents to retain their own supply.[24]

Ten acres of parish land at the Ridgeway was available in the early 1880s for two hundred houses of a rather superior class. At Windmill Hill, twelve acres of the Old Park estate had been bought by Mr Sugden for the construction of two hundred houses. The glebe lands, thirteen acres at the junction of the Ridgeway and Windmill Hill, were staked out for a hundred houses. Lower down the hill, opposite Chase Green, a small estate was set out for a hundred dwellings and there was room for another hundred on the four acres at Bridgen Hall. The Ridgeway Oaks estate came onto the market in 1889 (in the angle between the Ridgeway and Hadley Road); large and expensive properties were again stipulated.[25]

Much of the area along the Ridgeway was developed and all the houses were taken within ten years by businessmen migrating outward from the inner suburbs. The fine church, St Mary Magdalene, standing proudly on the summit of Windmill Hill, was completed in 1883 in memory of Philip Twells of Chase Side House, to meet the spiritual requirements of the well-to-do residents; it had taken only twenty months to complete. The architect was William Butterfield. It was, said the *Observer*, worthy of his reputation. The paper described everything as 'admirable', the Minton tiles used for the flooring, the walnut and oak pulpit and seating, the stencilled ceiling, and the background of the chancel in polished Devonshire marble, panelled and bordered with the letters IHS carved

✴ J. GARRARD, ✴

BUILDER AND DECORATOR,

Sanitary Engineer,

Winchmore Hill and Enfield.

⌂ ESTIMATES FREE. ⌂

The ENFIELD PHARMACY,

ENFIELD TOWN,

Is one of the best-known and oldest established Pharmacies in North London.

Dispensing of Physicians & Surgeons Prescriptions and Family Recipes specially attended to, the Proprietor having had the best experience in this department.

None but Qualified Assistants employed.

F. GOLDBY (late Gange)

PHARMACEUTICAL CHEMIST,

ENFIELD TOWN.

W. HALFYARD & Co.,

Lithographic, Letterpress,

AND

Copper=plate Printers,

BAKER STREET, ENFIELD

NOTE HEADINGS, BILL HEADS,

BUSINESS & ADDRESS CARDS.

HIGH-CLASS MATERIALS ONLY USED.

J. COMBER,

Pastry-cook and

. Confectioner,

FANCY BREAD & BISCUIT BAKER,

LANCASTER ROAD,

ENFIELD.

Families waited on Daily.

Wedding, Birthday, and Christening Cakes made to Order.

School Treats and Parties supplied on the shortest notice.

G. KING & SON,

Removal ∴ Contractors

(Pantechnicons and Covered Vans),

HIGH STREET,

Ponders End.

FURNITURE .

. WAREHOUSED.

From the Enfield Illustrated Magazine, July 1898

in relief. The social needs of the upper middle class were catered for by the building of the Bycullah Athenaeum, approaching completion in October 1883. The hall, 110feet by 55feet, could seat 750 to 1,000 people. Natural light was admitted by 'a lantern of immense dimensions'. At night the hall was illuminated by gas, two stars of twenty burners each suspended from the ceiling and twenty-four wall brackets with globes. Culloden Rowan, the originator of all this splendour, was bankrupt by 1892, with liabilities of £1,388 and no assets. Six months later he was dead.[26]

The increase in middle-class house building gave an opportunity to specialist tradesmen like J. Garrard, practical plumber, gas fitter and glazier, who advertised in the *Observer* (June 1872) offering to fit 'hot and cold baths of every description, water closets… hot houses and vineries with hot water pipes, and apparatus for steam and gas cooking'. A new sewing machine was advertised in October that year called the Beckwith Gem, 'the latest wonder of American ingenuity'. It cost 42s, carriage paid, and boasted a two-year guarantee. And what better Christmas present could an affluent and admiring husband devise for his middle-class wife than the new Harper Twelve Trees wringer-washer, three machines in one? It would do the fortnight's family wash in four hours without rubbing or boiling; it might also save a servant's wages. It was advertised in the *Observer* (20 December 1879) as costing five guineas, carriage paid. Even funerals were changing; light pretty cars were taking the place of the lumbering old mourning coaches. At the funeral of George John Pestalozzi, Thomas Hobbes provided 'a beautiful car with a rich violet pall which covered the coffin'. Upon it several handsome wreaths were placed, provided by friends.[27]

The local photographer proved an inestimable boon to families, linking up remote relatives and preserving the memory of the dead better than the most elaborate funeral monument, as well as providing much inspiration for late twentieth century family historians. R.L. Farr, portrait and landscape photographer, had opened his studio in the Town in November 1869. He made himself available to take portraits from nine in the morning until five in the afternoon, daily. He also sold 'carte-de-visite' views of Enfield at sixpence each, (picture postcards could not be sent by post until 1894). The Enfield Camera Club was set up in June 1890 with twenty-five members; D.G. Pinckney was appointed president. They held their first exhibition on 31 January 1891 at the lecture hall in Chase Side.[28]

Another elegant upper middle-class estate was developed at Hadley Wood from the 1880s. The Great Northern Railway Company in 1846 had planned to extend their lines from Peterborough south into London, passing through former Enfield Chase land belonging to the Duchy of Lancaster. Here the plans of the railway company were delayed until September 1847 by objections raised by Thomas Paris, the tenant at Greenwood Farm, but work began at the end of the year and was completed by August 1850. Kings Cross opened in October 1852 and stations were built at Hornsey, New Southgate, New Barnet and Potters Bar. It was in 1880 that Charles Jack, the owner of the Beech Hill Park estate and mansion, entered into negotiations to induce the railway company to build a station on his land. These negotiations had proceeded so far by 1884 that he was able to arrange a building lease from the Duchy of Lancaster to replace his former lease. By this he agreed to build ten houses before 1885 and thereafter two houses a year. He also agreed to contribute towards the expense of the station, estimated at £6,279, and the bridge estimated at £5,120. Hadley Wood

19. An entrance to Welch's livery stables (formerly Biscoe's) in Church Street. The shop next door is Graham Bros cycle manufacturers. The last buildings on that side of the road were the stables belonging to Chase Side House, demolished in February 1901.

station was opened in April 1885; twelve trains a day in each direction stopped there, but none later than 8pm. Forty upper middle-class houses had been erected by 1896 when Charles Jack died. Building continued slowly. There were just over sixty houses on the estate by 1901 and by 1914 the number had reached about a hundred. During the First World War Beech Hill Park mansion, by then in a dilapidated condition, was used as billets for the Royal Fusiliers.

The middle class required servants to clean their large houses and governesses to educate and look after their children. Miss Maria Halls was engaged by Mrs Thompson of Malmo House, Bycullah Park in 1887, to provide an all-round education for her four daughters in French, English, drawing, music and singing, elementary German, needlework and painting. In her spare time she was to attend to the mending and supervise the servants' work. Music lessons were to extend over three hours every day, the first session to take place before breakfast. She was required to teach, standing at the piano. This paragon was to be paid £20 a year and board. After ten days the mistress complained that her piano playing was not of a high enough standard and she was given ten shillings and dismissed forthwith. The young woman was forced to sue for her out-of-pocket expenses in the County court, where the magistrates admitted that the work demanded was worth £50 a year. W. Saville of Bruce Grove was advertising pianos in the early 1890s at from ten to two hundred and fifty guineas. (eg *Observer* 25 August 1893).[29]

Alfred Pepper, job and postmaster in Silver Street, offered horses, neat broughams and open carriages for hire by the day, week, month or year. James Biscoe of the Rising Sun in Church Street (later William Welch) could proffer the same facilities, but could supply in addition a fashionable circular brougham for wedding and other parties, and wagonettes for large and small excursion parties. He was willing to give estimates for transporting the Rifle Corps on days out and offered lessons in riding. Enfield had the services of a dental surgeon by November 1869, Mr Vinen, who advertised that he visited Enfield every Thursday and could be consulted at Mr Dixon's the chemist shop in Baker Street. Competition was provided a few years later (April 1874) by T. Evans, surgeon dentist, who attended every Tuesday and could be found, a little inappropriately, at Garrard's the plumber's workshop in Church Street. Among his specialities he offered 'incorrodable mineral teeth'. The following year Garrard let his accommodation to a Monday dentist, D. Stewart Mackenzie from Barnet, who offered painless extractions using nitrous oxide gas.[30]

6. Artisans' Dwellings:
Chase Side, Lancaster Road and Eastern Enfield

Chase Side was a country lane until about 1870, with scarcely any dwellings north of the British Schools (now, 1991, The Moon Under Water). Close to the site of the Six Bells, until 1863, stood Gordon House, behind a high wall fronting the road. The grounds extended half-way back to Baker Street. The house is shown on the 1754 map of Enfield parish at Trinity College Cambridge; it took its name from Lord George Gordon, the mad nobleman of the Gordon riots, who owned the property in the eighteenth century. It was an imposing mansion, entered beneath an Ionic portico. The ground floor comprised the entrance hall, the dining room, and a large drawing room with fine oak wainscoting and a statuary chimney-piece. There was a breakfast room and an anteroom. A 'noble oak staircase' led to the four principal bedchambers on the first floor. There were six more bedrooms on the top floor and a secondary staircase led down to the ground floor, so avoiding unnecessary encounters between servants and family. The stables provided accommodation for nine horses; there were roomy coach-houses, with a wash-house and a laundry alongside a spacious carriage yard. A melon house and a walled kitchen garden lay beyond the stables. The estate was first offered for sale in 1847; it comprised seventy-two acres and included the ancient moat called Oldbury. Gordon House was pulled down by 1858 and, a few years later, the grounds were laid out by the North London Society for development under the name of the Gordon estate.[31]

Gordon House, according to a writer in the *Observer* in September 1875, had been wastefully and uselessly pulled down to make way for modern buildings which did not show themselves for years afterwards. 'It might', he said, 'have lasted another century'. Very few houses, it is true, had been built in Gordon Road or in Halifax Road by 1868, but the sale of small dwellings was encouraged soon afterwards by the decision of the Great Eastern Railway Company to add third-class carriages to all their trains in 1872. This incidentally did nothing to diminish the railway company profits. The population of the area had so increased by 1874 that a new church (St Michael's) was considered necessary. A further five acres was set out for a hundred houses in the early 1880s. Building continued over the following thirty years until the whole of Chase Side was

GORDON HOUSE ESTATE FOR SALE 1847

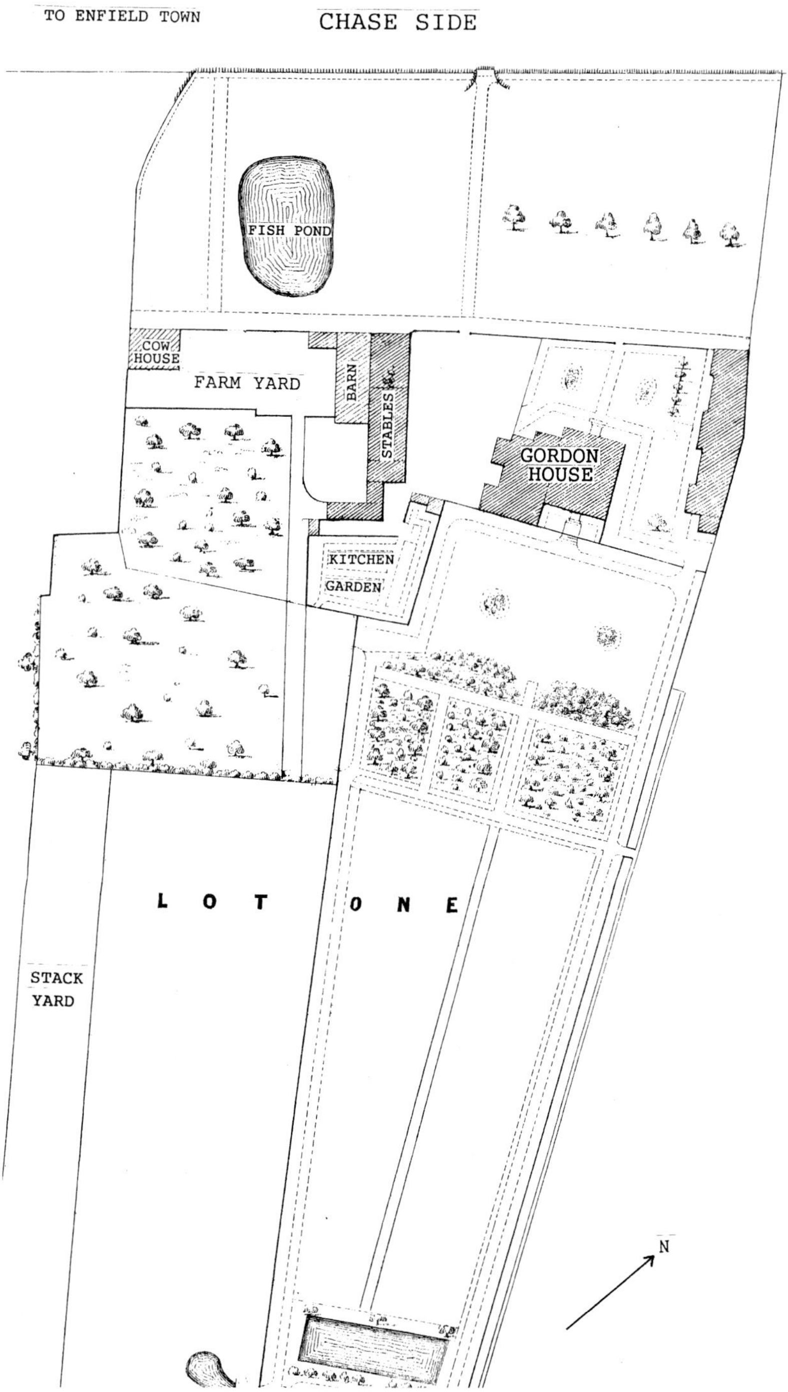

TO ENFIELD TOWN   CHASE SIDE

FISH POND

COW HOUSE

FARM YARD

BARN

STABLES &c.

GORDON HOUSE

KITCHEN GARDEN

L O T   O N E

STACK YARD

N

20.   *The contents of this ancient house, known as 'Raleigh's House' were put up for auction in 1886 and the building was subsequently demolished despite pleas that it should be saved. It stood on Chase Side Crescent by what was then called Lower Gordon Road.*

21.   *'Raleigh's House' from the back.*

occupied by shops and houses.[32]

Another ancient and historically interesting house lost in the building which ensued was the traditionally named 'Raleigh's House' at the junction of Gordon Road and Chase Side. Though it had already fallen into ruin, one correspondent at least, in July 1886, made a plea that it should be saved, but to no avail. Colonel Somerset, the owner, said that he would be willing to sell it to anyone who would restore it, but he declined to do so himself. The contents were auctioned by Richard Nye. One ancient flag-shaped weather vane, now at Little Park, Gentleman's Row, was knocked down to Mr Leggatt for £1; the curious oak panelling from the hall went to the same gentleman for £13 10s; and some antique chairs were bought for £10 4s by Mr Edelstone of Bush Hill Park. The remainder of the paintings, books and furniture were sold, and so ended Sir Walter's very tenuous connection with the parish of Enfield.[33]

The Birkbeck, New Lane, Woodlands, Cedars and Brigadier House estates were laid out for building in 1880 north of Lancaster Road (then New Lane) and plans showing the roads, footpaths and the drainage system were submitted and approved by the local authority. But although houses had been erected on the estates by October 1881 and more were being built, there was as yet little sign of the roads and the footpaths. Many of the properties were put up by small local builders, some living in houses they had themselves built on the estates. Many of them began building with such limited capital that the properties soon fell into the hands of mortgagees. Thus there were frequent changes of ownership and the new householders found it difficult to attach responsibility for the state of the roads and footpaths and even for the drains and water supply. The surveyor of the Local Board urged that a new bylaw should be passed to compel the freeholders to complete such essential works before building agreements were entered into.

An area of twenty-five acres north of New Lane (Lancaster Road) was laid out for development in 400 plots along Birkbeck, Lavender, Acacia and Hawthorne Roads, Woodbine and Myrtle Groves, Violet, Rosemary and Primrose Avenues (the very names redolent of rural tranquillity) and Morley Hill, in January 1879 by the Birkbeck Freehold Land Society. All the plots were sold immediately. Plans to construct a complete sewerage system, with separate storm water drains were submitted by the society to the Local Board of Health; the *Observer* hoped that these would prove more effective than the drains on the Gordon estate. By August 1880 a fifteen-inch sewer had been completed from the Hop Poles as far as Cocker Lane (now Browning Road) but the surveyor to the Local Board found fault and refused (July 1880) to allow connection to the Board's sewers until the defects had been remedied. He also found serious defects in the construction of houses built on the estate by F. Clarke of Tottenham. The first floor joists, he said, were so weak that the floors were scarcely safe to walk over and the greater part of the weight of the roof was carried on a piece of timber only three inches square, moreover the brickwork consisted of a large proportion of 'bats' improperly bonded. The houses, he said, would be 'absolutely dangerous to the public if allowed to remain'. Clarke was also building ten houses in Brigadier Hill where his flues were only seven inches square, totally inadequate to carry off the smoke. 'None of his work', said the surveyor, 'was in accordance with his drawings'.

Plans were submitted before the end of the year 1880 by the builder, J. Richards of Tottenham, for two cottages in Birkbeck Road, and by J. Brooks of

NEW ENFIELD ESTATE.

Birkbeck Freehold Land Society.

9 & 30, SOUTHAMPTON BUILDINGS, CHANCERY LANE, LONDON.

Francis Ravenscroft, Manager.

1887

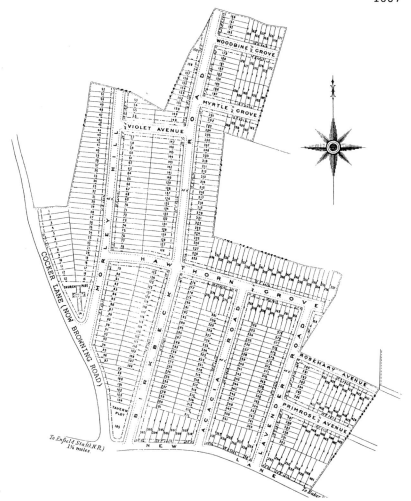

nearby Halifax Road for one cottage in Acacia Road. The following June Brooks submitted plans for three more houses in the same road. Edward Creake of Windmill Hill submitted plans for one cottage in Primrose Avenue and Henry Linzell of Tottenham for thirty-five cottages in Canton Road where he began immediately on the construction of ten. But when he applied to the Board, six months later, for the water supply to be connected, he still had not begun work

22.   *Primrose Avenue, one of the roads laid out in building plots in 1879 by the Birkbeck Freehold
Land Society; all the plots were sold immediately. Part of the road was known as Canton Road.*

on the remaining twenty-five. William Carey of Acacia Road submitted plans in
February 1882 for two cottages in that road, then another in March. George
Howard of Birkbeck Road planned to build two houses nearby in Morley Hill,
and soon afterwards John Crabb of Baker Street submitted plans for a cottage,
also in Morley Hill. A number of houses had been built in Birkbeck Road by
March 1883 when Dr Ridge came down to inspect a shallow well which served
nine new dwellings there. He declared that the water was contaminated and
unfit to drink; he was told that worms and leeches were frequently pumped up.
The estate was well developed by the time St Luke's Church opened there, using
an iron building, in 1885.[34]

The New Lane (Lancaster Road) estate of ten acres was set out for 300 cottage
properties in New Lane, Acacia and Birkbeck Roads and Rosemary Avenue. The
Woodlands estate, near Brigadier Hill, of thirteen acres, was to provide plots for
two hundred houses in Cocker Lane (now Browning Road), Merton, Sterling
and Burlington Roads. Sixty-eight lots on this estate were auctioned by Arthur
Jackson towards the end of February 1881. Fifty lots changed hands immediately
for a total of £2,000; the remaining eighteen were sold subject to negotiation.
Plans were submitted for forty-five houses there in the following June. A fifteen-
inch sewer was laid down by the Board in July 1881, 700 feet along Cocker Lane
and a twelve-inch pipe sewer was extended up New Lane. These were to serve
forty acres of the Woodlands and Cedars estates where a hundred houses were
at the time being built. Those being put up in January 1883 by Messrs Wheeler
(eighteen cottages in Burlington Road) were inspected and condemned by the
surveyor as unsafe and dangerous. The walls were out of perpendicular, bulged
in places, and were imperfectly bonded. The houses had to be demolished and
rebuilt. In April the surveyor served notice on J. King, also building houses in

23.   *Eighteen cottages in Burlington Road were inspected in January 1883 and condemned by the surveyor as unsafe and dangerous.*

Burlington Road, that his work did not accord with his plans as regards the thickness of the walls and the dimensions of the chimney flues. The nearby Cedar estate of fifteen acres was laid out in building plots. In October 1881 the surveyor had reason to complain of eleven houses being built there which infringed the bylaws because the height of the rooms in the back extensions was less than eight feet and the floor joists were too close to the ground. The builder had been warned, but continued to transgress. About this time six acres, which had belonged to Brigadier House, were divided into 200 plots. 'No part of Enfield' said the *Observer* (14 May 1897) 'if we except Bush Hill Park, had been more extensively developed during the last decade than the areas north and south of Lancaster Road.'[35]

The population of the eastern side of the parish trebled in the ten years 1851 to 1861, from 1,534 to 4,954. This was largely due to the expansion of the Royal Small Arms Factory. By 1871 the population of this eastern area had reached 8,027. Medcalf Road near the factory was laid out in 1861 and there were terraces of houses in Warwick Road by 1865. Warwick Road by November 1871 was described as in 'an unwholesome state'. The houses on the west side had forecourts but there was no pavement or footway and the east side was bounded by a ditch. Medcalf Road was in a better condition, having road drains and a footway for part of its length. The surveyor therefore suggested that its condition warranted adoption by the Board. (Surveyor's Report). A jute factory was opened at Duck Lees Lane, Ponders End about 1865. Ponders End mill and the estate attached had been put up for sale in 1853. The old water mill was still operated in two parts but both mills were now employed in grinding corn. One side, with three pairs of stones, was worked by Mr Young, the other, with four pairs, was worked by Mr Farmer. The mill was capable of grinding 350 quarters (500 sacks) of wheat a week. The land attached, when sold, was divided into building plots and Alma and Napier Roads were laid out by 1868. North of

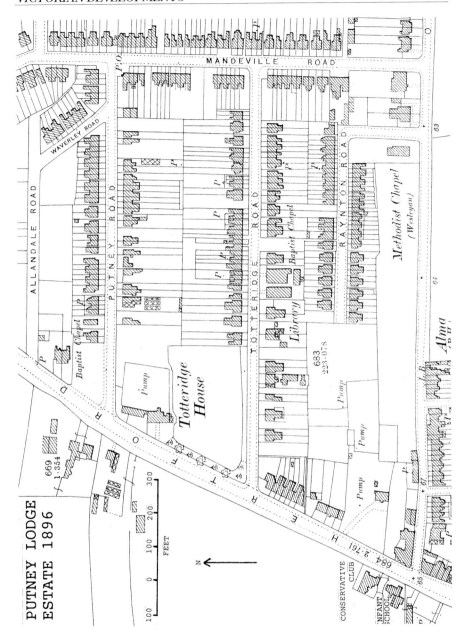

PUTNEY LODGE ESTATE 1896

Ordnance Road, the Putney Lodge estate was sold to the British Land Company in 1867. It was divided into 296 building plots for sale, marked out in Mandeville, Totteridge and Putney Roads. Six-roomed houses there were being advertised in 1869 as suitable for workers at the Royal Small Arms Factory. This estate was not finally completed until 1897.[36]

Vast areas of land, most of it in Enfield, were put on the market at the sale of the Connop estates in 1869, but few buyers were found. Some land with frontages on the main roads was sold; fourteen and a half acres, almost opposite St James's Church, for £5,000 (£345 an acre), for example. South of this, also with frontages on the road, forty-one acres sold for £9,500 (£232 an acre). Over four hundred acres of the land in Enfield offered for sale at this time were being used for market gardens and orchards.[37]

More land had become available for building in the eastern side of the parish by the early 1880s. There were four acres available in Green Street for 160 houses and four acres in Alma Road for 200. Land in Jasper Road was available for fifty, with a further fifty in Ordnance Road and a further fifty in Medcalf Road. Forty acres of market gardens belonging to W. Mitchell, including Broadlands the family residence, were sold in a hundred lots in 1881, and sixty-seven plots of freehold building land in St James Road and Old Road, as well as a brickfield in Southbury Road. By the year 1886 the number of houses for sale in Enfield greatly exceeded the demand. It would be no hardship, said the *Observer*, if the work of the speculative builder was suspended for a few years.[38]

7. Enfield Town and Market

Enfield market remained in almost total abeyance from about 1840 to 1870 and for a time it seemed likely to die out altogether. The market cross, erected in 1826, had been a cheap job (£200) made of Bath stone which proved too soft for survival. For years it had attracted the attention of the swarms of ragged children who pestered the neighbourhood, and forty years later it was in a state of advanced dilapidation. The vestry ordered the demolition in 1847 of the six old wooden houses in the Market Place and the erection, on the south side of the market cross, of a new cast-iron pump. About 1870 the market began to show signs of new life. 'For a long time past,' said a writer in the *Observer* in 1879, 'a few stalls had been erected in the Market Place, but not until the last few months have they been of sufficient importance to engage the attention of the authorities.' Tradesmen were now beginning to quarrel over pitches; some were even taking up places on Friday nights for Saturday. A meeting, convened by circular, was held at the George in April 1867 to consider a project for widening the London Road approach to the Town. It involved the demolition of five cottages and the old house at the corner of Cecil Road where William Winterburn lived. The churchyard in 1859, said Mr Sykes, a leading Enfield solicitor and conservationist writing in the *Observer* (May 1867) 'was an unfenced wilderness overgrown with nettles and weeds, the graves misshapen, the tombs mutilated and defaced'. With total lack of respect, the corner by the footway had been the site for years of a urinal. It was now proposed to put up a screen in the interest of decency. The churchyard had been railed in and put into better order in 1867 under the regime of the Reverend W.D. MacLagan, the curate in charge. Subsequently its state alternately improved and deteriorated over the years.[39]

Despite the changes and the street lighting, the Town after nightfall remained a dark and inhospitable place, according to a correspondent in the *Observer* (26 April 1879):

'After leaving the cheerful lights of the station', he wrote, 'the traveller plunges into the obscurity of Enfield High Street (The Town) where, but for the friendly lights of a few shops, he would be in impenetrable darkness. He

24.   The drinking fountain was erected 1884/5. It was found convenient to keep the fire-escape there until the advent of the trams created the opportunity for the local lads to get a laugh by pushing the apparatus against the overhead wires and it had to be removed. Photograph about 1907, Stansfeld and Co were brewers.

passes the Market Place, the parish church and the post office (near the George) shrouded in gloom. At the New River bridge the darkness is so profound that he must grope his way with a stick or umbrella through the numberless posts and bars and little wicket gates'.

There obviously he was referring to Gentleman's Row. The Board, in August 1880, came to a firm decision that it would provide effective street lighting in all public thoroughfares throughout the year, from sunset to sunrise. Eight persons were to be employed to ensure that the lights were lit and working efficiently. The price of street lighting had fallen (December 1881) to 1s 4d a night for each lamp, and it was expected that, when the new gas works opened, the cost would be further reduced. Notices were now to be put up throughout the parish displaying the names of the streets.[40]

Through the hot dry summer of 1884 people watched the slow progress of the drinking fountain which was being built in the Town under the auspices of the Drinking Fountain Association. The collection of money to pay for it proceeded even more slowly than the building and when the fountain was completed at last in March 1885, the subscription was still £20 short.[41] The Palace School (see Vol. 1 p.249) continued to flourish through the late nineteenth century. The master in 1860 was Nutter Barker who had succeeded his father and, before him, Dr May and Mr Tuke. Nutter Barker was followed by Mr Hogarth, assisted by two resident masters and various visiting tutors who gave instruction in drawing, drilling, music and singing. A chemistry class with laboratory practice had been added by July 1886. After Mr Hogarth retired in 1899 the building was used as a post office, until the new post office was built in 1906. Thereafter the 'Palace' housed the Enfield Town Constitutional Club. Great changes took place in Church Street around 1900 when the old brick wall on the south side of the road, extending from the 'Palace' to the houses adjoining Welch's livery stable, was taken down. Palace Gardens was subsequently built on the former playing fields of the Palace School, and a range of shops known as Palace Parade was put up along Church Street. The old Manor House, fondly though erroneously known as the 'Palace', survived until 1928.[42]

More and more, the Town became a place where people gathered on Saturday nights. 'We have lately had the Town of Enfield almost blocked to ordinary traffic', complained the *Observer* (20 October 1890) 'it being used as a mart for a certain commodity' (alas the coyness of the editor impedes investigation) 'and as a gathering place for people to witness men, women and children having teeth drawn'. Frequently disturbances occurred, sometimes blamed on the Social Democratic Federation, sometimes on the Salvation Army, and sometimes on the drunks.

> 'The flaming lights over the stalls ranged around the market cross', wrote a correspondent in 1893, 'threw a fitful and lurid glare… back in the darkness lay the old parish church. The Town is full of people, fathers and mothers are doing their shopping, boys and girls playing and spending their ha'pennies on sweets. By the fountain, at a Salvationist meeting, a 'sister' was relating her spiritual experiences. Crowds from Edmonton and Tottenham poured into the Town, and people from the villages to the north. There were stalls for provision dealers and fish merchants, crockery sellers laid out their wares on the ground and harangued passers-by. A cheap hosier was doing a brisk business, while on another corner a very voluble trader sold sweets, "one, two, three (he piled them up, some with medicinal ingredients of his own concoction), four, now, all this lot for one penny". A cheerful young damsel sold whelks at a penny a dish. Many an anxious housewife could be seen eking out her few shillings to the best advantage. The Town on Saturday nights was the scene of hard drinking and horseplay. But little by little the market emptied, one by one the lamps were put out and at last all was still, for the Sabbath approached. In the early hours the scavengers appeared to sweep up the refuse and by the time the Town awoke all was spick and span and the battered crumbling old market cross awaited a new day'.[43]

The market had grown so busy by 1895 that it warranted a statement from that almost forgotten institution, the Enfield manor court, recommending the parochial charities to exercise control. A set of rules was forthwith adopted. It was strongly felt that the approach to the west door of the church should be improved and the public convenience at the entrance to Church Walk should be moved to a less exposed position. 'A fine new building' (now Barclays Bank) said the *Observer* (2 July 1897) 'is nearing completion on the site of the old court house (the former Greyhound). The new George is to be flanked on the west with an ornate and lofty building which will take the place of that known for many years as Meyers's Library'. In July, workmen excavating at a depth of three feet in the Market Place, to lay down a drain from the new London and Provincial bank, came across brickwork foundations, presumably of The Vine public house, demolished in the reign of James I.[44]

The Enfield Parochial Charities in December 1896 invited tenders for an eighty-year lease of the Kings Head at £100 p.a., on condition that the lease-

25.   *A view from the church tower about 1905, showing the market and the old 'Palace' behind the shops on the far side of Church Street. Dr Uvedale's great cedar still dominates the skyline.*

holder spent not less than £3,000 on rebuilding the house. The lease was taken by the Cannon Brewery.[45]

The death of Mrs Philip Twells in 1900 led to the breakup of the estate belonging to Chase Side House, which had been built as recently as 1826 by a Mr Stedman. The mansion was demolished, shops were erected on part of the street frontage, and the land where the house had stood, now known as the Library Green, was purchased by the Urban District Council for a town hall; they paid £5,000. G.W. Marshall was given permission to make a road from Cecil Road to Church Street through the estate. On 15 February 1901 the local paper wrote 'Chase Side House is now no more'. The entrance gate on Church Street disappeared with the building of Sarnesfield Road. Cecil Road was extended and the old elms and the high wall opposite the Wesleyan chapel were ruthlessly destroyed. On the north side of the road, the grounds of Little Park were developed in the early years of this century with shops along the frontage in Church Street up to the present site of the post office. The house itself, (now the Registrar's office) had been purchased by the Local Board in 1888 to be used for offices. The name Little Park was subsequently transferred to the house next door. (5 Gentleman's Row).[46]

The state of the market cross had deteriorated by Christmas 1901. It was then leaning markedly out of perpendicular, which posture was attributed to excavations for a public lavatory near by. Further subsidence, it was held, would render it dangerous; underpinning, it was thought, would be too expensive. Thus the parochial charities decided on demolition and the parish lost the opportunity to rival Pisa or, at least, Chesterfield.[47] A new market house was erected in 1904, an octagonal structure supported on eight columns of teak. It bears an inscription on the cornice to declare that it was erected to commemorate the coronation of Edward VII.

Political meetings in the Town were banned in July 1903, but the prohibition was defied. At twelve noon on the Sunday after the prohibition, Mr Wrampling, a Social Democrat, undeterred, mounted the steps of the fountain and launched into 'abuse of sundry clerics and public men'. He was warned by Inspector Twigg and, refusing to leave, had his name and address taken. Following this he declared defiantly to those assembled that he was prepared to do a month for the right to free speech.[48]

Writing in the *Gazette* (29 January 1909) H. Dugdale Sykes lamented the loss of many picturesque and interesting buildings around Enfield Town. The seventeenth century Rummer had been pulled down in 1859. The Greyhound survived only until 1897 though it had ceased to be a public house after 1860. The George had been rebuilt in 1895. The former Cowden Clarke schoolhouse had been taken down in 1872 when a new railway station was built behind it in Southbury Road. The entrance to the Town from Southbury Road, said Mr Sykes, had for a long time been an eyesore and an obstruction to traffic. The road had been only fourteen feet wide. On one corner, the site subsequently taken by Lloyds Bank, had stood 'a rare old style of house and shop', occupied by Mr Grout the saddler. Close to the station there had been a piece of waste land used as a dumping ground for rubbish; it had lain desolate since the opening of the Eastern Counties railway in 1849. The buildings from Southbury Road to London Road, he said, 'had been of a uniformly squalid and mean appearance'. The old Nags Head and the two shops next to it were demolished when Southbury Road was widened in 1882. Mann and Crossman the brewer had contributed £1,250 to the scheme, and Nags Head Lane in 1882 had become Southbury Road. The new Nags Head had opened in March 1883 with a coffee room and parlour and facilities for billiards, pool and pyramids. On the western corner of Silver Street there had been old wooden houses with low doorways; the passing of these too were mourned by Mr Sykes.[49]

8. Banks, Post Office, Police and Telephones

Enfield had no bank for business transactions until the London and Provincial established a branch on the east side of the Town in 1875. It was open Tuesdays and Fridays. Their fine building on the corner of the Market Place was built in 1898, designed by the local architect W. Gilbee Scott. Lloyd, Barnet and Bosanquet's Bank followed in 1886 and the building now on the corner of Southbury Road and Silver Street replaced Mr Grout's shop at the beginning of the year 1892. Grout's moved to number two, Southbury Road. With the decline of saddlery, the business developed into an ironmongery and tool shop which many of the older inhabitants of Enfield will recollect with a sense of loss. A branch of Barclays bank was established in 1908. The Enfield Savings Bank had been modestly holding its own for many years; receipts in February 1859 amounted to £3,834, repayments to £3,806. The branch which had been opened at the Royal Small Arms Factory however, had been closed because of the hostility which existed there between the management and the artisans.[50]

The post office in 1840 was kept by Mr Jelly the baker, in the wooden premises which later became Ebben's (now, 1991, a carpet shop). After Mr Jelly's death, his widow became the postmistress and the office subsequently passed to her sister Miss Leech. Her shop was next to John Tuff's the chemist. It had an eighteenth-century bow window and was divided into two parts by a glass partition, one part used by the postmen, the other by the public. The General Post Office constantly complained of a shortage of space there and when the parcel post began, they commandeered Miss Leech's back parlour. Mr Cushing the builder had to build a sitting-room for the postmistress on her garden. All this is related in Miss Copeland's recollections, originally published in the *Gazette* as *Recollections of Old Enfield* (reprinted and republished in 1983 by Edmonton Hundred Historical Society.)

Miss Leech and her sister were paid only £75 a year and had to find their own accommodation and lighting. Miss Copeland, who lived with them and helped in the post office, was obliged to go out teaching in order to make ends meet. She became postmistress in 1871 and retired in 1896. Christmas day and New Year's day, she recalled, were not very busy in those early days, 'But on St Valentine's day; then we would have a pile to be sure'. Mostly the valentines were of a sentimental character, elegantly produced and often scented, displaying love tokens, usually a pair of doves. She remembered the beginning of the telegraph service. 'The instalment of the wires and instruments was a great ordeal'. They had to pick up the work of sending and receiving messages as best they could. What made it so difficult was that they had to deal with telegrams for the Royal Small Arms Factory. It took postman Webb an hour to get to the Lock with a message. This situation was remedied however in 1870 when telegraph lines were put up to connect the post office on Edmonton Green to the post offices at Ponders End, Enfield Wash and Enfield Lock. The line was carried along the main road on wooden standards, set a hundred yards apart. Each stood forty feet high and was painted green with a white base. After July 1871 the mail bags were brought down on the Great Northern Railway. The *Observer* noted regretfully, 'We have seen the last of the little red carts and the gold-laced-coated drivers'. The letters had to be sorted into eight walks, for there were eight postmen. As the parcel post developed, the premises in the Town became far too small and at last, in June 1883, they were forced to move into new premises

26.   The Nags Head had been rebuilt in 1882. The trees along the north side of the Town were
planted in 1884 and the drinking fountain was erected that same year. The George was modernised
in 1895 and the London and Provincial Bank, established in Enfield in 1875, moved to the corner
of the Market Place in 1897. The cart to the rear belongs to Singer's sewing machines.

27.   The Metropolitan Police in 1840 took over the Vestry House in the Town, which became the sub-divisional station.

built by Mr Fairhead in Southbury Road,[51] a move which was not popular, for it was held that the post office should be in the Town. 'As a temporary measure', said the *Observer* (7 July 1899) 'we hear that the old Palace School is to be fitted up as a post office'. There were pleas in the local press that the old house should be saved by conversion to a museum and public library, but the furniture at this time was sold by auction.[52]

The Commissioners of the Metropolitan Police in 1835 had not extended their area of jurisdiction north beyond Hackney and Newington, although the police patrols, like Watkin, a Waterloo man who lived in a wooden cottage in London Road, became part of the Metropolitan force from 1836. That year the gentlemen of Tottenham complained that their parish lay entirely unprotected except for a few night watchmen employed by the Commissioners of the Metropolitan Turnpike Roads. The gentlemen requested that the Metropolitan Police should establish a force 'adequate to protect the property and peace' of the Tottenham inhabitants, but Lord John Russell thought that such a move would be 'ill-advised'. The Act passed in 1839 extended the police area to up to fifteen miles from Charing Cross, its present limit. Enfield, Edmonton, Hornsey and Tottenham became part of the Metropolitan 'N' division on 13 January 1840. The police force in Enfield before 1840 had been under the control of the local magistrates sitting in petty sessions at Mr Sawyer's office in Silver Street. The Enfield constables were all above the age of thirty and so were precluded from appointment to the Metropolitan Police. Criminal cases arising in the parish, according to Mr Sawyer, were 'by no means numerous', and had been adequately dealt with at petty sessions. He hoped that this practice would be allowed to continue, which would avoid cases being sent to police courts outside the parish. The Metropolitan Police in 1840 took over the Vestry House in the

28.   *This new police station was built in London Road in 1872. Photograph 1909.*

Town. Five police stations were established in the new sub-division; at Edmonton, using the former watch house in Church Street; at Scotland Green in Tottenham; at Hornsey; at Turners Hill in Cheshunt; and at the Vestry House which became the sub-divisional station for the new area with an inspector in charge. A police sergeant and six police constables were deployed at Enfield Highway. A police station was built at Green Street in 1849.

The constables wore blue swallow-tail coats, blue trousers (white duck during the summer) and tall, shiny, black leather 'stovepipe' hats, reinforced, so it was said, so that officers could stand on them to see over high walls. Each constable carried a truncheon and a rattle. 'It was always the aim of the riff-raff,' wrote Mr Plume, 'to knock off the policeman's tall hat'. Police courts, following 1840, were held in the Greyhound Inn which, after it closed as a public house, became known as the court house. A revision of the outer districts took place on 30 October 1865 when Enfield became part of 'Y' Division. A new police station was built in London Road in 1872.[53]

A meeting was called at the beginning of May 1891, on the suggestion of Dr Ridge, to consider the viability of a local telephone exchange in Enfield. The National Telephone Company, taken over by the Post Office in 1912, promised to ensure that it would be manned day and night, including Sundays. Subscribers for £10 a year would be entitled to make local calls; for £20 a year they could extend the range of calls to London. Call rooms would be established for non-subscribers where local calls might be made for 3d, London calls for 6d, for a maximum of three minutes in each case. It was proposed that a canvass be made of potential subscribers, but the parish was as yet too conservative for the adoption of such advanced technology. The first telephone call box was installed at the Town station in March 1910.[54]

9. Outlying Estates and Great Houses

The introduction in the budget of 1894 of graduated estate duties presaged a new threat to the survival of large estates, though the burden on owners was at first only light. Fortunately for Enfield some great estates avoided the fatal embrace of the land societies and survived long enough to come under the protection, for ever one hopes, of the Green Belt. Most of these surviving estates, like Trent Park, lay remote from both population centres and public transport. Trent Park had originally been part of Enfield Chase. It was purchased when the Chase was enclosed in 1777 and the villa was built there by Sir Richard Jebb, physician to George III. He paid £2,220 for the lease and £2,955 for the timber. He proposed to use most of the land (altogether 350 acres) as a park. The villa was in the Italian style. He called it Trent Park in honour of the Duke of Gloucester on whom he had worked a miraculous cure at Trento in Italy. The *Gentleman's Magazine* described it disparagingly as 'a loggia', hardly large enough for a single man, only thirty feet by forty; the biggest room measured only twenty feet by sixteen. Jebb created paddocks and stocked his park with deer. On his death in 1787, Trent passed briefly to the Earl of Cholmondeley and in 1793 to John Wigston, who also owned Millfield House in Edmonton. After Wigston's death the estate was leased to Sir Henry Lushington a banker, and then to John Cumming who made improvements to the house and died there in 1832.

The following year David Bevan of Belmont at Cockfosters purchased Trent Park (now 471 acres) for his eldest son Robert Cooper Lee Bevan, on the occasion of his marriage. Robert was to live there until his death in July 1890. He was a partner in Barclays Bank; it was he who built Christ Church Cockfosters, and provided both the boys' school and girls' school there. Though he was wealthy, life in the mansion throughout the time of the Bevans was austere. There was no billiard room, no smoking room, and worldly amusements were shunned. No dances were presented, no theatre visits arranged, no race meetings, no card playing. Bible reading was a daily routine. Robert had been a convert to evangelicalism at the age of twenty-seven and often preached in the little Calvinistic Methodist chapel at Botany Bay. Emma, his wife, had been brought up High Church 'as befitted the daughter of the Bishop of Chichester', but she became a member of the Plymouth Brethren. It was Robert who planted the grand double avenue of lime trees and he who converted the house into a Victorian mansion of mauve brick and slate. Trent Park was always full of children; Robert's two wives bore him fourteen. His son Francis had three wives and ten children; he also was an evangelical. He sold the lease in 1908 for £12,000 to Sir Edward Sassoon. There was nothing evangelical about the Sassoons. Prime Minister Asquith spent the week-end there in June 1910 and played a mixed foursome with Miss Asquith on Enfield golf course. Sir Edward died in 1912, following a car accident. He bequeathed Trent Park to his son, Philip.[55]

The great ambition of Philip Sassoon was to erase his Jewish oriental background and to achieve acceptance in society at the highest level. Trent Park was to play a major role in his attempted self-transmutation, for hospitality of a rare kind was the instrument he was to employ and for this he needed a grand setting. Although an invitation to Sassoon's Trent Park became, in the nineteen-twenties, the hallmark which distinguished the important and successful from

29.   *Sassoon's magnificent Trent Park. Car parking is no longer allowed on the forecourt.*

those struggling to become so, or those declining from being so, no discerning eye could be deceived into believing that Sir Philip Sassoon was an English country gentleman.

The house, transformed from Bevan's ugly building, he touched with magic, 'so that where formerly had glowered a mid-Victorian mansion in mauve brick with designs in black brick covering its face ... now stood an old house in rose-red brick with stone cornering, long settled and stained with time'.

Jebb's original house had not been pulled down but incorporated. Between 1926 and 1930 Sassoon re-designed the mansion and encased it with bricks from the recently demolished Devonshire House. From there too came the portico and the stonework. Sassoon's re-fashioned Trent is so beautiful that few, seeing it, would doubt that it had been established there for at least two hundred years. The royal family were regularly entertained there; Lloyd George and Winston Churchill were many times Sir Philip's guests.

The park, ornamented with statues from Stowe, Milton Abbey and Wrest Park, was as true to the eighteenth century as the house. Occasionally Sir Philip threw the grounds open to the public in aid of charity, and visitors could savour for themselves the splendour of the park, the picturesque Japanese and Italian gardens, the greenhouses and the orangery, the lovely beds of water lilies, the wide lake ornamented with black and white swans, magnolias like huge trees, and the wonderful pergolas. His masterpiece of ostentatious hospitality was on the occasion of the visit of Prince George Duke of Kent and Princess Marina, following their wedding in 1934. For the honour and delectation of the newly-weds Sir Philip set up the three obelisks from Wrest Park which bear tribute to certain eighteenth century dukes of Kent. Sir Philip died a bachelor in June 1939 at the age of fifty; his ashes were scattered by an RAF squadron over his estate at Trent Park.

The house was requisitioned during the Second World War, emptied of its treasures, and used as an interrogation centre for high-ranking prisoners-of-war. When peace came it was requisitioned by the Ministry of Education, with five acres around it, as a teacher training centre to provide a six-month crash course for ex-servicemen. It became a residential teacher training college in 1950. Soon afterwards the park was acquired by compulsory purchase for the Middlesex County Council.

Those who would like to know more about Sir Philip should read Stephen Doree's delightful article '*The Sassoons of Trent Park*'.[56]

Whitewebbs too has escaped the developer. The mansion was built by Dr Abraham Wilkinson who had purchased the estate, Whitewebbs Farm, from the Bretons in 1787. The exterior was altered to a French Second Empire style, c. 1870-80, probably by his grandson Henry Cox Wilkinson who died at the mansion in 1887, just one century after his grandfather had purchased the place. An article in the *Observer* at that time described the house as magnificent. The internal decor, it said, was the work of Italian artists and the mansion contained works of art of immense value which were sold at Christie's in February 1888. The Wilkinson family continued to live at Whitewebbs until the estate was purchased by Lady Meux of Theobalds in March 1900. She cut down 'thousands of trees' and let the house intermittently; Frank L. Gardener was living there from 1902 until 1906. After the death of Lady Meux the estate was taken by Sir Frederick Orr Lewis, a Canadian, in August 1911. The house to which Sir Frederick travelled by car the fifteen miles from London stood in forty acres of park and woodland. It was a long white building with about forty rooms including servants' quarters. A generator was used to light the house and to pump the water. 'The gardens were beautifully laid out and an ornamental lake provided a shady retreat at the back of the house'. Maples were called upon to furnish the mansion and, when it was ready, Lady Orr Lewis invited the local gentry — Sir Henry and Lady Bowles, Colonel Sir Alfred and Lady Somerset, Colonel Bosanquet, and others from further afield, to a house-warming party. Sir Frederick held the estate until his death in 1921. It then passed to his son, Sir Duncan Orr Lewis, who retained it until 1931 when it was purchased by the Middlesex County Council and leased to Enfield Urban District Council as a public park. The house was retained by the County Council, intended for use as an old people's home.[57]

Old Park, though much diminished, has also survived. Edward Ford, the owner who died there in 1893, had been born in Lancaster and had taken the estate in 1837. He was a member of the commission of peace for forty years. John Walker Ford abandoned Old Park in September 1909, as the Grange Park estate encroached too close for his peace of mind. Hundreds of collectors and dealers

30.   *Old Park in 1888; Edward Ford died there in 1897. He had taken the estate sixty years earlier, it was abandoned by John Walker in 1909.*

attended when the contents of the house were sold by auction in November. Among the objects dispersed that day were three Roman amphorae and a great deal of Georgian silver. A stained glass panel from the dining-room, decorated with armorial emblems and dated 1606, was sold for £80; a similar panel, dated 1587, went for £156. A marble figure of Oliver Goldsmith fetched 280 guineas. The library, which was sold at Sothebys the following year, contained first editions of *Jane Eyre* and *Wuthering Heights* which sold for £28 and £48 respectively.[58]

Following the death of James Meyer, the Forty Hall estate passed into the hands of H.C.B. Bowles of Myddelton House who purchased it from Meyer's executors as a residence for his son, Henry Ferryman Bowles. Throughout the first half of the year 1897, Forty Hall was in the hands of builders and decorators who carried out a thorough renovation and made considerable structural alterations. The white plaster which covered the outer walls was removed and additions to the west made on the north side of the house. The former staircase was removed (alas no description was left for our benefit) and was replaced by what the *Observer* described (27 August 1987) as a very handsome staircase of oak. The hall from which the staircase springs was opened up by the removal of brickwork which had partly closed the arched entrance to the hall from the main passage through the centre of the house. The ceilings were cleaned and restored. The building work was done by Patman, the decoration by Washington of Turkey Street.

The Forty Hall and Myddelton House estates, which belonged to the Bowles family, comprised 500 acres in 1909 and included coverts and a deer park. The gardens at Forty Hall were tastefully laid out, the most notable feature being the magnificent box edging, at least two hundred years old. E.A. Bowles, the brother of Colonel Henry Ferryman Bowles, had constructed a wonderful rock garden at Myddelton House which had attained world-wide celebrity for the rare and beautiful plants seen there. The only lighting within Myddelton House was provided by candles.[59]

The line of descent of the family was from Henry Carington Bowles, a director of the New River Company who died in 1852. His property came to a nephew, Henry Carington Bowles of Myddelton House, who for many years was treasurer and became governor of the New River Company, until it was taken over by the Metropolitan Water Board. At that time he was elected chairman of the New River Lands Company. He was deputy lieutenant of the county, lord of the manor of Worcesters, and a member of the Local Board of Health. It was he who promoted the formation of the Enfield Local Volunteers in 1859. When he died in February 1918 his fortune amounted to £373,486. He left two sons, Henry Ferryman Bowles, usually known as Colonel Bowles of Forty Hall, and E.A. 'Gussie' Bowles who continued to live at Myddelton House.[60]

Following the death of Lady Meux, there was an auction of the furniture and contents of Theobalds Park in May 1911; the Egyptian museum there was sold for only £1,700. The house was taken by Admiral Sir Hedworth Meux. King George V was his guest there in November 1912 for a day's shooting. The estate, 104 acres, was leased about 1930 and developed as a first-class residential hotel. Most of the existing furniture was bought by the lessee for about £30,000. Hot and cold water was laid on to the bedrooms, a golf course was created, tennis, squash and racket courts were set up and swimming baths were built, covered and open. The house contained forty bedrooms, a dining-room to seat one hundred, three drawing-rooms, a library and a card-room.[61]

Dacre Lodge at Cockfosters, known as Buckskin Hall in the seventeenth century, was destroyed by fire in February 1895. It was a house of considerable size and value, the residence of Mrs Gladstone, widow of Robert, a cousin of William Gladstone. Most of the village of Cockfosters, cottages, blacksmith's shop, mission hall and workmen's club, was part of the Yeeda Grange estate, which was sold by Harrods (as auctioneers) in August 1911. The Grange itself, a large rambling Victorian mansion, was demolished in December 1972. A motor omnibus service was extended in November 1913 from Southgate to Cockfosters[62]

Wolverton, the residence of H. Trenchard J.P. in Hadley Road, was offered for sale by auction in June 1909 with grounds of four acres. The building, in the Jacobean style, was held to be of great architectural beauty. The design for the house had been exhibited at the Royal Academy and at the St Louis exhibition. It had cost £10,000 to build and to lay out the gardens; 'splendid' heating and lightings systems had been installed. The property failed to reach the reserved price and was withdrawn at £4,900.[63]

Capel Manor too survived. It was offered for sale in 1791 in the Court of Chancery. The former owner had been William Hart. It then comprised fifty acres including a modern brick mansion called Capel House, a dwelling house in Turkey Street. Also included was 'a new built brick and timber manufactory adjoining a capital head of water with every requisite for the dyeing branch'. Capel House, according to a survey of 1781, had been built about 1760; '£200 judiciously laid out', it was claimed, 'would make the premises in a fit condition to receive a purchaser or tenant'. The estate was purchased by Rawson Hart Boddam, formerly governor of Bombay. He demolished the mansion, keeping only the stables and a few other outbuildings, but retained the name for the new villa which he built there. The estate was purchased in 1840 by James Warren and the house remained in his family until it was sold to Lt Colonel Sydney Medcalf in 1932. Medcalf died in 1958 leaving the estate to the Incorporated Society of Accountants which used it for residential courses until 1966, when they rented it to the Enfield College of Technology. The grounds and outbuildings were leased in 1968 to the Capel Manor Institute of Horticulture. The whole property was purchased in 1973 by the London Borough of Enfield so that the house could be used by the Middlesex Polytechnic. This arrangement lasted until 1980 when the house too was taken over by the Institute.[64]

High rating, following the revaluation of 1929, contributed to the loss of many fine old houses. J. Neilson the agent, asking for a reduction of the assessment on Roselands in Turkey Street, claimed that any new tenant would have difficulty in keeping up the property in a proper way. Because of the high assessment he had been unable to find a tenant for the Manor House at Bulls Cross owned by Sir John French — less well-known as the 1st Earl of Ypres — and it had been pulled down. He asked for a reduction at Claysmore, Clay Hill, which had recently been let to Lady Tree at £158 per annum. There too he had experienced great difficulty in finding a tenant, and now her ladyship had asked to be released, so that house too looked likely to be demolished. He believed that the property had been built in 1608.[65]

10. Land Sales and House Building 1897-1903

After a lull which had lasted for about ten years, the late 1890s saw a surge in land sales and house building in Enfield. During the three years up to 28 January 1898, 480 houses were added to the rate books and the pace of building was accelerating. In the seven months between 28 January and 31 August 1898, plans for the erection of 463 houses were submitted to the district council. Land containing brick-earth became particularly valuable; thirty-three acres (most of it near Hoe Lane) were sold to a brickmaker in 1900 for £8,100 (£245 an acre). At the same time twenty-six acres of market garden and orchard in Carterhatch Lane sold for £3,350 (£126 an acre). Mr Bowyer, the auctioneer, on 25 March 1898 disposed of ten and a half acres on the south side of Lancaster Road. 'In a short time', said the *Observer*, 'it will be metamorphosed from market gardens into highways and artisans' dwellings.' There was an unprecedented demand for small properties in this area and the Brigadier House estate (Brigadier House stood on the site now, in 1991, occupied by St Luke's Church) was about to be put on the market. Plans were in preparation for the development of land in Browning Road where two and a half acres were offered by auction in fifty or sixty plots. Services were unable to keep up with the expansion. A petition from the residents of the Cedar estate in March 1898, complained of 'a total lack of street lighting'. 'Many new residents had moved into the area' and the householders demanded that their wives and daughters should have the protection of well-lit streets. The long suffering residents on the Birkbeck estate, in August

1900, were promised roads to replace the quagmires and tracks on their estate. Tenders were out to make-up Canton Road (now part of Primrose Avenue), Primrose Avenue, Birkbeck, Acacia and Lavender Roads. Select houses in Kynaston Road, under the management of a Mr Drake, were offered at 11s a week inclusive; careful judgement was promised in the selection of tenants. Five years later the rents had to be reduced to 10s. The old wooden house at the foot of Brigadier Hill (now called Brigadier House) survived. Its neighbour, known as 'Woodlands', a house built in a similar style, was used as the Ruth Elliott home of rest, where sick and crippled children were cared for by Doctors Ridge and Knox Souttar.[66]

A piece of vacant land known as Drapers which for twenty years had been a sort of no man's land, 'a refuge for derelict pots, pans and donkeys', was laid out for building by 5 August 1898. A carriage road forty feet wide would be constructed and planted with trees to form 'a grand avenue between the Ridgeway and Lavender Hill'; a splendid site, said the *Observer* (5 August 1898) for medium-class residences, detached or semi-detached, for sale or to let.

Sixty-three acres close by the railway to Enfield Town, lying between Southbury Road and Lincoln Road, were sold in July 1898 for £7,800. All the lots there were secured on behalf of Mr Williams of Swansea. Within a year or two, it was predicted, four or five thousand houses would be built. Development proceeded apace; freehold plots, for sale or to let, were offered there in September 1899 and responsible builders were invited to bid. 'Medium sized houses', said the *Observer* (16 March 1900) 'are let or sold as soon as, or before, finished'. All the frontages on Fotheringham and Lincoln Roads had by then been taken, and many of the fine frontages on Burleigh Road, which was nearest to the station.

Ten lots were sold in March 1900 with a frontage on a new road to be called Cecil Avenue. The estate included the Oldbury moat (see Vol. 1 p.70). When the moat was threatened in 1892 its preservation had been urged, yet the site remained undespoiled in 1897 though hemmed in on all sides by the developer. It was proposed at that time that it should be acquired as a recreation ground, but the urban district council remained paralysed by its penury. The moat was finally filled up and a road was driven across the site. H.S. Hardman's men, working nearby at the end of Burleigh Road, found a Roman lead coffin eighteen inches below ground level and, two or three feet away, two sepulchral urns of grey coloured pottery were discovered side by side and flanked by red tiles set on edge. Regarding discoveries from the Roman period (see Vol. 1 p.16) it should be mentioned that in 1908 further south, work on Cornish's brickfield, now the Raglan School playing field, uncovered a stone coffin containing two skeletons. Roman pottery had previously been unearthed in this field. It was estimated by July 1904 that 3,000 people now occupied the streets between Southbury and Lincoln roads and the population there was still growing.[67]

It was reported in April 1898 that a road was being constructed across the Manor House estate in Chase Side. On the Gordon estate the land formerly known as Clarke's fields, abutting on Gordon Road, was now laid out for building. C.H. Jacobsen proposed to build thirty-seven villas and three shops on the north side of Gordon Road down as far as the Gordon Road infant school (later the scout hut). The houses, with Bath stone bay windows and York stone sills, were to comprise six rooms with a bathroom (cold water only) the baths to be of a style known as 'roman'. Rents would be set at 10s to 10s 6d, but payment of 11s 6d would secure the lease of a 'villa' over twenty years, plus a moderate ground rent. No deposit was demanded and the occupier would complete his purchase of the lease merely by paying the higher sum over twenty years. Land at the rear was laid out for College Road, leading from a new road called Heene Road into Gordon Road; 150 houses in all would be built.[68]

Agricultural labourers' cottages survived in many places throughout the parish and many of them by the end of the century were in a dilapidated condition. Councillor J.J. Wilson thought that most of them ought to be condemned, but then what would happen to those who lived in them? There were too many already, he said (*Observer* 21 April 1899) labouring for £1 a week, who had to pay half their wages in rent. That was the reason why the poor still lived in places like Loves Row (now Chapel Street behind Gentleman's Row). There was no way to reach Loves Row by road. It comprised, built alongside a ditch, a row of cottages which were very old and badly in need of repair. The floors lay directly on the earth and some of them were lower than the ground outside. The ditch, used upstream by many dwellings as an open sewer, had been a recurrent nuisance there for years, and ought to have been piped long before.[69]

Dr Ridge, the medical officer, declared in March 1901 that housing was the most urgent problem facing the community; how to arrest the continual rise in rents which was forcing the poor to crowd together in ways detrimental to health and decency. The danger of indecency among the poor was likely to have weighed as heavily upon Dr Ridge as the danger to their health. The worst difficulties he added regretfully, taking the opportunity to bang the old temperance drum, were usually found among those given to drink, but even if, by increased sobriety, such people were able to pay more rent and could thereby seek separate accommodation, the landlords would respond to the increased demand by putting up rents. Dr Ridge was of the opinion that the remedy lay in compulsory acquisition and municipalisation: it is a debate that continues into the late twentieth century.

Some people certainly found difficulty with the rent. Arabella Chandler, aged forty-six of Montrose Terrace (Scotland Green Road), was charged with an assault upon the rent collector, using a hobbing foot; the man was left bleeding profusely from the head. He had come to give her notice to quit because her rent was in arrears. Mrs Chandler alleged that the rent collector was drunk and that he had forced his way in and struck her child. She called upon her daughter and a youth to corroborate her version of events, but she was fined 20s with the alternative of fourteen days.[70]

A campaign of meetings and petitions was pursued by the Housing League, to demand council housing for working men, but in reality the housing shortage was coming to an end, as it was at this time throughout the whole of the outer London area. There had been so much new building by September 1901 that eighteen to twenty houses for rent could at any time be found around Southbury Road, while at Fifth Avenue, Bush Hill Park, nine or ten cottages were on offer at 6s 6d a week. Councillor Hardman declared that month that he had six-roomed houses for which he had difficulty in obtaining 7s a week. Nevertheless the Housing League continued to press the local authority to provide council housing and in June 1902 presented a scheme for the building of a hundred houses on five acres. It was argued at the council meeting that a large number of houses were empty in poor areas like Alma Road and Scotland Green, but Mr Weston pointed out that, whereas five years before these houses could be rented at 4s 6d a week, the landlords now demanded 6s 6d. He claimed that the chairman (J.H. Saunders) who was the largest house agent in Enfield, would be unable to find a house for a low wage earner at less than 6s. Unwilling to agree, the chairman asserted that he had many to let at 5s 6d and there were others who had houses at 4s or 5s. The problem did not then exist, as it does in the late twentieth century in Enfield, of a scarcity of small cheap dwellings. Many of these were then being built, though men continued to argue whether the rents were too high for the poor. Mr Sutton of Gordon Road and Mr Burrage of Ponders End had each in course of erection forty specially designed workmen's cottages at Bush Hill Park between the school and the station; these would be completed in three months. Scores of small houses for artisans had recently been built in that locality.[71]

The Small Dwellings Acquisition Company was floated by certain members of Parliament to assist working men to become house owners by taking advantage of the terms of the Small Dwellings Acquisition Act of 1899. Land was acquired at Bush Hill Park in Landseer Road, and by December 1902 eighty-seven houses were being built. Each comprised six rooms and a bathroom; those on the west side of the road had a frontage of sixteen feet (slightly less on the east side) and a depth of ninety-six feet. The local authority by the terms of the Act was able to offer a mortgage at from three and a half to four per cent, of up to eighty per cent of the price; for example a loan of £240, repayable over thirty years, on a house costing £300. Few working men however were in a position to find the £60, but the company offered to lend a further £45, similarly repayable, leaving the purchaser only £15 to find. Repayments would then amount to 11s a week. Alternatively the houses could be rented at 8s 6d or 9s a week.[72]

Following their operations in Landseer Road, the Small Dwellings Acquisition Company in 1903 put up cottages with a twenty-foot frontage in Cecil Avenue — front parlour, dining room, kitchen and scullery, three bedrooms and a fitted bathroom and lavatory — on a ninety-nine year lease (£5 a year ground rent) for £273. Tenants wishing to purchase the lease would pay 12s 6d a week for five years; they would receive their deeds when the mortgage repayments had been completed. There were other schemes of purchase.[73]

An alternative plan that same year with the same objective, the purchase of the property or the lease by the householder, was initiated by Mrs Gordon Canning. Soon after Burton's farm came onto the market she secured several acres for the erection of artisans' dwellings in the roads which were to be known as Ladysmith, Kimberley and Sketty Roads. She employed A.E. Monk of Edmonton to erect in Sketty Road fourteen double fronted two-storied blocks with twelve rooms in each block, each to cost £1,000 and to accommodate four families. There would be a metal staircase at the back in case of fire. The first occupants took up residence in June 1903.[74]

Land and houses continued to change hands rapidly in eastern Enfield. At an auction in July 1898 sixteen acres at Enfield Lock were sold for £3,800 — £237 an acre. Seven cottages in South Street, together with five acres, were sold for £2,070, and twenty-two freehold cottages adjoining for £2,175, less than £100 each. There was a Local Government Board enquiry in November 1899 to sanction the borrowing of £2,710 for street improvements, including paved footpaths, in Mandeville Road and Mandeville Crescent. Mr Hall who was a property owner objected; Putney, Totteridge and Oakhurst Roads had all been made up without being paved, he said, Turkey Street had no pavements nor had

31.   This range of timber buildings, one of which belonged to a blacksmith, and the old cottages adjoining were standing in Hertford Road on the corner of Green Street in 1904. The notice urges a vote for David Weston, the bill poster.

parts of the main road. The Hertford Road, from the Edmonton boundary to Waltham Cross, was paved and kerbed after June 1901 by Middlesex County Council; the Urban District Council paid a quarter of the cost (£12,800).

Throughout the year 1903 extensive building operations were going on in Chesterfield, Catisfield and Beaconsfield Roads. Most of the houses were let, though some were purchased; yet there were said to be hundreds of empty houses in the area and many people unemployed.[75]

The range of old timber buildings at the corner of Green Street, one of which belonged to a blacksmith, and the old houses adjoining, were still there in July 1904. The parish lock-up had remained until a few years previously on the other side of the main road. It was described as a small, square, brick structure with a heavy nail-studded door. It had at one time been possible to walk to Sewardstone by way of Green Street, and a very pleasant walk it had been, but the bridge which had formerly spanned the Lea at the bottom of Mill Marsh Lane had fallen into ruin twenty-five years since. Still the water-wheel at Ponders End mill 'continued to give out its pleasant music'. Fuller House at Scotland Green yet survived, but the delightful old hostelry the Two Brewers on the corner of South Street at Ponders End had been pulled down and rebuilt in March 1896.[76]

Notes to Chapter One

1. H.P. White *Regional History of Railways* V.3 *Greater London* p171, Alan A. Jackson *Londons Local Railways* p25. *Recollections of Old Enfield* p11, 32, 40, *Observer* S 1864, Au 1865, Mr 1872, 4S 1875, 22 Jl 1904
2. H. Dugdale Sykes in *Enfield Gazette* 29 Ja 1909, *Recollections* p11, 16
3. *Observer* N 1869, H.P. White *op. cit.* p166, A.A. Jackson *op.cit.*
4. *Observer* 25 Ap 1885
5. *ibid* 21 Ja 1898
6. *ibid* 15 My 1880, 3Jl 1880, 30X 1880, 5N 1881, 7 Ja 1882, 23 Jl 1881
7. *ibid* 7 Je 1882, 23 S 1882
8. *ibid* 14 Je 1884, 25 Ap 1885
9. *ibid* 4, 18 Jl 1890, 1 Au 1890, 28 N 1890, 5 Je 1891, 3, 31Jl 1891, 7 Au 1891, 23X 1891, 2N 1894
10. *ibid* 14 Je 1884, 20S 1889, 7 Mr 1890, 2X 1891
11. HLG 25.10
12. *Observer* eg Je. Jl. Au. S 1870 Mr.Ap.Jl 1871, 10 My 1879, 31 Ap 1881, 6 Au 1881, 3S 1881
13. *ibid* 16X 1880
14. *ibid* 20F 1886, 10D 1886, 5D 1885
15. *ibid* 15X 1881, 8 Ja 1876, 21 Au 1880, 15X 1881, 14 Ja 1882
16. *ibid* 13 D1901, 8 Jl 1882, 26 Au 1882, 2S 1882
17. *ibid* 29 Ap 1904
18. Enfield, sale catalogue Je 1872, J.W. Ford *Bush Hill Park, Observer* 12S 1890
19. H. Dugdale Sykes in *Enfield Gazette* 12 Ja 1909, *Recollections* p11, 12
20. Enfield sale catalogue 1861
21. J.W. Ford *op.cit passim*, Enfield. Bush Hill Park estate sale catalogue, *Observer* 31 Mr 1883, 28X 1892, 21 Jl 1883
22. *ibid* 2 Je 1899, 22 Jl 1904
23. C.W. Whitaker *Enfield* p249, 250, *Observer* 29 Ja 1909, 4X 1879, 11X 1879, 21N 1885, 8Jl 1882, 9S 1894, 17D 1880
24. *ibid* 24 Mr 1883, 8S 1893
25. *ibid* 16X 1880
26. *ibid* 19 My 1883, 21 Jl 1883, 13X 1883, 22 Ja 1892, 15 Jl 1892

27. *ibid* 26 Au 1882
28. *ibid* N 1869, 6Je 1890, 16 Ja 1891
29. *ibid* 22 Ap 1887
30. eg *ibid* My 1872, N1869, Ap 1874, 13F 1875
31. Enfield. Gordon House estate sale catalogue 1847, *Observer* 22X 1892
32. *ibid* 4S 1875, My 1874
33. *ibid* 24 Jl 1886
34. *ibid* 4 Ja 1879, 24 Mr 1883, 19D 1885, Enfield Surveyor's reports 15 July, 6 Au 1880
35. *ibid* 26 F1881, 13 Ja 1883
36. VCH Middlesex V5 p219, MRO Acc 311.44, Acc 704.9.19, Acc 686.1-4, O.S. Middlesex II SE 1897
37. Enfield sale catalogue 24 N 1869
38. *Observer* 16X 1880, 11 Je 1881, 13 Ja 1883, 23 F 1881, 16 Ap 1881, 20 F 1886
39. *ibid* 22N, 6D 1879
40. *ibid* 28 Au 1880, 17D 1881
41. *ibid* 20S, 6D 1884, 21N 1885
42. *ibid* 12 Ja 1909
43. *ibid* 1S 1893
44. *ibid* 25X, 15N 1895, 8 Ja, 16Jl 1897
45. *ibid* 4D 1896
46. *ibid* H.D. Sykes 12 Ja 1909
47. *ibid* 6D1901, 31 Ja 1902
48. *ibid* 17 Jl 1903
49. *ibid* 24 Mr 1883
50. *ibid* H.D.S. Sykes 29 Ja 1909
51. *Recollections* p70-75 *Observer* N1870, Jl 1871
52. *ibid* 22, 29S 1899
53. MEPOL 2, 74, Bernard Brown *Damn Yankees* in *Haringey History Bulletin* 29, *Recollections* p25
54. *Gazette* 8 My 1891, 18 Mr 1910
55. *ibid* 2 Je 1910, 16 Au 1912
56. Edmonton Hundred Historical Society. Jewish Research Group *Heritage* 1. 1982
57. *Gazette* 30 Mr, 15F 1900 and information Enfield Local History Library
58. *ibid* 19 N1909, 3 Je 1910
59. *ibid* 8X 1909
60. *ibid* 8F, 3 Mr 1918
61. *ibid* 29N 1912, 13F 1931
62. *ibid* 8F 1895, 21N 1913
63. *ibid* 11 Ja 1909
64. Jack Edwards *The Story of Capel* 1985, *Gazette* 9 Au 1929
65. *Gazette* 29N 1929
66. *ibid* 29 Je 1900, 1 Ap 1898, 3 Au 1900, 10 Mr 1905
67. *ibid* 9D 1898, 24X 1902, 8 Jl 1904
68. *ibid* 22 Ap 1898
69. *ibid* 4S 1903
70. *ibid* 22 Mr 1901
71. *ibid* 13S 1901
72. *ibid* 5D 1902
73. *ibid* 10Jl 1903
74. *ibid* 26 D 1902, 19 Je 1903
75. *ibid* 22 Jl 1898, 17N 1899, 28 Je 1901, 4S 1903, 9X 1903
76. *ibid* 22 Jl 1904, 20 Mr 1896

Chapter Two

Edwardian Developments

1. Introduction

A surplus of houses existed throughout the metropolis and suburbs by 1905, and as many as seventy thousand were said to be unoccupied. There was a tendency among the middle classes to move further out, up to twenty miles, as long as the place was well served by a railway. There they could find lower rents and rates and ample gardens. The tendency within Enfield was for the middle class to migrate from the east of the Town to the west where a number of good class houses were going up near Windmill Hill and the East Barnet Road. According to Alfred Bowyer the auctioneer, middle-class houses on the higher ground were especially popular, while those at Bush Hill Park were now hard to let.

Landlords of smaller properties also found them difficult to dispose of. One estate agent complained (*Observer* 19 August 1905) that he had recently spent £30 on repairing six small cottages. Despite this he had had to lower the rents, yet he still found it hard to get respectable tenants. Even to retain tenants was difficult and he had to offer to paint, paper and whitewash his properties. House owners in Enfield were lucky to clear four per cent, he said. Other districts had better facilities, and he went on to cite Ilford where the streets were lit by electricity and they had a splendid service of electric trams. These, he thought, would be a great advantage to Enfield. Alfred Cole, who had a hat and clothes shop in the Town, complained that trade had decreased since the Royal Small Arms had been slack; the Boer War had been the best time for trade. Pessimistically he predicted that trams would take the trade to other areas. There were 10,604 houses in Enfield in March 1906, but nearly one in ten was vacant. As a result there had been very little house building over the years 1904 and 1905.[1]

Widespread improvements to local services were undertaken early in the year 1906 and this threw Enfield into a state of turmoil: a condition which seemed likely to last for quite a time. A sixteen-inch water main was being laid along Baker Street and London Road and in the Town, the road was up in one place for electric cables and in another for the laying of the National Telephone Company's wires. Soon there would be the demolition of the shops in London Road for the tramway and for the next two years the Great Northern extension would be causing chaos. Street numbering remained incomplete up until the First World War.[2]

The building of a station at Grange Park opened up that area for middle-class housing development. An electric tram service along Green Lanes to Enfield Town commenced in July 1909 and brought about a new surge of middle-class house building at Bush Hill Park. Building continued apace in middle-class

32, 33.   Edwardian scene in Enfield Town, two panoramic views. Above, from the left, the Nags Head built in 1882, Gomm the butcher 'noted for the best home-killed meat ...delivered to all parts including Clay Hill, Forty Hill and Winchmore Hill'; then John Beaven grocer and wine and spirit merchant; and Charles Walters mantles, jackets and costumes. On the other corner of London Road Mrs Schmidl 'cook, confectioner and ball and rout furnisher'. The ancient timber house once known

as Ansycles crouches behind the shops.
Below a view looking west about 1901. On the far side Alfred Cole tailor and hatter, George Brooks
the stationer, then Mrs Schmidl's and, beyond the cart standing near the drinking fountain, Miss
Davis had 'her fancy repository'.

ENFIELD AND WINCHMORE HILL DIRECTORY—1910-1911.   333

G. ELLIS & CO.,

Civil, Military and Ladies
TAILORS,
61, Church St., ENFIELD

Briefly, we may say that every effort is made to realize in practice what we believe to be the secret of conducting a business successfully—viz. that to study the interests of your customers the surest way to advance your own ; to this policy we owe our success, as by it we gain confidence wherever our name is mentioned.

Lounge Suits in variety, of our standard fine quality Indigo Serges, from 50s. We guarantee absolute hard wear, and the colour not to change until worn out. English Tweed Lounge Suiting from Two Guineas. Costumes in pure Indigo Serges from 3½ Guineas ; in face cloths, which we recommend, from 4 Guineas. We call your attention to our style, fitting and workmanship.

Testimonials can be seen at all times at our office.

The comment of the press after our first twelve months' trading.

Business Paragraph.

The progress the young firm of Tailors (Messrs. G. Ellis & Co., of 61, Church Street, Enfield) is making is such as to entitle them to be congratulated, and to induce a large number of City and West End shoppers to spend their money locally. This firm has a bright future before them in the way the business is conducted, under the entire supervision of Mr. Ellis, who claims the wonderful record of ten successive years without having had a misfit.

34.   From Kelly's Directory of Enfield 1910-11

suburbs like Southgate, but the building of houses which could be let to workmen at 6s or 7s a week had become an uneconomic proposition by this time. Builders found it almost impossible to obtain finance and although cheap land could be purchased, the cost of materials and labour had risen by ten per cent over the five years 1903 to 1908. The building of workmen's houses in Enfield virtually ceased. There was a housing shortage by 1914.

2. The Great Northern Extension

The acquisition of land for a projected Great Northern loop line to Stevenage had begun in 1902 with the purchase of the fields behind Chase Farm School and parish lands near Holtwhites Hill. The year 1904 saw the purchase of Chase Lodge on Holtwhites Hill, a picturesque mansion formerly the home of Admiral Tindal and before that of Mr Holt White, nephew of the Reverend Gilbert White of Selborne. Important steps were taken in December 1905 to clear the way for the new railway. Mr Bowyer, the auctioneer acting for the company, sold on site the materials from three houses demolished in Chase Green Avenue and also Chase Lodge where the valuable fittings attracted over two hundred would-be buyers. The auctioneer then set out along the line of the route, over hill and dale, selling trees here and there, until he reached Cuffley Hill. Two months later he sold Chase Park on Windmill Hill to the house-breakers. This was a fine mansion built in 1822 by a Mr Browning and subsequently purchased by Edward Ford; it had since been occupied by J.W. Ford who moved to Old Park shortly before the house was demolished. The Shrubbery was also pulled down, 'a snug old-world abode amid the trees on the western side of Chase Green', the avenue of trees which led up to the entrance can still be seen near the war memorial. The Railway Company transferred the site to the Council in exchange for a portion of Chase Green. It was proposed to span Windmill Hill by a steel girdered bridge, and it was the original intention to build the new station on the north side of the road. The line was to be carried by bridges over Chase Green Avenue and Holtwhites Hill from where it would take a more westerly course sinking into a deep cutting under Lavender Hill and thence between the cemetery and Chase Farm School fields to Crews Hill where a station would be opened, and so on to Cuffley Lane. The tender from Mr Nowell of Newcastle on Tyne was accepted for the construction of this railway. In compensation for some forty houses demolished, the Railway Company was to erect twenty cottages on the north side of Holtwhites Hill opposite the former site of Chase Lodge.[3]

The work began and with each passing day more labourers and gangers arrived in Enfield. 'Up to the present', remarked the *Observer*, (25 May 1906) 'they have proved an orderly and quiet body of men'. A navvy mission was established in a temporary building at the junction of Lavender Hill with Brigadier Hill, during the week it was used as a working men's club, and over Christmas 1906 it had been crowded. Nearly four hundred men settled in the neighbourhood, many bringing their wives and families, for they expected to remain for two or three years. Houses which had formerly stood empty were now occupied.[4]

Clearings were being made and temporary lines laid during March 1906. A

35.   Chase Lodge on Holtwhites Hill, formerly the home of Admiral Tindal and before that of Mr Holt White, was demolished in 1905 to clear the way for the railway to Cuffley.

36.   Chase Park on Windmill Hill was another fine mansion demolished to make way for the railway in 1905. It had been built in 1822. The entrance gates stood where Old Park Avenue now meets Windmill Hill.

large steam navvy was working through May building the embankment on either side of Holtwhites Hill. So extensive was the cutting required to carry the line beneath Lavender Hill that that road had to be closed for a time. The line

The Steam Navvy Cutting New Railway through Enfield.

37. The steam navvies cutting a way for the new railway towards Cuffley had reached the northern boundary of Enfield by May 1907, the date of the postmark on the card from which this illustration was taken. The location looks like the deep cutting immediately north of Gordon Hill station.

was making good progress towards Cuffley by May 1907 and the steam navvies had reached the Enfield boundary. The contractor was using six light locomotives which he housed in a shed alongside the line. About five miles of track had been put down from the point where the new work had started south of Enfield Chase station. The new station on Windmill Hill was now to be built east of the former terminus where a row of tumbledown cottages had been demolished. Another station was planned between the summit of Gordon Hill and the Lavender Hill bridge. The line ran on to Crews Hill near the temporary smallpox hospital; there Crews Hill station was to be built. 'Many choice building sites will come into the market' rejoiced the *Observer* (3 May 1907). 'This corner of Middlesex and Hertfordshire will undergo a great transformation'.[5]

Level crossings at Windmill Hill, Chase Green Avenue, Holtwhites Hill and other places had facilitated the use of a temporary contractor's line which had many steep gradients. The temporary crossing at Windmill Hill was taken up in October 1907. The temporary line was henceforth to be carried over the recently constructed bridge.

The building of the railway provided some difficulties. Four steam navvies were employed and two important viaducts constructed. The Rendlesham viaduct north of Lavender Hill, which carries the line over the little brook which runs through Hilly Fields park, is 600 feet long with fourteen spans, and eighty feet high; it cost £20,000. The Sopers farm viaduct near Cuffley is perhaps even more spectacular though not quite so high; it has eleven spans. The very fine bridge at Chase Green Avenue cost £3,000. The station at Windmill Hill had been begun by October 1907, also the one at Gordon Hill where the platforms were to be 400 feet long. Progress was being made at Crews Hill. The work ran into last minute difficulties when the embankment collapsed between

38. The Rendlesham viaduct, fourteen thirty-foot span arches supported by eleven piers and two stronger piles. It has semi-circular arches and is constructed of engineering bricks. It is 165 yards long and about 75 feet high.

Winchmore Hill and Enfield. A large gang of men worked day and night to repair the damage, hampered by continuous rains through December 1907. Trains to Enfield had to be confined to a single track which caused great inconvenience to passengers. Said the *Observer* (15 January 1909) 'the remaining work will soon be done on the five new stations from Winchmore Hill to Cuffley'. These included Park Grange (later Grange Park) with platforms 200 feet long. It had been provided to serve the estate being developed there by Metherell and Sons.[6]

On 4 April 1910 the line was opened to Cuffley and there construction work was abandoned in the middle of a nearby field. It was at first intended to run a steam railcar service to Cuffley station from Enfield, but the idea was rejected in favour of conventional trains. Fourteen trains daily reached Cuffley. The completion of the line to Stevenage was for a time postponed owing to the adverse financial condition of the Railway Company.

About six hundred men had been employed and the weekly wage bill had amounted to £800. Over two years later, in July 1912, the Great Northern Railway Company accepted the tender of McAlpine and Sons to continue the line as far as Stevenage. Work was to begin immediately. The navvies employed were housed in temporary huts and there they spent their Christmas that year with a phonograph for entertainment. In the afternoon on Christmas day the encampment was visited by two ladies who brought tobacco, fruit, chocolate, pies, tarts and a Christmas card for each man. Work was continued despite the outbreak of the First World War in August 1914. The contractor, during July 1915, was engaged on building a tunnel 2,684 yards long just north of Cuffley, which, he claimed, was only two or three weeks away from completion, so that it would not be long before the new portion of the line was ready for official inspection. Businessmen in Enfield, urged the *Gazette*, should look ahead to the day when a few minutes' railway ride would bring people from this newly opened-up countryside into Enfield (16 July 1915). The line opened from Cuffley to Stevenage on 2 June 1924. The old terminus at Enfield was retained as a goods depot until about 1970, although in October 1940 it was returned briefly to passenger use when an unexploded bomb fell on the through line. The old track was lifted in 1975.[7]

3. The Grange Park Estate

Old Park Grange, or Pike's Farm, was purchased freehold from Lord Currie by Richard Metherell in 1905 and it was he, in conjunction with his son W.R. Metherell, who developed the Grange Park estate. He had been quick to perceive the possibilities of the proposed Great Northern extension. Richard Metherell came from Bideford in Devon where he had been apprenticed as a builder, joiner and cabinet maker. He arrived in London in the 1870s to work for a large building contractor, He was placed in charge of small jobs, then quickly promoted to the control of important work in the City and the West End. He went into business on his own at Stroud Green where he purchased the Hall and Woodlands estates at Muswell Hill which he developed in the 1880s, being the first speculative builder in that area. He had bought in 1895 a house called Elmscott on the summit of Bush Hill and he came to live there, which put him close at hand to supervise the building of the Grange Park estate. By the exchange of land, and by an agreement to build a given number of good class houses within a specified time, he induced the railway company to build Grange Park station (he had made a similar arrangement earlier at Cranley Gardens, Muswell Hill). He purchased from John Walker Ford all the land on the western side of Bush Hill between Green Dragon Lane and Elmscott and diverted Salmons brook into a straight course, thus reclaiming an acre of marshy land.[8]

Land between Winchmore Hill and Enfield became available when the Chase Park estate was offered for sale at public auction in March 1908. The *Observer* (20 March 1908) described the estate as having an 'ideal situation', with two Great Northern stations, Enfield (ie Enfield Chase) at one end, and Grange Park at the other. It was the last area of open land immediately to the west of the Town. 'By the development of this picturesque spot' the paper went on, 'Enfield and Southgate will receive a substantial addition to their rateable values'. Eventually, it was promised, 'there will be a broad new road past the Presbyterian church leading directly into Green Dragon Lane'. Mr Metherell had already begun development at Grange Park. 'The magic hand of Metherell', said the *Observer*, expressing in September 1909 great admiration 'has metamorphosed the

39.   Richard Metherell, the builder of the estate at Grange Park, by an agreement induced the railway company to build a station there which opened in April 1910. Salmons Brook passes beneath the railway north of the station.

appearance of the district. It has transformed Green Dragon Lane, a narrow winding path, into Grange Drive'. The *Observer* was somewhat premature; the old name refused stubbornly to die, being loudly maintained by every tram conductor on the new electric cars along Green Lanes. The new name by contrast, being ignored, died young. A number of good class houses, 'neat and not too pretentious' had been built in the Chine and in Old Park Ridings and three impressive shopping parades had been begun. Many of the houses already occupied had been erected on land formerly used as an orchard, and fruit trees survived in great numbers. From Green Dragon Lane one could look north across the valley of Salmons brook to the old farmhouse (Pike's farm) which crowned the facing hill. The valley between was the scene of feverish activity. Two roads, the Chine and Old Park Ridings, were being extended across the valley and up the hillside opposite. Two ornate bridges had been built to take the two roads over Salmons brook.

  People were living in the houses on the Winchmore Hill side of the valley by March 1910. At the summit of the hill opposite, on which stood Pike's farm, a deep cutting was being made through the brow of the hill so that the new roadway lay ten feet below the original level of the ground. The object was both to reduce the gradient and to utilise, as the road surface, the bed of a shallow gravel pit in the field beyond the summit. Here, the road was spanned by a rough bridge which carried a footpath from Green Dragon Lane towards Enfield. The road would eventually lead out at the foot of Windmill Hill by the side of the petty sessional court-house. In another road at right angles to this last, the Grangeway, Mr Metherell proposed to build a block of ten, increased to twelve, handsome shops with flats above, near the station at Grange Park. It was intended that this road should eventually lead into Eversley Park Road. There were plans to erect forty-one additional detached and semi-detached houses during the year 1910, for which Southgate Council would provide the drainage. Grange Park station opened on 4 April 1910. Work proceeded through the summer of 1910 and £20,000 was spent on the estate, £500 weekly in wages alone. Fifty-six new houses had been completed by the autumn, as well as the twelve shops adjoining the station, two of which were already let. Work stopped with the approach of winter, the workmen disappearing from middle-class view until the spring. The new road opened from Chase Side, Enfield, to Green Dragon Lane in July 1912. The Chine was also being pushed along through the brow of the hill in a twelve-foot cutting; both this cutting and the one mentioned earlier have since been filled in. Houses could be rented at between £55 and £70 a year, or could be purchased at prices ranging from £750 upward. No fewer than eight designs were used and no two adjoining houses were alike; each had five or six bedrooms and two or three reception rooms. All the roads were completely made up. Seeing middle-class villas arising on all sides, J.W. Ford concluded, in September 1909, that the time had come to leave his mansion in Old Park.[9]

The war brought building operations to a standstill. Metherell and Sons in 1916 bought Thorney Island on the Sussex coast where they strengthened the sea banks, made extensive improvements, and went into agriculture on a large scale. They resided at Thorney Manor House until 1929 when they moved to Aldingbourne. Richard Metherell died in November 1932 aged eighty-two.

Another small development served by the Great Northern Railway was the East View estate, later called the Chase Court estate, between Windmill Hill and Chase Green Avenue. Plans were submitted in 1907. The houses were to be fitted for electricity and gas and would sell at from £500 each freehold.[10]

4. Electric Trams

The North Metropolitan Power Company announced in 1901 that an electricity supply generated in the vicinity, had been switched on in Hertford. At the same time plans were revealed to provide electric power for tramways in an area of north London covering 325 square miles. The power station at Brimsdown by 1904 was transmitting power at 11,000 volts. The tramway overhead wires were energised at 550 volts D.C. It was unusual that a tramway company should also be the electricity supply company. Electric power and light, it was promised, would be made available as a cheap by-product of the traction system. The first electric tramcar in these outer suburbs was seen in Wood Green in June 1904 running experimentally over lines still worked by horse trams. The new lines and the power transmission system for the tramways were to be provided by Middlesex County Council, which would then lease the system to the Metropolitan Electric Tramways Company, which would operate the service.

The project initially went forward at great speed. By August 1904 electric cars were running from Wood Green to Finsbury Park and the old horse tramway had been reconstructed from Manor House along Seven Sisters Road as far as Tottenham High Road. Through Tottenham as far as the boundary with Edmonton the wood blocks and new rails were in place, the poles had been

Enfield Town

40.   *The Town about 1904, before the trams. The bank on the corner of Silver Street and Southbury Road was erected in 1892.*

erected and the overhead wires fixed. The first 150 cars, 'handsome double-decked vehicles' to carry from sixty-eight to seventy-four passengers, had been supplied by the Brush Electrical Engineering Company. The line through Tottenham as far as Snells Park was opened by 26 August 1904.[11]

At this point construction came to a halt for a long time. 'Ensign' motor buses began running in August 1906 between Angel Road Edmonton and Waltham Cross, but the service quickly collapsed. 'The majority of the residents along the route', declared the *Observer* in August 1906 will not be 'anxious to see these lumbering stinking monsters on the road again'. The paper was undecided whether it was lack of punctuality or the high fares which had caused the failure.

It was June 1906 before the Middlesex County Council placed the order for the building of the line through Enfield to Waltham Cross, the contractors being Dick, Kerr and Company. The work was started at Waltham Cross 'on the instalment system' as one correspondent described it, a stretch being laid and a stretch missed alternately, until the line reached the Congregational church at Enfield Highway (now the Co-op Hall); then the workmen went back to Waltham Cross. The plan was to lay one track at a time in order not to totally disrupt the traffic. Councillor Weston pressed the contractor to use local labour, for there was widespread unemployment in the area.[12]

High Street Ponders End, said the *Observer* in June 1907 'looks as if it had been subjected to a rigorous bombardment'. The work of levelling to the dust several of Ponders End's better-known houses was just finished: Cotwells, which had belonged to W.F. Field, the Lodge the home of Dr Evans, and Abingdon House the home of Thomas Redburn. The two post offices had gone, one at Ponders End, the other at the corner of Green Street. Northcourt, Ponders End's most imposing building apart from Eagle House, had been demolished by September. It had been built by Mr Webb only twenty years earlier.[13]

The line through Enfield opened in December 1907 as far as the northern Enfield boundary. The short portion in Hertfordshire was due to be finished by the end of January. A special car carrying the Light Railways committee of the Middlesex County Council made a journey of inspection from Tramway Avenue to Waltham Cross. The route was divided into penny fare stages, Tramway Avenue to Southbury Road, or Putney Road to Waltham Cross. A twopenny fare took the passenger from Tramway Avenue as far as Putney Road, a fourpenny fare from Bounces Road to Waltham Cross, and there were workmen's fares of one penny on any single journey completed by 8am.[14]

A belated consequence of the opening of the tramway was the decision in September 1909 to close the Great Eastern Edmonton to Cheshunt line for passenger traffic. It had never paid its way and the company was unable to use it as an alternative main line. It had hoped for more housing, giving rise to more commuters, but the area remained almost entirely given over to market gardening which employed the population locally. Since the advent of the trams in December 1907 passenger traffic on the railway had declined by nearly fifty per cent.[15]

The widening and levelling of Green Lanes through Palmers Green began in the autumn of 1906. The main road had to be diverted through the garden in front of the public offices during the reconstruction of the New River bridge there; meanwhile a gang of workmen was engaged in widening the road outside the Green Dragon. A new road called Ridge Avenue, sixty feet wide, had been constructed by July 1909 from Green Dragon Lane to the northern end of

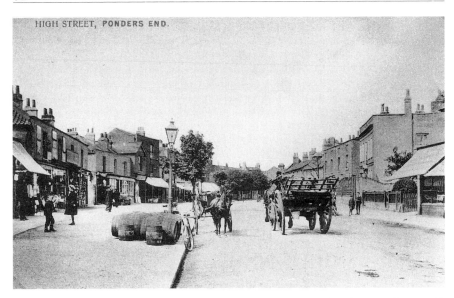

41. *High Street, Ponders End looking north. The photographer must have been standing outside the Swan, then a beer-house.*

42. *High Street Ponders End looking north towards Eagle House. The building with the chimney was Ponders End Brewery.*

Church Street at Bush Hill Park. The land required had been given by the owners of the Red Ridge estate and the County Council had paid for the construction of the road, the drainage and the sewerage. Village Road had been widened to sixty feet and a line of trees had been planted to replace those cut

43. The tramway through Ponders End to Freezywater was opened in December 1907 and completed to Waltham Cross in April 1908. A penny fare took you from Tramway Avenue to Southbury Road; it cost fourpence from Bounces Road to Waltham Cross.

44. A tramcar, about 1910, outside the gloriously ornate Two Brewers at the corner of South Street. It had been rebuilt to replace a rural predecessor in 1896 and was destroyed by a bomb on 30 September 1940.

down in the road widening. Park Avenue had been prepared and London Road widened to fifty feet through the grounds of Roseneath, Juglans Lodge and Beaufort Villas. The offices of the Stratford Brewery and half dozen cottages had been demolished near to the Town, as well as the eastern gable of the old house

45.   *London Road was widened to fifty feet, the offices of the Stratford Brewery and the cottages shown here were demolished to make way for electric tramcars about 1908.*

46.   *London Road looking south (towards Palmers Green) after the tramlines had been laid. All the buildings on the right, as far as the Baptist Tabernacle (subsequently Woolworth's) had been demolished in order to open out the junction of the Town and London Road.*

(Ansycles) at the corner of London Road and the Town. A surface water drain had been laid from the Market Place to the boundary brook to provide for the future development of land alongside the new tramway which at that time was used as a golf course by the Bush Hill Park Club. The tramlines were laid by

47. *Two special cars in the Enfield terminus; workmen are still laying tar blocks outside the George. July 1909.*

48. *The first electric tram made its way to Enfield Town on 1 July 1909. A great display was put on by the tradesmen with hundreds of flags suspended from Venetian masts.*

Wimpey and Co and the work was completed by Thursday 1 July 1909. That day a ceremonial car carrying County Council and Tramway Company dignitaries made its way from the Green Dragon to Enfield Town. Crowds lined the way and there was a dense throng at the terminus outside the George. A great display was put on by the tradesmen in the Town with hundreds of flags suspended from Venetian masts. The Town was bedecked from the railway station in Southbury Road to the end of Church Street, and from the police station in London Road as far as the Vicarage. The Great Eastern Railway Company responded to the challenge by reducing fares to 1s 1d for a third-class return to Liverpool Street and by running the trains at quarter-hour intervals through the day. The tramway from the Enfield Town railway station to Hertford Road, one and a half miles, was opened on Monday 21 February 1911 with a special tram driven by Councillor Weston. The fare was to be a penny each way.[16] It was the last new tramway built for the Metropolitan Electric Tramway Co.

5. Bush Hill Park and Winchmore Hill

The Bush Hill Park estate west of the railway had been begun before 1880 and from the first the land had been reserved for good class property. Roads had been cut and many handsome villas erected, but then the estate had been overtaken in popularity by developments west of Enfield Town served by the Great Northern railway. The likely advent of electric trams along Green Lanes now brought a revival of interest in the area; no fewer than 350 houses were built between 1904 and 1908 and let or sold almost as soon as they were built. New thoroughfares were being opened. Frank Bethell, the architect of the estate, planned a new road (Queen Anne's Grove, Gardens and Place) to run from Bush Hill Park station into Bury Street (Map p. 21). The completion of Park Avenue made it easier to get to Enfield. The new road being constructed for the tramway, it was said, would cut the walk to Grange Park station by eight minutes.[17]

A new club house for the Bush Hill Park Club was built on a site between Wellington and Abbey Roads in 1905, conveniently near the station, single-storied with a spacious entrance hall. It provided a billiard room, ladies' room and gentlemen's room, and it had a verandah at the back overlooking croquet lawns, tennis courts and a bowling green. There were facilities for quoits, badminton, clock-golf and archery. The tennis and golf clubs at Bush Hill Park were soon afterwards amalgamated with the new club. It became the social centre of the estate with whist drives, card parties, concerts and social functions through the winter. The annual subscription for a married couple was three guineas, for a single gentleman it was two guineas. The membership in May 1908 stood at 150. The club was disbanded in July 1912 and the premises (still there) were sold to new owners who carried it on as a private club. Its remaining funds, amounting to £85, were donated to Enfield Cottage Hospital.

The owners of the estate in 1900 had provided the land and given £500 for an iron church, known as St Stephen's to be erected. Once opened the congregation there grew steadily and a meeting was called at the Bush Hill Park Club pavilion under the chairmanship of J.W. Ford to promote the raising of funds for a permanent church. The foundation stone was laid by Lady Wolverton in

49. Delightful little stock brick cottages on the Cardigan estate where privet was supplied free to tenants for planting in their front gardens and an annual flower show was organised.

May 1906 and the church was consecrated in May 1907.[18]

A new scheme for presenting a pleasant aspect to Bush Hill Park east of the railway and also to encourage the working classes to take a pride in their homes was inaugurated by the Estates Trust Ltd, owners of the Cardigan estate in 1906. Privet hedging three feet high was purchased and supplied free to tenants for planting in their front gardens in Harman Road, John Street, Charles Street and Park Terrace. Another feature of this estate was an annual flower show. Many of the delightful little stock brick cottages in these roads have survived, though some have been ruined by recent 'improvements'. Later the company built a different style of house in James Street, using best red brick for the double bay fronts. These houses comprised six rooms and were let at 7s 6d to 8s a week. Other working-class estates in the neighbourhood took up the idea of a garden contest and in the summer of 1912 competition turned Fifth and Sixth Avenues into a blaze of colour. Three prizes were offered, a ton of coal, half a ton, and half a chaldron. The Cardigan estate that year presented its twelfth annual flower competition. St Marks Institute near by had been opened in 1907 by Princess Louise.[19]

Complaints about the early morning train service from Bush Hill Park station persisted. The last threepenny train arrived at Liverpool Street at 7.30am and this was usually full before it left Enfield Town. Some six thousand people lived near the railway station at Bush Hill Park before the First World War, and many of those who travelled in these early trains were young and impecunious office workers, boys and girls, who had to hang about Liverpool Street station in what seemed to their elders as unseemly promiscuity, to say nothing of considerable discomfort when the weather was cold and wet, until they began work at 8.30 or

50.   Halliwick, formerly Bush Hill House, housed a home for crippled girls from 1911. Its former occupants included Hugh Myddelton, Isaac Currie the banker, and Sir Samuel Cunard the ship owner.

9 o'clock. A petition circulated in the district was signed by 1,100 people; it asked the railway company to start a train at Bush Hill Park. There was no response to this suggestion, but return fares on the 6.57 and 7.05am from Bush Hill Park were reduced to five pence (fourpence from Edmonton).[20]

It was reported (*Observer* 11 August 1911) that Halliwick, formerly Bush Hill House, the old mansion on Bush Hill, was being renovated and new buildings added. When the work was completed it was to be used to house the Cripples' Home for Girls which had been established in Marylebone Road for thirty-five years. Halliwick had stood empty for a long time though it formerly had housed occupants of importance. Sir Hugh Myddelton, builder of the New River had lived there, Isaac Currie, the banker had enlarged the house; and her former resident was Sir Samuel Cunard the ship owner. A particularly fine house in the area, Bury Hall, was offered for sale at an auction in March 1914, but it found no purchaser and was demolished in 1920. Its magnificent ceilings and oak wainscoting were photographed by the Victoria and Albert Museum, though no record has been left of the great yew hedge in the garden. Bury Hall had once been the home of the Galliard family[21] (see Volume One).

Even Winchmore Hill was suffering change, the old Green Dragon had been demolished, and the Kings Head in May 1898 was about to be replaced by an imposing modern hotel at a cost of between £7,000 and £8,000. The pretty cottages around the Green had been swept away to make room for shops, the pond had been drained and the village green set out with a fountain at its centre. During the first three years of the century Green Lanes changed from a narrow gravel road with broad strips of grass down each side into a suburban main road. Once the decision to run trams had become known, builders became interested in every vacant frontage. Modern brightly lit shops at the Broadway Winchmore Hill must have offered a strange contrast to the dark country road which people remembered. Houses had been built, particularly along the west side, and many were occupied by July 1904. On the east side, a new road had been cut and work was progressing on the Fords Grove estate where formerly had stood the residence of Mr Busk.[22]

A most elegant development was the garden city planned at Grovelands to occupy over three hundred acres. The controlling syndicate commissioned Messrs Milner and Sons and White, the well-known landscape gardeners (they had laid out the Kaiser's garden at Potsdam) to provide a unique design in town building. No house was to cost less than £550. The principal road (Broad Walk), one of the only two straight roads on the estate, was to run from Winchmore Hill Green to Bourne Hill along the line of an ancient footpath through Winchmore Hill woods, nearly a mile in length. It was to be eighty feet wide and two avenues of old trees were to form a boulevard. The scheme was to cost nearly two million pounds. Not a tree was to be cut down except to make room for roads and houses. Each house would stand in its own grounds and would be divided from those adjoining by evergreen hedges and grassy banks. A private park for the residents was proposed, one and a quarter miles in circumference. It would embrace a fine sheet of water eight acres in extent and the old Georgian residence (Grovelands) which Captain Taylor had recently vacated. The mansion was intended to be used as a club house and a meeting place for Masonic lodges. The syndicate even planned a new railway station in Hoppers Road. The best laid plans however do often go astray; Southgate Council stepped in and secured sixty acres of the estate for a public park, paying £20,000. The syndicate's ambitious woodland city scheme had met with a severe setback.[23]

6. The Servant Problem

The servant problem became acute in the years before the First World War, probably because there was alternative employment available locally for young women, mainly in the electrical industry. Miss Bartlett's agency in the Market Place advertised situations for an experienced nurse (required immediately) to look after an infant, at £20 to £30 a year; also for a good cook, 'only two in the family and three indoor servants' at £24 to £28. There were vacancies for a great number of cooks-general, head parlour maids and general servants, at wages ranging from £8 to £25 a year. Servants were not what they used to be; they had become too independent. Mrs Ellis of Belcaro (Bycullah Park) found hers insolent. She employed two sisters, Dora Thornton as a cook and May Clark as a domestic servant. Things came to a head at Belcaro one day after Mrs Ellis had rung twice for Clark to come up and clear the lunch away. When she failed to appear, her mistress descended into the kitchen and reprimanded her. May was apparently unimpressed; she came up slowly and reluctantly and went about her work in what her mistress described as 'a very slovenly fashion'. Mrs Ellis, exasperated, took the sweeper from her and proceeded to demonstrate how work ought to be done in a lady's house. Her demonstration completed, she turned around to find that May Clark was no longer there. Seething with indignation she stormed down to the kitchen where Clark, totally unabashed, declared that as she (Mrs Ellis) had begun to sweep she thought she had better finish it, whereat the cook laughed uproariously. Mr Ellis, coming to his wife's

51.   Nurse with an infant along the Ridgeway about 1910; she might earn £20-30 a year.

rescue, insisted that he would not have his wife insulted and discharged them at once. Even then the mistress interceded (a respectable household could scarcely be without servants when visitors called) and said that they could stay until the end of the month. They stayed, however, only until the following Monday when, at seven o'clock in the morning, May Clark took tea up to the bedroom as usual. She and cook were dressed ready to go and when Mr Ellis appeared they asked him for their wages. He paid them the amount due to date and told them to leave. Subsequently they sued him for wages in lieu of notice, but judgement was entered for the defendant.[24]

7. Working-Class Housing

The population of Enfield in 1901 was 42,738; it grew by 1911 to 56,344, an increase of 13,606 or 31.8 per cent. There had been an average of 5.35 persons to a house in 1901; this number fell by 1911 to 4.34. There were, in 1911, 12,900 houses, an increase of 4,282 in the ten years since 1901, but decennial statistics can be very misleading. The building of small houses had been very rapid until 1903; it had then virtually ceased and the population of Enfield since 1903 had scarcely increased, indeed many of the schools had falling numbers. Few people now moved to Enfield, due in some measure to inadequate public transport when compared with suburbs served by underground lines.

During the five years ending 1908, 1,345 houses had been erected and certified as fit for habitation, but they were mostly for the middle class; in the five years which ended in 1913 only 768 were finished. Fewer houses were built in the year 1913 than in any one year over the previous twenty-five years. Mr Bowyer, a knowledgeable auctioneer and estate agent, blamed the systematic under-valuation of house property under the 1909 Finance Act which, he claimed, had depreciated the value of house property by twenty per cent. This valuation, and the land value tax, had been strongly attacked by the Conservatives in parliament as a deliberate tax on the landed interest. It had also frightened away the small investor from land and property. Nevertheless some suburbs, such as very middle-class Hendon and Finchley, continued to grow. Yet the inactivity in house building was a national trend and was an important factor in the creation of a nation-wide house famine after the First World War. Another impediment to building small properties was the rise in the cost of materials and labour by some ten per cent in the five years up to 1913. This made it difficult to build cottages to let at 6s or 7s a week even though eligible building sites could be bought cheaply. There was already a housing shortage by 1914. 'Several would-be residents in Enfield', said the *Gazette* (26 September 1913) 'have searched in vain for an empty house at a moderate rent and have applied to house agents to no effect'. Bowyer said that Enfield had suffered from a dearth of cottages for some years past. He was of the opinion that if any enterprising person were now (January 1914) to build two or three hundred they would readily find tenants at satisfactory rents. 'No sooner' he said 'is there an empty cottage than there are a dozen persons ready to take it at sixpence or a shilling more than was paid by the outgoing tenant. Should local industries expand, there would be an increased demand for houses, and rents would go up materially'. James Neilson, another well informed estate agent, pointed out the difficulties. Builders of small property, he said, found it almost impossible to obtain finance during construction and when they had finished building they were faced by potential purchasers who offered less than the cost of labour and materials. Many of those who sought cottage property as landlords were retired tradesmen, civil servants or policemen who wanted the property not for their own occupation but as a secure investment for their savings.[25]

Overcrowding inevitably became endemic; even respectable families tolerated conditions to which we have grown unaccustomed in the late twentieth century. Doris Shuttlewood, speaking of her grandparents' house in Connop Road, wondered how they managed to accommodate six children and a lodger with only three bedrooms and one outside lavatory. 'I do know', she said 'that the parents had the middle bedroom, the boys had the back room, and the girls had two double beds in the large front room'. Mr Coombes the lodger must have slept downstairs. The house had no gas upstairs; the girls used candles to go to bed.

Washing and cleaning facilities in working-class cottages were primitive. 'There were no bathrooms', wrote Sid Robinson, 'and the only source of hot water was from kettles or pans placed on top of a coal-fired kitchen range. There was, hanging on a nail in the scullery, a tin bath', Sid goes on, 'but it needed a lot of water for there were eight of us in the family. I have no recollection of my two older sisters using it and, to the best of my knowledge, I did not bathe from November 1917 until the early 1920s when the coal cellar was converted into a bathroom with a gas geyser'. (*Sid's Family Robinson*).

8. Edwardian Changes

The number of changes in Enfield multiplied from the turn of the century. Enfield House, long carried on by William Lock, was taken over by Pearson Bros in May 1902. Isaac Robinson whose family were said to have held the windmill

52.   *Church Street, on your left Palace Parade to the Rising Sun, on your right the wall of Burleigh House.*

53.   *Shops were opening in Palace Parade in Church Street in the autumn 1898, at that time workmen were busy fitting out 'the emporium where will be transacted commercial operations by the firm of Mr J. Sainsbury'. The postcard is dated 1910.*

since 1720 and whose father Benjamin had been tenant there for forty years, left the mill house in 1904, moving to premises in Chase Side lately occupied by Mr Pennyfather the dairyman. The Robinsons were originally at Old Park Farm and

54. The Town Park was opened to the public on 30 July 1902. Mowing the grass was no problem, Mr Wilson paid £6 a year to feed his sheep there. The illustration shows the splendid aviary.

held the windmill on a yearly tenancy. The mill had not been used since 1887 and had been dismantled in 1901 when it lost two of its sails. It was finally demolished in September 1904 and a large house was built on the site. A new petty sessions court on Windmill Hill, built to the design of the county surveyor, was finished by September 1900.[26]

The 'Palace' grounds had fallen to the builder and Palace Parade had been built along Church Street, 'the newest and finest block of shops'. In the late October of 1898 workmen were busily engaged in fitting out 'the emporium where will be transacted commercial operations by the firm of Mr J. Sainsbury'. Vast quantities of goods were being unloaded there while the shop was being beautifully tiled throughout, watched with great interest by hundreds of future customers. The 'Palace' itself had been taken over as a post office, the furniture there being sold by auction in September 1899. There remained a strong feeling that this old house ought to be retained. The Council conferred with the owner, Mr Lister of Hampstead, but in September 1906 the Urban District Council voted against purchase or lease, Mr Sykes alone standing out for purchase. It was taken by the Enfield Constitutional Club in April 1907 on a twenty-one year lease.[27]

Mr Leggatt, who owned five of the houses in Gentleman's Row, approached the Council in November 1902 with a proposal to close the footpath from the telephone office (next to the Stag) as far as the Archway Tavern, for it divided the houses from their front gardens. The owners in recompense offered to surrender an equivalent strip of land which could be used as a path, on the east side of the road from the Wesleyan Church to the Archway Tavern. Mr Leggatt claimed that the footpath had never been intended to be a public thoroughfare but was merely for the use of the occupants. It was unpleasant and unsafe for females after dark he claimed, being the haunt of undesirables. Enfield Council declined the exchange.[28]

Negotiations had been proceeding for the purchase of that part of the grounds of Chase Side House, recently demolished, abutting on the New River.

55.   In 1909 the Council purchased sixty-two acres of Park Farm for £8,000, from Archdeacon Potter to create Hilly Fields Park.

It was offered at £6,750 by the Twells trustees and subscriptions from the public were invited. J.W. Ford headed the list with £500, Mr Bevan offered the same. It opened to the public as the Town Park on 30 July 1902, providing the occasion for the first half-tone photographs printed in the *Observer*. The Council, in June 1902, applied to borrow £4,100 for the purchase of seventeen and a half acres at Enfield Lock for a recreation ground to be known as Albany Park. The area now known as Durants Park was acquired for £7,563 in October 1903. Mowing the grass was a problem which could be turned to advantage; an offer by Mr Bell to pay £15 a year for the grazing of Albany and Durants Parks was accepted. The grazing of the Town Park was let to H. Wilson for £6 a year. The grazing of parks ceased in March 1909. The Reverend V. Travers Macy in January 1907 offered to sell to the Council $6^1/_4$ acres of meadow known as Tuckers field for £2,000, which was £200 less than he had paid for the land seven years earlier. It was to be used as a recreation ground and would also provide a site for a school. The Council applied to borrow £16,725 in 1908 for the purchase and fencing in, for a recreation ground, of market garden land at Lincoln Road which bounded south on an area where a large number of working-class houses had been built over the preceding few years; it was felt that it would inevitably be developed unless purchased. A decision was taken in November 1909 to purchase sixty-two acres, part of Park Farm, from Archdeacon Potter for £8,000. Its use as a park, known as Hilly Fields, was welcomed in the hope that it would limit the expansion of small house building ever further northward in Enfield.

  Work was begun in November 1905 on the building of the new post office on the lawn of Percy House, Fairhead being the builder. The post office was opened on 30 September 1906, lit by electricity. Percy House was demolished by June 1907; the frontage was to be used for 'five handsome shops'. The work of

56.   Work began in November 1905 on building the new post office in Church Street on the lawn
of Percy House.

57.   Post office staff, from manager down to telegraph boy, photographed outside the new post office
on the occasion of the opening, 30 September 1906.

widening and improving Church Street continued eastward from the new post
office to the boundary wall of Burleigh House.[29]

Town Parade, another new parade of shops in Silver Street, was completed by
April 1907 and some local tradesmen moved there from London Road where

the projected widening of the road for the electric trams had put a blight on property. The proliferation of new shops caused difficulties in the years before the war. Retail trade was said to be in decline in Enfield and traders were demanding steps to halt the building of more shops or the conversion of further houses into shops. Colonel Bowles was struck by the number of these conversions, particularly numerous in Baker Street and Silver Street; it was usual among these small shopkeepers that the wife looked after the business while the husband went out to work. There were 941 shops in Enfield on the day the vote was taken in 1912 to choose Wednesday as early closing day. It amounted to one shop to every sixty people or one shop to every twelve dwellings.[30]

St Paul's Presbyterian Church was opened in 1907. The year 1910 saw the widening of the bridge over the New River at the end of Church Street. Patman, the long established family building firm which had been in the Market Place for some ninety years, sold out to Newby Bros who, in November 1911, vacated their newly acquired depot in Sydney Road and the premises in the Market Place. A few years later, in 1914, these premises were demolished and a palatial suite of showrooms and offices was erected on the site for the Tottenham and District Gas Company.[31]

Mr and Mrs Withers left Burleigh House in November 1912, having lived there for half a century. Demolition of the property, the site of which was thought likely to come on the market for building development, was begun in January 1913. The mansion had stood protected, for some three hundred years, behind handsome wrought iron gates which were subsequently sold for £90. The central block, ornamented by brick pilasters, was probably the oldest part of the house. The front entrance led into a fine hall in Purbeck stone, containing a fireplace with Flemish tiles (illustrations Vol 1 pp169, 171). In the kitchen was a roasting spit worked by hot air rising from the fire; it was about two hundred years old. There was a deep well which still produced water. The scullery had a ceiling beam four feet square. Above the hall was the drawing-room, lit by three circular headed windows. It contained a white marble statuary chimney-piece depicting Alexander the Great which fell to dealers for only £8 10s. Above was a suite of bedrooms. All the principal rooms were originally panelled but they had been modernised in 1848 when papered canvas had been stretched over the panelling. This had recently been removed revealing a message in chalk declaring that the work had been done by W. Dean of Enfield. Behind the hall was a gallery which gave access to other parts of the house. One bedroom in the east wing had an Adam style fireplace with Dutch tiles and in another room was the fireplace marked with the letters BDM, Benjamin and Margaret Deicrowe, the owners in the seventeenth century who had been so cunningly deprived of their property by the machinations of a crooked attorney (see Vol 1 p168). Inevitably the house was said to be haunted, the ghost it was claimed, being dressed in doublet, hose and ruffle, a little old-fashioned perhaps even for Benjamin's time. The site, after demolition, sold for £7,000. One lot, purchased for £1,235, was said to be intended for the erection of a picture palace. New shops on the frontage were nearly completed by July 1914; more shops by that time covered the site of Percy House.[32]

Demolition was begun in November 1912 of three ancient houses between the Rising Sun and Welch's stables; the site was to be used for the erection of three shops. Grout's shop in Southbury Road was destroyed by fire about the same time. The Archway Tavern (now Archway House, Gentleman's Row) lost

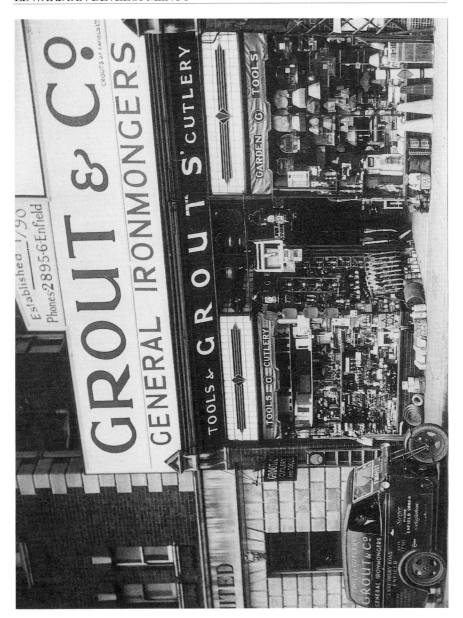

58. Mr Grout, the saddler, had occupied 'a rare old style house and shop' in Silver Street, on the corner of Southbury Road. The site was subsequently occupied by Lloyds Bank. Mr Grout moved to this shop in Southbury Road and became a general ironmonger, it was destroyed by fire about 1912.

its licence in 1913. The Hop Poles, another reminder of rural Enfield, at the junction of Lancaster Road and Baker Street, was pulled down in 1909 and replaced by a modern building. Wood House and Ivy House, on the corner of Chase Side by Parsonage Lane, were demolished in November 1905; they had

59. The old Hop Poles was rebuilt in 1909.

been ruined by a fire a few years earlier. Margetsons pond, in front of them, was filled in and Parsonage Lane was widened to forty-two feet. Brecon House was sold in December that year for £885, to R.H.C. Westmacott, the son of the occupier. The property included a detached piece of building land fronting the footpath from Chase Gardens to the Crown and Horseshoes. Beauchamp House was taken over for development in 1906 and ten houses known as River View were built on the site and fitted with 'electrical apparatus'.[33]

Baker Street still retained many fine houses. Fox Hall is said to have been built about the middle of the seventeenth century, and panelled walls and carvings survived in many of the rooms. The dining room had a low ceiling decorated with Tudor roses. To the north of Fox Hall lay an old courtyard bounded on one side by a long tiled barn surmounted by a small turret with a weather vane where once had been displayed a clock. The low wooden house next door belonging to Mr Bailey had formerly been used as a home for pauper children from Shoreditch. At the rear, still standing, were cottages which had been put up in 1829 by the overseers of St Leonards.

The cottages in Meeting House Yard were falling into ruin. Within the yard was the fine Congregational chapel with seating for four hundred. This was the oldest nonconformist site in Enfield and it was the third chapel built there. Opposite Fish's field was the house of Alderman William Challis, also Lee House, formerly a school known as Gothic Hall. Beyond lay the residence formerly of Dr Abernethy who died in Enfield in 1831. On the west side of Baker Street, towards Clay Hill, stood Cedar Cottage. The Firs, Holmwood and Pattensweir, and Burnham Cottage. Holmwood, which retained its fine wrought iron gates, had at one time been kept as a school by the Revd Stephen Freeman; Charles Babbage and Captain Marryat had received an education there. Gough

60. Parsonage Lane ran between the cottage with a cart outside and the weather-boarded Wood House on the far corner, demolished in 1905 after a fire (photograph 1889).

Park on the north corner of Clay Hill had been demolished in 1899. The picturesque old Rectory House, at the junction of Baker Street and Parsonage Lane, which had been vacant since the death of Mrs Barry, was taken in January

61. *Margetsons Pond, named after a nearby seller of sweetmeats, was filled in around 1906 and Parsonage Lane was widened to forty-two feet. The house next to Wood House was called Ivy House; it was demolished in 1905.*

62. *Fox Hall in Baker Street, described as one of the most interesting houses in Enfield, was said to have been built around the middle of the seventeenth century. The house, two lodges, stabling and paddock, with $2^3/_4$ acres was sold in 1898 to Mr Halsey the cricket-bat manufacturer. He proposed to use the premises as a factory.*

63. Number 164 Baker Street, weather-boarded with red tiles, had formerly been used to house pauper children from Shoreditch. At the rear were cottages added in 1829 by the overseers of the parish of St Leonards. In 1854 Hackney Union opened a purpose-built Poor Law School at Brentwood and closed their premises in Enfield.

64. Within Meeting House Yard stood the Congregational chapel. This was the earliest nonconformist site in Enfield and the third chapel on the site.

1910 by Captain S.W. Smith.

The ancient pest house on Chase Green was demolished in July 1910, its site was to be used for seven villa residences. Local tradition had always asserted that the little pond on the Green behind the house was the site of a plague pit. Old

65.   Eagle House, High Street, Ponders End was demolished about 1965.

photographs of Enfield show many small ponds, usually with one or two of the local urchins at play there. Wisbeys pond, at the top of Brigadier Hill was filled in about 1910. Hubbards lay between Grahams Cottages and the infirmary (ie St Michael's Hospital). Pinnocks, named after the landlord of the Six Bells, was in front of Raleigh Place. Margetsons, at the junction of Parsonage Lane and Chase Side, was called after a seller of sweetmeats close by, and Drapers was on Chase Green opposite Mr Purdey the vestry clerk's house.[34]

The Manor House in Chase Side was burnt out between four and five o'clock one Sunday morning in December 1910, the only occupant being a caretaker. The house, containing some fourteen rooms, stood some distance back from the road. At one time it had been surrounded by paddocks and orchards, but these had long since been sold for development and houses and cottages had been constructed in Manor Road. Its great neighbour, Gordon House, which had stood to the north, had been demolished long since and its estate built over. Baker Street was said, in April 1909, to be in a decline which had been going on for years. Seven shops were empty and five large residences. Ridler Road, with forty-two houses, had eleven empty; Canonbury Road with eighty-five had nine empty; Bell Road with twenty-four had seven empty. People complained of high rents and rates.[35]

The years before the First World War brought many changes to Ponders End with the demolition and rebuilding of the Goat and the building of the Technical Institute opposite. The cheap trams to Edmonton Green had taken trade away from Ponders End and there were empty shops and vacant places all along the High Street. Forty-four tradespeople petitioned the council in 1912 to allow stalls there, so that their area could compete. A new post office opened in the High Street in September 1913. Eagle House, formerly the home of Miss Harman, later of J.T. Whitley, which had stood empty for some years, was now occupied by Dr Barnes. Ponders End chapel had recently suffered 'improvements', the brick frontage having been covered with Portland cement mixed with white sand, and the facade divided up into a credible imitation of stone blocks.[36]

A local historian in 1900, perambulating the parish of Enfield with the 1572 survey before his eyes, would have been able to recognise many of the buildings listed by Twynhoe, or at least later rebuildings or modernisations on the sites. By 1914 almost everything had been swept away. Through the years 1900 to 1914 the heritage of past ages was recklessly and ignorantly destroyed; what was saved survived by accident. The necessity for conservation is by no means the least important lesson to be learned by the reading of local history.

Notes to Chapter Two

1. *Enfield Observer* 19 Aug 1905, 9Mr 1906
2. *ibid* 9Mr, 25F 1906, 24 Ap 1914
3. *ibid* 29D 1905, 2F, 29 Je, 9F, 23F 1906
4. *ibid* 11 Je 1907, 9Mr 1906
5. *ibid* 9Mr, 25 My 1906, 2 Au 1907
6. *ibid* 27D 1907
7. *ibid* 25 Mr, 1 Ap 1910, 19J1, 13 S 1912, 3Ja 1913, 16 J1 1915 4X 1907
8. *ibid* 11N 1932
9. *ibid* 26 J1 1912, 9 S1910, 17 S 1909
10. *ibid* 11N 1932, 31 My 1907
11. *ibid* 8 N 1901, 24 Je, 1J1, 26 Au 1904
12. *ibid* 10 Au, 31 Au, 29 Je 1906, 1F 1907
13. *ibid* 21 Je, 23S 1907
14. *ibid* 6, 27D 1907
15. *ibid* 20 Au, 24S 1909
16. *ibid* 2 J1, 11Je, 18Je 1909
17. *ibid* 29 My 1908
18. *ibid* 26 J1 1912, 14 J1 1905, 2 Mr, 4 My 1906, 3 My 1907
19. *ibid* 23 Mr 1906, 6 S 1912
20. *ibid* 30 My 1913
21. *ibid* 3 Ap 1914
22. *ibid* 29J1 1904
23. *ibid* 25 Mr 1910, 26N 1909, 1J1 1910
24. *ibid* 2J1 1909
25. *ibid* 23 Ja, 6F 1914
26. *ibid* 2 My 1902, 22 Ja, 9S 1904, 7S1900
27. *ibid* 1, 29S 1899, 28S 1906, 12 Ap 1907
28. *ibid* 20N, 4D 1903
29. *ibid* 7D 1900, 18J1 1902, 30 Mr 1906, 26 Mr 1909, 11Ja, 12 Ap 1907, 26N 1909, HG1.384 *Observer* 28 S, 5X 1906, 21 Je, 18X 1907
30. *ibid* 5 Ap 1907, 9 Ja 1912
31. *ibid* 20S 1907, 8 Ap 1910, 31 J1 1914
32. *ibid* 21F 1913, 31 Ja 1914, 13 Je 1913, 31J1 1914
33. *ibid* 8N, 29N 1912, 22X 1909, 3N, 8D 1905, 21S 1906
34. *ibid* 28 Ja, 1J1, 11N 1910
35. *ibid* 16D 1910, 12 Ap 1909
36. *ibid* 1S 1911, 15N 1912, 26S 1913, 24 Ap 1914

Chapter Three

Employment

1. Introduction

Industry moved into Enfield in the early nineteenth century. The first factory to be set up was the dyeing and finishing branch of a firm manufacturing black crape, a product essential in every decent household when paying their last respects to their dead. The company saw the advantage of being close to London, its biggest market. Transport from Ponders End, on the turnpike road, was as good as could be expected anywhere in the early nineteenth century. There were moreover plenty of respectable young females available and willing to work for moderate wages.

The second and much more important industry arose directly from Britain's inability to manufacture an adequate supply of small arms during the war against Napoleon. A manufactory of small arms under government control was decided upon, and the site chosen was at Enfield Lock. The River Lea supplied adequate power to work the machinery and gave easy access by barge to the arms stored at the Tower. The Royal Small Arms Factory, as it came to be known, was greatly expanded at the time of the Crimean War, when it was converted to mass production, using machinery imported from America.

The Northern and Eastern Railway Company opened the first part of its Lea Valley line from Stratford as far as Broxbourne in September 1840. Within a year or two the line was extended to Bishops Stortford and a branch to Hertford was built. Stations were opened in 1840 at Water Lane (now Angel Road, Edmonton) and at Ponders End. A new station called Ordnance Factory (now Enfield Lock) was added in 1855.

Despite competition from the railway, traffic on the Lee Navigation continued to increase, carrying a vast amount of grain, particularly barley, for conversion into malt. Immense quantities of malt from Ware were carried, 26,653 tons (213,224 quarters) in 1866, at a shilling a ton. The Navigation was able to compete with the railway when goods and materials had to be transported in large quantities, for example, stone, timber and iron. The barges brought both breeze for the burning of bricks, and ashes to mix with brick-earth, from the London ash pits. Manure was distributed along the Navigation in vast quantities from Ponders End up to Hertford. Factories, by the 1860s, extended up the Lea Valley as far as Ponders End. The Royal Small Arms Factory and the Royal Gunpowder Factory employed their own barges. The other barges, which served both the Lea and the Thames, were owned by lightermen. The waterway had been much improved by dredging. Tolls amounted to £8,104 in 1858, they rose to £10,431 in 1865, and in 1867 the Royal Commission on the

Prevention of Pollution in Rivers anticipated that it would increase even further, but still the Trust was unable to pay a dividend. (P.P.XXX111(1867) RCRP second report).

No further factories were set up in Enfield until the Jute Works came in the 1860s, attracted by easy access to London by rail and road and by a largely under-employed population in Ponders End, where the bedraggled children of the poor could be used as cheap labour. The skilled men in the factory were brought from Scotland, though some had originated in Ireland. The growth of London, and especially of middle-class suburbia, provided a market for linoleum, and a factory to make it was set up in the 1870s. The Jute Works ended its precarious existence in bankruptcy in 1882 leaving behind much poverty and many empty houses.

Its former works were taken over a few years later by Edison and Swan and thus began Enfield's long-lasting and profitable association with the electrical trades. A number of small workshops came into existence in the 1890s, many of them aiming to meet the new and popular demand for cycles. Others made cricket bats, tennis rackets, brooms and brushes. The availability of good brick-earth in the area between east and west Enfield, and two great booms in house building encouraged the expansion of brickmaking. Industry in the area was given a tremendous boost in 1906 by the opening of the power station at Brimsdown. Cheap electricity encouraged the construction of factories for the manufacture of white lead, varnish and chemicals. Thus eastern Enfield became industrialised before the First World War. With the outbreak of hostilities almost all the firms turned over to war production and a vast new factory was built to supply shells for the western front.

The rapid growth of London in the last quarter of the nineteenth century and the decline of arable farming in that period, encouraged in Enfield, and in the neighbouring parishes, the use of the land for intensive market gardening. Almost the whole of the glasshouse industry of this country, by 1913, was sited in the Lea Valley. Some fifty per cent of the glasshouses were producing tomatoes, twenty-five per cent cucumbers, and the remainder grapes, peaches and flowering plants. The industry employed eight or nine thousand men and boys. The needs of suburbia also encouraged dairy farming on the clay lands of the western side of the parish.

In this chapter I am not attempting a technical history of local industry, a task for which there are few less qualified than myself. My aim has been to portray the employees, the conditions under which they worked, and their efforts to protect and improve those conditions. Where possible, I have sought to show the opinions they held and their attempts to safeguard themselves in times of adversity, through friendly societies, co-operatives and trade unions.

2. The Crape Factory

The factory belonging to Grout, Baylis and Co. stood on the north side of South Street at the junction with Scotland Green. Robinson in 1823 wrote: 'In South Street, Ponders End there is a manufactory of crape established in 1809. It employs about a hundred persons, fifteen of whom are men; the rest are women and children'.[1] The firm Grout, Baylis and Co. was set up in Norwich in 1807 by

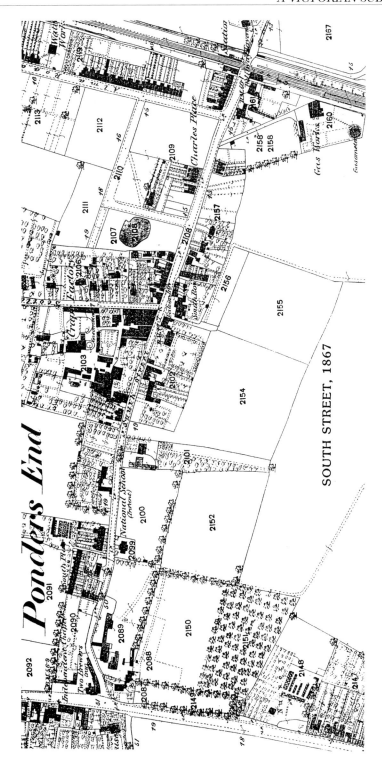

SOUTH STREET, 1867

66.   *The crape factory in 1841 employed thirty-eight men and seventy-seven women and girls. Females were not well paid. The highest wage was 12s; mostly on piece-work they earned 6s to 8s a week.*

Joseph Grout and his brother George who became two of the three partners who managed the firm. In 1809 they built a dyeing and finishing works at Ponders End. The firm extended the manufacturing side after 1815, establishing factories at Yarmouth and other places in East Anglia. They had 3,594 employees by 1824, mostly women and children, and their whole undertaking was valued at £233,000. John Baylis, the third partner, came to live at Ponders End and took charge of the plant in South Street where the crape was dyed, finished, inspected and dispatched to the London warehouse. Joseph Grout moved to Stamford Hill, from where he managed the company's finances and the London warehouse. George Grout controlled the manufacturing side in East Anglia.

For a time the firm had a virtual monopoly in the production of mourning crape. The custom of wearing black when a death occurred in the family started among the upper class and spread downward through the middle class to the working class. A widow, in the 1780s, if she wanted to be considered a lady, had to wear a black dress made of worsted and silk and decorated with black crape, a crape bonnet with a widow cap inside, and a crape veil. After a period of one year and a day she would change this for a black silk dress heavily trimmed with crape which she would wear for six months. In the following three months she would wear less crape, and so the display of grief diminished in regular three monthly stages until two and a half years had elapsed. The wearing of black crape was to a lesser degree incumbent upon relatives, and even door-knockers were trimmed with crape. It was moreover deemed unlucky to keep the material in the house after it ceased to be worn, so every burial meant the purchase of new material. This was very good for Grout and Baylis.

Crape was made from a plain silk gauze. It was embossed with various patterns by being passed between two cylinders. The upper one was of brass or gunmetal, hollow so that it could be heated by steam, and the design was engraved upon it. The engraving was done by hand and might take a year or more. It was then used to impress the design upon the softer lower cylinder, made of compressed paper. The crape was then passed between the two cylinders. Subsequently the material was steeped to set the design and then it was dyed using logwood to obtain a good black. Finally it was stiffened with starch and glue or shellac. The process at Ponders End needed a supply of clean soft water available from a deep well on the site. The crape was sold by the packet; a Ponders End stock list of 1825 shows 3,518 packets of crape, each containing about fifty yards. The South Street factory was valued that same year at £5,000, which included machinery to the value of £1,300.[2]

Pigot's directory of 1826, speaking of Ponders End, states; 'The large silk manufactory of Messrs Grout Baylis and Co. contributes to no small degree to its welfare by giving employment to a number of persons of both sexes'. In 1841 more than a quarter of all the households in the Ponders End area contained at least one crape factory worker. A great deal about the workforce is revealed at this time by the notebook of the new vicar at St James's Church, the Reverend John Fuller Russell,[3] compiled between 11 and 26 April 1841. Russell was of the High Church party and was secretary of the Cambridge Camden Society for whom he wrote several tracts. He names seventy-eight crape workers, and through the 1841 census a further thirty-seven can be added. The factory at this time employed thirty-eight men and seventy-seven women and girls. Many of the senior workmen received good wages and some were paid during sickness. The women were not well paid, the highest female wage recorded by Russell being 12s a week.

Russell's portraits of the people of Ponders End give an overall picture of poverty aiming at respectability, the existence of which he acknowledges even among those who would not come to his church. Many, of course, attended chapel. Mostly they sent their children to school, either to Sunday school or to day school. Russell was not over-generous in his comments on his parishioners, but he was a conscientious minister and went to see almost everybody in the district.

Betsey Nicholls was a married woman living opposite the White Hart in Ponders End. She had been employed in the factory since she was a child and now earned 7s a week making up packets of crape. She had a little girl six or seven years old, who it was whispered, was illegitimate; there had been another born since her marriage. The little girl went to the dissenters' Sunday school. Under pressure from the vicar, Betsey promised to come to church herself and to send the child to the Church Sunday school. The Sunday school belonging to the Independent chapel at Ponders End had been set up in 1830. The building survived as late as 1914; it stood at that time in a derelict condition in the High Street near the new technical institute. Apart from the Sunday school it had housed, from 1830 to 1885, an infant day school.

The vicar was even less charitable towards Mrs Carrington and her family who lived in Goat Lane (by the Goat at Ponders End). She earned 9s a week turning a reel to dry the crape. 'A slovenly ignorant woman, she never attends church', wrote the vicar, 'has three daughters married, all badly conducted before marriage — little hope of amendment'. Susan Hart too was denied the vicar's charity. She lived with her father in a house by the eight-milestone at Ponders End. He was employed in the factory at 15s a week. Susan had once attended both church and Sunday school but had of late neglected both, offering for

67.   South Square off South Street. In 1841 it was a hotbed of dissent.

reason that she looked after her brother who was an idiot. The vicar dismissed her excuses; 'she is idle', he wrote. Mrs Hart, her sister-in-law, had made a better impression by promising to go to church on Sunday afternoons and expressing to the vicar a wish to be better instructed in reading.

The vicar's stern eye fell disparagingly even upon some regular members of his congregation like Mr Bearman, a sound churchman employed regularly at the factory, a kind husband as the vicar admitted, and a good singer, but his failing was insubordination to those in authority over him, presumably including Mr Russell. Mrs Bearman he dismissed as a prejudiced churchwoman; maybe she held strong Low Church views. Another on whom the vicar's eye fell without total approbation was Annis the carpenter at Grout and Baylis. He often attended church, was described as a well-behaved man, but sometimes — not often — drank too much. Mrs Annis and Samuel their son passed unscathed. He was about sixteen years old, was fond of reading, could write and usually came to church. Many of the men who worked in the factory had a basic education. Henry Broomham, the colour dyer on 26s a week and paid during sickness, could write very well, as could his brother, a labourer; both often came to church. The vicar noted them as potential Sunday school teachers.

The vicar and his curate met with a less than enthusiastic response in South Square, for that place was a hotbed of dissent. At number one on the corner lived Henry Archer, employed at 18s or 20s a week with an allowance during sickness. His wife also worked at the factory and earned 8s. They never attended church and they probably did not go to the meeting; as the nonconformist services were known. Their children went to the meeting school, but it was said that they were paid for by some of the dissenters. Next door in number two lived old Henry Orme. He earned 20s a week at the factory, his wife 8s. They both attended services at the meeting and the vicar thought that there was little chance of conversion, either here or in the next house, number three, where old Lucas lived. He drove the van at the factory and got 18s a week. After speaking to him, the vicar declared that Lucas was too old to improve. His wife though 'was a smart woman for her age'; she did piece-work in the factory and earned 6s or 7s a week. They both supported the meeting. Mrs Pursel in number four went to the chapel because she was paid there as a pew opener. He described her as a civil woman, 'better educated than many'. Her father had been employed some years earlier as clerk to Mr Russell's father who had been the nonconformist minister at the Baker Street chapel. Because the vicar felt that there was hope of amendment, the curate left tracts.

Mrs Hardman, an aged widow, lived in number five. She was on piece-work at the factory though, owing to her age, was not always able to work. Henry, her son, was the gate-keeper at the South Street level crossing on the railway. The vicar was much interested in Rebecca Barton who lived with them. She had been abandoned by her mother who had left England 'in an adulterous manner' for America, some years earlier. The girl had refused to accompany her and Mr Hardman had taken in the child. She was then earning 3s a week. The Hardmans adopted her although they could ill-afford it. She now earned 5s 6d a week, had been educated at the Church Sunday and evening schools, and though she was fond of reading, she had the housework to do after finishing at the factory. She had formerly gone to the meeting school, but being favoured by Mr and Mrs Hubbuck, (George Parker Hubbuck was the manager at the Crape factory) she had abandoned the meeting and had long since been excommunicated. The vicar observed, perhaps regretfully, that she appeared to have broken off a love affair with young Wilson opposite the church, and that she now favoured James Ellis.

James worked at the factory for 15s a week and lived with his brother William on Scotland Green. The health of both brothers was poor but fortunately they worked in a warm room at the factory. James had recently begun going to church, but the vicar thought that this might be because of Rebecca. William attended the meeting house. He was employed by Grout and Baylis to examine the crape for blemishes, earning 20s a week and, very importantly for him, was paid for sickness'.

Thomas Orme in number six was described as a sharp, clever man, given to argument and heretical. He held a good position at the factory where he earned 28s a week and was paid for sickness. His wife worked there too, on piece-work at around 7s a week. They both went to chapel and their children attended the meeting school. Mrs Elliott in number seven was hostile; she told the vicar that she had been brought up in the church but went to the meeting for gospel. The vicar particularly disapproved of her; 'a self-righteous hypocritical dissenter', he wrote. Mrs Varden, the widow in number eight, earned 10s a week at the factory. She was very civil, but attended the meeting and Mr Russell thought that she was probably too old to mend.

David Conyard the black-dyer lived in number nine and earned 26s a week. He occasionally attended the meeting and his children went to the meeting school. The vicar on his visit found him a civil man, but a second visit by the curate brought out the worst side in David Conyard. Mr Haskell thought him 'very uncivil, disquietingly so, a complete brute'. His wife was a little less hostile, but she told the vicar firmly that she 'had been brought up to meeting and don't wish to leave it'. She was on piece-work at the factory and earned about 7s a week.

Alan Ball in number eleven was employed to attend to the steam engine at the works and was paid 20s a week. He was a hard-working civil man, and had married the widow Mrs Freeman who was employed in folding crape at 9s. They attended chapel very infrequently and church not at all. Only recently their infant had died. The widow's eldest daughter was twenty-five; she did piece-work, earning around 7s, and came to church only occasionally, though at one time she had been more regular. Emma, the other daughter, was nineteen. She had suffered a great deal of ill-health and was considered unlikely to live more than a year or two. She could read and write and regularly came to church. The vicar's highest accolade was reserved for her: she 'would do for a Sunday school teacher'. The widow's third daughter impressed him less favourably; 'A spoiled child — goes to the meeting school'.

In number twelve lived Spark the night-watchman; he was paid 15s a week. 'Professes to be a churchman', wrote the vicar, 'but I never see him at church'. His wife did piece-work at 7s and their child worked there too at 3s 6d a week. She went to the dissenters' Sunday school. Betsey Hart, an old maid in number thirteen, earned 7s a week at the crape works. The vicar found her in a bad temper and she told him brusquely that she always went to meeting, that is, when she went anywhere.

Mrs Hammerson, a cow keeper, lived at number eighteen, a respectable woman. Her eldest daughter worked at the factory under Mary Kirk (of whom more below) and earned 9s. She was a quiet well-behaved girl, but she went to the meeting. The second daughter had formerly been employed with her sister, but she had been discharged for inciting a young girl to discontent. She was now employed selling milk, and was seen regularly in the congregation at St James. She was a friend of Emma Freeman and usually they walked to church together. Mrs Green who lived in number twenty did piece-work, and her father was the porter at the factory gate. In number twenty-two lived 'Old Bean' and his wife; they worked together at the factory. He earned 20s 6d, she earned 12s a week. They were quiet, civil people who attended the meeting 'out of ignorance', according to the vicar.

The women in charge of the rooms were paid only 12s a week, even Mary Kirk the paragon of crape workers. She was mistress of the rolling room, a single young woman who had worked many years at the factory. A very steady discreet person, she kept a strict watch over the young girls working under her and 'would countenance no improper behaviour'. She lived with her aged grand-mother in a wooden house with casement windows in South Street. The old lady was on piece-work and earned about 7s a week. They both attended church.

The Frasers' house was in Scotland Green. The mother was a widow and did piece-work at the factory. Two of her sons, John and Joseph, lived with her. John suffered poor health; he worked at dyeing and dressing the crape at 16s to 18s a week. Jonathan Fraser, who had the house next door, was the foreman dyer. He earned 31s a week and had a bonus of £11 a year and was paid for sickness. James Fraser in the sixth house along sorted the qualities of crape when finished and earned 22s a week; he too was paid during sickness. A civil and well-behaved man when pleased, as the vicar described him, but soon put out. He played the clarinet very well and was uncommonly proud of his only son. The vicar considered this to be his weak point. His wife also worked at the factory folding crape at 9s a week. All the Frasers went to chapel, though James had had his boy christened at church.

One of their neighbours was old Mrs Pharoah, a widow who lived in a small wooden house belonging to Grout and Baylis on the west side of Scotland Green, right next to the factory. Her husband had held the leather mill and yard next to Mr George's corn mill at the bottom of South Street. He had been a man of some standing in the parish and had been a churchwarden. The vestry had granted her a small pension after his death, because she had been left poor. Her son, a tanner, said the vicar, 'appears to behave hard to her'. She attended the meeting but was 'not bigoted'. Her husband's former greatness in the parish was her weakness; she had 'a long tongue' and would talk incessantly of his former triumphs.

The house next door also belonged to the firm. Old Mr Coombs lived there with his housekeeper. He was so deaf that he couldn't hear ordinary conversation. They both went to the meeting. In the little old cottage next door lived Rayment, an elderly married man. The cottage belonged to the firm and he was employed there at 28s a week. Neither he nor his wife ever came near the church, though Lydia their daughter came occasionally. She earned 6s a week in the factory. Her little sister attended the National school at Enfield Highway. Her brother was employed at the corn mill; he came regularly to church and was a good singer.

The large house on Scotland Green belonged to Mr Gough the farmer who had married a Quaker. The couple had been heart-broken at the death of their daughter about eighteen months since, a very well-behaved child about fourteen years old who had been employed in the factory. She had been a regular attender at both church and Sunday school. Mr Gough's neighbour was poor Mrs Poyser, widowed eight months since with eight children. She earned about 6s a week at the factory, 'a quiet well-behaved woman'. Her eldest daughter had gone out to service. Eliza, the second, about eighteen, worked at the factory rolling crape and earned 7s. She had been taught at Sunday school to read and write and went to church. Mary, the third daughter, was sixteen. She earned 4s 9d a week, 'a very good child, very fond of her mother'. She too could read and write and the vicar persuaded her to become a Sunday school teacher. The family, said the vicar, were once under the domination of the dissenters, but the father had removed the children from their school because he was dissatisfied with their improvement. The vicar was sympathetic towards the widow who came to church on Sunday afternoons as often as she could. More he could not expect for she had a large family with little means and doubtless had much to do on a Sunday.

Langford Place was a row of respectable houses on the north side of South Street. The vicar did not bother to call at numbers one and two. Mr Langford who lived at number one was an Independent. At number two lived Mr Wilsden a preacher of the same persuasion. McDonald in number three was employed at the factory and earned good wages. His son, about sixteen, who was apprenticed there, could both write and calculate very well. Very occasionally they went to the meeting, but never to the church. James Peters, a young married man, lived in number four. He earned 23s a week at the factory and was paid for sickness. Quiet and very civil people, they had friends who were better off than they were. Sadly they had lost their only child about a year back. Old Conyard in number five had been pensioned off from the factory, where he had worked for many years as a dyer. Nevertheless he still went in from time to time and did a bit, just to keep himself amused. He worshipped at chapel and was adjudged by the vicar to be too old to change. In number six lived Walker another Independent, and in number seven Witham, a foreman, and his wife. They were regular church-goers and two of his children attended the National infant school. They had seen much affliction for they had lost two children about a year back.

Next door to the factory lived Chapman, a very quiet man who had come from Norwich. Both he and his wife worked for Grout and Baylis examining the silk as it came in from other factories. He could always be seen in St James where he sat at the south-west corner, but his wife was sometimes absent because of ill-health. She played the flute and the vicar thought that she might make a good Sunday school teacher. Edmonds lived next door. From time to time he went to meetings, even to church occasionally, 'a civil, stupid fellow' said the vicar a little ungenerously. Both he and his wife worked at the factory. She had more sense than her husband, thought the vicar, but she went to chapel. Then there was Judd the lighterman, a man of some little property, with a large family, whose wife did piece-work at the factory. It was Caroline their second daughter who caught the vicar's eye. She was about twenty, was on 8s a week, went to church regularly and was well-behaved and fond of reading. The vicar saw potential there for a Sunday school teacher. Her two younger sisters went to the National infant school.

On the other side of South Street lived Mrs Payne whose husband was a gardener. She did piece-work, as did her two eldest daughters. A younger sister went to the National infant school. The widow, Mrs Naughton, who lived next door became the door-keeper at the church for the Sunday evening service, though her husband had been a Roman Catholic. He had formerly been employed at the factory. She and her eldest daughter did piece-work and there were two younger sisters, one of whom earned 3s a week at the factory while the other went to the National infant school. Jackson and his wife lodged there. He was an agricultural labourer, 'a kind husband', said the vicar, 'but sometimes short of work'. Mrs Jackson did piece-work at the factory and they went to church from time to time. The vicar called at the house to baptise their child. Mrs Naughton had two other lodgers, Mrs Hunt who went to meeting 'but thinks it better to go to church' and Mrs Barber.

Mrs Goode lived opposite the works in the house next to that of Mr Baylis. She was the sister of Mrs Judd, but 'very inferior in manners to her'. She never went to church though her daughter went to the National school at Enfield Highway. She did piece-work at the factory. Ives the lighterman lived one or two doors up from the butcher's shop in South Street; he brought the coal up for the factory. Occasionally he went to church and two of his children attended the National infant school. His son, about sixteen, helped with the barges. They mostly worked on Sundays.

Mrs Upson, who lived in Holmes Alley off South Street, was the mistress of the black-dressing room. She sent two of her children to the meeting school and one to the National infant school. 'A useful orderly woman', said the vicar, 'but little care for religion'. The curate saw her husband, talked to him about dissent and left a paper on the duty of going to church. The vicar also described Mrs Harknet as orderly. She lived next door and was another of the women charge-hands, earning 12s a week. She never went to church and there is no mention of chapel. Her husband had formerly been the carman at the corn-mill. The only family to come in for untempered criticism were the Kirbys, up Cranes

Alley. Mrs Kirby, the vicar said, 'was a bad character and in debt', Mr Kirby was 'very bad'.

The late nineteenth century saw changes in the Victorian way of death; crape became less fashionable and Grout and Baylis less profitable. Over the years 1888-1893 the company losses increased annually. The Norwich mill was closed and sold in 1890. At Great Yarmouth a consortium of local businessmen, concerned about the effects on the town of any closure of the mill, bought the works and, when the Ponders End factory closed in 1894, they purchased the machinery from Ponders End, and had it carried by rail to Yarmouth.[4] The factory at Ponders End was taken over by the lately formed United Flexible Metallic Tubing Company.

3. The Royal Small Arms Factory

The manufacture of military weapons by the government began in 1804. Before that time the State had to depend on private industry, and when that failed arms were purchased in Germany. The production of military arms differed fundamentally from the making of fowling pieces and was carried on by a distinct class of mechanic. Without direct employment by the government this class of workman could become virtually extinct in times of peace. During the wars from 1793 to 1815 the procurement of arms from the Continent became very uncertain. There was not a musket left in the Tower by 1802 and according to Lord Chatham the art of making military weapons had been lost in this country. The government was forced to purchase some 300,000 very clumsy and inferior muskets on the Continent.

To remedy this crisis a manufactory was set up in the Tower, but the space there was too limited and part of the works was transferred to Lewisham in 1808; there the barrel branch was established. Lewisham also had disadvantages for it lay at a distance from water transport and there was no water power to work the mills. A steam engine had to be used, the operation of which cost £2,000 a year.

A better site was found at Enfield Lock and, in the late spring of 1812, Captain John By of the Royal Engineers was ordered to make a survey. He found that the fall of water on the River Lea was more than adequate for the needs of the factory and work began. The move from Lewisham was undertaken in March 1816 and by the end of April fifty-four men, with the stock, machinery and equipment, had arrived in Enfield. The transfer was completed by the middle of May. After the end of the war it was decided that a nucleus of a manufactory for small arms should be retained in public ownership, and that it should be concentrated at Enfield. In consequence, the gun-finishing branch was taken there in 1818 and the buildings at Lewisham were demolished. Twenty-two men and their families, with some of the machinery, were transported by cart to Deptford and thence by barge up the River Lea to Enfield. The remainder of the men at Lewisham were discharged; they were given a month's pay and also their travelling expenses to find other work. A sword-making branch was added to Enfield in 1823 and sixty-three men were employed there. The purchase of land and water had cost £7,330, the buildings and machinery £61,543. The establishment was sited immediately below the conflux of the Small Lea and the Old Lea

68.   Government Row. From the start, the workmen employed at the Small Arms Factory at Enfield Lock lived on the site. The Board of Ordnance built sixty-two cottages, those for artificers of one storey containing two rooms, those for the foremen of two storeys and four rooms.

69.   The ferry and ferry house near Enfield Lock from a postcard dated 1906

and thus had the use of water from both streams with a fall of seven feet nine inches, which was equal to ninety horsepower. There was access by water to the storehouse door, and being close to the Royal Powder Mills at Waltham Abbey, one set of barges could serve both factories. The machinery, of cast iron, consisted of two undershot wheels, each of forty-eight horsepower, which drove boring and turning benches calculated to bore 50,000 musket barrels a year. It was also used to work grindstones and polishing gear for swords and bayonets, rifling machines, and machinery for the preparation of tools.

The Enfield works were under the direction of George Lovell. He described Enfield Lock as 'remote and picturesque'. The men and their families lived within the factory compound where the Board of Ordnance had built sixty-two small cottages. Those for the artificers, each of one storey, contained two rooms for which they paid 2s a week rent. Cottages for the foremen had four rooms. On the river bank the Swan and Pike had been purchased by the Board of Ordnance in 1811. It was felt that it would be better that the workmen should have a public house nearby where the landlord was under the control of the Board. No other public houses were nearer than the Sun and Woolpack on the turnpike road nor any church nearer than Waltham Abbey or St Andrew's at Enfield Town. Payments were made in 1825 to a 'reverend gentleman' which suggests that he may have been holding services in the factory.

When the artificers were first transferred to Enfield they were paid by the day, but since the object of the establishment after the war was to maintain a check on the prices charged by private manufacturers, it was felt necessary to follow the practice of private trade and to employ the men on piece-work. There had been a large stock of arms and barrels remaining after the final defeat of Napoleon and the requirements of the peacetime army were small. Nevertheless, since it was considered essential to maintain the establishment at Enfield, the gun-makers were employed on the production of various other articles for military and naval consumption. George Lovell could claim in 1823 that this had been done without cost to the public, even with a profit to the State, and that with any expansion of production his costs would diminish.

George Lovell the storekeeper (manager) on a salary of £350 a year was forty-five in 1834. He was married and had eight children and a house at Waltham Abbey. He had entered government service as a clerk in the Royal Carriage Department in 1805 and had since acquired a wide knowledge of the manufacture of firearms and of factory administration. His original duties at Enfield lay in the care of the stores, the issue of receipts and the payment of cash; but with the abolition of both the posts of inspector and assistant inspector of small arms, their duties had fallen on him. He was widely read and could translate French and German technical papers. He travelled a great deal for the Board, visiting France, Belgium and Germany, and he played a major role in the redesigning of British arms and in the replacement of the flintlock by percussion weapons. His costs compared very well with those of private manufacturers, and this was the cause of the antagonism and hostility which greeted the introduction of the sword branch at Enfield Lock. Swords had been made at Birmingham, though the best steel was made at Sheffield. Private manufacturers too often colluded to fix the price when they produced for the Board of Ordnance. The contract for the new pattern swords had been offered to the trade in 1823 and all the masters had agreed to set a price of 31s 6d per sword, but the swords had been made at Enfield for 22s and they were judged to be superior.

The Royal Small Arms Factory at this time was making percussion pistols for the Coastguard service using old materials at the Tower, but with new bolts. They also made carbines for infantry sergeants (altered from light infantry muskets), land pattern musket barrels and brass locks for sea service guns. They filled in the time cleaning, varnishing and embellishing ancient weapons in the King's Palace of St James, making spear lances for the light cavalry, doing repairs to old cavalry swords and scabbards, and even making iron bed trestles and leg irons. The store was filled with 13,000 pistol, rifle and musket barrels, 5,000 pistol and rifle bolts and other parts. There was a shortage of work.

A committee consisting of the Surveyor General of Ordnance and high-ranking army officers made a visit to the factory in 1834. They recommended that the men should be retained on a six-day week, but that they should be paid for only five days, for it was asserted that 'the men, having no means of procuring other employment on Saturdays, would be left in idleness to brood over what they considered a grievance'.

A system had been worked out for requisitioning materials and fixing the prices paid for piece-work. All materials required but not in stock had either to be requisitioned from the Tower or other stations, or purchased from a contractor. On receipt it was inspected by the superintendent before being issued to the foremen, who then allocated to the men as the work progressed. It was the duty of each foreman to make a daily report of the work done by each piece-worker under his control, no item being recorded until it had passed the reviewer and had received his stamp. The workmen had to pay for damage done by careless handling, the money being deducted from their earnings.

The men on day work were mustered at regular hours, a roll call being taken and a record of attendance kept. The superintendent was constantly passing through the workshops examining progress and watching that the day workers did not loiter. Towards the end of the week he collected the daily reports and records of attendance from the foremen and compiled a list of articles made and passed by each piece-worker up to Thursday night, allocating to each item its proper price from the price book. From this list wages were paid by the storekeeper in person at eleven o'clock on Saturday morning, each man coming up to the pay table and being called upon to state the amount which he considered due to him. This process must have demanded a widespread degree of numeracy. Every individual received his own money in cash and signed the list; the men were never paid in gangs. Day work men were paid at the same time and in a similar manner. The arms were handed to the storekeeper when finished and the unused materials returned to him. The arms were then sent to the Tower by the Waltham Abbey barges or by carrier's cart.

The workforce in 1834 comprised the storekeeper, superintendent and clerk and forty-three employees including four foremen and viewers, thirty-four artificers, first to third class, a day warden and four labourers. Top wages were 39s a week, labourers being paid 2s a day and upward.

An opportunity to expand production came in 1837. The number of weapons held in store had been greatly reduced by this time and the percussion musket was about to replace the flintlock. George Lovell urged that all services should be issued with the improved weapon, and this would require 140,000 muskets. He calculated that five years' war consumption ought to be held in store. Weapons, he considered, ought to last fifteen to eighteen years in the hands of a soldier, though the regulation period was twelve years. On this basis he worked out that 198,000 muskets should be produced, and strongly urged that the Royal Small Arms Factory should play a major role in the supply. The barrels, rammers and bayonets, he said, should be made in Birmingham, for it would be imprudent to make them at Enfield Lock at so great a distance from supplies of

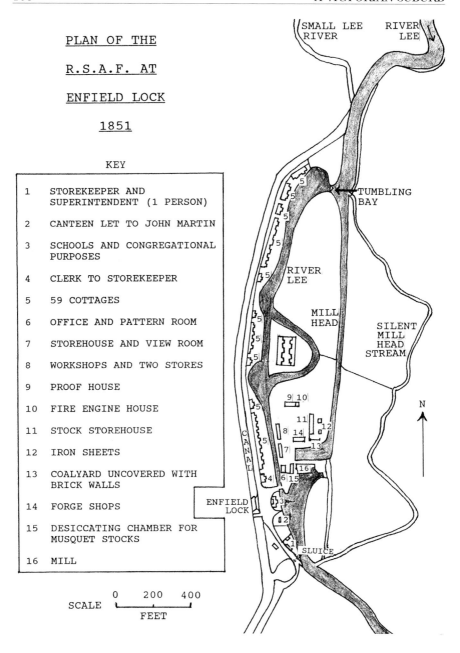

PLAN OF THE

R.S.A.F. AT

ENFIELD LOCK

1851

KEY

1	STOREKEEPER AND SUPERINTENDENT (1 PERSON)
2	CANTEEN LET TO JOHN MARTIN
3	SCHOOLS AND CONGREGATIONAL PURPOSES
4	CLERK TO STOREKEEPER
5	59 COTTAGES
6	OFFICE AND PATTERN ROOM
7	STOREHOUSE AND VIEW ROOM
8	WORKSHOPS AND TWO STORES
9	PROOF HOUSE
10	FIRE ENGINE HOUSE
11	STOCK STOREHOUSE
12	IRON SHEETS
13	COALYARD UNCOVERED WITH BRICK WALLS
14	FORGE SHOPS
15	DESICCATING CHAMBER FOR MUSQUET STOCKS
16	MILL

SCALE 0 200 400 FEET

coal and iron. The locks could be manufactured both at Birmingham and at Enfield Lock. He expected that 12,000 could be made in the first year and that the numbers would grow to 20,000 after two or three years. The buildings at Enfield Lock would require only minor extensions.

George Lovell in 1839 was still urging that an increased share of the manufacture should be allotted to the Enfield Small Arms Factory; 'seeing the difficulty in getting military arms set up by private trade and the very high prices charged'. He proposed that the factory should be capable of meeting all government requirements if it was found that production by private trade was being restricted by collusion between employers or combination among the men. He proposed to provide more space at Enfield by raising the roof over the barrel and lock shops and by adding a storey in wood. He further proposed to put up a new building as offices for himself, the superintendent and the clerk, also to add an upper floor to two blocks of single storey cottages for the use of artificers. The viewers (foremen) employed at Enfield, Birmingham and at the Tower had their salary increased in 1841 according to their length of service; the new salaries were to be £110 per annum for those who had served up to seven years, £120 for seven to fourteen years, and £130 for over fourteen years. George Lovell in 1840 was appointed inspector of small arms in charge of production.

As the Royal Small Arms Factory at Enfield Lock grew, taking on more work, it came under virulent attack from the representatives of private industry, and personal attacks were made on Lovell. A rifling machine was purchased in 1845 from Evans and Sons for £110.[5] A school was opened at the factory in 1846, consisting of one large schoolroom with two small rooms adjoining for a master and mistress. Control was transferred to the National Society in 1855, though it continued to be paid for by the government. At this time it became a mixed school under a mistress with a staff of pupil teachers.[6]

The Crimean War had become inevitable by the end of 1853 and it was launched on a wave of patriotic anti-Russian fervour. The long years of peace, however, had left Britain ill-equipped to secure military success. The army had been reduced in size and active service revealed many weaknesses. Small arms were urgently required, yet it was discovered, somewhat late, that this country, proudly proclaiming itself the workshop of the world, lacked the capacity to supply them. Machinery for the economical production of interchangeable parts for small arms was available only in America. The use of interchangeable parts would mean that rifles could be assembled rapidly by semi-skilled labour, without the necessity for individual adjustments which could only be made by skilled engineers.

Thus it was that on 18 February 1854 authorisation was given to purchase machinery for 'a new small arms manufactory at Enfield'. Colonel Burn, the assistant inspector of artillery at Woolwich, was required to obtain from Mr Whitworth details of gun factories and the makers of machinery in the United States. It was essential that there should be no delay. The speedy completion of the new factory was regarded as a matter of the greatest importance to the public interest. Colonel Burn, with Lieutenant Warlow and Mr Anderson, were sent immediately to America with instructions to bring back a model or a 'specimen' (specification?) of every machine used in that country for making muskets. Lieutenant Warlow was to superintend the examination and boxing of all machinery ordered. Mr Burton, an American expert, and three first rate artificers were sent to Enfield to oversee the setting up of the machinery and to instruct the workmen. The Robbins and Lawrence Company of Windsor (Utah) agreed to make and deliver on shipboard, machinery able to manufacture 250 musket barrels a day. It included;

> Eight rough boring machines at £475 each
> Four second boring and reaming machines capable of 1,500 revs a minute at £285 each

Twelve barrel lathes for turning the barrels to shape at £425 each
Six barrel lathes for turning the butts to exact size at £325 each
Two double hand-lathes at £400 each
Fifteen milling machines at £375 each
Four drill presses at £250 each
Two machines to mill the end of the tang at £200 each
Two machines to counter-bore the barrel at £200 each
Two machines for cutting the thread at £175 each
Two machines for tapping and counter-sinking at £115 each
Sixteen rifling machines at £500 each
Six inside polishing machines at £400 each
Four outside polishing machines at £500 each

The total cost of this one order was £36,045. In all there was lavished on the establishment, from January 1854 to March 1857, £240,593. This included £75,986 for buildings, £64,667 for machinery, £27,270 for stores, £4,716 for salaries, and £67,952 for wages. About 1,250 men and boys were employed.[7]

The machinery was installed by the beginning of July 1855. In preparation for the change to mass production notice was given that from 21 July the engagements of all workmen employed at the factory would be terminated. Several of the old hands were granted pensions, others 'with long and faithful service' were given gratuities, some were found employment in London or Birmingham. The remainder were re-engaged on altered terms. The new system came into operation on 23 July. Working hours were to be the same as in private industry: Monday to Friday 6am to 6pm with half an hour breakfast and an hour for dinner, Saturday 6am to 1pm with half an hour breakfast, making a fifty-nine and a half hour week. The gates were opened at five forty-five and any workman who entered after five past six lost a quarter of an hour; after six-fifteen he lost half an hour. The gates were closed at six-thirty. Wages were still paid on Saturdays before dinner.[8]

The immense importance of the new works, both locally and nationally, can be seen by the reaction to a serious accident which occurred there on 7 July 1859 when the great engine was put out of action by the breaking of the shaft. Seven or eight hundred men had to be laid off for a fortnight. They managed to keep on five or six hundred others because the machinery had prepared sufficient work to employ them on hand labour. To meet the emergency the management was able to procure several small engines from Woolwich. They also sent to Stratford, to the railway workshops, to borrow a thirty ton engine. It took three days and, on parts of the journey twenty-four horses, to drag it to Enfield Lock, only to discover that the bridge over the Lea was not strong enough to bear the weight. It had to be taken back to Stratford. A new shaft had been fitted by the beginning of August and the works were quickly back in operation.

Around a hundred thousand weapons a year were produced at Enfield, mostly rifled muskets of the 1853 pattern. Production costs ranged from 37s to 39s 8d which compared most favourably with prices charged by the gun trade in London and Birmingham, where weapons cost on average 65s. Those purchased in Liege cost 56s 10d. By 1859 the Enfield Rifle was the pride of the parish. 'Enfield' said the O*bserver* (June 1859) 'has very great reason to be proud of its rifle in the construction of which a vast and exquisitely perfect series of machinery is daily at work'. The article speaks of the sight-seers and of the enormous steam engine 'which sets the apparently complicated machinery in

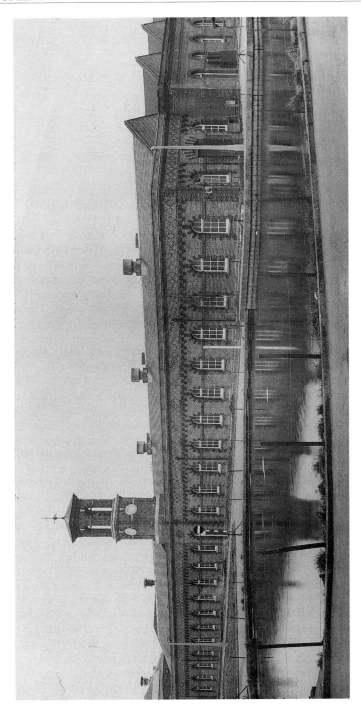

70. *At the time of the Crimean War nearly a quarter of a million pounds was lavished on the Small Arms Factory in Enfield and it was entirely and elegantly rebuilt as can be seen in this photograph.*

motion'. Along the Lee Navigation about six hundred yards of wharfage had been constructed with three cranes capable of lifting fifteen to twenty tons. A fine basin in front of the main buildings had been built. The demand for rifles was increased by the formation in many parts of the country of volunteer rifle companies.[9]

The *Enfield Observer* in January 1862 reported that the factory was very busy; a great deal of overtime was being worked and several hundred men and boys had lately been taken on. The factory, now re-equipped, brought a vast influx of money into the parish. Wages paid there in the year ending 31 March 1863 amounted to £136,193 and salaries to £3,150.[10] An advertisement in the *Observer*, directed at the well-paid workmen, announced:

> Six roomed houses, 1-5 Typo Cottages, Nichol Road (now Jasper Close) three beds, parlour, kitchen and wash-house, garden back and front, good supply of water.

The factory was busy in 1866 on the conversion of the old Enfield rifles to Snider breech-loaders which were said to give thirty per cent greater accuracy and a rapidity of firing improved in a ratio of five to one.[11] But the good times were coming to an end. Despite the fact that the government was the sole purchaser, the workmen, over the ensuing years, suffered from repeated fluctuations in the level of demand. Lay-offs began to reduce the numbers employed in July 1869 and several families were given free passage to emigrate to Canada. Twenty more artisans left for Constantinople, engaged by the Turkish government for two years to take charge there of the production of Snider rifles.[12]

There was no State provision for those thrown out of work, only the ignominy of the poor law. The more careful and intelligent of the workmen sought to protect themselves by membership of friendly benefit societies. There were four principal ones in Enfield at this time with a combined membership of 840. The largest was the Royal Cedar Tree Lodge of the Oddfellows, established in 1842. It had 388 members and the receipts for the year ended December 1870 amounted to £1,034. It had paid out that year in sick benefit £399, for funerals £72, and to widows £130. Subscriptions in 1859 were 8d a week; £12 was paid on death and £6 to widows. Members were cared for by the surgeon of the lodge during illness. The Oddfellows had 1,800 members in Enfield by May 1885 and its funds then amounted to £18,000. An example of the advantages which membership could bring is provided by George Hawkins who died in 1873. He had been one of the eighteen founder members of the Enfield Lodge of the Foresters when it was set up in 1843. He had paid 30s a year for thirty years, a total of £45, and during that time he had received from the sick fund no less than £200 and his family was to receive £20 for the funeral.[13]

Early in the year 1872 the army decided that the Martini Henry rifle, the first satisfactory breech-loader, should replace the Snider. This created another upheaval because new machinery had to be brought in and existing machinery adapted and altered. At this juncture Major General Dixon was given notice to retire after seventeen years' service as superintendent. Many of the men were left with little work for months and during the time when the changes were being made they were unable to earn more than a few shillings a week. Many found themselves obliged to run up crippling debts in the local shops. The tool-makers meanwhile were doing more than thirty hours a week overtime, paid at time and a half, but still the refitting went slowly. Work in the filing room came to a complete standstill at the beginning of January and the men, facing a prolonged lay-off, demanded to be put on day work to help with the re-tooling, but this was turned down because the Amalgamated Society of Engineers objected strongly to gun-makers being allowed to work in the toolroom. The foreman supported the union, and while men who had been employed there for years were taking starvation wages, he engaged more tool-makers from far off parts of the country.[14]

The behaviour of these strangers was remembered in Enfield for years. According to correspondence in the *Observer* in January 1882, they had been 'the roughest elements from the worst districts of the Black Country ... imported into the parish regardless of character or civilisation, so highly paid that they drank their earnings from mid-day Saturday until Tuesday night and were constantly in trouble with the law'. The management had to issue a warning that any man whose name appeared in the papers, having been charged in the police court, would be immediately dismissed. When the re-tooling was at last completed they returned to Staffordshire and elsewhere.[15]

Although some of the machinery was ready by the beginning of March 1872, the piece-workers could still earn no more than an average of 15s a week. Production remained at only 500 rifles weekly and many of these were inspected and condemned. The gun-makers sought a meeting with the superintendent and, although he himself could do nothing, he assisted the men in securing the support of the Conservative member of Parliament for the county of Middlesex, Lord George Hamilton, who came down to Enfield for a meeting in the Totteridge Road school-house. The men told him that it would be another three months before they could earn their money, and that many of them were already deeply in debt and would inevitably have to seek further credit. If it were to be refused then 'God only knows what would happen to the women and children'. The management had said that the men could leave if they liked, but this was out of the question because of the cost of moving. Besides some were entitled to superannuation or gratuities and if they resigned they would forfeit all claim on the government. Lord George Hamilton listened to their complaints and promised to do what he could. [16]

The re-tooling of the factory for the manufacture of the Martini Henry rifle was still proving difficult. The barrel, made out of solid steel, had to be drilled with great accuracy through the centre of the rod. Every attempt to do this at Enfield had failed. The only place having the necessary technical know-how was Mr Frith's works in Sheffield from where the barrels were brought to Enfield to be set and rifled with seven grooves. The new rifle had a smaller bore and a flatter trajectory which gave greater range and increased accuracy. The action body was made from a solid block of steel and a large cavity had to be made to receive the breech block. Great difficulty was experienced in bringing machinery to bear to carry out this operation in mass production, but this was overcome by November 1872. The solid bar was made hot in a furnace, then placed over a die of the required shape under one of Nasmith's steam hammers, which fell with a force equal to five tons. The ponderous steam hammer worked night and day. At last 1,200 rifles a week were being completed and it was predicted that the figure would soon be doubled. Two important improvements were made to the weapon at Enfield, an indicator to show when the rifle was cocked and a safety catch.[17]

The men were now busy again and earning good money, though most of them were left heavily in debt. It was at this juncture that the workmen decided to make another attempt to set up a retail co-operative. The *Enfield Observer* was scathing, demanding, to know 'was this the way these people expressed their gratitude to the Enfield tradesmen who had so recently stood between them and starvation?'. One may look in vain through the local newspaper to discover what motivated the men to take this action so soon after the end of the crisis. Perhaps the shopkeepers had taken advantage of their customers' indebtedness to raise prices. The *Observer* continued to sneer, declaring that, 'Past experience teaches the tradesmen that they have little to fear... three previous attempts to set up co-operatives have proved miserable failures and large sums remain due to those that supplied them and to those who took shares'. The writer urged that the shopkeepers should learn a lesson, and that in future they should refuse to grant credit, then, the writer adds, perhaps telling the truth without meaning to, 'they could supply goods over the counter for cash at as cheap a rate as any co-operative store'.[18]

The idea of a co-operative had been revived at the suggestion of the management. The men had found themselves in such straights after all the short-time working that they had applied to Major Dyer, the assistant supervisor, for an advance of pay. They complained to him of the high prices which they were forced to pay in the local shops. The Major replied that then they must be fools to shop there; they should combine and with their joint capital set up a co-operative, 'Similar to those achieving so much for the people in the north of England'. Twelve years earlier when a co-operative bread society had been formed, it had failed disastrously. Nevertheless they now went ahead and founded the Enfield Lock Co-operative Association. Until such time as they could afford to purchase for themselves, they accepted the offer of the New Supply Association to provide the stock.

Shares were issued valued at 10s each and no member was allowed to own more than ten, they were to be paid for by weekly instalments of not less than 3d; thus the Co-op could serve also as a savings bank. The first purchase consisted of a chest of tea which arrived just before Christmas 1872. It was held at the secretary's house in Bell Lane. Members pledged themselves to buy one pound each to give the business a good send off. Further purchases were made: a cask of paraffin-oil, two cwts of soap, six dozen of 'Prices snuffless dips' (candles), and a further half chest of tea. All these were articles for which they had been overcharged in local shops. Business could be transacted only in the evenings for it was all done from the secretary's house. Cocoa, coffee, sugar, rice and tapioca were added to the stock. Sales improved when the secretary moved house to a better position on the corner of Bell Lane and the Highway.

The Co-op however almost came to an untimely end in 1873 when stocktaking showed that stock to the value of £18 was missing. The secretary resigned and moved away.

A full-time shopkeeper was appointed in 1874. This was a hazardous step, for the weekly trade amounted only to £13, but it meant that the store could be kept open all day. The Rochdale system was adopted which signified selling goods at market prices and returning the surplus to members as rebate on purchases. A coal department was opened in 1875, and in 1876 a drapery department, though for this latter not more than £5 was to be expended on stock. A new store was opened in 1881 in Mandeville Road. Membership by this time stood at 110 and the weekly trade at £40. The society was burdened by a mortgage of £350 and it was at this inopportune moment the shopman resigned to set up his own business, taking much of the trade with him.

The society had 358 members by September 1889, its income during the previous quarter having been £1,923 and its capital amounting to £1,651. A meeting was held to establish a branch at Ponders End. New members would pay a shilling entrance fee, 3d for a share book and 3d for a rule book. Dividend (profits) would be retained until members had accumulated £1. By 1893 the Co–op was paying 2s in the pound to members.[19]

The skilled workmen were now (1873) learning how to voice their own grievances. For some years the cashier at the factory had acted as income tax collector, deducting tax from wages whenever he found workmen in receipt of more than a hundred pounds a year. The men considered this to be an injustice. Their earnings were subject to wide fluctuations from year to year and, although they might earn £100 one year, the following year it might only be £50. They believed that it was illegal to stop tax out of pay and between them they raised sufficient money to seek advice. Counsel's opinion gave support to the feeling of the men: he declared that, since their earnings were casual, they ought to be assessed over three years. The men therefore instituted proceedings against Mr Clapham, the cashier, in the county court, but before the case was heard the Board of Inland Revenue caused the money to be returned.[20]

The Martini Henry was being produced at a rate of nearly 3,000 a week by early 1874 but the modernisation of the machinery had enabled management to dispense with much of the hand labour; some men were discharged, others were pensioned off. A cloud of uncertainty hung perpetually over the prospects of the workforce. Orders fell off and, by April, were so low that a crisis meeting of local property owners, shopkeepers and workmen was held at the Bell. It was rumoured that the order for 1874/5 was for only 673 pieces a week, although the stock in hand was said to be smaller than at any time since 1797. The Martini Henry was not so popular as had been hoped; it was heavy and the recoil was violent. Declining prospects led to a fall in the value of property in the area. It was a situation unheard of near a government factory which had cost more than half a million. This situation had arisen because the government was purchasing arms from private contractors and from Germany. The men demanded that the Railway Company should provide workmen's trains like those running to Enfield Town and Edmonton; this it was thought might attract new industry into the area.[21]

The year 1874/5, however, proved better than had been forecast because more orders came in for new weapons and some 140,000 Martini Henry rifles were returned for modification. In fact there had never been so much work at Enfield Lock. The men were eager to earn money to pay off their debts, but management reduced the prices paid for piece-work, so much so that the workmen complained that they could barely earn a living and could put nothing aside for the future. They accused the management of replacing skilled men by semi-skilled in order to reduce wages. A thousand extra hands had been taken on. The *Enfield Observer* waxed lyrical over the brilliant illumination provided by thousands of gas burners glowing late into the night, but the heat which these generated, with the lack of ventilation, made the factory unpleasant and unhealthy to work in.[22]

A great effort was being made to complete the year's order by 1 April, with artisans working until nine on weekdays, and six on Saturdays. The reduced prices paid for their work, the men argued, meant that when overtime came to an end they would be on starvation wages. Another grievance was the rigidity of management's code of discipline. Though they were on piece-work they were locked out if they were a few minutes late. The rules had not been imposed so harshly when Colonel Dixon had been in charge, they said; he had instructed the police to apply the rules more leniently.

The value of orders had fallen away again by May 1876 and great numbers of artisans and labourers were discharged. Many found their gratuities to be less than they had expected because, in calculating their service, the government had made deductions for time lost which had occurred when machinery was changed, and also when there had been a shortage of work. The men had at other times put in many hours overtime, even on occasions working all night, but this was never taken into consideration. In one case, because a man had been sick for three weeks seventeen years previously, the Treasury had deducted a year's service.[23]

The workmen remained constantly under threat of sudden dismissal and some of them either could not, or would not, save. One woman, who was sued in May 1880 for a debt of £3 10s, pleaded that her husband, who had been earning £2 a week at the factory, had been discharged eight weeks before when work had been slack. He was now away in Birmingham looking for a job and she had nothing coming in to feed the children. Wages at the factory certainly had been reduced. Twenty years earlier, wrote one correspondent in the *Observer* (14 January 1882), obviously pleased about the change, men had earned in half a week more than many of them now did in three weeks. He said that in the old days the men had 'worked Wednesday, Thursday and Friday like horses and had spent the money like asses from Saturday through to Tuesday, and their wives and families were left worse off than those of bricklayers' labourers. 'The artisans of today', he claimed, 'and the workmen of twenty years ago are as different as is the present government establishment from the old building that gave place to it... No one now has any fear of living too close to Enfield Lock, nor do landlords as a rule refuse to accept the factory hands as tenants'. The present artisans he thought were an industrious and saving class of men.[24]

The vacillating policies of governments which brought alternate rumours of short time and threats of dismissals, followed by reports of substantial orders, continued to render life uncertain for the employees at the Small Arms Factory. The decision in January 1885 to equip the Volunteers with a hundred thousand Martini Henry rifles, of which 80,000 were to be made at Enfield, gave promise of full employment for five years. Only a year later however (27 February 1886) came a report that 300 hands were to be discharged, despite the fact that an order had just been received for the manufacture of new arms for the regular army. The *Sunday Times* complained that a quarter of the swords and bayonets supplied from Germany failed the 'bone and muscle test'. 'Is it right', the paper demanded, 'to secure warlike supplies from abroad when Englishmen are prepared to take up contracts?' The expansion of the Enfield factory was advocated, so that there would be 'more English hands employed to do England's work'.[25]

Nevertheless only a few weeks later a notice was pasted up in the works stating that it would be necessary to discharge 800 hands. The *Enfield Observer* (6 March 1886) expressed dismay:

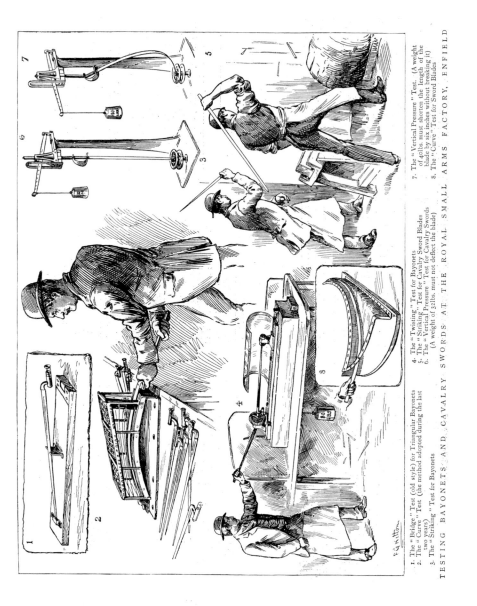

1. The "Bridge" Test (old style) for Triangular Bayonets
2. The "Curve" Test (the method adopted during the last two years)
3. The "Striking" Test for Bayonets
4. The "Twisting" Test for Bayonets
5. The "Striking" Test for Cavalry Sword Blades
6. The "Vertical Pressure" Test for Cavalry Swords (A weight of 32lbs. must not deflect the blade)
7. The "Vertical Pressure" Test. (A weight of 40lbs. must shorten the length of the blade by six inches without breaking it)
8. The "Curve" Test for Sword Blades

TESTING BAYONETS AND CAVALRY SWORDS AT THE ROYAL SMALL ARMS FACTORY, ENFIELD

71. *The* Sunday Times *in 1886 complained of the importation of inferior swords and bayonets from Germany. Such weapons were well made and tested at Enfield, said the paper, and an expansion of the Enfield works was demanded.*

'By the establishment of the Government Small Arms Factory' it declared, 'some thousands of the best and most skilled artisans have been attracted from the large manufacturing centres, and there has grown up what may almost be called a town of considerable importance in the district of the Highway. It was confidently believed that this neighbourhood would enjoy immunity from the prevailing depression. Only last year the government determined to arm the whole volunteer force with the improved rifle, to be made at the Enfield factory. The work is not completed and will take five years at least. Many of the men, by frugality and industry, have been enabled to buy their own houses; others have become small shopkeepers. Many have their small savings invested in building societies. The 800 ordered to be discharged is but a slight proportion of those affected, for their families represent 3,000 to 4,000 souls'.

A delegation from the Enfield Highway Conservative Working Men's Club was dispatched immediately to Edmonton to see Lord Folkestone, the Conservative member for the constituency. He received them warmly and promised to raise the matter in Parliament. There were letters in the *Morning Post* and the *Daily News* from Mr Littler of Broomfield Park and by Friday morning, according to the *Daily News*, a telegram had been received at Enfield causing the superintendent to withdraw the notice. But uncertainty remained. Sir Henry Campbell Bannerman declared in the Commons that the order had been issued as a warning to the workmen of an impending reduction of wages, but he hoped that abrupt dismissals on a large scale could be avoided.[26] The rumours began again; yet within weeks came an announcement that the War Office had decided to extend the factory and it was reported in May 1886 that a large number of workmen were engaged on new building, and that the new workshops would be fitted up with the latest patterns of machinery. Messrs R.E.Crompton and Co. supplied three large dynamos, in August 1886, for lighting the works with electricity. It was stated, however, that it was not intended to use these new buildings in the immediate future.[27]

The centre of the dilemma was indecision concerning the weapon to be produced for the army. According to the *Daily Telegraph*, no fewer than eight structural changes had been made in the new Enfield Martini rifle. At least 20,000, some said 70,000, of these weapons had been stored, yet every one of them would now have to be altered, 'lock, stock and barrel'. The newspaper found it incredible that, 'in a practical nation like our own', weapons continued to be manufactured by tens of thousands only to be altered within a month or two. It was confidently predicted that, when General Smith's Small Arms committee was able to agree, the Enfield Martini would be rendered obsolete by the introduction of a magazine rifle. The manufacture of the small Gardner and Nordenfeldt machine gun was being undertaken at the factory. The extensive low-roofed workshops now covered several acres, a big forge had been added, and an electric lighting workshop. Twenty-three hundred hands were employed, but the repeated alterations to the Enfield Martini, involving the remaking of forging blocks, cutters and other tools, necessitated periodic discharges and suspensions among the workmen, while machinery was being changed. This state of affairs, the *Observer* predicted, would continue. 'When all has been done and a hundred to a hundred and fifty thousand rifles have been remade, should General Smith's committee favour a magazine gun, all these weapons will be useless.'[28]

The following month (July 1887) a meeting was held in the Albany Hall chaired by J.C.Watts chairman of the Edmonton Radical Association. It was attended by some five hundred men who protested against further sweeping

Ordnance Road Enfield Lock.

72.   *The approach to the Royal Small Arms Factory along Ordnance Road in 1913. The roof and bell turret of the church can be seen.*

discharges. The government, it was alleged, were to turn a thousand men adrift out of 2,400, many of whom had been induced to come from Birmingham on a promise of two or three years regular work; they would be faced with ruin. J.H.Matthews, secretary of the John Morley Club, who worked in the RSAF, claimed that for many months these men, now destined to be discharged, had been doing overtime. The system turned out 2,500 rifles one week and two or three hundred the next, and it was always the workmen who suffered. A letter from the meeting was sent to Lord Folkestone and questions were submitted in Parliament where it was pointed out that a whole community depended upon the factory. Under pressure, Northcote, the Under Secretary for War, denied any decision to discharge, but his denial, according to Matthews, was based upon a false distinction between suspension and discharge. 'If a man is put off with no wages it is the same thing', he asserted. 'These men are on piece-work and get paid according to the work turned out.'[29]

The questions in Parliament and the publicity in the press, especially in the *Pall Mall Gazette*, delayed the discharges, but within two months the process was resumed. The Secretary for War, replying to Lord Folkestone, defended the dismissals, claiming that the number of hands was nearly double the number normally employed in peacetime. He blamed the long delays in settling the pattern of the new magazine rifle. Further questions were asked in Parliament in September 1887 in an endeavour to reveal the extent of the muddle. Had the manufacture of the Enfield Martini ceased, and if so when? Were those rifles already made being converted to Martini Henrys and if so were there not already more than enough of them, since a magazine rifle with a smaller bore was about to be adopted? These matters were pursued by the *Daily Telegraph* but the situation remained obscure.[30]

As a measure of self-protection a provident society had been set up in the works. Again the idea came from above, from Lord Folkestone when he spoke at the recently established Conservative Club in South Street. He suggested that the employees should put a small sum by each week which could be put out to interest. Mr Raitt the cashier at the factory became treasure and remained so until his retirement in February 1900. The society's income over the first three years up to March 1889 was £1,372, of which £1,272 had been paid out in benefits. There were no facilities for eating in or around the works; the wives cooked meals for their husbands at midday and these were collected by carmen like John Burchall and taken to the factory.[31]

Rapid progress was being made by May 1889 in installing machinery for the manufacture of the new magazine rifle and by June day and night shifts were being worked in some departments. Additional men had been taken on and by September 3,200 men were employed and 1,500 to 1,600 ILMH rifles were being turned out weekly. It was intended to expand production to 2,000 a week; £6,000 was paid out weekly in wages at this time.[32]

The new rifle was finally issued to the army at the end of December 1889, including the European infantry in India, but not to the native troops. It had been on the stocks for three years and was the fifth new rifle introduced to army service since 1851. There had been the Enfield rifle from the beginning of the Crimean War, and this had been issued to the Volunteers when these units were set up in 1859. The 'Enfield' was superseded in 1864 by the 'Snider' which was the muzzle loading 'Enfield' altered to a breech loader. The Martini breech loader was adopted in 1871 but was not issued until three years later, and it was not until 1877 that the whole army was equipped with it. It was thought at the time to be a perfect weapon. 'Now', said the *Observer*, 'there is a new rifle which has no hostile critics.' After a moment's consideration however, the paper added 'as yet'.[33]

Towards the end of each financial year as orders were completed and the budget expanded men were laid off from the Small Arms Factory until the new year brought new orders. A hundred and fifty were discharged in January 1891, but things were not so bad as they had been some years earlier. Expectations for the financial year 1891/2 however, were disappointing and the estimate for wages at the factory had been reduced by £75,000. The labourers were worst hit; many of the skilled men laid off found work at the small arms factory at Old Ford, and the Great Eastern Railway ran a cheap train daily at 6 am to take them there. They were home soon after seven in the evening. But there were more dismissals. A mass meeting held in the market place at Enfield Lock in February 1892 was addressed by Henry Barrass who claimed that the government was about to reduce production at Enfield from 2,000 down to 500 a week. Henry Bowles brought the matter to the attention of Parliament, asserting that rifles which could be made at Enfield for £3 10s were being purchased from private industry for £5 10s. He believed that the government order placed at Enfield was lower than it had been for twenty-five years. A deputation from the RSAF attended at the House of Commons and a number of members of the Commons visited the factory.

The works were now entirely closed on Saturdays. Labourers paid by the hour, whose full money was only 18s to 20s a week, suffered, yet the men remained staunchly Conservative. On the day of the general election in July 1892 the works closed at midday and a long procession of carriages was laid on by the friends of Colonel Bowles to take the men to the polling booth in the main road where for an hour the polling was brisk. Unionist checkers confidently claimed that the voting was four to one in favour of Henry Ferryman Bowles the Unionist candidate. He was returned by a substantial majority.[34]

The movement to secure sixpence an hour minimum pay for labourers at the factory, to equal what the dockers had won in 1889 and what had lately been conceded by the LCC and generally in the Metropolitan area, was set on foot by a meeting at the Greyhound in Ordnance Road in December 1892. The cost of living in the Metropolitan area, it was pointed out, was one-third lower than it was in Enfield. A deputation was appointed to seek the support of Henry Bowles. Another meeting was held early in February 1893 when Bowles shared the platform with Keir Hardie. It is quite remarkable that this occasion should have brought in such close proximity a Unionist landowner and a socialist ex-miner, by then the Independent Labour MP for South West Ham. There were 155 labourers employed at the factory; most received between $4^1/_2$d and $5^1/_2$d an hour, only a few got sixpence, and some men with families receiving only 3d. Labourers were on day work, paid at an hourly rate. Tom Mann, who had done so much to help the dockers win the 'tanner' in the 1889 strike, addressing a large open air gathering outside the works in April 1893, called for a forty-eight hour week.[35]

The works remained closed on Saturdays and the labourers, able to work only five days a week, found their money reduced from 19s to 17s 7d. In answer to a question, Parliament was informed that the lowest wage paid at the RSAF during the previous week was 11s $1^1/_2$d to a lad of eighteen doing piece-work, but twenty-two men over twenty years old were earning less than 18s, the lowest being paid 16s 8d. 'We are informed', said the War Office spokesman, (Campbell Bannerman) 'that the current rate for labourers in the neighbourhood is 16s'. 'The farmers' he added, 'have in fact complained that we are raising the rates in Enfield and Waltham'. This assertion was strongly denied by a correspondent in the *Observer* who obviously had firsthand experience of local conditions. He pointed out that the market gardeners in the area, Messrs Wilson senior, Wilson junior, Mitchell, Humphreys and others paid 18s to 20s a week. Over and above this their men had many opportunities considerably to increase their pay, such as planting, bunching and gathering, all of which tasks were done on piece-work, enabling the men to earn 30s a week. The current wage for a sewage worker in this area was 20s 3d and builders' labourers were paid 5d or $5^1/_2$ an hour for day work. Campbell Bannerman moreover had made a comparison between a skilled labourer, working in unhealthy conditions in the factory, and an unskilled labourer working in the fields. The hardship caused by low wages was added to by ever increasing rents. The London Trades Council lent its support to the sixpence an hour campaign and a committee was set up with J.H.Matthews as chairman; Henry Barrass was a member.[36]

The fortunes of the work-force continued to fluctuate. The Liberal government (1892-1895) was accused of running down the Enfield factory. It was reported in the *Evening News* in March 1893 that the management was about to discharge a further 300 men. "The RSAF", said the paper, "presents a woeful spectacle with hundreds of big machines lying idle." The estimate for wages for the year 1893/4 was £120,000 against £160,000 in the previous year. A valuation of the buildings and machinery at over £200,000 was given in the House of Commons. Some work was created when all the serviceable Martini Henry rifles which had been exchanged for Lee Metford magazine rifles were returned either for store or for conversion to carbines at Enfield. In March 1894 however a large order for rifles was transferred to Birmingham. After a while work picked up temporarily and by July six-day working had been resumed. Short time working nevertheless recurred in March the following year and Major Bowles relentlessly resumed his questions to the Secretary of State for War. The uncertainty of employment held wages down. Those employed in the 'big room' claimed that their rate of pay had not increased for twenty years. The men held a meeting in the canteen in March 1896 to secure an extra penny an hour; there was no strike threat, only the appointment of a three-man delegation consisting of Henry Barrass, J.Moxam and J.Adams, to see the manager, Mr McGee, who gave them a sympathetic hearing.[37]

By January 1898 conflict between the British and the Boer republics of South Africa was becoming inevitable and overtime was being worked at the Royal Small Arms Factory. The Boers were importing arms from Germany and engaging German artillery officers. The work load at Enfield had so increased by April that men were being brought into the district and there was a surge in house building. Said the *Observer* (22 April 1898) 'stacks of bricks and building materials are being carted on to various open spaces'. An order for twenty thousand rifles was rumoured in May. The optimism was premature and by March the following year the government, with its usual lack of wisdom and foresight, was laying off men because the new orders couldn't come in before the beginning of the new financial year in April. In May, however, came an order for 114 machine guns. Demand for rifles remained low although they could be turned out in Enfield at £2 12s against a cost of £3 4s at Sparkbrook in Birmingham. The editor of the *Observer* (6 October 1899) expressed his pleasure to find 'that the alarming reports... that a state of war had been precipitated by a Boer invasion of Natal is nowhere confirmed'. The rumours of war may have alarmed the editor but they presaged good fortune for the artisans at Ordnance Road. The machine-gun shop began working overtime, as did the smith's shop and toolroom, making parts for wagons and tent shoe pegs, but orders for rifles still did not come in. Collections were made in the works, and also at Ediswan's, to provide for the wives and families of fellow workmen recalled to the colours. The events of the South African war were given wide coverage in the local press. It was going badly and a series of reverses and surrenders in December 1899 brought gloom and despondency throughout the country. Seven marksmen from the Enfield Lock detachment of the 1st Battalion Middlesex volunteers embarked for South Africa on 13 January 1900.[38]

Orders for rifles at last began to come in with the new year. Some departments of the factory were working until midnight. Soon a night shift had to be employed and Sunday working began. Further work was provided when imperfect sights on the Lee Enfield had to be replaced. By this time a seven day week was being worked at the powder mills. The spring brought a series of British victories which culminated in May with the relief of Mafeking. Enfield rejoiced; flags and bunting were hung out, bonfires were lit and there were fireworks. The Foresters band and the boys' band from Chase Farm School played patriotic music. The Royal Small Arms Factory was thrown open to the public, each department competing in decorating the workshops. Patriotic fervour brought thousands on a pilgrimage to Ordnance Road; on the first day nearly four thousand sightseers crossed the bridge. The war engendered in the middle class a concern for national defence with the result that rifle clubs were set up

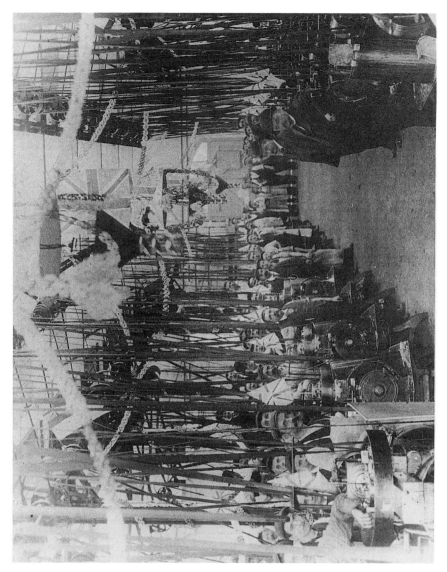

73. May 1900 saw the relief of Mafeking. Patriotic fervour brought thousands on pilgrimage to Ordnance Road, where departments competed in decorating the workshops.

throughout the country. Mr Devine, the schoolmaster, offered the range at Claysmore for the use of the Enfield Rifle Club. The factory changed over to the production of a new rifle, based on the Mauser, which was lighter and shorter than the Lee Metford. Through August 1900 the men were working until eight o'clock every night. The flight of Kruger into exile in the autumn seemed to presage the end of the war, but guerrilla fighting continued for a further eighteen months. It was a time of glorious prosperity at the RSAF. Peace was not established until April 1902, after which the prosperity faded.[39]

The wages estimate for the year 1902/3 was down £27,000 on the previous year, foreshadowing less overtime and less employment. At the beginning of 1903 an order for 25,000 Lee Enfields was cancelled and the War Office ordered the retooling of the factory for the production of the newly adopted Lee Enfield Modified rifle. Much of the machinery had to be adapted and new machines were laid down. Production was not resumed for many months, during which time the workmen had to exist on reduced pay while the imposition of unreasonable conditions added to their grievances. J.H.Matthews became their self-appointed spokesman. At a meeting in the large hall at Chesterfield Road School, he shared the platform with James Branch the Liberal parliamentary candidate. He told the piece-workers that they should be organised to resist the employers. He and Henry Barrass had been employed at the factory for nearly thirty years, he said, and formerly when a man had no work on a Friday the management had paid him his wages and let him go home. Now, men were forced to come in on Saturday mornings to get their pay. In former days workers were paid whenever they were unable to get into work because of floods; now if they were unable to get in, they got nothing. The following week there was a public meeting to protest against the run-down of the works for it had also hit the local shopkeepers who were forced either to give credit or to sell nothing. Many of the men had worked only one to three days a week since Christmas and they were coming out of the gates every Saturday with only 5s to 15s in their pockets. The Urban District Council dispatched a letter to the War Office telling of the extreme distress among piece-workers. J.H.Matthews called a meeting in the dinner hour one day towards the end of September 1903, to urge the formation of a union branch. Matthews had played a leading role in every dispute at the factory since 1886 and in 1907 he was selected by the United Workers Federation as a parliamentary candidate.[40]

A reduction of the labour force from its wartime level was inevitable; a year after the fighting stopped 2,600 men were still employed at the factory, against 2,100 before the war. The War Office was of the opinion that at least three or four hundred men would have to be discharged, but in the meantime hundreds were kept on though earning £1 a week or less. They hung on in the hope that the factory would return to full employment when the plant for the new rifle had been laid down. A question in Parliament from Colonel Bowles at the end of March 1904 revealed that 152 men had earned, on average, less than 22s a week over the previous six weeks. If they were family men, they must have been living in poverty. Many men had run into so much debt that when they were finally discharged their debts exceeded their gratuities, for which they often had to wait five or six weeks without a penny coming in. They complained that these gratuities were calculated in such a way as to rob them of their due; for while management deducted the time when men were laid off because there was no work, it took no account of the overtime they had put in. Thus men who had worked the required seven years qualifying time were, by dubious adjustments, often robbed of their gratuities. J.H.Matthews led a deputation to the War Office representing the United Government Workers Association to voice these grievances. With the impoverishment of the workforce, houses were falling vacant as people crowded together to save on rent. House building ceased and the distress spread to the building trade. Much of the trouble was said to be caused by imperfections in the design of the new rifle; production could not start until solutions had been worked out.[41]

74. *David Weston began work at the Royal Small Arms Factory at the age of eleven. He was a member of the Urban District Council for twenty-seven years and became its chairman; he was also a member of the Board of Guardians for twenty-three years. He drove the first tram down Southbury Road.*

Short-time working continued throughout the year 1904; the works remained closed on Saturdays, reducing the hours to forty-four a week. The average wage for the week ending 3 December 1904 for the general run of skilled and semi-skilled workers (excluding labourers, foremen, leading hands and viewers) was £1 15s 6d. Four hundred men were discharged in March 1905. Seventy-five per cent of the shopkeepers in the Lock area, declared Councillor David Weston, were on the verge of bankruptcy. Men who had tried to purchase their houses through building societies had been unable to keep up repayments. Children were going to school ill-fed and poorly clad. Two-thirds of the machinery at Enfield was standing idle. The number of empty houses in the area was shocking.

David Weston was a self-made man. He was born at Darlaston in Staffordshire and his family came to Enfield in 1863. His father got work in the RSAF and David joined him there at the age of eleven. Later he took a job as a road contractor's foreman and timekeeper. Then he went into partnership with his brother in a coal business opposite Brick Lane. He became manager and steward of the Liberal Club at Franklyn Villas, Ordnance Road. He did bill posting in his spare time and, after a brief interlude as a refreshment caterer, he decided to get his living by bill posting. This business he expanded through Enfield, Hertford, Ware, Chelmsford, Brentwood, Finchley, Barnet, Southend, Clacton and even further. He had leanings towards Liberalism, was a member

75.   The funeral of David Weston.

of the Board of Guardians for twenty-three years and of the Middlesex County Council for twenty-one. His energy and his ambition were apparently unlimited. He died in September 1927 at the age of 73.[42]

The Murray committee, appointed by Balfour in 1905, set a figure for the number of employees at Enfield at between 1,900 and 2,000 and limited the weekly wage bill to about £4,000. The United Government Workers Federation continued to demand that labourers' wages be increased from 22s 6d to 26s. This, claimed J.H.Matthews, the president, was the money paid by other local firms. He cited John Rochford, Ediswan's, the London Brick Company and others. The Royal Small Arms Factory remained short of work. Production was held up by doubts about the efficiency at long range, of the new short barrel rifle. According to the *Daily News* the minister, Haldane, was being pressed in Parliament to place more orders for bayonets at Enfield where they could be made for 8s 1³/₄d each as against purchase from the trade at 9s 8d. Four hundred men were dismissed from the Waltham Abbey Gunpowder Factory between March 1905 and May 1906.[43]

An attempt by the War Office in 1910 to rationalise production at its factories was met with stubborn opposition from the Small Arms Union and the Amalgamated Society of Engineers. The War Office refused any longer to guarantee the maintenance of 2,000 jobs at Enfield and the numbers now fell to 1,900. All men over sixty had been discharged, and all those under twenty-one. A great demonstration was organised supported by five to six thousand people with banners and bands to protest against the 'sweating methods being adopted and the heavy reductions in wages at the Royal Small Arms Factory'. There was much concern throughout the town that any serious reduction of the wages paid at the factory would hit both shopkeepers and landlords.[44]

Prospects in May 1913 hung in the balance, dependent upon the adoption or rejection of the new service rifle which was about three inches longer than the current design and had a peephole sight instead of the 'V' shaped. There was the promise of a new machine gun more deadly than the Maxim and so light that

76. *A great demonstration against the sweating methods being adopted at the RSAF, held at Enfield Wash on 2 April 1910, organised by the Small Arms Union and the Amalgamated Society of Engineers and supported by between five and six thousand people.*

one man could carry it. The rationalisation had left the workforce disgruntled; it was a 'speed and feed' system, each work process being watched and timed by the management. The staff in the sword and bayonet department had been cut by half and those remaining were mostly boys. The unions contested the savings made and criticised the quality of the work produced. Union effort was now concentrated on securing a 30s minimum wage. Many of the older hands found themselves transferred from the workshops to what they called the 'labour gang' doing semi-skilled work at reduced pay. A new process for drilling rifle barrels was introduced in 1914 and many barrel setters, who had been earning £2 a week, were put on other work and found their wages reduced to 26s. The factory was in the unhappy position, as late as March 1914, of being equipped to do work and having the prospect of little to do. No progress had been made with the new rifle. Why, it was asked, should the factory be confined to the manufacture of arms when motor transport could be made, or aircraft? The Birmingham Small Arms, now under private enterprise, and Armstrong Whitworth, had both gone into motor production. Obviously war was not foreseen, except perhaps in Germany.[45]

Colonel Tisdall resigned as chief inspector of small arms at the factory early in the year 1914, to be replaced by Major Brown. Government estimates for the factory for the year ending 31 March 1915, announced in May 1914, foretold no worsening nor improvement in the prospects, the allocation for wages remaining the same at £200,000; for materials less money was allocated, £75,000 against £80,000 in the previous year. The government was certainly not preparing for a war that year.[46]

4. The Gas Company

The Enfield Gas Company was formed in 1850 with a share capital of £2,000. The original works in Slaughterhouse Lane (renamed Gashouse Lane, now Sydney Road) were built to the design of Jabez Church, well known at the time as a gas engineering consultant.[47] The changes caused a great upheaval in the Town; a row of cottages which had very long front gardens extending on to Enfield Green, had to be demolished. Charles Plume in his 'recollections' tells that one of the tenants by the name of Dunkling, employed as grave digger and bell ringer at the church, refused to move and sat it out until his roof was taken off. Gas supply began in 1852. 'At first there were a lot of funny ideas among the old people about the new light. Once or twice something occurred to put out the lamps and they were in great excitement, fearing that the Town would be blown up.' On one occasion it was found necessary to let the gas out of the gas holder, just as the Enfield militia were marching past smoking their pipes. That event caused great consternation.[48]

The Ponders End and Enfield Highway Gas Company was formed in 1859 and the works, also designed by Jabez Church, opened in January 1860. The *Enfield Observer*, in an ecstatic mood, looked forward to a chain of light from the Highway to the Town. The reality proved less entrancing. Many years later one writer, remembering his early days in Enfield, recalls that 'there were but few street lamps and they were poorly lighted'. The time for extinguishing them was eleven o'clock, not surprisingly for the gas cost 6s 3d for a thousand cubic feet.

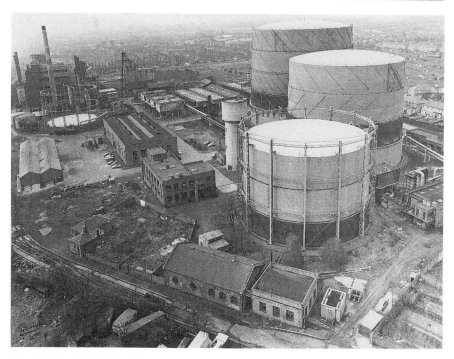

77. *The Ponders End and Enfield Highway Gas Company was formed in 1859; the works in South Street opened in January 1860. The local newspaper looked forward to a chain of light from the Highway to the Town.*

A further economy was achieved by leaving the street lights off for four nights on each side of the full moon. Most people used candles indoors for gas was far too expensive.[49]

The Enfield Gas Company obtained power in 1879 to purchase the land and plant of the smaller Ponders End and Enfield Highway Gas Coke and Light Company. For a time the supply was produced by the two works jointly, but in 1882 the Enfield works were closed and the supply came entirely from the Ponders End works. Both the old plants were worn out and it was decided to erect an entirely new plant on land adjoining the old Ponders End works. The new premises were built by Fairhead and were laid out to admit of expansion up to an output of one million cubic feet a day. The retort house was built near the Great Eastern Railway line, with coal stores on either side and access by sidings. The cost, including the land and several miles of new mains, was £25,000. The engineer, again Jabez Church, expressed his pride in the achievement. The town was growing at an ever increasing rate, which created the opportunity for expansion, but the firm had to keep an eye open for competition from electricity. Terms had not yet been arranged to serve the developing middle-class estate at Bush Hill Park where they were using oil lamps in the elegant, newly built villas. Reassuring all those gathered to celebrate the opening of the new works in October 1882, the company secretary declared that electric light, unless it was materially cheapened, would never be brought into general use, and if it could be made to pay, Enfield Gas Company would itself seek the means to supply it. Meantime they were more interested in expanding the production of gas for heating and cooking. The challenge from electricity, however, loomed larger and more immediate than had been anticipated. A few months later it was revealed that the Bush Hill Park Company had laid mains in preparation for lighting their estate with electricity, indeed Tayler Smith, the architect and manager, had it already installed in his own house. Perhaps it was this looming threat of competition which induced the Company, in September 1882, to reduce the price of gas from 5s 6d to 5s per thousand feet in the hope, it was said, that the inhabitants of Bush Hill Park 'may now be more willing to take gas, as many are quite out of heart with their oil lamps'.[50]

It was reported in August 1886 that Messrs R.E. Crompton had supplied three large dynamos for lighting the Royal Small Arms Factory. That same year an impetus was given to the use of gas for cooking and heating by an exhibition of gas stoves and gas heaters held at the Riding House, Enfield Court. The results were so encouraging that the Enfield Gas Company in September decided to open a showroom at their offices in Sydney Road. Cookers were offered for sale or hire at nominal rentals, and could be fitted for only 7s 6d; gas at a lower tariff was offered to users of gas cookers. The great impediment restraining the Company's progress was the straggling layout of the parish. In the early days endless trouble from leaking mains had robbed the Company of one-third of its returns, but a new start had been made, and consumption of gas was rising rapidly by February 1887. The price was down to 4s 6d per thousand cubic feet by 1892. Nevertheless this compared most unfavourably with the Tottenham Gas Company at 3s 2d, the cheapest in Middlesex. The Enfield Company still had only 1,051 private consumers, and although there were 5,859 houses in the parish only 176 of these used gas for cooking. Fifty-eight new stoves had been installed since a second exhibition of cookers in May 1891.[51]

The Company had not been exempt from the labour troubles which had disturbed the gas industry throughout the country, following Will Thorne's successful organisation of the London gas workers in 1889. A claim by the National Union of Gas Workers for three eight-hour shifts, instead of two of twelve hours, and an extra sixpence a day, was agreed nationally, but the agreement was broken by the Enfield directors in August 1890. They re-imposed the twelve-hour shifts and offered the stokers a further sixpence a day compensation. The men would not accept and were discharged with a week's pay instead of notice. Their places were immediately filled by other workmen, obviously brought from a considerable distance, who were boarded and lodged on the factory premises. Strike pay was paid, augmented to £1 a week by collections made at the Royal Small Arms Factory, but the strike collapsed and the men's belated offer to accept Company terms was rejected.[52]

Gas, by 1906, was facing the challenge of electricity now generated at the new power station. The Enfield Gas Company nevertheless continued to expand. During the last half of the year 1905, there were 716 new consumers and 495 additional cookers had been installed; gas sales had increased by nine per cent. Prices were cut to 3s 6d per thousand cubic feet (3s 3d to users of gas stoves), but competition from electricity ultimately forced rationalisation on the gas undertakings and a bill was introduced in Parliament in November 1912 to transfer the Enfield Gas Company to the Tottenham and Edmonton Company. The take-over was accomplished 1 January 1914. The price of gas in Enfield was reduced to 2s 8d per thousand cubic feet. Owners of penny meters, it was announced, would get three extra cubic feet for a penny. A new showroom was to be erected in Church Street on the corner of the Market Place.[53]

5. The Jute Works and The Cortecine

The jute factory was being built in July 1866 when the surveyor recommended that the repair of Alma Road be deferred 'till after the Jute Company have finished their works'. It was operating by April 1867 when the Local Board of Health was urged, because of the difficulties of the poor work people, to consider the improvement of 'the Jute Works road'. The factory lay isolated and hardly accessible in Duck Lees Lane in the area which became known locally as Spike Island, probably because of a poverty existing there (a 'spike' being a popular term for a workhouse). George Barnes, general secretary of the Amalgamated Society of Engineers and later to be a cabinet minister during the First World War, came to Ponders End at the time the factory opened in 1867. His father was the engineer in charge at the Jute Works. George received his education in the National school at Enfield Highway and joined his father in the factory at the age of eleven. The London Jute Works Company was to lead a precarious existence; it had the liquidators in for a time from March 1869 and this was followed in July 1871 by a serious fire, but the premises were well insured. The Company finally went bankrupt in 1882.[54]

The Jute factory workers were of the very poorest class and a large number of children were employed. The families lived in the crowded terraced cottages in the neighbourhood of Alma Road. Eighteen people for instance lived in number six Talbot Terrace, fifteen in number fourteen Hales Cottages, and no fewer than twenty-three lived in number eleven Jute Cottages, all in Alma Road. The Jute Cottages owned by the Company comprised twenty-six cottages and three beerhouses on the east side of Alma Road. Many of the dwellings were unfit to live in, according to the surveyor, so damp that the plaster had fallen down in large patches from the walls and ceilings. Brick clay had been used instead of mortar when they were built. Lavatories had been installed but now there was no water supply. In one house the kitchen had no floor and was occupied by tame rabbits in cages, while in the back bedroom the tenant kept caged birds. In many of the houses the handrails on the stairs and landings had disappeared, probably up the chimney. The surveyor reported on one inhabited house and two unfinished houses in June 1870 because the party wall between a finished house and one of the unfinished houses was concave. The surveyor proposed that the three houses either be shored up or taken down. Every day bricks were being taken out of the walls by children. 'If this went on all three would soon fall down' he said. Mr Harman, the wealthy vicar at St James, protested about 'the dirty state of the inhabitants of Alma Road and their dwellings'. (Surveyor's Report 25 August 1870). So poor was the building work that four houses partially erected on the south west corner of Alma Road blew down during a heavy gale in May 1882. The surveyor described the construction as inferior and protested to the estate surveyor. The builder, he reported, was in temporary difficulties which accounted for the work being suspended. (Surveyor's Report 11 May 1882)[55]

Many of the Jute workers had been born in Scotland, particularly in Dundee, but there were workers from Inverness, Aberdeen, Forfar and Charles Town. A smaller number had been born in Ireland, though some of these had worked in Dundee. These workers were quite unlike those employed in the Crape Works, let alone the artisans of the Royal Small Arms Factory. Jute working was an unhealthy occupation because of the dust. Mostly they made sacks. They may also have provided canvas backing for the Cortecine Floor Covering Company which later moved to Wharf Road in Ponders End, and also to the Angel Linoleum Works in Edmonton.

The factory children are listed euphemistically in the census records as scholars, for they spent half their time at a school provided by the company in South Street, which was used almost entirely by the factory children. They were ill-cared for and unkempt, 'with whom clean, well-clothed boys would not associate'. We glimpse a picture, (December 1867) of the swarm of ragged little ruffians, a hundred to a hundred and fifty boys and girls, who surrounded and attacked Sarah Croft for some obscure offence. They tore off her clothes and would have gone on to further violence, but several men intervened and protected her. Some of the girls were prosecuted at petty sessions; Annie Lieden got a month in the house of correction, Maria Fagan got ten days, Mary Macdonald, Elizabeth Clarke, and many others were fined £2 each and 10s costs and damages. In August 1874 the company took all their employees to South-end for the day by train from Ponders End station, six hundred in all, accompanied by the Ponders End brass band reinforced for the occasion by musicians from Enfield Lock. It became a regular annual excursion, but the tiny taste of the good life was too much for some of the employees. After the outing on 17 August 1879, to Walton on the Naze, three of the men absented themselves on the day following, one of them having worked for the company for eight years. The whole industrial process depended on the work of their section, and the mill was brought to a standstill. Fifty pounds was paid daily in wages and, instead of the seven or eight tons of jute usually manufactured, little over three tons was produced. The firm had strict rules which stated that workmen absenting themselves without permission would forfeit all wages due to them and might be dismissed without notice. Normally a week's notice, or wages, was given. These men were summarily dismissed, even the eighteen hours' pay, held back as a safeguard, was not paid to them, and they were prosecuted before the magistrates, presumably for breach of contract. Captain Clarke, the manager, relenting a little in court, offered to withdraw the case if the men paid the costs. His only object, he said, was to set a lesson to others, but the bench of wealthy evangelical magistrates, Meyer, Ford and Bevan, insisted on the full rigour of the law. The manager telegraphed to Dundee for two or three skilled men to replace those dismissed.[56]

Duck Lees Lane was often flooded in winter and the workers, including the children, had to wade through the water and work all day long in wet clothes. The Local Board would not undertake any remedy because it was not a public road. Eventually repairs were paid for by holding a concert at the factory in the large dining room which could hold four to five hundred people.[57]

The Baptist minister, the Reverend A.F. Cotton, made a house visitation in the area following the closure of the Jute factory in 1882. He reported that there were 680 houses in Ponders End of which 130 were then unoccupied. Many of the families had moved away when the factory closed and some had been forced to move into rooms to save on the rent. The hope remained alive for some time that the Jute Works would reopen, but it did not, and the building was taken over by Edison and Swan in 1886.[58]

The year 1873 saw plans submitted for an oilcloth factory on land 'nearly opposite the Jute Works'. T.C. Clarke, who was a director at the Jute, had been instructed to erect the building. The Local Board of Health had approved the plans, though stipulating that only linseed oil should be boiled there. The new Cortecine factory was opened in May 1874, having taken ten months to build. It was described in the *Enfield Observer* as a handsome, lofty building on the Middlesex bank of the River Lea. Cortecine was made of strong waterproof canvas upon which a mixture of vegetable oil and ground cork was rolled. The fabric thus produced, it was claimed, possessed advantages over ordinary floor-cloth.[59]

A serious fire broke out there on Good Friday, April 1897, in one of the drying shops. The factory had closed on the Thursday evening and all the young workers were free until Tuesday morning, although some of the adults had been working over the holiday. The drying shops were rectangular, three storied, brick buildings, 150 feet long by only five feet wide and positioned near the centre of this extensive works. An immense amount of valuable stock was stored there. Great bursts of flames shot through the roof, and soon a second building, lying parallel and to the north, was ablaze. The Ponders End brigade was the first to arrive, then the Ediswan brigade followed by Edmonton, Enfield, Waltham Abbey, Tottenham and Cheshunt brigades. There was no lack of water and many of the working departments with the machinery were saved. Nevertheless the resulting unemployment caused considerable distress in the neighbourhood.[60]

6. Edison and Swan

Edison and Swan was certainly an improvement on the Jute Works. Joseph Swan had begun the manufacture of incandescent electric lamps at a factory near Newcastle in 1880 and the following year he joined with Thomas Edison to form the Edison and Swan United Electric Company. By 1882 electric light was installed in the Savoy Theatre, the Mansion House, the British Museum and the Royal Academy, but every such installation required its own generating plant and storage cells. Edison and Swan decided to take premises nearer to London, and plant, machinery and the lamp stock were transferred by goods train. *The Observer* (2 January 1886) reported that the Edison, Swan Electric Lighting Company, 'fortunately for the poor people of Ponders End', had begun to fit up the former jute works. Production of lamps on this site soon reached five thousand a day. Power was derived from a ponderous 1,000 h.p. mill-type steam engine with a twenty-foot wood-toothed wheel driving on a main shaft which ran the whole length of the factory. Production was rigidly compartmentalised, each process being kept strictly segregated to safeguard trade secrets.

The early efforts of the firm had been distracted by a long legal battle against competitors who attempted to break its monopoly. The case eventually reached the Court of Appeal which visited Ponders End to investigate matters at first hand. Edison's patent was finally upheld and the competitors left the field. London had thirty-six electric supply undertakings by 1889 and there was even

78.   *Despite its liability to flooding, Ediswan's, by 1906, was the largest manufacturer of incandescent lamps in the United Kingdom.*

talk of the Enfield Gas Company building a generating station. The earliest lamps had carbon filaments made from parchmentised cotton thread, but Swan soon replaced this with a much stronger thread (artificial silk) carbonised. An industrial exhibition was held at Alma Road School in 1900 and the Edison and Swan Company displayed incandescent lamps in all sizes up to a nineteen inch diameter. One pounder pom-pom shells produced there for the Vicars-Maxim Company and used in the Boer War were also exhibited. The Royal Small Arms Factory exhibited a collection of rifles and bayonets, some manufactured as early as 1862. The exhibition was in aid of the wives and children of reservists called up for the war. Ediswan's set up an institute for their staff and workmen at The Elms in Ponders End High Street. In the years after the Boer War business was badly hit for a time by competition from Germany, but by 1904 it was picking up. A large order was on hand and more workmen were being taken on with the result that parts of the factory which had been shut down were now reopened. The firm in 1906 was the biggest manufacturer of incandescent lamps in the United Kingdom, with large factories at Ponders End and Newcastle on Tyne: it could boast appointment to the King and to the Prince of Wales. The factory attracted some of the best researchers of the age. Sir William Thompson (later Lord Kelvin) worked there on his mirror galvanometers, and Professor Fleming pursued research there which led to the invention of the thermionic valve in 1904. The prototype of the commercial vacuum flask was made there. The change from steam power to electricity occurred in 1906, by which time the Company headquarters had moved into central London.[61]

The Edison and Swan works, in 1913, stood on eleven and a half acres of land between the Great Eastern Railway and the Lee Navigation. The Company's

79.   Dinner hour exit Edison and Swan, 1912, but why the straw hats, collars and ties? Is it Saturday or is there an excursion arranged?

annual output was greater than that of all other British incandescent lamp manufacturers put together. The old building, formerly the jute factory, still survived. Glass blowing was the first part of the operation. The crucibles — eight of them were used at a time — were made on site, the clay being delivered by rail. Each weighed half a ton and when built they were raised by lift into a specially constructed room in which they were kept at white heat for a week. Each crucible would contain 18cwt to a ton of glass, enough to make 7,000 to 7,500 lamps. The filaments were attached to platinum wires and, after the glass bulb was sealed to its holder, the air was extracted by a mechanical pump. Great technical expertise had been built up in packing the fragile bulbs for transit to markets at home and abroad. The company was keeping to the fore in the manufacture of metal filament lamps which offered a seventy-five per cent economy in power consumption.

The 'Light', as the factory became known locally, was engaged in the manufacture of a large variety of articles other than lamps. The new aviation

80.   Cabinet shop, Ediswan's 1914. Charlie Wootton, in charge, wearing smockcoat; in background stands Enoch Wootton holding drawn wire lamp display board. They subsequently formed a woodworking company, starting in sheds next to the slaughterhouse in High Street, Ponders End, afterwards Alma Road.

industry had brought a wide demand for appliances, from the broad wing to the small screw and finely tempered wire, and a whole range of miscellaneous parts used in aeroplanes. Wire binders were produced for Australia where they were needed to make miles of wire fences. The Admiralty placed orders for switchboards to control electric current and gun fire. The firm was making indicators to show when watertight doors were closed on ships. Other products were commutators requiring the assembly of 100-132 parts, a stamp affixing and effacing machine, and mechanical pianos; designers were even working on electrical piano-players, and a new pneumatic piano-player was being patented. Hundreds of household butter-makers had been exported to Russia. In 1914 the firm was producing an electric iron for which they offered a twenty-one day free trial.

A large proportion of the workforce was girls who mostly lived locally, but the machines were manned by two hundred men and boys who travelled to work from Enfield Lock, Edmonton, Chingford, Waltham Cross, Botany Bay and western Enfield. There was a brass and iron foundry, turnery and joinery shops and a machine shop 108 feet by 106 containing 280 machines, 'a very inferno of noise', with bewildering lines of moving belts and hundreds of feet of overhead shafting. Electrical power was used. The men had a canteen near the entrance to the works, and close by were two large rooms for women and girls furnished with tables, chairs and kettles. The clerical staff had separate facilities.[62]

7. Strikes and The Unions

Nearly forty years of almost unbroken industrial peace from the early 1850s ended in the late 1880s. Low unemployment and a strong demand for labour encouraged labourers to join trade unions. The year 1889 saw the national dock strike. A meeting of the workmen at the Royal Small Arms Factory, held in September that year and addressed by James Rowland MP, expressed sympathy for the dockers and offered support so that they might win 'a great victory on behalf of the working classes'. In the following February, the engineers met at the Albany Hall to consider setting up a trade union at the factory, and soon afterwards a well attended meeting of the labourers from the Royal Gunpowder Factory, held at the Three Tuns, agreed to form a branch of the Southside Labour Union. This encouraged the labourers at the Royal Small Arms Factory, and two weeks later they too held a meeting to consider combination for better wages. The meeting was addressed by a Mr Sullivan of the Labour Protection League, an organisation which had branches in other government establishments, now including Waltham Abbey. Each branch had its own rules and kept its own funds. Some of the RSAF men asserted that they were paid as little as 15s to 17s a week. They complained that the government had saved money by the abolition of former pension arrangements. Now it made a compulsory deduction of two per cent of wages (the government contributed the equivalent of five per cent), yet after ten years service, men would get only 3s a week pension; after twenty years it would be only 6s, which was not enough to live on. Thus, they argued, the men would end up in the workhouse and the money would go to the Guardians. It was unanimously resolved that a union branch should be formed.[63] Soon afterwards the pension scheme was withdrawn and the unions spent the following fifty years fighting for its restoration. The men remained without a pension scheme until the outbreak of the Second World War.

Labour disputes were widespread in 1890; the stokers were out at the Enfield Gas Company and there was a strike at Barrett's sweet factory in Wood Green.

The main grievances there were the fines imposed for petty offences, 3d for being one minute late, 3d for taking a sweet from a tray, and a shilling for being caught in the wrong room. Barrett's management attributed the trouble to 'the comrades of the Social Democratic Federation who had imported themselves into the dispute'.[64]

Trade union membership in Enfield grew only slowly through the 1890s. The trade cycle turned downward from 1891. The Enfield branch of the Amalgamated Society of Carpenters and Joiners held a meeting at the Stag in March that year to mark the first anniversary of the branch. Membership in Enfield, it was remarked, was much smaller than it ought to be. The Operative Bricklayers had set up a branch here, as had the General Labourers Union, but the unions sought to avoid strikes. About twenty men employed by Jackson, the contractor working on the new reservoir at Holtwhites Hill, left their work after the dismissal of a man for insolent behaviour. The men had but recently joined the Union. Police assistance was invoked by the contractor. The men received no support and were forced to return to work. The Navvies, Bricklayers, Labourers and General Labourers' Union denied that it had called the strike; they knew nothing of it, they said, until they read of it in the *Observer*. 'This union', wrote A. Humphreys the secretary, 'does not encourage men to come out on strike without consulting headquarters. If they do, they get no support'.

The growth of trade unionism among workers was a national and not merely a local phenomenon following the success of the London dockers' strike in 1888. At a single meeting of the Gas Workers and General Labourers Union in Enfield in 1893, twenty-six labourers became members.[65]

There was a strike at the Edison and Swan factory in September 1892 when sixty out of 150 men in the fitting shop walked out. The strike committee, which had union backing and financial support, asked if it could send a deputation to negotiate, but the manager refused to see men who, he said, had left his employ. There was another dispute at Ediswan's in June 1895. The Electrical Trade Union sent in a memorial signed by sixty-five lamp-makers and exhausters asking the firm to pay trade union agreed rates. The firm asserted that it was unable to pay more because of competition from Germany. It claimed that £1 0s 7$\frac{1}{2}$d was a fair wage in that department. The trade union rate was 7d an hour for lamp-makers, 8d for exhausters and 8$\frac{1}{2}$d for skilled workers. The men passed a resolution condemning the 'sweating system' which, they alleged, was in vogue in the factory. Two weeks later all the girls, who had been laid off when the men and boys went on strike, had been re-engaged, and fifty more had been taken on. Although a number of the strikers remained out, there was a slow drift back to work, though some found employment elsewhere.[66]

Among the longest hours worked in Enfield were those worked by shop assistants. Shop owners were trying to reach an agreement to close at 2pm on Wednesdays. This was adopted by the butchers in May 1890. The Shop Act 1911 failed to limit the number of hours worked but it gave workers a statutory half-day holiday. The Factory Acts gave some protection to young factory employees. Ediswan's were prosecuted in April 1897 for employing three lads later than seven o'clock in the evening; two were aged fourteen, one thirteen. The hours of work allowed by the Factory Act in this district were 7am to 7pm, and the youngsters were not permitted to work overtime.[67]

Serious disturbances in industrial disputes were rare and when they occurred it was usually among workmen brought in from other parts of the country. Men from Cambridge employed on building a new infirmary at the Edmonton workhouse in 1899 came out on strike when their foreman was replaced by a local man. The new foreman was brutally attacked and seriously injured. At this same time work was held up by a strike on the building of Enfield's new isolation hospital at Worlds End.[68]

The Trades Dispute Act of 1906 made peaceful picketing legal, even if it led to a breach of contract. Eley's in Angel Road was hit by a strike in October 1906. The firm, which employed several hundred women, had decided to reduce wages. There was a strike of painters and labourers in November 1906 at the Northern Convalescent Hospital Worlds End. The painters had been offered $7^1/_2$d an hour, the labourers 6d; they demanded $8^1/_2$d and 7d. The strike was supported by the Painters Society and the men demonstrated with a band and flags outside the hospital gates. A trades and labour council was set up for Enfield in July 1907; there were forty delegates representing fourteen unions with 2,500 members. Enfield Urban District Council, in 1910, fixed a minimum wage of 26s a week for male employees over the age of twenty-one.[69]

The years 1911-13 saw the country ravaged by industrial disputes. The national railway strike in the summer of 1911 did not badly affect the commuters of Enfield and Bush Hill Park owing, as the *Observer* put it (25 August 1911) 'to the loyalty of the Great Northern and Great Eastern men at Enfield'. A subscription was subsequently raised to reward them. The strike fever however did spread to Enfield in September, when eighty boys from Southbury School walked out and spent the afternoon marching around the district behind a board bearing the short message, 'We are on strike'. They did not state the cause of the dispute. They created some commotion in the Hertford Road by holding up a tram at St James's School, where they called upon the scholars to join them, but they met with no response. The ringleaders were punished, Horace Shaw the leader being forced to stand upon a chair with a paper pinned on him declaring 'this is the biggest coward in the school' which, even if true, appears somewhat irrelevant. The incipient revolt smouldered all the week with revolutionary meetings in corners of playgrounds, but finally it died away. The national coal strike of 1912 had little effect locally; it lasted from February until April. 'It had not caught Enfield firms napping' declared the *Observer* with satisfaction. The Enfield Gas Company at that time had coal to last another two months. Ediswan's, where two thousand were then employed, ran entirely on electricity, as did Wright's mill at Ponders End. The Metallic Tube Company in South Street still had two or three months' supply, and the Cortecine factory had good stocks. The Brimsdown Lead Company had sufficient coal for about a month: work was very brisk there at that time. The Royal Small Arms Factory had its coal delivered by barge and had large stocks. By the middle of March the price of coal for domestic users had gone up by 14s a ton. The poor were the worst hit, for they mostly bought in small quantities from week to week. The price had risen to 47s a ton by the end of March and many householders were running out. There was an increased demand for coke, but then the strike ended.[70]

The lock-out of the London building trade workers throughout the early months of 1914 left many families in distress. Weekly collections were made in eastern Enfield and distributed in the form of food tickets. A large but peaceful demonstration was held in March. Building workers from Enfield Wash, headed by the North Enfield Military Band, paraded along Hertford Road to join a second contingent from Ponders End. Thence they marched by Southbury Road and along Baker Street, Lancaster Road and Chase Side to Enfield Town Park. The rain poured down in torrents throughout. The men had refused to work with non-union labour, and accused the employers of an attempt to crush the trade unions. The lock-out continued through the months up to the First World War, though the numbers receiving relief from the collections in Enfield slowly diminished as workers were forced to find other employment.[71]

8. Smaller Firms

Small firms were set up and seized any opportunity which arose to provide services or manufacture goods for sale. Gilbert of Enfield Highway in 1866, made electro-magnetic machines, the use of which was recommended as a remedy for 'rheumatism, indigestion and nervous disability' (debility?). Olley's engineering workshop was in Baker Street; they installed a new engine and shaft there in 1870. Albert Olley was quickly into the field when cycling became popular in the early 1890s, manufacturing a wide range of models which he advertised weekly in the local press. Everything, the *Observer* reported (15 October 1897) from the making of the frame to the last bit of plating, was done in his workshops by skilled mechanics. The firm made costly additions to the plant in their workshops where the handlebars, cranks and brake rods received a covering of nickel silver by electro-plating. Mr Olley acquired a powerful motor car in August 1899 which made its first successful run to Cambridge, then to Yarmouth. Thus tested, it was made available for hire, long or short distances. The firm offered to teach driving, maintenance and repairs. They also offered to install electricity or incandescent gas lighting in houses.[72]

The Mountjoy cycle works at Enfield Highway was set up by E. Croft about 1895. A couple of years later, Sidney Graham announced his intention to erect large workshops with enamelling plant in the Town. Graham already produced 'a well built and attractive cycle' known as the 'Parade' and as well as a tandem, and in February 1903 he secured a patent for a motor cycle with a sidecar, the 'sociable motor cycle'. A chair carriage drawn behind a motor cycle was already in common use, but this improvement allowed 'a lady and gentleman to take trips sociably alongside'. The sidecar could be detached. Armed with his patent, Sydney Graham set off for Birmingham to arrange for its manufacture on a large scale. Graham Bros, in 1912, issued a catalogue showing their range of motor vehicles available for hire, from the sumptuous Daimler to the useful taxi. By ringing Enfield 82, cars could be hired at a cost of 7s 6d an hour, including the driver who 'would await your orders at your own front door'. Enfield of course was not alone in its endeavour to take advantage of the surging demand for cycles, nearly every town in England possessing its manufactory. Large scale production of bicycles began in the 1890s and by 1909 Britain overtook Germany as the leading exporter.[73]

Seamer Bros, which was set up at Bush Hill Park about 1892, took premises in Palace Parade (The Town) in 1900 and invested in valuable plant including dynamos and baths for plating. All the enamelling there was done by brush, and baked in capacious ovens. The firm's catalogue, issued in October 1902, listed motor cycles for sale. They also made electric light fittings, and a four horse-

81.   Sidney Graham and his sociable motor-cycle in February 1903. It was an upholstered basket chair in a steel frame on the side of the motor-cycle costing £13 13s. The photograph was taken in the yard of the Rising Sun in Church Street.

power gas engine was installed there capable of producing 2,000 candle-power. Electric lighting was thereafter offered to neighbouring shops and private houses. By 1909, Seamer Bros had a motor works in Baker Street, in the former nonconformist girls' school of industry, subsequently known as Kingdom Hall. It was there that they constructed an aeroplane to the designs of W. Britain of Wildwood in Rowantree Road, a well-known manufacturer of mechanical toys. The frame was made of bamboo strengthened by steel wires, the joints of wood glued and bound with special cords. It was covered with balloon fabric, the tail looked something like that of a bird, and to it a rudder was attached. The propellers were situated behind the wings and the machine was powered by two thirty-six horsepower JAP engines. The wheels were like bicycle wheels, with pneumatic tyres. The first trials were made in the grounds of Myddelton House by R.M. Seamer and were confined to lifting the machine a foot from the ground. Hopes ran high. The *Observer* (13 August 1909) thought that possibly its performance might overshadow the historic flight of Bleriot from Calais to Dover which had just been made. Later tests were carried out on Chingford marsh (where the William Girling reservoir was later constructed). The machine achieved a number of hops, but it finally came to grief in a meadow and had to be left where it landed until the farmer had gathered his hay crop. But so many essential parts had been purloined by that time that no further progress could be made in Enfield's endeavour to conquer the air. Seamer's was acquired, in February 1916, by Gale and Plummer motor engineers.[74]

The Enfield Chase works in Chase Side, in April 1905, were producing the 'Royal Enfield' bicycle at from eight to sixteen guineas. Motor cycles could be purchased for thirty-five guineas while motor cars cost between 200 and 475 guineas. In 1905 H.J. Drage had a motor and cycle works in London Road, and Miles and Fortescue were carriage builders in Chase Side. There were 151 workshops, seven laundries and thirty-eight bakehouses in Enfield by March 1906. Mr George Halsey, at his factory in Baker Street, made cricket bats for some of the leading players in this country, and exported bats as far as Melbourne. A visit to the works in the summer of 1895 made a pleasant afternoon excursion for the reporter from the *Observer*. A huge pile of cleft willows lay in the yard, no less than 36,000 in various stages of seasoning. They would eventually be taken into the shop to be rough shaped and afterwards placed in a powerful press to compress the fibres and to produce the final form of the blade. The handles comprised sixteen pieces of cane glued together. The firm also made tennis rackets and hockey sticks, and had taken an agency for ABC rubber tyres which could be fitted to the wheels of horse-drawn vehicles at a cost, for a pair of four-foot wheels, of £4 13s 6d. The factory comprised an engine shed, smithy, wheelwright's shop, paint shop, circular saws and band saws, an oak crusher, lathes and the press. Much of it was destroyed (to a value between £5,000 and £6,000) in a great fire in January 1900. The losses included hundreds of one-guinea cricket bats, though onlookers saved many of the clefts by throwing them over the wall into the yard of the Baker Street chapel. The firm continued, and the name Halsey was said, in 1914, to be famous throughout the Empire. The firm was still in business at least as late as 1939. The Graphotone printing works was set up in Abbey Road, Bush Hill Park, in the 1880s and was in business until destroyed by a fire in February 1907. At that time there were about thirty employees, half of them girls. Much valuable machinery was destroyed.[75]

A brush manufactory was established in the grounds of Yarra House in Baker Street. Broomstocks (broomheads) were made from beech, birch and alder, mostly imported from Scandinavia. Some forty or fifty different patterns of broomheads and brushes were being made. In the autumn of 1913 the factory was busy on a large order for road brooms for street clearing. The London Cocoa-nut Fibre Manufacturing Company had a works in Ponders End in 1879, and was reported as being in the county court for a debt of £12. A blood-drying works had been set up in 1887 between Ponders End railway station and the Cortecine factory. It consisted of a brick building to house the drying ovens. It had a forty foot chimney stack, and there were also a number of temporary buildings. The smell gave rise to many complaints. Plans were submitted early in the year 1893 to build a white lead factory at Ponders End. Some members of the Local Board were worried about the effect on the water supply, some about the noxious gases likely to be emitted, and although Dr Ridge did his best to reassure them, the Board refused to sanction the plans. The firm nevertheless went ahead. The Board found itself powerless to prohibit the building it could only hope that, through some contravention of the by-laws it would be able to intervene. The white lead factory on the banks of the canal was a timber-framed building with a roof and sides of corrugated iron, standing on a concrete base. Ebenezer Marshall wanted to know why everything unpleasant had to be put at

Ponders End. They had gypsy vans encamped on the road leading to the Cortecine factory, two stabbings had just occurred there, and there was the stink of the blood drying works, the stench arising from the sewage farm (complained of by the management of the Cortecine factory) and the stench of the Cortecine factory complained of by everyone else. Now the white lead works arose like an ugly apparition on the canal's edge.[76]

There were nine factories at Ponders End by the end of the year 1906; Ediswan with 1,400 employees, the Cortecine with 250, the Gas Works employed 50, the Flexible Tube Company, which had taken the premises formerly occupied by the crape works, employed 250, the chemical works 50, Barnard and Company 20, the flour mill 40, the marble works 40, and the printing works 30, making a total of 2,130.[77]

9. The Power Station

The North Metropolitan Electric Power Supply Bill was before Parliament in 1900; it would authorise the building of a generating station at Enfield to supply power in bulk over a wide area. The bill was opposed by Hertfordshire and Middlesex county councils and by nearly all the local authorities, including of course Enfield, blind as always to its own interests. The Urban District Council even joined with Tottenham and others to promote a joint scheme to supply municipal electricity, though it had never been able to manage its water supply or sewage systems with any success.[78]

Despite municipal opposition the bill passed into law. The North Metropolitan Supply Company was to cover an area eighteen miles square. It aimed to produce cheap electricity using riverside sites where coal and water were obtainable under the most favourable conditions. Enfield Council, reviewing the situation, decided that the time was not propitious to risk municipal supply. Plans for the power station at Brimsdown were ready by November 1901, and a start on the building was predicted for 1902. In July 1903 the Enfield surveyor received notice that the Northmet proposed to lay mains along Millmarsh Lane, Green Street and Hertford Road. The installation of the generating plant was well advanced by September, a vast army of navvies and other workmen were laying cables, and piles of materials were daily deposited on the road sides. The power station was designed by C.W. Gray with space to accommodate further machinery and plant in anticipation of growth. A dock was constructed for the delivery of coal by water, other materials could be delivered by the Great Eastern railway. The 3,500 kilowatt turbine was said to be the largest of its kind yet constructed and equal to five thousand horsepower. Supply began in September 1906. A sub-station with a transformer to reduce the voltage from 10,000 to 400 volts and to convert alternate to direct current, was put up in Ladysmith Road. From there current was distributed to users; fifteen and a half miles of cables had been laid and fifty consumers connected by February 1907. The threat of this competition resulted in a further reduction in the price of gas. The sales war with the gas companies was to continue over the years up to and beyond the First World War. In July 1912, the Northmet offered a special flat rate of one penny a unit for cooking purposes. By 1914 cables were being extended northward to furnish current for electric lighting in Cheshunt and Waltham

82.   *Enfield Electricity Works, Ladysmith Road, housed transformers to reduce the voltage from 10,000 to 400 volts, also to convert alternate to direct current.*

Abbey.[79]

Extensive building operations were going on between Brimsdown railway station and the River Lea. Four or five new factories were planned. A white lead works, using a new process, was being built in 1906, a varnish factory was erected and opened and, further south, a centre with tanks for the treatment of sleepers with creosote. The smell, it was hoped, might even overwhelm that coming from the sewage farm. Morson and Son had opened a chemical factory at Wharf Lane, Ponders End, known as the Summerfield Works.[80]

Work in the new white lead factory was extremely hazardous. An inquest on John Easter the furnaceman was held in November 1906. The jury attributed his death to lead poisoning and added a rider recommending (but not insisting) that it would be advantageous to employees' health if the firm were periodically to change their duties. Workmen could now claim compensation for injury at work and there were a number of claims against the Brimsdown White Lead Company. Frederick Hannaford was an Edmonton man who had worked there as a press hand at $6^{1}/_{2}$d an hour, which represented 34s a week. He had been taken ill 4 October 1907 and, until 21 February, the company had paid him 17s a week compensation. This was then reduced to 10s, and soon afterwards the payment ceased. He had, he said, to test a certain liquor in a glass tube which he filled by sucking the liquor up into a tube, but sometimes it came up too fast and got into his mouth. He had begun to feel ill after he had been at the factory three months, suffering internal pains and loss of memory. He had a fit while working the night shift and Dr Wade had ordered him to take a rest. He returned to work when he was better. He had another fit in September (1906) and four sound teeth dropped out of his top jaw. He was home for three days and when he returned to work he was given a week's notice; the manager said

83. Cosmos factory originally built for the manufacture of varnish in 1906, was taken over soon afterwards for the production of electric light bulbs.

he smoked too much. He was now (April 1908) too weak to work. Judgement was reserved, presumably to await medical opinion.[81]

The Brimsdown Lead Company again appeared in the county court in December 1908. James Groom had worked in the factory for only six or seven months, earning 50s a week, when he was taken ill with lead poisoning in March 1908. The company paid him a pound a week until August; this they then withdrew on the grounds that he was no longer ill, though he claimed that he was suffering from paralysis. The death of another workman occurred there in 1909. He had been engaged in the building and repair of litharge furnaces at £2 6s 8d a week, and the company claimed that the lead poisoning had been caused because he had not worn the regulation mask. He left eight children and although the eldest was twenty-four, the four youngest were entirely dependent on the widow. She claimed £300. That same year William Moggs claimed in court that he had been suffering from lead poisoning since January 1905. Before that time he had been earning £2 15s a week, and since he had been off work the company had paid him £1 a week up to December 1908. He now received nothing. Sixty-four factories in Enfield were inspected by the Council in 1907.[82]

Plans were submitted (January 1908) for a nitrogen factory between the Lea and Stockingswater Lane. The Sandringham motor and engineering works opened at Enfield Highway in September 1910 specialising in gear cutting. The Ruberoid Company submitted plans for a factory in Stockingswater Lane at Brimsdown in 1910; it was an offshoot of the Ruberoid Company of America. The varnish factory, opened in 1906, did not last long, and the building near Brimsdown station was taken over by the Brimsdown (or Imperial) Lamp works (Cosmos). Ranges of new workshops, 350 feet long, were put up around the old factory which was then used largely for storage and offices, also for glass-blowing. A lift was installed. The company aimed to manufacture the new patent (Wirum Tungsten) metallic filament lamps, the filament being a delicate hair-like wire which gave off a brilliant light. 'Wirum', the trade name given to this new alloy produced in the laboratory at Brimsdown, was said to possess all the strength and efficiency of drawn tungsten wire, without the disadvantage of becoming extremely brittle after only a few hours' use. The firm employed several hundred, mostly women and girls, who were said to earn good wages on piece-work, many travelling from as far as Tottenham, even Hackney, by rail. They had a strike there in October 1911 when thirty young women in the vacuum pump room walked out over the dismissal of one of their number. The company, German owned, as the rival Edison and Swan were eager to inform everybody at the outbreak of the war, decided to pay off the strikers, but the girls refused the money. Police were called in to afford protection for one young woman who refused to join the strike and she was escorted home, followed by the strikers. Cosmos boasted of having supplied lamps for the Czar's Winter Palace in St Petersburg (Leningrad) and for the Summer Palace in Peking. They were proud of conditions in their workshops which were equipped for ventilation and temperature control. Cloakrooms were provided for the girls and women and rooms where they could take their meals. In July 1914 the firm chartered a special train out of Liverpool Street to take their employees to Yarmouth.

Notice of the impending closure of the Ridley Whitley floor-cloth factory at Angel Road Edmonton was given in April 1914. Eight hundred hands faced unemployment, many of them coming from Ponders End and the Highway. The firm had been in existence for 120 years. There was a protest meeting at Edmonton Town Hall. Service industries like the Birkbeck Laundry in Trinity Street expanded rapidly in the years before the war, presumably as the difficulty of getting servants became more acute. Its up-to-date buildings covered two acres. The laundry was collected and distributed in six motor vans. Within six years up to 1914 the work-force grew from eight to 112, mostly women and girls.[83]

10. Market Gardens and Other Farms

Market gardening in the area has been treated in some detail in an excellent paper by Dr Juanita Burnby and Audrey Robinson, '*Now turned into fair garden plots*', from which much of this section has been gleaned. The trade was widespread in Enfield throughout the nineteenth century, but it was not until the last quarter of the century that the Lea Valley developed into the most important concentration of glasshouse industry in the world. By the late 1880s it covered hundreds of acres of land in Edmonton, Enfield and Cheshunt where arable crops had formerly been grown. With the coming of cheap railway fares in the 1870s and the consequent spread of working-class housing, the nurseries migrated slowly northward from Tottenham, as land there became increasingly valuable for building. In 1870, there were only ten acres of glass in Edmonton; by 1898 there were a hundred. L.G. Bennett, in his thesis '*The Development of the Horticultural Industry in Middlesex*' wrote that in the 1890s 'There were hundreds of acres of glass in the parishes of Edmonton and Enfield, some growers having up to twenty acres of glasshouses.' Even on modest sized holdings, growers annually produced vast quantities of pot plants. Enfield in 1874 had 219 acres of orchards; by 1890 this had increased to 733 acres, including 326 acres of soft fruit (strawberries, raspberries etc). There were 485 acres of market gardens in Enfield in 1874, and by 1890 this had increased to 1,554 acres.

Market gardens were distributed across the whole parish except on the clay lands in the west, the former area of Enfield Chase. Joseph and John Thirgood were listed as market gardeners at Ponders End as early as 1849. Joseph was then living in the High Road near the White Hart. His son Henry took over the business and by 1871 was employing seven men, three women and two boys. He moved in the following year to a larger holding just out of the parish, at Nightingale Hall in Edmonton. John, another son, lived at Scotland Green, where he held a six-acre market garden and employed six men and three boys. Within ten years he had increased his holding to twenty acres.

Joseph Matthews of Ponders End is named as having taken two stands at the Covent Garden Flower Market, at £7 a year, in 1872. His son Amos held the Durants Arbour Nursery in Derby Road as well as the Old Nursery in South Street in 1905. He was still in horticulture there up to about 1925. The Matthews family not only grew flowers but cucumbers and tomatoes. The Guiver family held Durants Nursery on the site of the present Ambrose Fleming school playing field. In 1893 they were offering roses for sale in $8^1/_2$ and $9^1/_2$-inch pots at £5 and £6 the hundred. The Andrews brothers held twenty acres of market gardens on the south side of the Queensway at Ponders End and by 1902 they had extended their interests as far as Freezywater.

The Mitchells of Enfield Highway were market gardeners from the early nineteenth century. The census of 1851 shows that William employed fifty-eight men, although he was also engaged in brickmaking. His son, William John Mitchell of Broadlands Enfield Highway, took over the nurseries in 1881 with assets to the value of £3,500. The following year he advertised in the *Chronicle* for an 'Experienced man understanding the cultivation of tomatoes and cucumbers under glass... also a successful propagator of roses'. The business survived for twenty-five years only to fall bankrupt in 1906 following a run of bad seasons. When the railway (the Cheshunt loop) passed through his farm the Great Eastern Railway Company paid him £8,500, but he spent it all on improvements. At the time of his bankruptcy he owned thirty-seven acres freehold valued at £10,000; seven or eight years earlier, at the height of the building boom, it had been worth £15,000. Mitchell also held by lease 120 acres adjoining his freehold. The lease had recently expired and although he had expected £4,600 compensation for his crops, the arbitrators had granted him only £1,300. Another branch of the family remained in business — C. Mitchell was growing fruit in 1907. This comes to notice because one of his fruit pickers fell from a twenty-five rung ladder and was awarded £16 5s compensation, also £1 11s 6d to meet his doctor's bill. The fruit pickers were paid by the sieve, this man earned an average of 25s each week.[84]

Another family of market gardeners at the Highway were the Wilsons. Josiah, John Josiah, and Joshua were named in a directory of 1860. There was also a John Wilson in Green Street and another Josiah near Enfield Town railway station. John and Mary Wilson had been market gardeners at the Highway as early as 1816. Throughout the century the family held market gardens in various parts of the parish. Josiah Wilson held Moat Farm, later called Southbury Farm in Southbury Road. John Josiah his son lived on until 1914. An obituary in the *Enfield Gazette* tells that John Josiah had started in business in Carterhatch Lane, from where he had moved to Home Farm Enfield Highway. He had become one of the most successful market gardeners in the neighbourhood, famous as a strawberry grower, and was the first in the district to grow strawberries for the London market. Enfield, it was claimed, had become well known for vegetables and much of the credit was due to John Josiah Wilson. He became chairman of the Enfield Local Board of Health in 1894 and was later chairman of the Urban District Council. Home Farm was sold by auction in July 1914.[85]

Joseph Winterburn was named as a market gardener in Pigot's Directories of 1832 and 1839. He lived in the farmhouse on the corner of London Road and Cecil Road, where the Roman Catholic church was later built. It was one of those very old houses where you had to go down a step or two to enter. Joseph's business flourished throughout the first half of the century but it ran into extreme financial difficulties in 1861, the year that Joseph died. Severe frosts had destroyed his crop of greens, and his horses had to be sold off to pay outstanding taxes. His son Charles was left with only about five acres in Lincoln Road at Bush Hill Park.

Stuart Henry Low was among the most financially successful nurserymen of all time. He built up the business in Clapham but in 1879, because the whole of that area had already been covered with glasshouses, he bought sixteen acres near the station at Bush Hill Park. Within eighteen months he had planted fruit trees, roses and shrubs, and thirty-three glasshouses were either built or almost finished, 'all side by side, north to south, with just adequate space between for ventilation'. This came to be known as the Royal Nurseries. When Stuart Henry Low died in 1890 his son, of the same name, was living in Lincoln Road. The firm remained in Enfield until 1990, in Theobalds Park Road.

Another nursery was that of Henry Ironside who held eight acres on the east side of Churchbury Lane and on the south side of Southbury Road in 1881. The Gibbons, both father and son, were self-made men, true representatives of Victorian England. Ebenezer Gibbons was born at Bethnal Green in 1796 and came to Enfield in 1813. He is listed in the directories as a fruiterer, though in 1832 he appears as both fruiterer and pastrycook. Old Ebenezer died in 1881 having lived sixty-eight years in the parish. The *Observer* says that he was the first Sunday School teacher in Enfield. His second wife was Mary Genotin, probably of French Huguenot descent. Ebenezer the son was an enterprising young man. At first he assisted his father in his trade as confectioner, while at the same time he traded in fish and invested his profits in pigs. He was eventually able to buy himself a horse and cart with which he extended the range of his activities. He bought further transport and built a wider connection twenty miles north into Hertfordshire and Essex. He became well known as an open-air preacher. His enterprises grew rapidly as did the number of his employees. Eventually he grew fruit and roses on a large area of land on both sides of Southbury Road and owned a confectionery shop near Enfield Town railway station. He also came to acquire considerable house property in Enfield, including what were described as 'model or artizan dwellings', a block of twelve tenements for the poorer classes in London Road. He founded, with Ebenezer Marshall, the Royal Chase Building Society, and was instrumental with John Vincent in setting up the first

84. Ebenezer Gibbons grew fruit and roses on a large area of land on both sides of Southbury Road. A self-made man of enormous energy and enterprise, he played a prominent part in the religious, political and charitable life of his parish. The illustration shows Mr John Gibbons with some of the workers.

Baptist church in Enfield. He helped in the creation of the Enfield Town inter-denominational Christian mission, still successfully in business. He was a member of the Burial Board, the Local Board of Health and the first School Board. He died in 1911 at the age of seventy-six.

The Cracknell family of market gardeners lived in Enfield from 1784 until around 1935. Thomas Cracknell, a market gardener in Turkey Street, died in 1827. John, his son, took a holding in Baker Street in 1826, and at least four of his sons became market gardeners. Old John died in 1865, aged seventy-six. Four days later his son John committed suicide; he was found by his daughter, having hanged himself from a beam in the shed. Practical problems immediately arose, for he had been appointed executor to his father's will. The duty now fell upon his mother Elizabeth, for the younger John's widow was confined in the county lunatic asylum. A grandson Thomas was still living at what was known as Churchbury Farm in 1935. The area is now occupied by Chase School and playing field.[86]

The rising value of land which might be used for building caused problems for tenant farmers like John Bennett. About 1854 he had taken a yearly tenancy of thirty acres on which there were eight hundred fruit trees, for which he had had to pay £600 when he had taken the tenancy. During the last twenty years he had invested his profits in new planting, increasing his stock to 1,748 standard fruit trees, 14,161 gooseberry bushes, 3,718 currant bushes, two acres of strawberries and six acres of rhubarb. In June 1884 the owners of the property gave him six months notice to quit; this he could not dispute, but he asked for compensation. The trees, he claimed, were worth £1,700 and the bushes £2,700.

85.   The farmhouse of the unfortunate Cracknell family stood alongside what is now Tenniswood Road on the present Chase School playing field. It was demolished c1952/3.

The owners, two women, refused to meet this claim and sought an order to eject him. The court denied the order but the owners re-applied again and again, so that at length, through the cost of employing counsel, his savings were exhausted and he was forced to agree to arbitration. He was awarded £620, scarcely sufficient to pay his legal costs.[87]

Some nurserymen set up in business with very little capital indeed. Merchant and Elston, of Fords Grove Nursery at Winchmore Hill, began trading there in 1899 with only £100 each, which they had borrowed from Elston's wife. They took four acres on lease and rented two and a half acres more, purchased heating apparatus for £163 and bought the materials needed for six greenhouses which they erected themselves. But the business failed and in November 1901 they were £100 in debt. They disposed of their assets to Mr Cole, to whom they owed £16 10s for pots; he paid them only £67. They appeared before the bankruptcy court in May 1903. Both men were at this time employed by Cole and it was claimed that they earned only £1 a week. The sale of the Oatlands Nursery in Carterhatch Road, with a shop in Ponders End High Street, was announced in February 1909, due to the bankruptcy of the owner. Twenty-two glasshouses and other buildings, together with six acres freehold, were sold for £2,200, but this proved only sufficient to pay off the mortgage. it was claimed that the annual turnover in 1907 and 1908, from nursery and shop, had been between £2,000 and £3,000 a year.

The bankruptcy of another market gardener was due to the acquisition of his land for house building. His case was heard in 1919, when he was sixty-eight. As a young man he had been the publican at the Stag and Hounds in Bury Street Edmonton, but he gave this up after seven years to start farming. He had £50 capital when he took the Bush Hill Park farm about 1890 and he worked it for fourteen years at a profit, until it was sold as a building estate. He was left with only twenty acres and was so short of meadow that he made a heavy loss on his cows. He took Nightingale Hall Farm of sixty acres in 1903, at £135 a year and carried on market gardening there for fourteen years, but then his landlord died and the executrix gave him six months notice. His claim for £900, for improvements and tillages, was denied for so long that eventually and unwisely he refused to pay £120 owed by him in rent. The executrix took action in the High Court and recovered judgement for £160 and £124 costs.[88]

Chaplin's nursery, along the Hertford Road at Freezywater, in the summer of 1910 was described as a mass of variegated flowers. Amos Perry, who contined to win innumerable awards, had 40,000 delphiniums at his hardy plant farm at Holtwhites Hill, probably, said the *Observer* (24 June 1910) the most extensive show in Europe. He retired about a year later leaving the business in the hands of his two sons, the elder being another Amos. Old Amos had started life as a pupil teacher in a British school in Gloucester, but for health reasons he took up farming at Winfield nearby, and soon afterwards (in 1858) he joined his father at Tottenham Hale nurseries where he remained for thirty-five years. He was among the first to realise the possibilities of hardy plants and he began systematically collecting specimens from all over Europe. These formed the basic stock of the Winchmore Hill Hardy Plant farm which he established after leaving Tottenham about 1893. He met with considerable success at Winchmore Hill before he moved to Enfield in 1903. Since that time his foreign business had grown so much that Perry's herbaceous plants had become widely known on the Continent and in America. There had been a time when Amos Perry had been hardly tolerated by the Royal Horticultural Society, but in later years he became one of its largest and most successful exhibitors.[89]

Something like six-sevenths of the glasshouse industry in this country was concentrated in the Lea Valley in 1913. A traveller on the main road to Hertford, or a passenger on the Lea Valley railway line, could not have failed to notice the glint of the glasshouses spread out over the countryside between the road and the railway all the way from Ponders End to Cheshunt. Almost all the houses had been put up in the previous twenty-five years. From Tottenham in the south to Broxbourne in the north, there were two hundred growers, with glass covering nine hundred acres. This represented an investment of some £1,300,000 in glasshouses and other buildings. About fifty per cent of this area was down to tomatoes, twenty-five per cent to cucumbers, the remainder to grapes, peaches, flowering plants and foliage plants. A single acre, in a good season, would yield forty tons of tomatoes, or twelve tons of grapes, or nine thousand dozen cucumbers. Each acre gave employment to about ten men or boys, which made a total employed of some eight or nine thousand, and the average wage bill amounted to between £8,000 and £9,000 a year.

Tomatoes were sown from seed in December. When ready they were picked, graded and loaded into baskets called 'strikes', each containing 12 lbs. Cucumbers were planted out in February in houses twelve to fifteen feet wide and varying in length from one hundred feet to three hundred. Thousands of baskets were filled each evening ready for removal to market. Motor transport was first used for this job in July 1901 when H.Seal of Enfield Highway hired a heavy lorry from Messrs Milnes and Co. of Oxford Street. He drove it to the premises of H.Larsen at Waltham Abbey whose glasshouses provided tomatoes for Covent Garden. Growers from all around came to watch. In half an hour 360 'strikes' were stowed under tarpaulin, $2^1/_2$ tons in weight, and the lorry set off at a steady eight miles an hour. Its arrival at the market caused a sensation. It was back in Edmonton an hour after leaving Covent Garden and it was re-loaded and back in the market within twelve hours. The experiment was held to be a triumph; it could save the cost of six horses, carmen, stables and stablemen.[90]

Many of the growers who had set up in eastern Enfield twenty-five years earlier remained in 1913. There was G.Prickett whose speciality was flowers, and J.Tully of the Rose Nursery who had come to Enfield just before Mr Prickett. These two gentlemen were associated with men from the Small Arms Factory in setting up the Highway Chrysanthemum Society. J.W.T.Baker was another of those who had been twenty-five years in Enfield, as was C.Banks; they both specialised in choice ferns and flowers. Alfred Smith had a reputation for carnations like Charles Perry, M.Larsen and Douthwaite grew both exotic plants and carnations. Amos Matthews at Ponders End was among the earliest growers in the area, and grew ferns. Parson and Co in Carterhatch Lane grew tomatoes, cucumbers and chrysanthemums. The largest grower was John Rochford, whose firm had a world-wide reputation as a grower of grapes. He held three nurseries in eastern Enfield ; at Durants, at Green Street and at Turkey Street. The trade gave rise to ancillary industries, like the basket factory near the station at Enfield Lock where they made baskets for strawberries, raspberries and other soft fruits. The building was destroyed by a fire in April 1914 and although the thirty-five hands, mostly girls, were safely evacuated, valuable machinery was destroyed. Much produce was carried by rail, and the level-crossing in Ordnance Road caused chaos to traffic, then as now. There were complaints (30 March 1906) that a long goods train was halted right across Ordnance Road while three men loaded a truck with baskets of cucumbers. 'If this is allowed now', said the *Observer*, 'what will it be like in the busy cucumber season?".[91]

Before the outbreak of the First World War, local growers were facing strong competition, especially from overseas. They complained of the high cost of transport to Spitalfields, Covent Garden or Borough markets. Motor transport was widely used and though there were firms which specialised in carrying the produce like Barton and Adamson, many growers had their own vehicles. Growers complained of the increased cost of heating and some had changed from coal to oil. The local soil was exhausted and growers had to purchase compost at considerable expense. The Nursery and Market Garden Industries Development Society announced in May 1914 that it would establish an experimental station at Crossbrook Street in Cheshunt to carry out work similar to that done at Rothamsted, but with special application to the glasshouse industry, putting emphasis on plant diseases and the selection of manures. A vast sum of money had been invested in the industry. The land was valued at £200 an acre, the glasshouses at £1,500 an acre, and a growing crop of tomatoes or cucumbers, valued on 30 April, was worth £750 an acre, making a total of £2,450 an acre. Thousands of foreigners were employed in the Lea Valley greenhouse industry, but with the outbreak of the First World War there was a mass exodus. Most of these men were Danes or Swedes and there were a few Germans. It was hoped that the war might favour the industry since supplies of cucumbers and tomatoes from the Continent would inevitably be restricted, but this seemed not to be so, for some reason people no longer bought tomatoes and cucumbers, let alone chrysanthemums, and many of the greenhouse hands took better paid jobs in the Small Arms Factory.[92]

Arable farmers throughout the country, in the late eighteen seventies, had been hit by cheap American imported grain and those in Enfield were no exception. The *Observer* reported (12 July 1879) that a great deal of wheat growing was still carried on, but farming on poor soil was no longer a good investment. Reuben Cook took the Ridgeway Farm in 1881. He had capital of £1,000 in cash and he raised a further £1,000 by a mortgage on the property, investing both these sums in the farm. He made a profit in his second year, but spent it in an effort to improve the land which was London clay and very poor. In no year since that time had he made any surplus, and in 1885 the drought cost him £700. By the beginning of the year 1886 he was bankrupt.[93]

The wages of farm labourers, except those employed in market gardening, were low. A case in 1874 shows a married man earning 12s a week, another in 1875 was earning 16s, both were in full time employment. William Hutchins, a farm labourer, appeared in court for a debt owed to James Garner who had a clothes shop in Baker Street. He was said, in June 1887, to be earning 14s to 15s a week. At harvest time he could earn more, for farmers paid piece-work. Two labourers at North Lodge Farm were employed by Thomas Blinko in 1879 to cut, by machine, 156 acres of grass at 2s an acre; this was in addition to their standing wage of £1 a week. They told the court that they had got up at four and had cut the whole 156 acres, allowing for the outsides which could not be cut by machine, but Blinko said that they were drunk and had only cut fifty acres for which he had paid them. They sued him for £5 12s but the county court found for the farmer, with costs. Grass was selling well at this time. Two hundred acres growing at Chase Park and Rectory Farm sold that year at 50s to 55s an acre, though previous sales had not been quite so profitable.[94]

The Enfield cattle fair was held on St Andrew's day every year. Farmers and dealers would come from miles around. The livestock stood in Silver Street, along Church Street and in the Market Place. The fair held in 1884 was reported in the *Observer* (which was unusual) only because the weather was so bad. Though it was thinly attended most of the stock sold at a good price. J. Phillips, who had his stand in the Market Place, had attracted a good-sized crowd and announced that he intended to sell live and dead stock there on Monday afternoons at 2pm until further notice. The 1886 fair had a good attendance of farmers and dealers and an excellent show of horses and cattle. Mr Nye, from his pens in the Market Place, sold thirty horses as well as a large number of shorthorn and other cows, also heifers, calves, pigs, goats, ducks, fowl and vehicles.[95]

Dairy farming increased after the turn of the century, especially on the clay lands in the western half of the parish, due to the growth of suburbia. H.W. Middleton, of the Raleigh and Ridgeway Farm Dairy, purchased in 1901 the old-established connection, and the herd of sixty cows, from Hawkins of Raleigh Road; he also took over, from Pocock, the recently opened dairy depot in Palace Parade. He then acquired the rounds and business of Messrs Stephenson of Home Farm, of Benson on the Ridgeway, of Clarence Tucker in Southbury Road, Garnett of Botany Bay and Hayes of Baker Street. In September 1906 he added his eighth dairy round, taking over the lease from Mr Moyle of Notts Farm on the Ridgeway. Thus he acquired some of the choicest and best situated pastures in the parish. He had employed six men in 1901, but by 1906 he had fourteen horses busy on rounds, and thirty employees. His aim was to sell purely local milk from pastures within two miles of the Town. In addition to his own farms, he received supplies from other local dairy farmers at Parkside farm in Hadley Road, North Lodge farm, Stephenson's Home farm, Holly Hill farm, Oak farm, Clay Hill and Botany Bay farms. His own dairy farm of 120 acres maintained a pedigree stock of ten very choice Jerseys, also two hundred hens. He received five churns of milk daily from Lord Salisbury's farm at Hatfield and a similar quantity from Lord Rayleigh's herd at Hatfield Peveril. There were in 1912, 457 cows kept in Enfield, by twenty cowkeepers. Hygiene in the dairy industry had greatly improved. The cows were inspected twice yearly and there had been an improvement of hygiene in retail milk shops. It was rumoured that the Maypole Dairy Company had secured premises in Church Street.[96]

A small holdings and co-operative group was formed in Enfield Wash in 1908. It had eight members and they applied to Middlesex County Council to hire sixty-one acres. Presumably they must have thought that the project made economic sense, or was it perhaps a last flickering survival of that old romantic longing for four acres and a cow? Most of this land lay between the New River and the Cheshunt loop. It belonged to Trinity College Cambridge and was part of a farm of 330 acres held on a yearly tenancy. The County (under the Small Holdings and Allotment Act 1908) ordered compulsory purchase.[97]

11. Brickmakers

Much of which I write in this section is from Sidney M. Beadle's '*Bricks and Brickmaking in Enfield, Edmonton and Tottenham*' (in preparation 1991).

Brickmaking had been a considerable industry in the parish certainly since Tudor times. Like the market gardener, the brickmaker was pushed outward from London as building encroached upon one suburb after another. The trade prospered or declined with the local house building trade. Its ups and downs can be followed in the career of Charles Stotter, formerly a journeyman and illiterate, who made bricks in White Hart Lane Tottenham, and moved out to Hoe Lane Enfield in 1896. There he took a field of seven acres for which he paid £250 a year rent and a royalty of 2s 6d for every thousand bricks. He had capital and stock to the value of £1,000. He went bankrupt in May 1903 with debts amounting to £2,337. Things in the building trade, he said, had gone very bad recently, his business had fallen off by thirty per cent. There were too many brickmakers. Only three years earlier bricks had fetched a good price, he could make a profit of sixty or seventy per cent. He was now left with 300,000 bricks in stock, and a large quantity of prepared material. Six and a half acres in the field remained unworked, he estimated that there were thirteen million bricks to each acre.[98]

Brickfields are shown on the 1867 Ordnance Survey plans. One lay on the north side of Lincoln Road, just east of where it is now crossed by the Cambridge Road. Directories show that this field was held by Edward Newman from 1855 until 1878, and by William Newman until 1898; by that time the part near Lincoln Road had been exhausted. It was then taken over by the London Brick Company, owned by John Cathles Hill, a Scot, who came to London in 1878 at the age of twenty-one. He became a successful speculative builder in the north London area, particularly in Hornsey and Highgate. Because he needed large numbers of bricks, he began manufacturing them himself at Fletton, near

Peterborough. With inspiration, he called his firm the London Brick Company. He moved into Enfield in 1898 to manufacture good quality red facing bricks. The decline in house building in the years before the First World War ruined him, and he became bankrupt with debts amounting to £1,202,000; he died in 1915. The bankruptcy was discharged after the First World War and the company, London Brick, is now the largest brick producer in the country. Their Enfield works closed about 1937.

The 1867 Ordnance Survey plans also show a brickfield on the north side of Southbury Road, east of where the Cambridge Road now crosses. It was owned in 1845 and 1855 by Thomas Sanders, and was later held by Bernard Mitchell whose father, William Mitchell, a market gardener at Enfield Highway, also made bricks. Another brickworks is shown north of Southbury Road. It was owned by Charles Bloom Dearsley (listed in a directory of 1898) who lived at Hereward House which stood at the entrance to his brickfield in Southbury Road. After the turn of the century the firm became the Crown Brickworks. The plans also show a brickfield west of Old Road, on the south side of Palmers Lane. It was taken over in 1886 by Charles Brown who having taken all the brick-earth there, moved to another field on the west side of the railway which he worked until 1903. Brown's brickfield was later used by the Council as a rubbish dump and is now a sports ground. North of Palmers Lane another brickfield was worked from 1910 to 1937 by James Frederick Rainer. It was called the Orchard brickfield; Roedean Avenue and Roedean Close are built on the site.

A brickfield at Bush Hill Park was set up south of Bush Hill Park Station in 1875 by the Northern London Estates Company, which was building a middle-class estate there west of the railway. The works were taken over by George and John Drake who, having worked out that site, moved south along Wellington Road to take over the land now used for Raglan School playing field. The Drakes were bought out by William Delhi Cornish in 1907. He gradually extended the field eastward across what is now Delhi Road and the little recreation ground to its east, and on to the site where Edmonton Upper School (formerly Edmonton County) was built in 1931. He finally took over land on the other side of the railway (the area around Trinity Avenue). The Bush Hill Park brickfields were nearing exhaustion by the late twenties (though the beehive kilns were still there in the early thirties) and Cornish purchased a field on the north side of Hoe Lane. The virtual collapse of the building trade in Enfield in the years before and after the First World War sent the brickmaking industry into hibernation from which it did not begin to recover until 1924.

Notes to Chapter Three

1. Robinson W. *History of Enfield* 1.19
2. R.G. Berry *Grout and Baylis*, mss at Enfield
3. Enfield D 1032
4. R.G. Berry *op cit*
5. W044.682, J. Burnby and A. Robinson *Early days of the Royal Small Arms Factory at Enfield Lock* (unpublished) Bowbelski M. *The Royal Small Arms Factory* 1977 WO44.133, 132, SUPP5.689
6. see section on education
7. WO44.535
8. WO44. 701

9.   Meyer's *Observer* August 1859, June 1859, Robert Smiles *The Royal Small Arms Factory, Enfield*
10. P.P. 1864. 35.595, 36.82
11. Meyer's *Observer* Feb 1863, July 1866
12. *ibid* June 1869, July 1869, Jan 1871
13. *ibid* Mar 1871, May 1859, May 1885, Mar 1873
14. *ibid* Mar 1872, May 1872
15. *ibid* 7 Jan 1882
16. *ibid* May 1872
17. *ibid* July 1872, Nov 1872
18. *ibid* Aug 1872
19. H. Chas Smith Cooperation in Enfield, Meyer's *Observer* 6 Sep 1889, 10 Nov 1893
20. *ibid* Feb 1873
21. *ibid* Apr 1873, Jan 1874, Apr 1874
22. *ibid* Sep 1874, Oct 1874, Dec 1874
23. *ibid* 1F 1875, 31 July 1875, 13 May 1876
24. *ibid* 15 May 1880, 7 Jan 1882
25. *ibid* 10 Jan 1885, 27F 1886
26. *ibid* 6, 13, 20 Mar 1886
27. *ibid* 15 May 1886, 20 Au 1886
28. *ibid* 3 Je 1887
29. *ibid* 1 July 1887, 5 Au 1887
30. *ibid* 15 July 1887, 2 Sep 1887
31. *ibid* 19N 1886, 15 Mr 1889, 24 My 1889
32. *ibid* 24 My 1889, 14 Je 1889, 20S 1889
33. *ibid* 27D 1889, 12 Ja 1890
34. *ibid* 16 Ja, 6 Mr, 8 My 1891, 12, 19, 26 F, 1 Ap, 25 Mr, 15 Ap, 15J1 1892
35. *ibid* 2D 1892 3F, 7 Ap 1893
36. *ibid* 15, 22S, 3N 1893, 30 Mr 1894
37. *ibid* 10, 24 Mr 1893, 20 J1 1894, 20 Mr 1896
38. *ibid* 7 Ja 1898, 17 Mr, 19 My, 8S, 10N, 22X 1899, 5 Ja 1900
39. *ibid* 26 Ja, 25 My, 15 Je, 6 J1, 3 Au 1900
40. *ibid* 18 Ap 1902, 9 Ja, 4, 11, 25 S 1903, 7 Je 1907
41. *ibid* 3 Je, 4 Mr, 1 Ap, 15 Ap, 24 Je 1904
42. *ibid* 3 F 1905, 16 F 1906, 30S 1927
43. *ibid* 15 Je, 18 My 1906
44. *ibid* 25 Mr, 1 Ap, 13 My 1910
45. *ibid* 23 My, 26D, 20 Au 1913, 23 Ja, 13F, 20 Mr, 6 Mr 1914
46. *ibid* 6F, 15 My 1914
47. Much of this information is from H.W. Merrison *A Brief Account of the Tottenham and District Gas Company's First Hundred Years* 1947
48. *Recollections of Old Enfield* p13
49. *Meyer's Enfield Observer* Ja 1860, *Recollections* p22
50. *Observer* 17S 1881, 9S, 7X, 30D 1882
51. *ibid* 20 Au, 3S 1886, 15F 1887, 4 Mr 1892
52. *ibid* 20 Au 1890
53. *ibid* 2 Mr 1906, 15N 1912, 19D 1913
54. Enfield Surveyors Report 20Je 1866, *Observer* Ap 1867, George Barnes *From Workshop to War Cabinet* 1924 *Observer* Mr 1869, Je 1870, J1 1871
55. Census enumerators schedules 1871, Enfield Surveyors Reports, 7 Ja 1870, 9D 1880
56. ED 16.209, *Observer* D 1867, Au 1874, 30 Au 1879
57. *ibid* 18X 1879

58. *ibid* 12 Au 1882
59. *ibid* Ap 1873, My 1874
60. *ibid* 28 Ap 1897
61. Edison Swan Ltd *The Pageant of the Lamp* 1950, *Observer* 4 My 1900, 18X 1901, 29 Ja 1904, 9N 1906
62. *ibid* 13 Je, 27 Je 1913, 9 Je 1914
63. *ibid* 6S 1889, 14F 1890, 28F 1890
64. *ibid* 12S 1890, 29 Au 1890
65. *ibid* 6 Mr 1891, 8 My 1891, 23F 1893
66. *ibid* 9, 16S 1892, 4 Je 1895, 28 Je 1895
67. *ibid* 29F 1890, 28 Ap 1897
68. *ibid* 7 Ap 1899
69. *ibid* 19X 1906, 2N 1906, 19 Jl 1907, 29 Jl 1910
70. *ibid* 15 S 1911, 1 Mr 1912, 15 Mr 1912, 29 Mr 1912
71. *ibid* 20 Mr 1914
72. *ibid* 11 Au 1898
73. *ibid* 5 Ap 1895, 19N 1897, 6F 1903
74. *ibid* 27 Jl 1900, 24X 1902, Enfield cuttings file, *Observer* 4F 1916
75. *ibid* 14 Ap 1905, 1S 1905, 23 Mr 1906, 27 My 1898, 12 Ja 1900, 1 My 1914, 15F 1907
76. *ibid* 5S 1913, 11X 1879, 28X 1887, 23 Ja 1893, 10F 1893, 6 Mr 1891, 23S 1892
77. *ibid* 15N 1906
78. *ibid* 3 Au 1900
79. *ibid* 25 My 1906, 22F 1907, 19 Jl 1912, 31 Jl 1914
80. *ibid* 11S, 9X 1903, 3 Au 1906
81. *ibid* 23N 1906, 10 Ap 1908
82. *ibid* 11D 1908, 26F 1909, 11D 1908
83. *ibid* 2S 1910, 10 Ja 1908, 14 Ja 1910, 15 Ap 1910, 6 Oct 1911, 15 Au 1913, 17Jl, 1 My, 15 My 1914
84. *ibid* 18 My 1906, 13D 1907
85. *ibid* 10 Jl 1914
86. *Ibid* 24S 1881, Enfield cuttings, *Observer* 5 My 1911
87. *ibid* 21 Je 1884
88. *ibid* 29 May 1903, 6F, 5 Mr 1909, 14 Mr 1919
89. *ibid* 13 Je 1913, 20 Je 1913
90. *ibid* 11, 25 Jl 1913, 6 Jl 1901
91. *ibid* 11, 25 Jl 1913, 10 Ap 1914, 30 Mr 1906
92. *ibid* 1 My 1914, 20 Mr 1914, 21 Au 1914
93. *ibid* 12 Jl 1879, 23 Ja 1886
94. *ibid* Je 1874, 4S 1875, 17 Je 1887, 8N 1879, 19Jl 1879
95. *ibid* 6D 1884, 3D 1886
96. *ibid* 21S 1906, 17 My 1912
97. *ibid* 4F 1910
98. *ibid* 12 Ap 1889, 8 My 1903

Chapter Four

Poverty

1. Introduction

The purpose of the Poor Law Amendment Act 1834 was to discourage men and women from becoming paupers, but there was little new about the new Poor Law except its large and forbidding new buildings. Throughout the eighteenth and early nineteenth centuries parish vestries had repeatedly endeavoured to solve the problem of expensive paupers by means much like those on which the legislators of 1834 pinned their faith. They had tried to abolish outdoor relief, they had from time to time reduced the food allotted to the paupers in the workhouse, they had imposed upon them more rigid disciplines, and they had used degradation to deter applicants for parish relief, but these means had never succeeded in lowering, for long, the cost of poor relief. The new Poor Law persisted throughout Queen Victoria's reign and survived, anachronistically, until 1929 and beyond. It was costly and inefficient and was regarded with dread by the self-respecting poor. Boards of Guardians for nearly a hundred years were fettered by the original aims of the Act under which they were set up and the finest achievements of the boards were marred by the stench which arose from the degradation they imposed. It even pervaded, in the twentieth century, the expensive new wards of their infirmaries into which many self-respecting patients would enter only when facing death.

Private charity was by no means dead in the nineteenth century. Charles Wright in 1848 set up six almshouses at Enfield Highway to accommodate six old widows, stipulating that they must have lived for more than a year at Enfield Wash, Enfield Highway, Green Street, South Street or Ponders End. Rent charges on houses in the City parish of St Luke (sold in 1964) were to provide each widow with £10 a year and a ton of coal at Christmas. This neat brick terrace remains with us in 1991 (VCH Middlesex V5 p258). More poor families, especially the children, were relieved by private charity in Victorian times than were assisted by the Guardians. Hard winters would see soup kitchens set up all over Enfield. Blankets, coal and boots were distributed, moreover the poor helped each other and men thrown out of work were able to exist for weeks, apparently on nothing, before they were driven to seek relief. Those who were forced in the end to apply at the workhouse, faced long hours of granite-breaking in the stoneyard for a few shillings and a loaf. Since even this might fail to deter a man whose children were starving, the Board, in the severe winter of 1890-91, determined that the head of any family applying for relief must enter the workhouse. Some of the local unemployed emigrated to Canada and many of the children from the Chase Farm Workhouse School were sent there.

*86.   The south entrance into the Edmonton Union. There was little new about the new Poor Law
except its large and forbidding buildings.*

Public works by local authorities (authorised by the Local Government Board
in 1871) came to be used, from the 1880s, as an antidote against unemployment
but there were arguments, then as now, as to whether the higher rates needed
to pay for such works did not deter industry from providing real jobs. Unemployment was endemic in the area up to 1914. Conditions in the neighbouring
parishes of Edmonton and Tottenham were even worse than those in Enfield.
    Slate clubs and friendly societies were used by many as a means of self-
protection against ill-health, unemployment and old age. It was not until 1909
that the State intervened, first to provide old age pensions, then in 1911 to
afford protection, for some, against sickness and unemployment.

2. The New Poor Law

The Enfield vestry met on 30 March 1836[1] and passed a strongly worded
resolution declaring that the institution of a union for the relief of the poor was
founded upon reasons inapplicable to Enfield. Enfield parish was of a size and
population equal to many of the unions, and it was the owner of a fine
workhouse built only 1827 at a cost of over £3,600. The select vestry claimed that
it had managed its poor with economy and efficiency and ought therefore to
retain full control over the spending of the parish rates. It had a duty not to
relinquish its responsibility for the care of its aged and infirm. The management
of the poor, it was felt, must deteriorate when controlled by a body meeting
outside the bounds of the parish, for its members would have less knowledge of
the circumstances of applicants for relief and must depend upon the reports of
a relieving officer. The vestry complained of the distances which the aged poor

might have to walk to secure relief.

Despite such opposition the Edmonton Union came into existence in January 1837. It comprised seven parishes: Hampstead, Hornsey, Tottenham, Edmonton, Enfield, Cheshunt and Waltham Abbey, an area sixteen miles from end to end and six miles across at its widest part, with workhouses in every parish. A preliminary meeting of the newly elected Board of Guardians took place in February at the Edmonton workhouse in Church Street (the site later occupied by All Saints National School) and Henry Philip Powys of Broomfield Park was elected chairman. It was decided to dispense with four of the workhouses and to use only those in Edmonton, Enfield and Hampstead. The aged and infirm were to be housed in Hampstead, the able-bodied at Edmonton and the children at Enfield.

The new poor law was to be based upon two guiding principles, first that no able-bodied man should receive relief outside the workhouse, second that relief inside the workhouse was to be dispensed in the most uncongenial manner possible. The first was intended to result in the abolition of outdoor relief, an objective which had been sought before in Enfield without success; the second was strongly reminiscent of the 'reforms' introduced by Enfield vestry a quarter of a century earlier.

Management from outside the parish caused difficulties almost at once. This was demonstrated by the case of R.C.Morrison in 1838. He had dwelt for sixty years at Winchmore Hill and had once owned considerable property. He had been for twenty-seven years a member of the Honourable Corps of Gentlemen at Arms and had resigned only because of his advancing years. Subsequently he had held a large and reputable academy at Hope House in Winchmore Hill Road near Southgate, but a long series of troubles and losses had reduced him to penury. He was now in his eightieth year, his wife was nearly the same age and of a very ancient family in Berkshire. For some years past they had been obliged to receive parochial relief; this had recently been reduced to two loaves of bread and 2s 6d a week. Even this pittance had now been removed by an edict of the Guardians and the couple had been left in great distress. An order had been made to admit them into the Union workhouse but they had declined to enter. Such people might have been dealt with differently by the parish where they would have been known personally by overseers and vestrymen.[2]

The former parish workhouse in Edmonton was soon found to be inadequate and in May 1838 it was decided to put up a new building at a cost of around £9,000. The site chosen lay south of Silver Street (Edmonton) and east of Bull Lane; the infirmary there was eventually to evolve into the North Middlesex Hospital. The proposed cost caused consternation in the Enfield vestry, moreover it was feared that the Guardians might now decide on the demolition of the Enfield workhouse. Enfield vestry pointed out that in the year ended March 1837 the poor rate in Enfield had raised the sum of £2,994 of which £2,114 had been spent on the poor. In the first year under the Guardians the rate had produced £3,262 yet only £1,770 had directly benefited the poor, the remainder had been swallowed up in administration and overheads. Here indeed was the beginning of modern local government. Again Enfield vestry called for separation from the Edmonton Union.

The Board of Guardians however decided to retain the Enfield workhouse to be used for the pauper children. The staff at Enfield originally comprised a master and mistress as well as a schoolmaster and schoolmistress, but after a

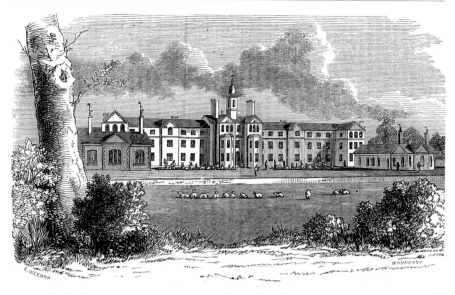

THE EDMONTON UNION.

87. It was decided in 1838 to build a new Union workhouse on a site south of Silver Street Edmonton. The workhouse infirmary there was later to become the North Middlesex Hospital.

short time the master and mistress were dismissed and a matron was appointed at £30 a year. Henry E. Parker's salary as schoolmaster was raised to £50 and in March 1840 he took over the duties formerly carried out by the master. An infirmary had been added at Chase Side and it was now proposed (December 1838) to enlarge the building to accommodate 230 children at an estimated cost of £1,000. Two schoolrooms were built with a boys' dormitory over, having a ground area eighty-five feet by thirty feet; this was in addition to the existing schoolrooms. The Board, in February the following year, purchased a cottage and several acres of land south of the workhouse and also rented the field behind at £15 a year. A fortnight later the Guardians purchased the land to the north of the workhouse which had formerly been leased to the Enfield Spade Husbandry Society. New building was commenced there in September 1839 and was completed by Christmas.[3]

3. Enfield Workhouse School

The emphasis at the Enfield workhouse was on cleanliness and order. The children's feet must be washed 'once a week, and their persons made thoroughly clean'. The whole establishment was to rise at six o'clock. The children were to dress, make their beds and say their prayers by 6.20, then to wash and comb their hair and assemble in the day room by seven o'clock for breakfast. After breakfast they were allowed into the playground until a quarter to nine when they assembled for prayers and school. Dinner was at noon and school resumed at two, until five. They were again allowed into the playground until

88.   The parish workhouse in Enfield was entirely rebuilt on the same site in 1827. Ten years later it was handed over to the Board of Guardians to house the pauper children of the Edmonton Union. Now it is known as St Michael's.

six. Then they had supper and played again until, at seven, it was time to wash and, at a quarter to eight, they assembled for prayers and bed. That was the summer routine. In the winter the day was shortened by two hours; they rose at seven and went to bed at seven.[4]

Despite praiseworthy efforts to maintain standards of cleanliness, epidemics proved difficult to eradicate. Disease was often brought in by newcomers. Many of the children who were moved in from Hornsey in 1838 had ringworm and although the worst cases were separated, the disease spread. In October that year there was an epidemic of the 'itch' (scabies) which, being cleared up, was brought in again by new entrants. Dr Asbury, the medical officer, attributed this to 'a want of cleanliness among the lower classes', though it was more probably spread by a number of children using the same blankets, and by the lack of laundry facilities and baths. The visiting committee recommended that two baths should be provided, with an apparatus for warming the water, but even this was not as effective as it might have been. Indeed the committee felt that the disease could even have been spread by 'as many as twenty boys being bathed in the same water'. An epidemic of measles in January caused three deaths and its after-effects brought on much illness. Out of about a hundred and fifty children, seventeen died that year. The registrar in Enfield faced considerable difficulty in registering the deaths of some of the younger pauper children who died in the workhouse, because their names were not known to the master. Dr Kay, an assistant poor law commissioner, in June 1840 advised the visiting committee that more vegetables should be included in the children's diet and in November a new weekly menu was ordered. It was adequate, if unexciting.[5]

Despite all efforts at eradication, epidemics, principally skin diseases, recurred year after year. Mr Stanlen, surgeon at the Cutaneous Institute, was

	Breakfast	Dinner	Supper
Sunday		4-6oz. baked beef 3oz. bread, vegetables	
Monday	1 pint milk	10-14oz. boiled suet pudding	
Tuesday	gruel*	4-5oz. boiled mutton, veg.	3-5oz. bread,
Wednesday	thickened	4-6oz. baked beef, veg.	butter, milk
Friday	with flour	12-14oz. rice pudding	and water
Thursday	3-5oz. bread	4-6oz. boiled mutton, veg.	daily
Saturday	daily	1 pint soup thickened with flour, 3oz. bread	

* oatmeal boiled in water

called in, in 1850, and recommended an ointment containing mercury. He advised the disinfection of the rooms, the bed linen and the clothes, which should be washed and placed in a room containing a pan of burning charcoal with an ounce of flowers of sulphur put on it. Perhaps more importantly, he also proposed that each child should have a separate towel.

Comments made at this time by Mr Everett of Chase Side House throw a little more light on possible causes of the contagion. He noted that the boys had only one shirt a week, that the bed linen was often damp, being never allowed to air, and that many of the children slept together. Nevertheless Mr Stanlen's remedies appear to have worked for a time, for the incidence of the disease diminished until in 1854 it was brought in again by the arrival of ninety-two children from Poplar, sixty-four of whom had scabies. Their stay was short but they left the disease behind them.[6]

The regime was liberal by the standards of the time. Corporal punishment was limited to the worst offences and a register of punishments had to be maintained. Lesser offences by children over ten were punished by deprivation of food for twelve hours, the younger children were 'put in disgrace'. *Meyers Observer* in August 1859 reported an examination of the schoolchildren in scripture, arithmetic (mental and written) dictation and writing. The maps made by the boys and the needlework done by the girls were highly praised. Boys were taught tailoring, shoemaking and field labour, the girls were taught to make and mend clothing, and domestic work. Thirty to thirty-five boys and girls were annually sent into situations. Having set down and considered these modest achievements, the approbation of the reporter so overcame him that, in an ecstacy of enthusiasm, he declared 'I felt proud of my poor rate'.

The boys remained at Enfield until they were fourteen, the girls until sixteen. The boys could be employed for a maximum of four hours a day on horticultural work in the workhouse grounds. All girls over twelve, and those under twelve thought by the mistress to be capable, worked alternate weeks at housework. A journal was kept of the hours worked to ensure that they did not spend too much time away from their lessons. Girls who were sent outside to do domestic work had to be paid a shilling a week. Some householders thought that this was an imposition. Mrs Joslin of Goffs Oak was of the opinion that the service ought to be free. She paid a great deal in poor rate, she said, and was entitled to some compensation, but Mr Parker remained firmly opposed to 'slavery'. Boys over fourteen who were more than four foot nine were eligible for recruitment into the Army or Navy. The Board made a grant of £2 to any boy entering the Navy, towards the cost of his outfit, and the recruit was taken to Sheerness. Boys entered the Army as drummers and were paid a shilling a week with board and uniform.[7]

A proposal in September 1880 that the Guardians should spend £5,000 on a separate infirmary at the Chase Side Schools to isolate cases of porrigo (skin diseases of the scalp) endemic among the children for many years, shocked the members of the Enfield Local Board; they strongly approved when central government refused to sanction borrowing for this purpose. Their former consternation however was nothing compared to the horror with which they received the next proposal, for the Edmonton Union now proposed to build an entirely new school[8] and immediately undertook the consideration of a number of locations, most of which were situated high up on the Ridgeway. Particularly favoured was the Springcroft estate, but this was purchased for a housing development by Mr Culloden Rowan. The Guardians next turned their eyes to Chase Farm on Lavender Hill. 'What will be its fate', muttered the Observer with forboding,[9] 'we do not know'. Petitions poured in protesting that high-class residential property in the area would be depreciated to the tune of fifty per cent, nevertheless the Local Government Board gave its sanction to the move. The forty-acre farm cost £12,000, the building £55,500. The opening ceremony took place at the end of March 1886, the building having been designed by Mr Knightley, the Guardians' own architect.[10]

Industrial training at the new Chase Farm Schools consisted of tailoring, shoemaking, a little gardening, instrumental music, sewing, cooking and laundry work. The workshops, according to Dr Mouat the inspector, were good and 'the means to make it a thorough success would not be expensive'. No schools were better adapted to turning out skilled artisans, he said, provided the children were not forced out into the world too early. Every child now had a separate towel, comb and brush. The swimming and washing baths were all that could be desired, though unfortunately none of the industrial trainers were able to swim and therefore they were unable to teach the children. The school was at last free from contagious diseases, except for the ever persistent porrigo. The death rate stood at twenty-five per thousand. It could even be claimed (Observer 16 August 1889) that porrigo itself was on the point of dying out, as only nine cases then existed.[11]

The Guardians sent children to Canada from 1892. Fifty-eight boys and girls went out during the year 1899 through the agency of Dr Barnardo. The following autumn (1900) the Reverend D.Fotheringham, chairman of the Guardians, told the Board that thirty-three boys and thirteen girls had decided that they would go, 'but for one reason or another many of them had withdrawn' and now only twelve remained willing. He attributed the defections to the new insistence by Dr Barnardo that all applicants for emigration must reside for two or three months in one of his homes before departure. It was the chairman's opinion that in most cases Canada was the best thing for the youngsters and to confirm his opinion he decided to take his holiday there the following year so that he could get in touch with the children on the farms in Ontario (Observer

89.   Chase Farm Schools opened at the end of March 1886; the building and site had cost £67,500.
It is now Chase Farm Hospital.

20 July 1900). Good as his word he visited Toronto, the town to which all the boys from England were brought before being sent on to the farms. Once they had begun working, they were encouraged to send their savings back to Toronto so that the money could be accumulated and, when a boy's engagement with the farmer was completed, he would have £5 or £10 with which he could make a start. The girls on arrival were received at Peterboro. The Reverend Fotheringham reaffirmed his view that the Guardians could not do better for the children (*Observer* 20 October 1900). Many parents however appeared unconvinced and as soon as they were notified that their children would be sent, they came to the workhouse and reclaimed them (*Observer* 11 September 1903). Nevertheless some children continued to go, twenty-eight being selected in 1909.[12]

The Guardians wrote to the Enfield School Board in November 1898 expressing an intention to place workhouse children in Board schools. This unprecedented proposal created a unanimity, almost unique, between the conservative and the progressive members of the School Board as they all hastened to reject the scheme. The very conservative vicar was first, as always, into battle: 'The question is answered at once' he pronounced decisively, 'there is no accommodation'. He was followed by the liberal George Spicer. 'If they sent a large number to one school', he pleaded, 'it would ruin it, for there is a strong dividing line' (*Observer* 18 November 1898).

Chase Farm School by November 1902 was full to capacity. There was even talk of renting a 'seaside abode' for some of the little ones, but the *Observer* (7 November 1902) deplored such extravagance. There were now 516 children in the school, the editor pointed out, each costing the ratepayers 7s or 8s a week; the responsibility should be thrown back upon the parents or other relatives. The Guardians sought another way out. On a Monday early in December 1902 all the children in the House belonging to the parish of Enfield were marched to the new Chase Side Board School. 'Fortunately', said the *Observer* (12 December 1902) 'admittance was barred as the school was full'. The Guardians, complained the editor (*Observer* 12 December 1902), 'have a fad' that the workhouse children ought to mix with other children. The next attempt to secure entry into council schools came a month later. This time the Guardians proposed to send only one child, but an outbreak of scarlet fever at Chase Farm delayed the operation. In December 1904 they took over Fortescue Villas in Gentleman's Row. Originally they intended to use it as a receiving house but, in the event, they housed selected children there, those with a long record of good health and good conduct. The exemplary behaviour of these children in church was noted in the local press as a proof of 'the good and careful training they had received'. Application then being made for school places for them, the education committee was forced to relent. The Guardians agreed to contribute towards the cost of their education.[13]

Due to the overcrowding at Chase Farm many workhouse children had to be boarded out, often in the humblest of homes and far removed from the area of the Union; an average of 5s a week was paid for each child. The relieving officer in his report in 1905 regretted that better-class homes could not be found where the small payment would not be so much a matter of necessity. Boarding out had become a business in some villages. He had heard stories in country pubs and had heard people laughing together, boasting how they had deceived the visitors. Mr Rutherford moved that no further children from the Edmonton Union be boarded out. He demanded that adequate relief should be granted

90. *A fortnight at the seaside: the workhouse children from Chase Farm School set off.*

to widows of good character to enable them to maintain their own children at home. There had been two cases in the previous week, he asserted, where the mothers had agreed to take out their children provided they were given adequate relief.[14]

An inspection of the school in March 1909 revealed the deteriorative effect of segregation on workhouse children. HM Inspector reported a feebleness in oral answering. 'Very little power of producing and using knowledge has been acquired', he wrote. 'There is a want of freedom, self-reliance and resourcefulness in speech'. In his opinion the children at Chase Farm Schools should associate with other children and some arrangement should be made to take them into council schools where they would get better teaching than at present.[15]

The management of the children under the jurisdiction of the Guardians was coming under scrutiny. There were 1,224 children on the outdoor relief list (July 1909), 235 more than in the previous year, while there were a hundred more in the Chase Farm Schools. The relieving officers reported that very few of the widows who had children in the workhouse were willing to take them out but, as Mr Metivier pointed out, the 1s 6d allowance granted to the widows was insufficient; it cost 2s 4d just to feed a child in the workhouse. What was even worse was that a widow on out-relief found her miserable 1s 6d cut off immediately her child reached the age of fourteen, while at the same time the Guardians maintained sixty children in the house aged between fourteen and sixteen.

The Guardians advocated the increased use of 'scattered homes', to these they proposed to send sixty more children of whom fifty could then be sent to local public elementary schools. Mr Metivier contended that the cost of keeping a child in one of these scattered homes, 11s 3d a week, was too expensive; the Guardians paid out £225 a year in rents alone. Mr Dewey had visited the Board's houses in Tottenham where there were fifty children, in six cottages, looked after by six foster mothers, two of whom were missing when he called. He found a little girl of eight cleaning up. 'One of the best cleaners I've got', the foster mother told him. The foster mothers received an allowance of $4\frac{1}{2}$d a day for food for the boys and 4d for the girls. Tottenham was the poorest parish in the Union, yet it received nothing for the education of these children. Parishes like Hornsey, very middle class, would not take pauper children, 'because the people would not stand for it'. With the onset of winter, accommodation at Chase Farm became further strained. There was a proposal to rent more scattered homes and a counter proposal to erect temporary buildings at Chase Farm. Some Guardians pointed out that the maintenance of a child in the schools cost 12s a week while out-door relief for a child was only 2s. Mr Metivier again urged negotiation with Enfield education committee; everything possible should be done to reduce the difference between workhouse children and those outside.[16]

School classes at Chase Farm were constantly changing with children leaving and new ones coming in. Many of those admitted to the junior mixed school were very backward. They had previously attended school irregularly and their level of reading and arithmetic was described, in 1912, as 'disappointing'; there was plenty of reading matter available, but the children were too backward to benefit. The senior department, it was said, undoubtedly was improving and the children had become more natural and less constrained than formerly.[17]

4. The House in Chase Side
and the Workhouse Infirmary

Following the opening of Chase Farm Schools, the former workhouse building in Chase Side became a haven for privileged paupers, the more deserving and respectable poor, mostly from Enfield — a 'pauper House of Lords' according to the O*bserver* (3 July 1896). It had only 150 inmates in April 1897 compared with 600 in the Edmonton house. That month the Guardians had a proposal before them to sell the establishment, but vicar Hodson opposed this strongly. 'It was the brightest spot in the whole management of the Union', he declared, and demanded that it should be retained for 'deserving poor people in their old age'. A correspondent for the *City Press* described a visit there in April 1901. He found six old ladies in the ward, sitting in comfortable chairs around a blazing fire. There was a table-cloth and pots of ferns on the window sills. The walls were brightened with chromos (coloured lithographs) and illustrated papers. A few years before, such old people had lived and slept in one room, but now they had the use of a sitting-room all day.[18] The demise of the Board of Guardians in 1930 did not fundamentally alter the nature of the institution. As late as 1939 it was still known as Enfield House. At that time it was a Public Assistance institution, and after the Second World War it became known as St Michael's.

Increasingly, workhouse infirmaries were being used as general hospitals. Mr Crusha, one of the Guardians, called attention to the case of William Hart, a labourer, taken to the Enfield workhouse infirmary with a broken leg, instead of to a hospital; his son had guaranteed to pay 7s a week maintenance and any funeral expenses. It seemed deplorable to Mr Crusha that the workhouse was being used by people who were not paupers, who were only taken to the workhouse infirmary because they got good treatment there. A number of local doctors on the other hand were urging that such people should be admitted by right. Dr Foster Burns of Edmonton, at the inquest of John Wade Scott, aged twelve, complained that when the mother had applied to the relieving officer to admit the boy to the Edmonton infirmary, she was told that they 'didn't take children there'. The infirmary was the proper place for him, pursued the doctor (*Observer* 17 July 1903) but he was driven away. 'I have cases day after day' he went on 'that ought to go into the infirmary'[19] but were not admitted. The Guardians and their servants remained rigid in their approach to poverty, often acting with unpremeditated cruelty in their unwillingness to bend the rules. Thus it was in the case of little Martha Fowler, aged eleven. She was given oxygen and brought from Tottenham to the Edmonton infirmary in May 1909, suffering from double pneumonia. Admission was refused, the child was sent all the way to Enfield, nearly five miles, in agony with every jolt of the vehicle over the rough roads; she arrived almost dead.[20]

Although the infirmary at the Edmonton workhouse had been built only three years, and at a cost of £25,000, there was a strong movement afoot to build a new, much larger infirmary there. Likely costs were bandied about, mainly by those who were opposed, ranging from £150,000 to £250,000. It was pointed out that many sick people were living in misery who ought to be cared for in the infirmary, but there was no room. The population of the Union had increased by 100,000 over the previous ten years and stood, in January 1904, at 348,000 and it was now growing by some 20,000 each year. There were 480 beds in the infirmary, that is one to every 725 people. Despite strong opposition it was decided to erect the new infirmary, to be sited on land adjoining the Edmonton workhouse. Plans were to be prepared for four blocks, each to accommodate 200 patients, bringing the number of beds up to 1,280. There would be a residence for the medical officer, a kitchen and stores, and a nurses' home on the site then occupied by Bridport Hall in Silver Street Edmonton. The Guardians borrowed £74,000 and by January 1909, 256 men were employed on the building. Tenders were invited for electric lifts and coloured tiles for the front administrative block and May 1909 found the building almost completed. The Local Government Board wanted the infirmary to be separate from the workhouse and to facilitate this demanded the appointment of a matron and a full-time resident medical superintendent. Dr Benjafield, who had for some time been medical officer to the Board of Guardians, was not a full-time officer for he had a flourishing private practice and, although he protested vehemently, the Guardians invited candidates for the appointment of a medical superintendent to the following meeting. There the proceedings were disrupted at the last moment by an angry dispute as to whether any appointment ought to be made. The issue was put to a vote and the Guardians having divided seventeen on each side, the chairman E.G. Cole used his casting vote in favour. Dr Spencer Mort was appointed and took up the appointment in April 1910. Poor law infirmaries throughout the country had provided 22,452 beds in 1891; by 1911 the number had risen to 74,013.[21]

At the opening of the new infirmary in July 1910 Sir William Job Collins, vice-lieutenant of the county of London and related to the Huguenot family of Garnault in Enfield, claimed that poor law infirmaries now differed only in name from general hospitals. 'The time will come', he anticipated, 'when they will be spoken of as municipal hospitals, for far too many people to be sick is to be poor'. Sadly he failed to understand how difficult it would be to eradicate the stigma attached, by the policy of the poor law unions themselves, to anything provided in their names. Despite the up-to-date, expensive facilities installed, the 'workhouse' odour hung about the establishment and people would not enter. Mr Metivier, usually on the side of the angels and now chairman of the Guardians, endeavouring only six months later to account for the very high death rate among the patients there, told of the shocking state of most of those who came in. 'If only people would overcome their repugnance to the poor law' he lamented, 'and send patients in while there was a chance of staying the disease....'[22]

It was the practice of the Guardians to issue orders which allowed the sick poor to see a district medical officer. One such was Dr C.H. Browne in Derby Road at Ponders End, who held eight surgeries a day and had two partners and an assistant to help him. He had attended 125 paupers in February 1912; they had made 151 visits to his surgery while he had made 144 visits to their homes.[23]

Many of the Guardians were not as progressive as Mr Metivier and seemed determined that the stigma which he deplored should in no circumstances be removed from their infirmary, thus when a motion was put forward that the Silver Street gates should be used as a separate and distinct entrance to the infirmary, it was strongly opposed by the Reverend G.W. White of the Baptist Tabernacle in London Road. Those in favour argued that the Local Government Board had only agreed to the siting of the hospital there on condition that it should be dissociated from the workhouse; there were nearly a thousand visitors to the infirmary on Sundays and self-respecting people were unwilling to be seen going through the workhouse gates. There were said to be sick people who allowed themselves to be admitted, thinking that they were coming into the infirmary, who then found themselves, against their wills, consigned to that pit of degradation, the workhouse. No wonder the expensive facilities provided in the infirmary were poorly used. Miss Debenham declared that if the two institutions were separated they might be able to induce the sick and respect-

able poor to come in for treatment. The Reverend White and his supporters had
no such objective, the infirmary, he insisted, was a poor law institution. The
Guardians agreed and the motion was lost. There had been talk for years about
the abolition of poor law boards but no reforming hand had yet been raised
radical and brave enough to sweep them into oblivion.[24]

5. Stoneyard and Charity

The Enfield Philanthropic Institution, set up in 1837, held its fourth annual
meeting at the George in January 1841. That week 120 bushels of potatoes and
220 quartern loaves had been distributed among the families of agricultural
labourers at Ponders End and Enfield Highway thrown out of work because of
the severe weather.

The hard times in the winter of 1842 again caused serious unemployment
among the agricultural labourers and forced the Poor Law Union to find work
for them at the workhouse. Many families were again thrown on relief during
the bad winter of 1845/6; during the week ending 16 February, 814 were forced
to seek help. Again in January 1847 the Board of Guardians had to distribute
relief to the unemployed. In the course of the week ending 17 February that
year, £126 in relief was paid to 800 families to provide sustenance of a sort, to
say nothing of rent, for 1,742 persons; their sustenance amounted to 18d a week
a head. Stone breaking was the task set for this princely reward and to ensure
that there were no slackers, each man was allotted his pile of stones. Payment
was made according to the number in his family. Most families would seek help
from the Poor Law only when facing death by starvation.[25]

Hampstead seceded from the Union in January 1848. The main workhouse
at Edmonton subsequently admitted the old and infirm as well as the able-
bodied poor. The building could house 480 paupers. During the winter months
it was full but in the summer the numbers diminished; in the September of 1849
for instance there were only 152 men and 140 women with thirteen babies. The
poverty which continued to exist in the parish was no no longer the responsibility of the vestry. It is on this account less apparent to the parish historian, yet
there appears, from time to time, evidence of considerable distress among the
agricultural labourers. Occasionally the poverty obtruded unpleasantly upon
the respectable parishioners, as when a gang of ragged boys and girls, clamber-
ing over the graves, shouting and laughing, followed a funeral procession to and
fro in the churchyard, coming close up to the mourners, scrutinising their faces
and making ribald remarks thereon. This happened in November 1860, but this
sort of behaviour was said to be common around Enfield.[26]

In an attempt to civilise, even to educate, the children of the poor, a ragged
school had been opened in Bonnetts Yard, nine tenements of wood, lath and
plaster, off Baker Street. There between twenty and thirty children were taught
the simple rudiments of reading, writing and arithmetic and the 'word of God'.
These children were described in the *Observer* (March 1865) as 'the outcasts of
society who could not, in their present condition, be taken into other schools
where it is desirable that the children should be decent'. The school was open
only on Sunday afternoons during the summer; presumably the pupils worked
throughout the week. In the winter months the school opened on several nights

during the week. It was maintained by voluntary subscriptions. James Biscoe the postmaster provided a treat during the summer (*Observer* July 1859) taking the children out to his field where he provided a good tea with nuts, oranges and currants, for both the teachers and the youngsters, and afterwards they played football.

A penny bank was set up at the school in April 1859, according to the *Observer*, in an endeavour to persuade the children of the poor to save their money instead of spending it on sweets. They were encouraged to deposit their pennies with the teachers for the purchase of clothes. Only the very poor were allowed to join and not more than one shilling could be deposited, because the interest paid, one penny in a shilling, was above the normal. Every year a party was arranged for the children and held at the British School in Chase Side, where they were each given a pair of boots or an article of clothing. The Enfield Philanthropic Institution helped to relieve distress. The bad summer of 1860 was followed by a winter of extreme severity, and many farmers found it difficult to provide employment even for their regular hands. Soup kitchens were operating throughout that winter and provided 3,580 quarts of hot soup and bread. Poverty existed even in the western side of the parish. A soup kitchen was set up at Mrs Staker's in Baker Street, open on Wednesdays, and another at Hicks Bakery in Chase Side, open on Saturdays. Tickets, available to the poor from subscribers, enabled them to get a quart of soup with bread for a penny. The winter of 1865/6 was another difficult one because of the high price of meat; 239 families were relieved by charity. The last week of October 1869 had seen continuous falls of snow and piercing cold winds. In *Meyers's Observer* the Enfield Loan Blanket Society appealed for funds 'For the sake of those to whom the comforts of life are barely supplied'. The need, it was said, had not been diminished by the introduction of brown paper blankets for the poor; the writer doubted whether these could ever supersede 'the coveted woollen blanket'. The Enfield Lying-in Charity had been in existence since 1797; it provided 'a skilful person' to attend poor married women in their confinement. All requirements were furnished for a month, and nearly eight thousand women had received assistance by 1867.[27]

As the century progressed the need for private charity did not diminish. The country suffered a series of poor harvests from 1873, though cheap imports of grain from North America kept prices low. The editorial in *Meyers's Observer* (11 December 1875) pleaded for continued generosity 'at this time when biting frost and drifting snow has closed the channels from whence the labouring classes, in a semi-agricultural area like our own, derive their daily bread.' Collectors had been seeking money to maintain soup kitchens, the coal club and the bread club, for it was by these means that many families survived through the long cold winter. Despite the existence of industry in Enfield some agricultural labourers were paid starvation wages. One example was quoted in *Meyers's Observer* (June 1874) of a man, described as honest and hard-working, who earned only 12s a week and had a large family, all quite young. After a long and bitter struggle he found that he could no longer maintain his children on his miserable earnings and he was compelled to apply to the Guardians for relief, but his application was automatically rejected. He was told that because he was in full employment and in receipt of the ordinary wages of his class, it would be necessary for him to give up his work, whereupon he and his family could be taken into the workhouse. The stupidity of the system was again drawn to the attention of the public the following year (*Observer* 4 September 1875). The man concerned was earning 16s a week with the possibility of extra pay at harvest and at other times and although he had six children, one of them brought in 6s and another 3s 6d a week. He had only asked for help because his wife was confined with twins. The relieving officer had offered medical assistance upon condition that he paid for it by instalments. The repayments however were more than the man could afford and his wife had to do without the help.[28]

For those employed in industry the years 1880 to 1896 saw a considerable rise in real incomes, but the unemployed and the agricultural labourer suffered stark poverty. The Revd F.C. Lloyd at St Matthew's Church, in the *Observer* (29 January 1881) appealed for help for the many poor in Ponders End not employed in the factories, who had been thrown out of work by bad weather. That month saw the worst snowstorms of the century driven by bitter winds from the east. Sixty quarts of soup were being distributed at St Matthew's three times a week and more was needed. Coal too was badly required. Every winter the soup kitchens opened their doors to the hungry; in January 1885 soup was served from the Duke of Lancaster Coffee Tavern in Silver Street and from Mr Gripper's brewery store (Sutton's warehouse) in Chase Side. A quart of soup and half a pound of bread was provided to those with a ticket, for one penny. The Reverend Mr Cotton did much for the children of the poor at Ponders End. 'Last Thursday' he wrote, 'we had seventy, some of their fathers had been out of work for three months'. He complained that he had not received a farthingsworth of help from elsewhere. Other places in the parish however had their own troubles. Many 'good workmen' were unemployed at Bush Hill Park (east of the railway of course) and soup kitchens there were serving eighty to a hundred quarts to the children, every Tuesday and Friday.[29]

Every winter unemployed labourers in desperation applied at the workhouse for work. The chairman of the Guardians, M. Latham Esq, complained that the more the Board did for these men in bad times, the more poor people would come into the neighbourhood. It was indeed a serious problem for the gentlemen of the Board and the master of the workhouse was called in for consultation. He advised that there was plenty of granite to be broken. Granite was often used to deter applications for relief. The Guardians in earlier years had paid a married man with one child 6d a day for this work and had provided him with four pounds of bread. Men with two children had had 7d a day and five pounds of bread, and thus the reward had increased with each dependant child. The men themselves also got two ounces of cheese a day, and on Saturdays there was a double allowance of bread to cover Sundays. The previous winter (1884/5) when the stoneyard had opened, they had paid the men a shilling a day with the same allowance for children and the same bread and cheese, but Mr Latham thought a shilling was too much, as it was more than was paid by most other boards. He proposed that it should be reduced to ninepence. Mr Mitchell urged the Guardians to pay the same as they had the previous year; he was sure that no man would go to the stoneyard for a shilling if he could find employment elsewhere. Mr Biscoe was for discretion on behalf of the ratepayers, and the chairman's proposal was adopted. Some of the Guardians found it difficult to understand how it was that many of these men had been able to survive for weeks before they applied for relief. It also puzzled some Guardians how these men could continue to survive on relief amounting to only a few coppers a day and a small allowance of bread and cheese. Their survival, it was thought, could only be attributed to the fact that the poor helped each other; they were much more generous in relation to their means than the more wealthy in the parish. Charles Booth[30] was of the opinion that the poverty line, for a 'moderate family', was between 18s and 21s a week. February 1886 had seen a great demonstration of the unemployed in London. It had developed into a riot and for two days London lay under the threat of mob violence. Two days before Christmas 1886 the Reverend E.W. Kempe of Jesus Church, Forty Hill, appealed on behalf of fifty married men from Enfield 'compelled, for want of work, to break stones for a pittance ... to give them a good Christmas dinner and something besides'. Yet Enfield was better off in this respect than the neighbouring parishes. There were 375 men from Edmonton and 209 from Tottenham, working in the stoneyards.[31]

Employment exchanges, known as 'free registries', were set up in May 1886 by Mr Latham in Edmonton, Enfield and other places in the Union. Unemployed men could have their names registered on a classified list, so that they would no longer be obliged to tramp endless miles in search of work. The service was free, but those who found work were asked to contribute a shilling, at the rate of 3d a week. The Enfield registry was held at the court house (the former Greyhound) and was maintained by Mr Purdey the parish clerk.[32]

6. Poverty in the Nineties

The winter of 1890-91 was exceptionally severe, and many agricultural labourers were off work for months. Despite widespread poverty the Guardians maintained the same policy, aiming to deter applications for relief. They now insisted that the head of any family granted help would have to go into the workhouse. Thus the Guardians protected themselves from false claims by deterring the genuine claims of those unavoidably unemployed. Mr Haines, pointing out that there were people starving, proposed that the Guardians might help by lending them money. This was resisted by the chairman on the grounds, no doubt true, that no one had applied for relief. There had been no applications because self-respecting labourers preferred to see their families starve rather than to seek help that would result in the degradation of entering the workhouse. It was essential, even among the very poor, that they should be able to maintain their social status among their neighbours. 'A good man,' in the opinion of the *Observer* in January 1891, 'may be prepared to incur the terrible stigma of residence in a workhouse and the social ostracism that follows, for the sake of his family', but most 'would rather endure destitution, or fall back on the inadequate resources of private benevolence'. Ebenezer Marshall pleaded that the Enfield Local Board should employ men to clear the snow and some extra men were taken on. Public works had come to be regarded as the main antidote against unemployment. Ponders End was as usual the hardest hit. The Reverend Cotton provided children with more than a hundred bread and milk breakfasts every day. He had been working with the poor for more than twelve years, he said, but had never seen such distress. The employees at Ediswan's sent him £11 3s 6d, the workers at the RSAF £9 8s 9d, and from the Cortecine factory came a gift of £2. He complained of the lack of help from the more wealthy parts of Enfield, with the consistent exception of Mr Ebben the baker in the Town. But charity also had its problems there. Over 2,500 tickets for provisions had been issued to the poor, and 160 tickets for coal, entitling them to one cwt each. Free dinners were laid on at the Lancaster Hall in Silver Street by Mr Gribble the manager of the late Coffee Tavern, and sixty needy children each day were taken there from the elementary schools. Free soup was provided at the Chase Side kitchen, also at St Mary Magdelen, at Christ Church and at the Baker Street Chapel. The Enfield Distress Fund committee was set up to deal with the problem in all parts of the parish. Major Bowles acted as chairman; the committee was to remain in existence after the end of the emergency.[33]

A harsh winter was again the cause of severe distress in February 1895 when twenty-six degrees (Fahrenheit) of frost was recorded in Enfield. Hundreds of tickets for food and fuel were distributed and soup kitchens were opened in the eastern side of the parish, in Bush Hill Park and at Chase Side. About a thousand people received relief from voluntary groups. In Edmonton a procession of three hundred unemployed men led by a drummer was broken up by the police

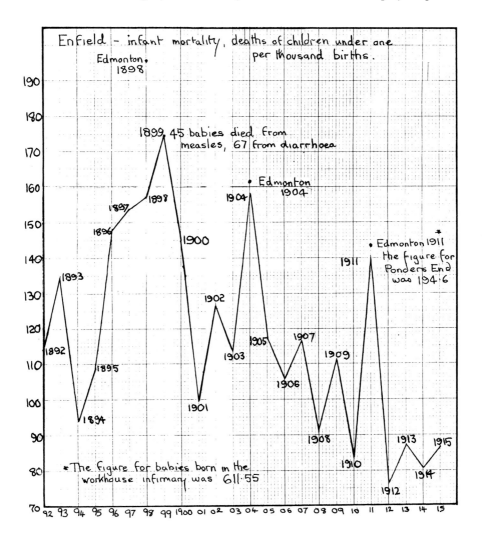

and two labourers, Jiggins and Fincher, both of West Street, carrying collection boxes, were taken into custody. The unemployed in Edmonton had set up a committee which included the vicar and other gentry. A.J. Wrampling, who was a social democrat and a local councillor, had been elected secretary. It was he who defended Jiggins and Fincher before the magistrates at petty sessions and the charges against them were dismissed. Later the unemployed demonstrated outside the workhouse demanding work. Wrampling threatened that unless something was done the men would bring their families into the workhouse, thus they turned the tables on the Guardians. Under this threat the Board joined with the urban district councils in seeking to create employment. Within one week the Enfield Urban District Council had found work for forty extra men. Another hundred were set to work trenching land at Ponders End acquired for allotments. Preference was given to married men with families and the labourers were paid the recognised rate for piece-work. Enfield rates for the year 1898/9 went up by 3d and at the same time the abatement on rates offered on small property (when the rates were collected by the landlord together with the rent) was reduced from fifty to twenty-five per cent. Some landlords refused to continue participation in the scheme, preferring to make their tenants pay the full rate direct. Thus the rents of many small properties increased by sixpence a week; the price of bread also went up. These extra costs fell directly upon those least able to afford them, that is those who lived in small cottages and had little else to eat but bread.[34]

7. Edwardian Poverty

The revival of trade and the increased work at the RSAF during the war in South Africa brought prosperity to Enfield between 1896 and 1902. Slate clubs were springing up all over the parish, providing for members a measure of self-protection and a little extra money at Christmas. Many of them were associated with the PSA (Pleasant Sunday Afternoon) movement. The Enfield PSA had 235 members in 1900, thirty-nine had received sick pay averaging about 3s a week, and there had been no deaths. The club felt able to pay 25s to each member at Christmas. The Kings Head (Market Place) PSA had seventy-eight members and had paid out £10 in benefits from January to September 1900 (*Observer* 30 November 1900). At the Spotted Cow, a little hostelry in the remote agricultural hamlet of Bulls Cross, Bert Everett the landlord acted as treasurer and distributed a dividend (in 1907) of 23s 1d. Undoubtedly this did no harm to his Christmas trade. Slate clubs (dividing friendly societies) shared out the greater part of their funds at the end of each year. Unlike the permanent friendly societies, a slate club member could not enter into a contract for life and thus insure his old age. Ill-health might cause a slate club to refuse membership and it might be forced to raise a member's subscription in old age.[35]

Severe weather and short-time at the RSAF following the cessation of fighting in South Africa again caused distress in the early months of 1903 and about a hundred of the unemployed paraded through Ponders End with collecting boxes. Many were forced to seek relief and the labour yard was re-opened. Mr Wrampling angrily exhibited a ticket issued there for eight hours work rewarded by 1s 6d in kind and 1s in money. The cost of out-door relief in the

91. Bert Everett, the landlord of the Spotted Cow, a little hostelry at Bulls Cross, acted as treasurer to a slate club and distributed a dividend every Christmas; in 1907 it amounted to 23s 1d. It was good for trade. The house is still there though it is no longer a pub.

Edmonton Union had risen by 171 per cent in the ten years 1893 to 1903. In Enfield, where the population had increased by 34.4 per cent, the cost of out-door relief had risen by 108.6 per cent. In Edmonton (with Southgate) it had increased by 539.7 per cent while the population there had gone up by 40.7 per cent. The magistrates complained repeatedly about the activities of bookies' runners (off-course betting was illegal) on whom heavy fines made no impres-sion. This year (1903) £150 had been paid by the bookies in fines at Enfield police court; they were making a fortune out of 'the class of people who could least afford it'. One man was cited 'who earned 24s a week and had only 2s to take home to his wife'.[36]

The slump of 1903-5 caused unemployment in parts of Enfield. So many were out of work in Bush Hill Park by December 1903 that a labour bureau was set up to help men to find work. Soup kitchens were operating there in the early months of the year 1904 issuing 140 quarts on two days each week. Ponders End was again hard hit. Teachers at St Matthew's School were paying for dinners twice a week for about fifty children. The education committee was asked whether it could make a grant towards the cost, as the London School Board did, but the committee replied that children were coming to school hungry and without boots or shoes throughout the whole of eastern Enfield and, at St James also, the teachers had clubbed together to provide meals.[37]

Charity, complained the Reverend V. Travers Macy, encouraged the increase of 'professional beggars'. He took a high moral tone when discussing the difficulty. 'There are people in my own district (St Luke's) who begged when I first knew them' he said, 'seven or eight years ago and still continue begging, though nothing has caused their poverty but drink and reckless extravagance, the help that has been given them by the well-to-do in Enfield has been their ruin. Their homes are invariably dirty, their children ill-fed and ill-clothed. Such people get no help from our parochial funds… but they go round to various houses in Enfield where they are not known and obtain gifts of money and clothes…. So many children have been sent to St Luke's vicarage in ragged clothes and without boots, and always in the wettest weather to excite pity, that we have to refuse to see all children who come' (*Observer* 18 March 1904). There was nevertheless very real poverty, caused by unemployment which had become endemic and short-time working which had reduced wages. The Enfield Relief Committee in November 1904 reported hundreds of cases of starving families at Ponders End. The Guardians had opened up their labour yard again and a hundred men were employed there, now paid 3s a day. At Bush Hill Park, said Charles Peploe (vicar of St Mark's, later of Christ Church, Southgate) 'a child in our junior mixed school fainted for lack of food. He was miserably clad, the father, like many others, being out of work. Our helpers have on two mornings given a cup of hot cocoa and bread and butter to 147 little ones recommended by the teachers. Distress here', he went on 'is now nearly as bad as it was in 1895 and the hardest pinch is yet to come'.[38]

At Grove Road, Enfield Wash a hundred boys and girls were given a free hot dinner on Tuesdays. 'Hungry and shivering they come into a warm room and pitch in at a bowl of soup, meat, dumplings and bread, of ten gallons not a drop was left'. This was paid for by Colonel Bowles until Christmas. The District Relief Fund was set up at the beginning of December 1904 and within three weeks fifty-nine families had been helped, including the families of some former Royal Small Arms Factory hands who had been discharged. Much of the money was collected in the factory. Unemployment and poverty gave rise to racism; scarcely distinguishable from anti-Semitism, it was encouraged at times by those in positions of responsibility. The vicar of Edmonton, the Reverend E.A.B. Sanders, interviewed by the *Morning Post* and the *Morning Leader,* pontificated that 'the immigration of foreigners was at the bottom of a good deal of the present trouble, it caused an overflow into places like Edmonton and our own people were thrown out of employment by cheaper labour'. Worse still was A.T. Williams, a member of the LCC who lived at Hill Lodge, Clay Hill. He roused a crowded audience at the Enfield Lock PSA held incongruously in the Co-op hall, with an unpleasant attack upon the enormous hordes of foreign Jews who… 'work for wages on which no Englishman could keep a wife and family' and lived six or eight in a room 'on what was practically bread and grease'. Now they were arriving at a rate of six or eight thousand a month. He hoped the day was not far distant when 'there would be at the mouth of the Thames a huge placard: "No foreign rubbish admitted here"'. A great many Jewish workers were crowded into tenements around Tottenham Hale and were employed in Jewish firms; on cabinet making at Lebus's in Ferry Lane, or in the manufacture of boots and shoes at A and W Flateau at Tottenham Hale. There was indeed very great distress in Edmonton where it was thought to be worse than in Tottenham. There were houses there denuded of everything saleable or pawnable, the remnants of the furniture had been broken up and burned because they had no fuel. Many of those who lived in Edmonton worked in London; out of 12,000 adult males in the parish 3,000 were unemployed.[39]

The Urban District Council in Enfield decided that it should double its funds to employ those out of work. It could only find jobs for unskilled labour, but it recommended some twenty tradesmen for employment at Alexandra Palace, to the building of which it had contributed money. Two hundred and eighteen of the unemployed, led by Walter Gammon a prominent local socialist, marched from Edmonton to the West End and collected £25 17s 10d. Twenty-two men were summoned before the magistrates for collecting in the streets. An unemployment exchange, now maintained in Enfield by the Permanent Relief Council (presumably under the Unemployed Workmen Act 1905) had on its books labourers, carpenters, painters, handymen, gardeners, clerks, caretakers, errand boys, carmen, charwomen, laundry women, domestic servants, shop assistants and warehouse men.[40]

In February 1906, 180 Tottenham unemployed were assisted to emigrate to Canada by Lord Rothschild, and that same month the Salvation Army sent 1,400 emigrants from Tottenham. The *Observer* (13 April 1906) printed a letter sent by an Enfield bricklayer living at North Bay in Canada:

> 'When we know there is an emigrant train going through', he wrote, 'we go to the station and walk through the train to see if there is anyone we know... saw one lot from Tottenham, a bricklayer and his family... had 4d between them with 1,400 more miles to travel. He wanted to sell his cardigan jacket to get tobacco... "Look at this", he says, "£20 to pay back for the passage". "Put it back in your pocket mate", says I, "and when you get to Manitoba, stick to work and keep out of the saloons and a month will see you a free man". I left them in better spirits and plenty of tobacco'.

Some men left their families behind. An Enfield woman with five children applied for assistance to emigrate in September 1908 because her husband had found employment in Canada. The Enfield Relief Council was prepared to make a grant towards the cost; in the meantime the Guardians granted her 7s 6d a week and some bread. Emigration to Canada was severely restricted in 1908 by the refusal of the Canadian government to accept further emigrants sent by charitable organisations.[41]

Many unemployed men trudged the roads seeking work, at night taking what shelter they could find. Some were even reduced to using the casual ward at the Edmonton workhouse, which remained a blot on the administration. The Reverend G.W. White (Baptist), one of the Guardians, visited the place just before Christmas 1906 and found twenty men huddled together in a small room waiting their turns for a bath. They had been there for hours and had had nothing but cold water out of a can in the centre of the room. Two men were put into each cell where there was only one bed, with two blankets each. They were given eight ounces of bread and cold water. Some Guardians, said Mr White, 'had been trying to get broth or cocoa but were defeated by men whose eyes stood out with fatness' (*Observer* 21 December 1906).

Poverty and unemployment remained endemic and the associated problems were off-loaded by government on to local authorities and local charities; these had to take what measures they could to mitigate suffering. Enfield Council, in January 1908, contributed a further £1,500 to the Alexandra Palace renovation fund on condition that a large proportion was spent on the wages of men recommended by Enfield. The building of the new George V reservoir at Ponders End which, it had been hoped, would provide a thousand jobs for labourers in that area, only increased the hardship, for the expectation of finding work brought in a small army of unemployed from elsewhere. The influx pushed up rents and led, according to the medical officer of health, to serious overcrowding 'which might deteriorate the health of the inhabitants'.

92. *Plans to build the King George V reservoir, with the promise of employment for a thousand men, brought an army of unemployed into the area seeking work. Construction was begun in July 1907 and completed in 1913, when it was opened by King George V.*

93. *The bust of Dr J. J. Ridge, who spent his life fighting on behalf of the people of Enfield for total abstinence, improved sanitation, purer water, decent housing, and more hospital beds. He died much respected in May 1908 at the age of sixty-one.*

Dr Ridge lamented that much of the distress was traceable to drink, and what made it worse was that there had been a serious increase of drinking among women. The good doctor had spent most of his life, when he wasn't fighting for better sanitation, improved housing conditions, purer water, or better care for the sick, in campaigning for total abstinence. He died in May 1908 aged sixty-one. Dr J.J. Ridge had been born in Gravesend where his father had twice been mayor. He came to Enfield in 1872 and joined the Congregational church in Chase Side. He had been medical officer of health since 1881, was highly qualified and had been consulting physician to the London Temperance Hospital for twenty-five years. He was also superintendent medical officer at the Edmonton and Enfield Isolation Hospital. The Cottage Hospital had been founded at his suggestion.[42]

The trade depression deepened in 1908 and the onset of winter left vast numbers without work. In Tottenham, 15,000 to 17,000 persons were said to be on the verge of starvation. Free meals in Enfield schools had to begin by early October; by the middle of the month 5,784 meals had been provided including three thousand breakfasts of cocoa or hot milk with bread and butter or jam. Soup and dumplings (an excellent filler) or meat and vegetables were provided for the dinners. Enfield Distressed Children's Fund had distributed 259 pairs of boots, issuing a strong injunction against pawning them, but to do justice to the parents there had been only one case where this was known to have occurred.[43]

The *Enfield Observer* (20 November 1908) urged increased contributions to the Enfield Distressed Children's Fund, warning that the council might be forced to adopt the Education (Provision of Meals) Act. This Act of 1906 allowed the levy of a halfpenny rate towards the provision of free meals and thus transferred the costs from charity to the rates; the *Observer* warned its readers of the additional expenditure that this would involve. The Fund not only had to distribute meals early that winter (1908-9) but the average cost of a dinner had risen from $1^1/_4$d during the previous winter, to $1^3/_4$d. January 1909 saw the labour yard again in use and men reduced to breaking stone, six cwt a day, for eighteen pence in food and a shilling in money. From the beginning of that month the post offices were busy paying out old age pensions for the first time; 480 claims had been allowed in Enfield. The pension was 5s a week for a single person at the age of seventy, 7s 6d a week for a married couple, but only those who had yearly incomes of less than £26 (single) or £39 (married) qualified. Later a sliding scale was introduced, from £21 to £26, thereafter a single person with an income of £26 a year received only 3s.[44]

The Enfield Relief Council established a skilled employment and apprentice-ship committee, which sought to train youngsters with the co-operation of industry. Attempts were made to persuade parents to forgo the immediate benefits of sending their children to work in exchange for the long term advantages of teaching them a trade. Government employment exchanges under the Board of Trade were set up locally in February 1910 but were not widely used until the introduction of unemployment insurance in 1912.[45]

The Board of Guardians continued to treat crises in families with bureaucratic rigidity. Thomas Manning had lived for some years at Manor Road; his case was reported in the *Observer* (4 June 1909). He had formerly worked for Hawkyns the builders' merchant in the Great Northern station yard on Windmill Hill, but he had met with a severe accident by a fall which had brought on spinal paralysis and rendered him incapable of work. He had nine children, five little ones under twelve at home and four older ones of whom three were girls in service; they contributed £2 a week to the household budget. Rather than become a burden on the rates, and in an endeavour to keep the family together, he had secured a barrel organ and a donkey, but then he had been compelled to enter hospital again. During this time his wife and the little boys had taken out the organ, but the law had intervened, allegedly to protect the children. His application to the relieving officer for help was turned down. He managed somehow to get to Edmonton and appeared before the relief committee asking for assistance so that he could employ a lad to help him get the barrel organ around. The Guardians were unhelpful. If he sold his donkey and organ, they told him, they might grant him a few shillings, but he would be required to move out of his house into a smaller cottage, and he would have to be entirely dependant on poor relief. He naturally wondered how much more it would cost the ratepayers if his five younger children had to be taken into Chase Farm Schools. State sickness benefit was introduced in May 1911, 10s a week for men, 7s 6d for women, for twenty-six weeks. Disability benefit at 5s a week could be paid indefinitely, and free medical treatment under a panel doctor was provided. Maternity benefit was 30s. This National Insurance Act 1911 also gave protection against unemployment, though it was confined at first to certain trades; 7s a week was paid for fifteen weeks in any one year. The health insurance was operated through friendly societies and trade unions (until the 1946 National Insurance Act), men contributed 4d a week, employers 3d and the state 2d.

The voluntary system for the provision of free meals for children was still functioning in the winter 1911/12. The Schools Canteen Fund provided 16,228 meals for necessitous children at a cost of £134 17s 6d, and 295 pairs of boots at £52. Poverty existed even among those regularly employed. At the end of the year 1912 council labourers, some married and with children, earned only 20s a week, so that after they had paid superannuation they had 19s 4d to take home. More than twenty years earlier Charles Booth had defined poverty in London as an income of 18s to 24s for a moderate sized family. Councillor Metivier urged that men could not live on such a wage and the council increased their pay to 24s. Where men were irregularly employed things could be much worse. The coroner, at the inquest on an infant named Ivy Blackford, declared that he had never seen a baby so thin. The family lived at Bell Lane, they had two other children but had already lost three. Reuben Blackford was a decorator but not in regular employment, sometimes he earned 30s but he did not average more than 15s, and the rent was 5s. (Cf R. Tressell *Ragged Trousered Philanthropist*)

Thus it was that by 1914, though poverty was still a major problem, relief had largely been taken out of the hands of local Boards of Guardians. Nevertheless the Boards survived until nineteen-thirty and the unpleasant odour of poverty and degradation that pervaded every institution with which they had been associated persisted almost up to the outbreak of the Second World War.[46]

Notes to Chapter Four

1. a list of vestry minute books in volume 1 p XV
2. S.I. Richardson *Edmonton Poor Law Union1837-54* p11, 23, MH 12. 7025
3. *ibid*, Richardson *op cit* pp 28-30
4. Board of Guardians Edmonton Union minutes 22 Ap 1840
5. Richardson *op cit* p67, 47
6. *ibid* pp 57-61
7. *ibid* p44, 45
8. *Observer* 11S 1880, 17D 1881
9. *Observer* 7 X 1882
10. *ibid* 6 Ja 1883, 25N 1882, 2 Ap 1886
11. *ibid* 2 Ap 1886, 14 Ja 1887, 16 Au 1889
12. *ibid* 27 Au 1909
13. *ibid* 8S, 16X, 10N 1905
14. *ibid* 30 Je 1905
15. *ibid* 26 Mr 1909
16. *ibid* 16 Jl, 12N 1909
17. *ibid* 14 Je 1912
18. *ibid* 12 Ap 1901
19. *ibid* 10 Jl 1903
20. *ibid* 28 My 1909
21. *ibid* 1 Ja, 15 Ja, 25N 1904, 29 My 1908, 5 Mr, 30 Ap, 12N, 19N 1909, 1 Au 1910
22. *ibid* 27 Ja 1911
23. *ibid* 10 My 1912
24. *ibid* 2 Ja, 27F 1914
25. MH 12. 7026, Read *op cit* p407, *Hertfordshire Mercury* 16 Ja 1841
26. Richardson *op cit* p17, PP 1849 XLV11 p14, 34, *Observer* N1860
27. *ibid* Mr 1865, Jl, Ap 1859, F, Je 1861, Mr 1865, Ja, F 1866, Mr, Ap 1867, F, My 1869, 11D 1875
28. Feuchtwanger E.J. *Democracy and Empire* p 112
29. *Observer* 17 Ja, 14F 1885, 10D1886, 14 Ja 1887
30. *Life and Labour of the People in London* 1889-1902
31. *Observer* 13F 1886, 17D, 23D 1886, 14 Ja 1887
32. *ibid* 15 My 1886
33. *ibid* 30 Ja, 2 Ja, 9 Ja, 23 Ja 1891
34. *ibid* 8F, 15F, 22F 1895, 6 My, 13 My 1898
35. *ibid* 27D 1907, 2N 1906
36. *ibid* 16 Ja, 31 Jl, 2X 1903
37. *ibid* 18D 1903, 4 Mr 1904
38. *ibid* 25N 1904
39. *ibid* 25N, 23D 1904, J. and B. Baum *The Jews of Tottenham Before the Great War* in *Heritage* 1 Jewish Research Group EH HS 1982, *Observer* 20 Ja 1905, *Enfield Chronicle* 14N 1902
40. *ibid* 15D 1905, 5 Mr, 13 Ap 1906
41. *ibid* 11S 1908
42. *ibid* 17 Ja 1908, 29 Jl 1910, 20N, 24 Ap, 1 My, 22 My 1908
43. *ibid* 25S, 16X 1908
44. *ibid* 20N 1908, 15 Ja, 8 Ja 1909
45. *ibid* 25 Mr 1910
46. *ibid* 11X, 9 Au 1912

Chapter Five

The Environment and the Ratepayers

1. Introduction

It was the cholera epidemic of 1848/9 which concentrated men's minds and made them aware of the need to establish a local Board of Health in Enfield. The health of the people of this parish was largely to depend for nearly half a century, on such sanitary measures as were taken by the Enfield Local Board of Health. It was set up in 1850. By this time, because of the rapid increase in population (which grew in the first half of the nineteenth century by sixty per cent) conditions in the parish had deteriorated badly. The new Board proposed to undertake the improvement of the water supply, the removal of human excrement and refuse, the protection of the people from infectious diseases and their homes from fire. It proposed to make provision in a sanitary way for the burial of the dead, to insist on certain standards in new houses and in old, and to maintain and light the roads. The new Board had scant experience to help it undertake these tasks, which were made particularly difficult in Enfield because of the unusually large size of the parish. The Board had to create administrative machinery from nothing. Being elected by the ratepayers, it was as reluctant to increase the rates as the ratepayers were to pay any increase. Therefore the Board sought to meet each problem in the cheapest rather than the best way possible. It sanctioned large expenditure only when driven to do so by the threat of an injunction or by the imminent collapse of a service.

For thirty years the Board was governed by the same gentry who had formerly ruled through the vestry. This remained acceptable to the ratepayers until the gentry became infected with ideas of improvement which induced them to spend more liberally. These ideas were introduced by the advent to the Board in 1879 of Sir Roland MacDonald Stephenson, an eminent engineer, and with the appointment under his influence of professional staff. New horizons opened up in local government but as the rates rose to pay for improvements, the deference shown by the middle class towards the natural rulers of the parish, evaporated. Middle-class ratepayers gained power at the local elections in 1883 largely through the vote of the new enfranchised working class. Once in control the new members displayed an alarming arrogance and an even more alarming ignorance, rejecting good professional advice with contempt and treating their former rulers with scant respect. Their behaviour soon became too preposterous for their own good and created a strong reaction which swept them out of office in 1885. The Board's work thereafter went on more smoothly but without that fervour for improvement which had flowered in the three years 1879 to 1882. Parsimony prevailed once more, the Board built no town hall, the water supply remained intermittent, the problem of sewage disposal was never adequately solved, refuse was still dumped close to people's homes and infant mortality remained high.

County councils were set up in 1888 and local government was reorganised in 1894 when the functions of the Local Board in Enfield were assumed by a new Urban District Council. Following this the provision of amenities was undertaken. A public library had been set up in 1893, Chase Green was taken over in 1897, parks, bandstands and swimming baths were provided and, with the demise of the School Board in 1902, elementary education was added to the responsibilities of the Council.

2. A Rural Slum

Enfield in 1841 was home for 9,367 people, forty-six per cent of whom were under the age of twenty. The numbers of the young however were inflated a little by the existence in the parish of fourteen high-class boarding schools, 219 pauper children in the Edmonton Union workhouse on Chase Side, and seventy-eight in the Shoreditch workhouse in Baker Street. The population had grown by sixty per cent since the beginning of the century. The growth had been rapid at first, from 5,881 in 1801 to 8,227 in 1821, forty per cent in twenty years. Thereafter the rate had slowed and over the next twenty years it grew by less than fourteen per cent. Between 1841 and 1851 the population grew by less than one per cent.

The number of houses in the parish had risen from 993 in 1800 (sixty-seven of them not inhabited) to 1,793 in 1841, an increase of eighty per cent. Essential services had not improved to keep pace with this growth and in consequence Enfield had become a rural slum. The squalor rendered the parish unpleasant and the people vulnerable to epidemics. The Reverend F.G. Sturgis, the curate at St James (Enfield Highway) wrote to complain in September 1849 to the General Board of Health. He had visited the sick and others in his parish over the previous two months and had been shocked by the accumulation of filth. He had found cases of malaria and cholera among families living in 'insalubrious penthouses adjoining stagnant water with cesspools and manure heaps at their doors'. He had buried three children dead of typhus in a yard of small cottages called St Patrick's Terrace opposite his own church where a heap of refuse almost blocked the entrance. Both in South Street and in Green Street stagnant ditches, full of malignant filth, were within yards of people's homes.[1]

Early in the year 1849, a petition was submitted to the Board of Health asking that a local Board of Health be set up; it was signed by more than ten per cent of the ratepayers. William Ranger, a superintending inspector, was dispatched to Enfield to hold a public enquiry, and the assembly room at the King's Head was placed at his disposal. The districts where epidemics had been most frequent were singled out for his attention; Loves Row behind Gentleman's Row, Parsonage Lane, the area around the Holly Bush, Meeting House Yard and many other courts and yards off Baker Street, Windmill Hill and Slaughter House Lane (now Sydney Road). Even Forty Hill, Hadley Green and Whitewebbs Lane, spots which we of the late twentieth century visit on fine Sunday afternoons to savour the sweet country air, were spoken of as plagued with

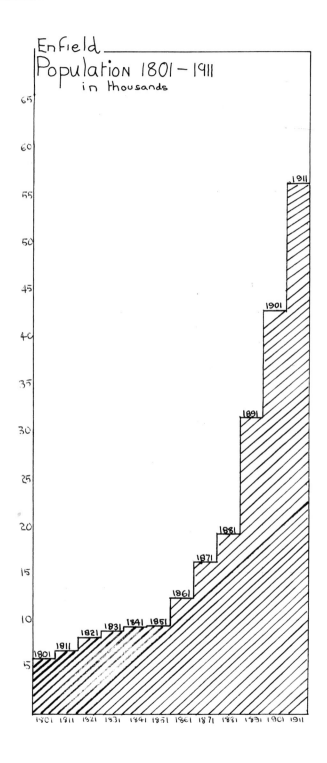

erysipelas, typhus and scarlet fever; the ditches there overflowed with filth and the stink was abominable. The smells were strongly emphasised by those who wanted the place cleaned up. Smells which arose from the putrefaction of organic matter, according to the widely held miasmatic theory, were the cause of epidemics. Edwin Chadwick and Florence Nightingale both shared this view.

Water was obtained in Enfield from wells; these sometimes had pumps, but more often the water had to be drawn up in buckets and it frequently had to be carried as far as three hundred yards to people's homes. In one small community the inspector was told that they obtained their water from a public house, but only upon condition that they bought beer there. The water from many of the wells was polluted by nearby cesspools and was unfit to wash in, let alone to drink. Those who lived near the New River were fortunate, for they could obtain an adequate supply by dipping, but many had to make do with the rain water collected off their roofs.

The sewage from many dwellings was fed into open ditches and was carried on a slow circuitous journey to the River Lea. One such open sewer, known in more pleasant circumstances as Saddlers Mill stream, began at Brigadier Hill. It crossed New Lane (Lancaster Road) by the Holly Bush and drew its stinking burden southward behind the workhouse, across Parsonage Lane, and to the rear of Gentleman's Row. Another little stream rose near the Hop Poles, flowed slowly along Baker Street and joined with the one from Brigadier Hill to deposit its insalubrious contents into the boundary ditch between Enfield and Edmonton. Thence it was carried to the East London Waterworks cutting alongside the railway near Ponders End station. Ponders End sewage was carried in an open ditch behind the houses on the west side of the High Street, thence behind the houses on the north side of South Street and into this same cutting by the railway.

Many of the houses had their privies built over such ditches, often with little attempt made to screen their users from public view. Pigs were kept within yards of human habitation, and farmers purchased night-soil from London which they piled up by the roadside; adding vegetable and other refuse to make great heaps of compost. All this contributed to the stench which, particularly in hot weather, pervaded the parish.

3. Enfield Local Board of Health

Under the Public Health Act of 1848, a local Board of Health was established in Enfield in 1850. Its first task, in order to eliminate the threat to public health which had developed at this time, was to provide pure and wholesome water, where possible available within people's homes. The second requirement was a system of enclosed public sewers connected to roads, courts, yards and houses by means of tubular pipes. The Board was to be responsible for the main sewers, but road drainage would be at the expense of any estate developer. It was hoped to enforce the installation of water closets to replace the cesspools and privies.[2] Thus, it was to take on these worthy tasks that men came forward to offer their services as members of a Local Board in Enfield. Twenty-eight candidates presented themselves for the first election in 1850. The gentry were well represented among those chosen. At the top of the poll was James Meyer of Forty

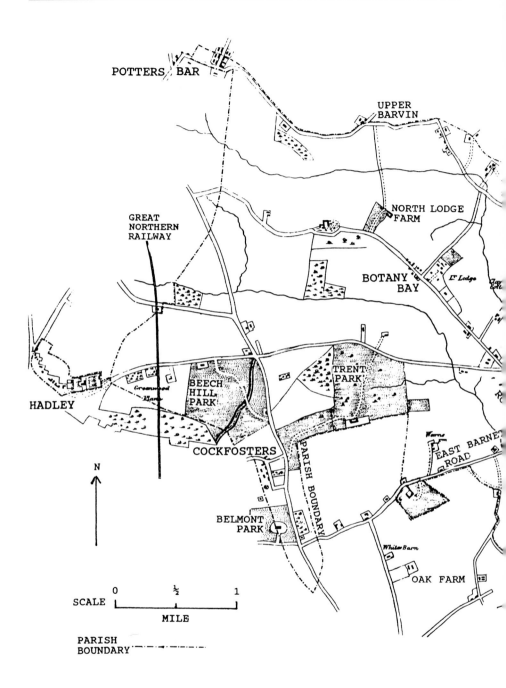

Hall, also elected were Daniel Harrison of Chase Hill, William Everett of Chase
Side House, Robert Cooper Lee Bevan of Trent Park, Dr John Millar of Oak
House, John Moore Heath the vicar and two of the lesser gentry. Three farmers
were elected, a builder and a wheelwright. James Meyer was chosen as chairman,

ENFIELD 1850

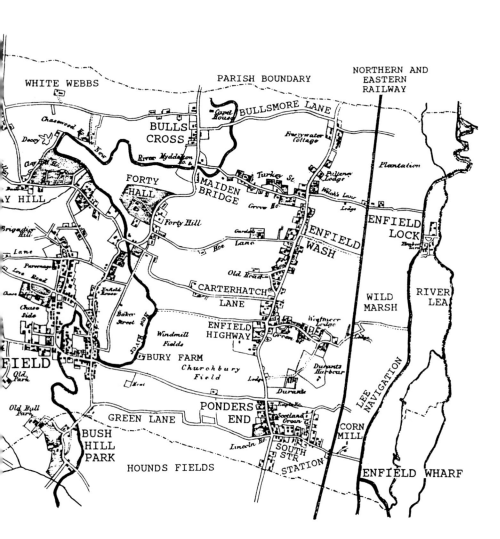

John Sawyer was appointed clerk.

The Local Board had its very modest plans ready by June 1854. It proposed to provide a water supply and a sewerage system in the Town and adjacent parts; also in Ponders End, the Highway and Turkey Street. There was to be a brick sewer to serve the Town and in the rest of the district fifteen-inch and six-inch stoneware pipes were to be laid. A filtration plant was to be set up in Lincoln Road near the railway crossing to remove the solid matter from the Town sewage. The residue, without further treatment, was now to be discharged nearby into Saddlers Mill brook, adding ever more pollution to that once delightful stream as it meandered on its picturesque course across the neighbouring parish of Edmonton. Pure water was to be found by sinking a deep well at Alma Road, from which the water was to be raised by a steam pump to a reservoir at the top of Holtwhites Hill. The estimated cost of this work was £12,500. An attempt had first been made to avoid the expense of a new source of water by coming to an arrangement with the New River Company, an obvious and very logical solution, but the Company refused to consider any proposal.

The Local Board soon concluded that its initial aims had been too ambitious and that it ought to confine its endeavours to the Town quarter and Ponders End. This more limited area, containing 932 houses, was created a special district on which higher rates could be levied to pay for the new services provided. Enfield Highway, it was said, 'being a rural district with few houses', would be best left without sewers, for the imposition of a rate for such a purpose would be highly unpopular there. The Local Board now obtained permission to borrow £12,000 and the work was begun.[3]

The superintending inspector, Alfred Dickens (the brother of a well known author) visited Enfield in March the following year (1855). By then fifty houses had been connected to the main sewers and in these, water closets had replaced the old privies and cesspools. Many property owners preferred to do the work themselves, but Alfred Dickens urged upon the Local Board the benefit of careful and skilful supervision of these private works where one bad junction might lead to endless trouble for the whole system. The Board having once accomplished this initial plan, thereafter made not a single improvement for the next thirty years, except it had been imposed by legal action or the threat thereof, or by an impending breakdown of the service.

Reading Watts complained on 10 October 1857 to the General Board of Health about the state of Enfield Highway. 'I never saw a place so bad off,' he wrote, 'for it is nothing but open privies and cesspools and the sewage from the houses runs from the cesspools into the wells. There is no water supply for the inhabitants'. The 'beautiful spring' in Old Road has a cesspool running into it. The dwellings along the High Road from the Sun and Woolpack to St James Church, including those in the lanes, alleys and yards leading off the main road, were crowded with humanity. The stench from the open ditches and from the filth on the sides of the highway, caused by the long accumulation of human and horse manure, was insufferable in hot weather. The state of the area was deteriorating, he claimed, because the population of the district had increased of late 'from the great addition made to the Ordnance Factory'. The General Board could only refer the matter to the Local Board. The Local Board sent Mr Watkins to investigate, but he couldn't see much wrong, although people did mention that the water from the spring in Old Road was sometimes not sweet. Suspecting that they might have been prejudiced, he brought a bottle of it back for the examination of the members but they declined to taste it, all save John Sawyer, who must have felt that it was his duty as clerk and who wrote in the margin of the minutes 'the water was exceedingly poor'. Mr Ironside, the surveyor, explained that when the spring in Old Road had last been put in order an old tar barrel was used; this was now rotten and the water ran straight into the ditch so that it became bad before the inhabitants could get at it.

The ratepayers at the Highway and Enfield Wash nevertheless remained willing to put up with the stench and the polluted water rather than accept a higher rate. Mr Cole, a tailor from Enfield Town, in October 1860 wrote to the General Board. He had a business at the Highway managed by his son whose sister kept house for him there. The area was so unhealthy that they were continually unwell. There had never been a sewer or a road drain in Enfield Wash between the Bell and the Woolpack bridge, he said, and the place was swamped with filth. He had written to the Local Board and was informed that the work could be done for £120 if he could get his neighbours to pay half, but the neighbours refused. 'They say they pay the Board of Health rate and the highway rate, and have no business to pay for a sewer'. Between the two Mr Cole could make no progress. Conditions continued to deteriorate, for the population was increasing. Two thousand workmen were now at times employed at the Royal Small Arms Factory. The land was flat and the open ditches, stinking of sewage, stood almost stagnant. This sewage, at the end of its protracted journey, fell untreated into the East London Waterworks cut at Ponders End. Even such conditions could only raise from the ratepayers a plea that the Local Board should clean the ditches, 'without burdening the unfortunate ... highly rated land holders'.[4]

4. Penny-Pinching Policies

By September 1859, 497 houses in the Town had been connected to the sewers and it was intended to connect a further hundred during the following two years. The Local Board could insist that any landlord, whose houses lay within a hundred feet of a sewer, should provide drains connecting to that sewer. The Town sewage, though filtered, was not deodorised or treated in any other way before being discharged into Saddlers Mill brook. There had long been complaints from residents living near the brook in Bury Street, Edmonton. These complaints were now taken up by the Edmonton Local Board of Health and an injunction was obtained to prevent further discharge into the stream. The Enfield Board was thereby forced to take some action, and it chose the least expensive means available to comply with the injunction. A contractor (Arthur Sawyer, the brother of the parish clerk) was employed to lay a stoneware main to carry the sewage in a straight line eastward to the corner of South Street. Thence it was taken by a fifteen-inch sewer, which also served the south side of South Street, and was discharged into the East London Waterworks cut near the railway station at Ponders End.

This cut had been constructed in 1853 in order to divert sewage which would have entered the River Lea above that Company's intake. It carried the Enfield sewage, some of it not even filtered, through the parishes of Edmonton and also Tottenham, where they had spent more than £30,000 over the previous nine years on an elaborate sewerage system. This Tottenham system however was not working and had not been in full use for some years. Nevertheless the Tottenham Board complained. Alfred Dickens, after examining the situation, came up with a most unwelcome proposal that the Enfield sewage should be properly treated at the Ponders End outfall. Tottenham Local Board applied for and obtained an order in Chancery to this end.

The Enfield Board at once petitioned the Secretary of State for a postponement. It pleaded that it would not be fulfilling its duty to the ratepayers if it was to spend the great sum required in adopting Mr Dickens's plan. It was urged, hopefully, that the sewage was already deodorised by the dye water from the crape works in South Street or, unconvincingly, that the responsibility for taking away the sewage in an inoffensive manner belonged to the East London Water Works Company. New works at Ponders End, it was stressed, could not be ready in less than three years and if the Secretary of State ordered that it must be built, Enfield Board would find it necessary to borrow £1,500. Thus the Board prevaricated until further pressure was applied by the River Lee Conservancy Act in 1868.

The ratepayers of Ponders End remained highly critical of the service rendered by their Board. Their views were expressed by John Tibbs in August 1863. As part of the special district, they were paying more than double the general rate, but in the village of Ponders End their only sewer was the one built to take the Town sewage into the East London Waterworks cut, and it was of little service to Ponders End. Conditions in parts of the village were awful. On a piece of land called the Alma there was a stagnant ditch close to the backs of a row of cottages and it received all the filth and sewage from the cottage privies. At the back of South Place there was another such ditch, (see map p96) and in many other places. Contagious diseases had been rife throughout the spring and summer. 'In the Town itself,' complained Mr Tibbs, 'the system of sewerage appeared to be everything that could be desired'. His contrast was not altogether just. The Board failed in its duties even in this more privileged area, as a writer in the *Observer* had pointed out (October 1862):

> 'People who go by the footpath which leads from Chase Side [ie Gentleman's Row] to the Church [that is by the present Chapel Street] must see a row of privies overhanging an open sewer. They may be sometimes sensible of an unpleasant odour. These privies are attached to the houses which make Loves Row and it is rumoured that the place has for some time been infested with fever, that many deaths have occurred, some of them from the terrible diphtheria, and that the infant school there has for these reasons been closed.'[5]

Nothing was done. A case of cholera occurred there in November 1866 but the state of the cottages was still not remedied. This was unwise since contagion is not restrained by any barrier of class and in 1879 typhoid fever spread from Loves Row to Gentleman's Row where there were three cases in Fortescue Lodge, two in Elm House and one in Fortescue Villas.[6]

The surveyor William Ironside (appointed 1856, retired 1870) considered the Enfield sewerage system to be 'very perfect indeed'. He was giving evidence in 1867 before a commission on the River Lea (P.P.xxxiii 1867). The sewers, he said (meaning the sewers serving the Town district only) emptied themselves into six settling tanks and from thence the sewage passed through a filter bed of stone and ballast. A hundred and fifty tons of solid matter were removed from the settling tanks every three months by manual labour and loaded into wagons. Farmers who took this sewage had to plough it in within two days (it was forbidden to use it on grassland) and they were paid to take it; the cost to the council was between £70 and £80 a year. Mr Ironside didn't think it did the farmers much good. The fluid which remained passed without further treatment down a stoneware glazed pipe and into the East London Waterworks cut. Along this, with the completely untreated sewage from all the other districts in Enfield, it made its way into the Lee Navigation below Tottenham Lock. The water there was black with filth and the smell in hot weather was appalling.

Mr Ironside also explained the system of refuse collection. 'Several people' he said, 'get a living by having an old pony and cart in which they collect the ashes from door to door and take them to the brickfields'. They sometimes had to pay the lower orders a penny or two for the rubbish. As for the road scrapings, he was glad to give them to anyone, though occasionally he was able to sell them to bricklayers. 'If all else fails', he said, 'we shoot them where we can'.

The water supply was carried in galvanised iron pipes, installed about 1856. William Ironside pointed out that the Board was unable to secure sufficient water in dry weather. It had been found necessary to put in several land springs about sixteen-feet deep to supplement supply. Everyone in Ponders End who wanted water had it, he claimed, and any landlord who lost a tenant would find that he had to instal a water supply in order to get anyone to take the house.

The River Lee Conservancy Act was passed in 1868 and created another crisis. Under its terms no sewage or other offensive matter was to be allowed to flow into the River Lea or into any of its tributaries. The Enfield Local Board was given thirteen months (subsequently increased to twenty) to find a new way to dispose of its sewage. It was a desperate situation but, to the members' joy and amazement, a means was presented to them which would cost them little. The Board entered into a contract with James Fortescue Harrison, who proposed to take the sewage and to use it to manure and irrigate his estate of 163 acres at Nightingale Hall in Edmonton. The proposal drew strong objections from his neighbours. He had recently purchased Nightingale Hall farm for £15,000; he now spent a further £2,000 on irrigation. He contracted to disinfect and clarify the water before it was discharged into the River Lea, and he even offered to indemnify the Local Board against any actions at law. All the Board had to do was to construct a network of sewers to bring the sewage to a point in South Street at the corner of Alma Road. It was necessary for this purpose to borrow £7,000.[7]

Mr Harrison's optimistic venture was a failure from the beginning. In March 1871 the farm was under two feet of water in places and the Board was forced to seek, from the River Lee Conservators, a further three months extension. This proved totally inadequate. The Conservators brought a summons against the Board in May 1872, and the Board brought a summons against Mr Harrison. The case against Harrison was heard before petty sessions and he was fined £10. The Enfield Chemical Manure Company, which was processing the sewage for Mr Harrison, gave notice that it would cease operations in September 1874. Harrison thereupon cut off the sewage to his farm and diverted it back into the East London Waterworks cut. He offered to sell the farm to the Board. The Board replied that it could see no justification for Mr Harrison's violation of his contract and again summoned him before the magistrates at petty sessions where a fine of £40 was imposed. The magistrates could scarcely be considered impartial, three of the four were members of the Enfield Local Board and James Meyer, the chairman of the bench of magistrates, was also chairman of the Local Board. Not surprisingly, both Mr Harrison's fines were quashed on appeal, with costs against James Meyer. Harrison accepted the sewage once more, but it remained untreated. At last, in July 1875, after the Edmonton Board had threatened to seek an injunction to prevent further nuisance in their district, the Enfield Board agreed to arbitration. The arbitrators declared that the contract with Harrison was valid, nevertheless they terminated it. The Board was given permission to continue to use the site for twelve months longer. The problem remained however of how to deal with one million gallons of sewage a day without polluting the River Lea and without creating a nuisance in Lower Edmonton, all which had to be accomplished at a cost which would not offend the Enfield ratepayers. The surveyor was sent to Hertford and to Leamington in the hope that he would find a solution there.[8]

The state of some of the farm labourers' cottages in the rural areas of the parish remained as bad as ever. In January 1867 the surveyor (W. Ironside) following up complaints about an abominable stench at Brigadier Hill, called to inspect Mrs Sanders's dwelling, where she kept nineteen pigs. He found the trouble already alleviated through the good offices of Mr Cracknell, a farmer in Baker Street, who had been called in to remove the manure, but Mrs Sanders fiercely denied the surveyor access to her house (Surveyor's Report). Smallpox broke out in February 1868 in Evans Yard, a court of dilapidated cottages 'unfit for human habitation' off Baker Street, owned by Ebenezer Gibbons. Mr Edelston, in January 1871, called the attention of the Board to the condition of Barn Cottages near his home at Bulls Cross. During the summer months the cottagers had been without water, and there was no proper drainage from the houses. Scarlet fever and smallpox had been raging there, in one house two children had died and the father and four children lay ill. The Guardians had not provided relief in time and had it not been for local families the poor cottagers would have died of starvation. The clerk was instructed to communicate with Walter Scott, the agent for the owner. Ebenezer Gibbons's cottages in Baxters Yard (in Baker Street opposite the end of what is now Tenniswood Road) had been condemned by the surveyor who described them as 'deficient in almost every requisite which should constitute a home.... The walls are giving way and the roofs are in a dangerous state', they are 'so full of drafts as to generate any amount of rheumatism... unfit for human habitation... as such', continued the surveyor 'I condemn the lot'. Ebenezer felt that the condition of his buildings could not possibly warrant such drastic action. He appealed and was given time to repair them to the satisfaction of the surveyor. The surveyor also complained (September 1871) about the water supply to Mrs Green's four cottages at Charles Buildings (on the west side of Hertford Road north of Carterhatch Lane). The two pumps there were within a few feet of the privies, the water was coloured with and smelt of sewage, yet there was a sewer available within a hundred feet. Complaints by the surveyor did not automatically result in a remedy. Situations were often complained of more than once and in similar terms, thus a remedy was sought in December 1871 for the poor state of the water in Old Road, which had been the subject of a complaint in 1857. An estimate was accepted (£6 15s) for a well to be made opposite the White Lion, sixteen feet deep and four feet in diameter (Surveyor's Reports). Occasionally buildings were closed down, like the cottage in Baker Street which had formerly been the Fox beerhouse. It was used in July 1870 as a public lodging house but it was in so dilapidated and dangerous a condition that an order was affixed to the premises declaring it to be unfit for human habitation. Plans for new houses on the site had been submitted by the following March.[9] It seems always to have been premises which had reached the last stages of decay that were used as public lodging houses. One had been condemned at Mill Corner near Hadley in 1866, described as 'in a dilapidated and foul condition'; it had comprised five cottages, owned by Mr North and kept by Mr Hacket (Surveyor's Report 3 August 1866). H.T. Lewis, recently appointed surveyor, also complained (September 1870) of the state of cottages in Grove Road, Enfield Wash, where 'solid filth encumbered the surface and liquid refuse saturated the subsoil'. The air in many of these cottages, he said, 'was strongly contaminated by the effluvia arising from the privies'. The cottages had no water supply for all the local wells had run dry; out of eighteen pumps in the area the surveyor couldn't get a bucket of water. The owner of the property was instructed to have the wells made deeper. A sewer had been laid to Enfield Highway by this time but it was found to be 'choked with ashes and other refuse'.

There was a further outbreak of smallpox at Whitewebbs at the beginning of the year 1871. The Edmonton Union made a strong recommendation to the Enfield Local Board of Health that a carriage should be purchased for use as an ambulance by those suffering from infectious diseases, and in consequence a brougham was secured for £16 from Mr Logsden the coachbuilder in the Town. Alma Road suffered an outbreak of smallpox in July 1872. Captain D.R. Clarke, the managing director of the Jute works, fearful that the epidemic might spread to his factory, demanded the removal of every case to hospital and offered £5 towards disinfecting the houses, but the Board had no power to enforce removal, nor any hospital to which, by right, it could remove the patients. The Guardians also urged that smallpox patients be isolated; they attributed the spread of the disease to the overcrowded state of many dwellings in the Alma Road area, also to the breakdown of the sewerage system. The Local Board had at that time no regular medical officer. Medical gentlemen were reluctant to undertake the duty, it being occasional and unsalaried, and the authority, for this reason, had been unable to take legal proceedings to abate the overcrowding.[10]

Dr Agar finally took on the duties of medical officer in February 1876 without a fixed salary, but receiving a fee for each occasion when his services were called upon. The Local Government Board therefore could not regard his appointment as conformable with the terms of the Public Health Act 1875 which required such officers to be paid a fixed salary. The Local Government Board also objected because Dr Agar was already the district medical officer for the Edmonton Union. The new MOH nevertheless took on the duties on the terms laid down by the Local Board and immediately drew the attention of the Board to sixty cases of fever which had occurred at Ponders End. Thirty-two were sick at that time and the number was growing daily. He had visited many of the houses in Alma Road and South Street where cases had occurred. He found them in a filthy state, the water-closets poorly supplied with water, some without any water at all. Most of the rooms were overcrowded at night, vegetable refuse had been thrown out and had accumulated in heaps near the back doors. The inspector of nuisances ordered the heaps to be removed and the houses to be lime-washed and cleaned with copious use of disinfectants.[11]

The Local Government Board again threw the cat among the pigeons in February 1877 by requiring to know what facilities the Local Board had available for the isolation of patients suffering from contagious diseases. The Board of

High Street Ponders End.

94.   *Dr Agar's house and surgery in the High Street. He became medical officer to the Local Board of Health in 1876 but was paid no fixed salary, receiving a fee whenever his services were called for.*

course had none and the Guardians made it plain that the isolation wards at the workhouse infirmary were for pauper patients only. The prevalence of fevers continued to concern the parish. October 1879 saw an outbreak of typhoid at Ponders End. Rosa Bradford with her two children, and Fanny Fraser, had been taken to the workhouse infirmary, the Guardians protested. Within a few weeks a hundred cases had occurred, three quarters of them in Ponders End, and five had died. Dr Agar blamed overcrowding, the water supply, the drainage and 'the number of poor and dirty people in the place'. The epidemic had died out by November. The Local Board in June 1881 drew attention to the great risk of contagion incurred by those who carried coffins at funerals. It was proposed that steps be taken to induce undertakers to provide hand-biers for the removal of the dead.[12]

The supply of water was proving as difficult and as expensive as the disposal of sewage. No housing estates had been built in Enfield before the establishment of the Local Board of Health, but soon afterwards development was begun on the estate known as Enfield New Town (the area including Sydney, Raleigh, Essex, Cecil and London Roads). Sewerage and iron water pipes were laid on the estate in 1862 and fire hydrants were set up, all of which cost the Board £400. The demand for mains water increased. Four hundred houses were being supplied with 58,000 gallons a day in June 1857; by July 1860 793 houses were supplied with 110,000 gallons a day. This was more than the system could bear, for although the engines could theoretically move 160,000 gallons a day if worked for twenty-four hours, the well was never designed to bear more than ten to sixteen hours draught. The output had fallen to only 84,000 gallons a day by 1865.

Mr Beardmore, an engineer, was called in for an opinion. He found that the engine was faced with two incompatible tasks. On the one hand, to feed the high level reservoir at Holtwhites Hill which supplied the houses in the Town district, the pumps had to be worked at a pressure high enough to lift the water 170 feet while, at the same time, the system supplied the low-lying area of Ponders End and there the high pressure caused the mains to leak. The wastage was often so bad that the reservoir at Holtwhites Hill would be empty in the mornings and consequently there would be no water in the Town quarter. The engineer recommended a new engine and pumps capable of supplying 1,500 houses with 150 gallons a day each, or 240,000 gallons in a twelve-hour day. Because two-thirds of the water would have to be lifted 170 feet, and one-third only sixty feet, he advocated that the two services should be separated and a second reservoir should be built in Nags Head Lane (Southbury Road) to hold 65,000 gallons. 'Owing to the new lines of railway to be commenced immediately in your area', Mr Beardmore went on, 'building is likely to increase greatly and, with the experience of last year (1865) it is unlikely that there will be sufficient water'. He therefore recommended sinking a deep well into the chalk 185 yards east of the turnpike road with pipes at a low level to take the water 900 yards to the pumps. The inspector from the Privy Council agreed that the work was essential and recommended sanction to borrow £5,000. Costs rose by £2,400 while the work was in progress, largely because one landowner refused to allow the pipes across his land, but also because large building operations begun in the area forced the Local Board to provide sewerage to avoid pollution of the water supply. Moreover it was found necessary to install a yet more powerful engine.[13]

The efforts of the Local Board still met with scant approval in Ponders End. Josiah Pascoe wrote in January 1868 complaining that although the Board had recently borrowed £7,000 to improve the water supply, the improvement at Enfield had decreased the supply at Ponders End. He now demanded to know whether the Board could compel the people of Ponders End to contribute to the repayment of the loan. He went on to complain about the fire hydrants. Ponders End now had a volunteer fire brigade but it was unable to exercise because the hydrants were rusted, having never been moved in thirteen years. Meanwhile the Local Board of Health was facing yet another problem, an extension of the water supply to the Highway, Green Street, Enfield Wash and Ordnance Road; £8,000 was borrowed in 1871 to meet the costs.[14]

The churchyard at St Andrew's was becoming a hazard to the health of the parish by the middle of the century. The original acre of ground lay crowded with the dead of a hundred generations. What had been scarcely adequate for a large village was now hopelessly inadequate in the semi-urbanised Enfield of the mid-nineteenth century. The burial ground had been extended in 1846 when one acre had been added, but burials in the ensuing years averaged well over a hundred a year and the danger to health recurred by the mid-1850s. The schoolmaster, in 1857, complained that there existed 'two public schools, numerously attended, on the edge of the overcrowded graveyard. The earth is completely saturated, no grave can be opened without disturbing human remains', he went on, 'the water in the Grammar School well is impure and not fit for the boys to drink'. The new ground, which had come into use twelve years earlier, had not solved the problem for, 'so long as the old yard remains unclosed, many insist on interring their dead in or near family graves'. There were 257 family graves and 178 family vaults in the old yard. Burials were still occurring inside the church, five over the previous twenty years. It was decided to discontinue burials in the old part of the churchyard from 1857, save under the most rigorous conditions, and burials inside the church were henceforth prohibited. The little burial ground attached to the old Chase Side Chapel was also closed; it had been opened in 1780. There had been only eleven burials there in the previous seven years, but the ground was very full.

A burial board was set up in October 1870 and a site was sought for a cemetery. Parish land at Lavender Hill was proposed, for land there was considered less valuable for building than other parish land. It was part of the Hundred Acres and the leases, granted in 1777, would expire in 1876. Negotiations were undertaken with lessees willing to accept compensation for the early release of twelve acres. The cemetery was opened in July 1872; it had cost £9,000, and a further three acres were added in July 1897. Burials in the churchyard were finally discontinued, except for existing vaults and walled graves, in February 1874.

Burial of the dead from eastern Enfield at Lavender Hill was expensive and inconvenient. The population in the east was by this time at least as large as that in the rest of the parish; the people were mostly artisans and agricultural labourers. A churchyard of three-quarters of an acre had been opened at St James in 1834. Deaths in this part of the parish, around 1860, averaged eighty-four a year from a population of 5,500. An acre was added to the churchyard at the end of the year 1861. The need for a cemetery at the Highway became more and more obvious; there were 160 interments there in the year 1879 and the population had risen to 8,000. Two more acres were consecrated for burial near the churchyard in 1880 and a further sixteen acres were added in 1901, by which time the population of eastern Enfield had risen to 21,000.[15]

The idea of a cottage hospital to be built by voluntary subscriptions had been floated by November 1873. It was intended to provide accommodation for six patients, three men and three women. Local medical men would have the option of treating their patients there. Patients would be admitted on presenting a letter from a subscriber, countersigned by a doctor, they would pay 2s 6d to 10s 6d a week depending on their means. Domestic servants could be admitted on payment of 7s 6d to 10s 6d guaranteed by their employers.[16]

The opening of the hospital in August 1875 was marred by the worst storm in Enfield since 20 July 1859. Lord George Hamilton, the member for Middlesex, was to have performed the opening ceremony but before his train arrived there was thunder and lightning and the rain came down in torrents, the roads were under sheets of water, no one could venture out of doors between one-thirty and three o'clock. The drains were unable to cope. A torrent of water flowed down Windmill Hill into Chase Side. Parsonage Lane, Gordon Road and Lancaster Road were converted into rivers two to four feet deep. The water poured into the New River by the Crown and Horseshoes like a cataract. No one could approach the Cottage Hospital and the opening was postponed until 12 August. The building had cost £1,632, the furniture £215. The committee entered into an arrangement with Dr Laseron who sent two sisters from the teaching hospital of the Evangelical Deaconesses Institution in Tottenham (later the Prince of Wales Hospital) initially for six months, though the arrangement appears to have become permanent. Doctors Agar, Mugliston and Ridge acted as honorary medical officers.[17]

The Queen's jubilee was celebrated by the opening of a new Jubilee ward, with three beds, in 1887. New bedrooms were added in 1892. Two years later a

95.   The Enfield Cottage Hospital was opened in August 1875 at Chase Side. The building had cost £1,632, the furniture £215

96.   The Queen's jubilee 1887 was celebrated in Enfield by the addition of a new wing to the Cottage Hospital. The former Primitive Methodist chapel was later incorporated as an annexe.

97.   Damage resulting from a fire in Silver Street opposite the Vicarage in June 1868. Seven cottages were destroyed, only two of which were insured.

workshop adjoining, formerly a Primitive Methodist chapel, was purchased and in 1898 the wards were enlarged to hold six beds each. A children's ward was opened in July 1906, paid for by a public subscription initiated by the Enfield Town Co-operative Society.

Antiseptic surgery, pioneered by Lister, did not become general until 1870. Enfield Cottage Hospital had to wait until 1895 for the gift of an operating table suitable for modern antiseptic treatment. The first use of X-ray locally occurred in January 1899 when Dr Distin brought a patient from the Cottage Hospital who had run a small piece of needle into her hand, to the studio of Milton Meyers in the Town. The photograph successfully located the needle, shown endwise, and it was removed.[18]

As the number of houses increased it became imperative that means should be improved to fight any outbreak of fire. Responsibility for the Enfield fire service, with the keys to the engine house, had been transferred from the vestry to the Local Board of Health in June 1856, because the churchwardens had no funds to maintain the fire engine. The by-laws of 1865 set out the duties of the fire engine keeper in some detail. The engine was to be taken out for practice at least once every three months. Regular volunteer firemen should be selected to man the engine in preference to others who turned up on the off-chance when there was a fire. The volunteer was entitled to 5s gratuity if he got to the fire within half an hour of the arrival of the engine. It was the duty of the keeper to despatch a messenger to the waterworks in Alma Road without delay, to ensure a plentiful supply of water. From 1865 no charge was to be made for the use of the engine within the parish. Fire fighting certainly needed to be well organised and efficient. Lincoln House, an ancient mansion at Ponders End, the residence of T. Spreckley, had been gutted by fire in March 1864 and its valuable contents had been destroyed. This gave rise, in December 1867, to a letter from several persons at Ponders End who aimed to set up a volunteer fire brigade for the protection of their own and neighbours' property.

Enfield had suffered a most alarming conflagration in Silver Street in June 1868, within a hundred yards of the engine house in the churchyard. It broke out at a quarter past eight at the back of premises owned by Mr Heath, a hay and straw dealer opposite the Vicarage. It was a quiet summer evening and many people were hurrying by to a concert at the Riding House. Within a few minutes the backs of a whole row of cottages were enveloped in flames. The parish engine was brought out and, though there was an ample supply of water from stand-pipes and from the New River, the operation dissolved into confusion as one person directed the water to the right and another directed it to the left. Seven houses were destroyed, only two of which were insured. The Enfield Philanthropic Institution did its best to organise relief, collecting £125.[19]

This lack of adequate organisation was emphasised by a letter to the Local Board in August 1870 wherein the writer pointed out that all four wheels of the fire engine were so wormeaten and decayed that it was not safe to take it out of the engine house. He also complained that the hose was constantly being used to flush drains and for other purposes, so that the engine was scarcely ever found complete in case of a fire. When a conflagration occurred at the Jute Factory in July 1871, one of the poles broke because it was wormeaten. Mr Meyer subsequently remedied the situation by seeking out a carriage pole from his stables.[20]

The Local Board of Health in 1870 consisted of five gentlemen; James Meyer of Forty Hall, Henry C. Bowles of Myddelton House, R.T. Ingersoll of Enfield Highway, H. Parry of the Elms, Ponders End, and Rear Admiral L.S. Tindall of Chase Lodge. There were two market gardeners, John and William Mitchell; Morton P. Eden was the superintendent at the Small Arms Factory, Charles Smith was a wine merchant in Baker Street, Frederick Bugbird a contractor in London Road, Ellis Hall a wheelwright from the Highway and William Nutter Barker was the proprietor of the Palace School. Six members were from the western side of the parish and six from the eastern. The Board met once a fortnight. It was elected by the ratepayers only; moreover plural voting was allowed in proportion to assessed property values. The Assessed Rates Act 1869 had extended local franchise to tenants of properties of a lower rateable value, thus it gave the vote in local elections to many skilled workmen like those employed at the Small Arms Factory.[21]

The Victorians preferred local to central government, for it was believed that local expenditure was more easily controlled by those who paid. Above all they aimed to avoid the appointment of an expensive bureaucracy. Grants in aid from central government remained small. Nevertheless over the first twenty-five years of the existence of the Enfield Local Board a small professional staff had been assembled. The bylaws of 1865 (re-issued 1875) laid down their duties. The surveyor was to examine the plans and sections for proposed new buildings to ensure that they were conformable with statutes and bylaws. The office of road surveyor was combined with that of inspector of nuisances whose duty it was to keep a register of slaughterhouses and inspect all shops where meat, poultry and fish were sold. As road surveyor he had to report obstructions and nuisances on the highway. The collectors must collect the rates and keep accounts. The policy of the Board aimed not so much at achieving model local government as at getting by on the lowest possible rates.[22]

5. Progress and the Ratepayers

The long sequence of penny-pinching policies on such matters of vital importance as sewerage, water supply and fire-fighting, was transformed for a short time by the advent to the Board in 1879 of Sir Roland MacDonald Stephenson of Hill Lodge, Clay Hill. He had been knighted in 1856. His reputation, he having carried out some of the largest engineering undertakings in the world, was of sufficient weight to persuade members to do what he considered necessary, even if it might cost money. He insisted that Lewis the surveyor should be replaced. It was essential, he stressed, that the Board should employ a surveyor with professional knowledge. Advertisements for the post were to be placed in the *Builder* and in other technical journals. A foreman too was required, experienced in pipe-laying and brickwork. To each of Sir Roland's proposals the Board acquiesced without demur. The advertisements brought thirty applications for the post of foreman. A hundred sought the office of surveyor and a Mr Kitteringham was appointed. Within days he had provided a provisional estimate for dealing with the problems of sewage disposal and water supply at a cost of £4,000. All the work which had previously been done in Enfield he declared to be below standard and requiring overhaul. The Board made no complaint even when Kitteringham increased his estimate to £4,520. Certainly the appointment of a professional surveyor was not before time, for house building was accelerating and in his first year plans for over three

98.   *Sir Rowland M. Stephenson, an eminent engineer who became a member of the Local Board in 1879. He inspired progressive thinking, at least for a few years, among the formerly conservative members of the Board.*

99. Hill Lodge, the home of Sir Roland Macdonald Stephenson, on the south side of Clay Hill near the Fallow Buck. Demolished in the early nineteen-sixties.

hundred new dwellings were submitted for his approval.[23] Even the conservative *Observer* was won over for reform.

> 'No one acquainted with the parish', declared the editor (3 July 1880) 'can fail to see that great change is rapidly taking place in its character. The value of land and house property has enormously increased and building operations are carried on in all directions'.

Overcome with very new-found enthusiasm, the newspaper reversed its accustomed role and itself proposed that money should be spent on improvements. It praised the work done in Mandeville, Raynton, Totteridge and Putney Roads, which had been remade, kerbed and channelled. They were now, it proclaimed, the best in the parish. There was a marked improvement in the sixty miles of roads within the district. The Board applied to borrow £1,500 to complete the paving and kerbing in the Town, Baker Street, Silver Street, Church Street, Windmill Hill and South Street. The surveyor was constantly on guard against jerry building and faulty sewers.[24]

The cost of local government was beginning an apparently infinite upward spiral. Spending for the year 1879/80 displayed a new liberality likely to arouse hostility among certain ratepayers. Despite its recently expressed enthusiasm, a certain anxiety may be detected in the *Enfield Observer* that the new professionalism could lead to higher rates. Still, the editor felt able to reassure his readers; 'so long as Enfield Board is composed of a large majority... of the largest owners of property in the parish, there is a guarantee that rates will not unnecessarily increase'. Then, as though to quiet his own remaining doubts, he added, 'The aggregate assessment of the twelve gentlemen is little under £6,000'. The following few months were to demonstrate that this was no guarantee against rate increases.[25]

View showing road going from Enfield

100.   Silver Street was paved and kerbed in 1880. On the right stood a fine mansion called Silverton (the present site of the Civic Centre). It had formerly been the home of John Sherwen, surgeon, poet and literary critic (see vol 1). On the other side of the road is Redlingtons. Beyond that lay the premises of William Binstead corn merchant while in the distance one can just see Pepper's stables.

Dr Parsons's report of 1881 (Dr Parsons was an inspector for the Local Government Board) usefully provides an overall view of the parish at this time. The population stood at 19,119, there were 3,573 inhabited houses, an increase of 680 in ten years, while 222 more were in course of erection. In the western part of the parish, formerly the Chase, dwellings were scattered, there was no public water supply and no means for the disposal of excrement but cesspits. The central part of the parish comprised the Town and the two parallel streets, Chase Side and Baker Street, also the outlying hamlets of Brigadier Hill, Clay Hill and Forty Hill. Many inhabitants in the area of the Town belonged to the professional, commercial and artisan classes, a large proportion being employed in London. The houses were not built in continuous rows but were distributed irregularly, alone or in groups of three or four, usually with a garden attached. A number of new estates had been laid out for building. Parts of the winding course of the New River had been piped and straightened, but the bypassed loop through the centre of Enfield had been retained by the Company for use as a storage reservoir. The public water supply was provided by the Local Board from a high level reservoir at Holtwhites Hill, the water being pumped from a well 360 feet deep at Alma Road. Supply in this central area was turned on for a period of four hours each day, staggered by districts. Cisterns were used for storage in the larger houses but in the smaller, buckets were used. A few of the houses got their water from wells, while those who lived close enough obtained a supply by dipping in the New River. Most dwellings had water closets, though many were insufficiently supplied with water and there were still a few cesspits. Sewers had been laid throughout central Enfield except in the outlying

NEW RIVER - ENFIELD LOOP

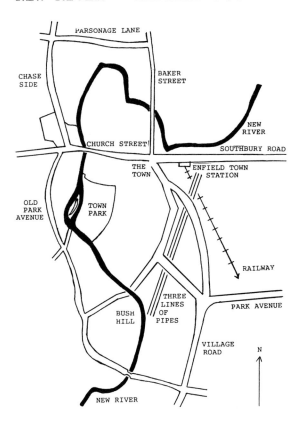

hamlets. The sewage was collected into a trunk sewer and delivered by gravitation to the Board's sewage farm at Cuckoo Hall in Edmonton.

A belt of market gardens about a mile wide separated the Town from eastern Enfield, which was low-lying, some of the streets there being liable to flooding. The population lived mostly near the main road, and the people were almost wholly of the working class. There were four factories employing labour in the area. Recent years had seen a good deal of building, including many small dwellings in continuous rows with back space. Sub-letting of one or more rooms was general, and overcrowding commonplace, (the Registrar General defined overcrowding as more than two persons to a room). Most of the houses had water closets. Sewage was drained into a tank at Cuckoo Hall Farm and at certain hours of the day it was pumped up and distributed over the land. Water from the artesian well was pumped to a reservoir in Southbury Road and was turned on from 6am to 6pm. Most of the houses in Ponders End were connected to the supply, but further north, in the Highway and at Enfield Wash, few made use of the Board's water and although the mains were laid in these areas, shallow wells with pumps were the normal source of supply.[26]

101.   The New River loop through Enfield was bypassed before 1881, but it was retained by the Company as a storage reservoir.

102.   The Crown and Horseshoes standing on the New River and looking much as it did at the time of the notorious Danby murder. (See Volume 1)

It will thus be seen that Enfield, like Tottenham and Edmonton the neighbouring Middlesex parishes to the south, by 1881 had a largely working-class population in the east and a largely middle-class community in the west, where the people were better educated and more articulate. The two communities, in all three parishes, inevitably developed conflicting interests, for the more prosperous west had to pay most of the rates. The seats of administration in both Tottenham and Edmonton lay in the east. Therefore the west, the area of Southgate in Edmonton and Wood Green in Tottenham, received less in the way of services and paid more in the form of rates. This led, in the 1880s, to the division of both these districts and new local boards of health were established in Southgate and in Wood Green. The administration in Enfield was in the Town and in that area, where they paid the most rates, the Local Board provided its best services. That is undoubtedly why no division occurred in Enfield, despite the fact that it was much larger in area than either of its neighbours.

The death rate in Enfield was below the average for England and Wales and approached that of a standard rural district. It stood in 1881 at fourteen per thousand per annum (compared with 27.2 in Liverpool, 26.6 in Glasgow or 20.4 in London). Though urban in name, Enfield remained to some degree rural; there was, in 1871, more than three-quarters of an acre to each inhabitant. Even death rates from epidemics were below the average for England and Wales, except for scarlet fever, diphtheria, diarrhoea and typhoid. There had been 260 cases of typhoid within the five years up to 1881, including forty-eight deaths, of which two-thirds occurred in the eastern side of the parish. Non-fatal cases were also more frequent there. Many of the stricken houses had sewers connected direct to the house without traps, an arrangement which allowed the gases from the sewage to seep into the house. Where houses were not connected, the likely cause of contagion was water from shallow wells, often sited near cesspits. Foul privies and filthy ditches were also blamed. Fever occurred in Alma Road in every year from 1875 to 1881. Another black spot was Meeting House Yard off Baker Street where seven old cottages of lath and plaster were served by two filthy water closets used in common; the standpipe from which the cottagers took their water was at a lower level than the closets. Dr Parsons described the water from a pump well at Gilbert Terrace (on the west side of Hertford Road, north of Carterhatch Lane) as 'black and stinking', yet those who lived there drank it until their children were taken ill of enteric fever (typhoid) in 1880. The surveyor had complained about this same pump ten years earlier, describing it then as impregnated with sewage, yet even at that time (June 1871) the Local Board's sewer had been laid within eighteen feet of the cottages (Surveyor's Report). At Eastfield Road, fever had recently occurred at numbers 27, 28, 29 and 30, caused by a shallow well only six feet from a cesspit. The Guardians had objected in 1879 when three cases of typhus had been sent to the workhouse infirmary. It was pointed out that the Guardians made provision only for paupers; the isolation of those suffering from infectious diseases among the rest of the population was the responsibility of the local boards.[27]

The system of sewerage had been extended to all populous parts of the parish, yet there were many houses not connected. The Board had borrowed £63,645 for permanent works up to March 1879 and since then (ie up to 1881) a further £1,200 for water supply, and £6,320 for sewerage. The medical officer of health had been appointed with no definite term of office and with no fixed salary; he

103. *Fever constantly recurred in Meeting House Yard off Baker Street where seven old cottages of lath and plaster were served by two filthy water closets used in common. It was found that the standpipe from which the cottagers took their water was at a lower level than the closets.*

was merely paid a fee when his services were required by the authority. He presented no annual report and received no return of deaths. There was no systematic inspection of nuisances and little time was allowed for this necessary work, because the official responsible had his hands full with overseeing the maintenance of the sixty miles of roads within the parish. The by-laws merely required that complaints against nuisance should be delivered to the surveyor Mr Kitteringham. Dr Parsons described him as 'an able officer', and 'in the habit of noting any sanitary defects', but his duties were heavy and incorporated building inspection, waterworks, water courses, sewers and drains. He also, said the inspector, had to cope with the consequences of the incompetence of his predecessor. There had been at least thirteen cases of typhoid fever in Gordon Road between December 1877 and March 1879, although the houses had then been erected only three years. They were built to a pattern still familiar in this area, with two living rooms and a scullery on the ground floor, and a water closet adjoining the scullery but with access from the backyard. There were normally three bedrooms, the back bedroom projecting over the scullery and water closet. The cistern, which supplied water both for flushing and for drinking, was situated below the floor of the back bedroom and the floorboards above it were left loose for ease of access. The cistern therefore was very likely to become contaminated by sweeping or washing the floor above, as linoleum was by no means universal. Another cause of complaint in Gordon Road was the foul pond at the junction with Chase Side.

The Local Board did not undertake to empty cesspools, but it had a covered wagon which could be borrowed for this job. A staff of workmen were employed to carry out sanitary work as required. There was no public arrangement for the removal of refuse, but the brickmakers now sent round their carts, every so often, to collect it, occasionally they even paid for it. The rubbish had to be heaped up in back yards until collected for there were no dustbins (or plastic bags) and it usually had to be taken out through the house. Overcrowding was widespread. The district had no isolation hospital. Many cases of enteric fever were taken into the Cottage Hospital. There were wards for infectious diseases in the workhouse infirmary at Silver Street Edmonton, but only paupers were supposed to be admitted. Carbolic powder and Condy's fluid were furnished to houses where fever had occurred but the rooms were not fumigated or lime-washed and there was no apparatus for disinfecting bedding and clothes by heat; it all had to be destroyed.[28]

The rate declared in April 1881 to meet the requirements of the Local Board of Health was 4s 6d in the pound. To this would have to be added water rate and poor rate, so that the total was likely to be 7s or 8s. Only nineteen years before, the Local Board of Health rate had been 1s $1^{1}/_{2}$d. There was resentment among those who were required to pay. A meeting was called at the new coffee tavern opposite the Vicarage in Silver Street. Those who attended were numerous and much aggrieved, their intention being the foundation of a ratepayers' association. Mr Fowell was voted into the chair and after a short address he called upon Ebenezer Gibbons. Mr Gibbons was not part of the deferential electorate. The difficulties, he told the ratepayers, were caused by the irresponsible borrowing of the Board. It was time they elected different men ... not gentlemen, but men who knew what it was to earn a sovereign for themselves ... men of the middle classes ... men who worked for their own money. Was it necessary to pave Windmill Hill to make a clean path for the *gentlemen* who had to go to the Great

Northern Railway station? Salaries of the Board's servants last year had amounted to £1,330 (cries of 'Shame'). Why were the Board's main roads so bad that the County refused to make a grant towards the cost of maintenance?[29]

Sir Roland MacDonald Stephenson, about to leave the parish for a few months before Christmas 1881, was worried by what he termed the ill-considered and vociferous arguments of the newly formed Enfield Ratepayers' Association. In an open letter to James Meyer, printed in the *Observer* (17 December 1881) he pleaded that the affairs of the Enfield Board were in a transitional state, moving out of the old rut in which it had floundered for years and now upon the high road to improvement. He was an advocate of economy consistent with efficiency, but efficiency must come first, retrenchment afterwards. Large expenditure would be required for some time to come, though it would not remain at the present high level. So far from deprecating the newly formed Ratepayers' Association, he claimed that he welcomed it as a valuable auxiliary in all the Board's undertakings. If he spoke with sincerity, he had yet to apprehend the wealth of confidence and the weight of ignorance that certain members of that organisation would be able to bring to bear upon the problems facing local government.[30]

He attempted to justify to members of the new Association, in simple, logical terms, the necessity for the high rate. There had been a recent and fundamental change of policy. It had been impossible to meet the requirements of the Public Health Act and the Lee Conservancy Act with a staff of officers whose technical knowledge had been utterly inadequate. He explained the objectives which the Board had set for itself; hygienic sewage disposal for the whole parish, pure water supplied to every house and cottage, gas at a reasonable price, and good roads and pavements. It would require another two or three years effectually to carry out this policy of improvement. The rateable value of the parish was only £65,000 and he described how the 4s 6d rate was arrived at;

	£	Rate in Pound
Loans, repayment of principal and interest	4,444	1s 7d
Highways (fifty-seven miles) and main roads (three and a half miles)	3,775	1s 2$^1/_2$d
Sewage disposal, renewal and repair of water mains	900	3$^1/_2$d
Gas (street lighting)	1,000	4d
Administration and salaries	1,200	4$^1/_2$d
Poundage (£400), occupant's rate allowance to owners (£900)	1,300	5d
Miscellaneous	900	3$^1/_2$d
	£13,519	4s 6d

Local Board elections were held in April 1882 and, although the retiring members clearly indicated that they were willing to stand again, the Ratepayers' Association persisted in nominating four candidates to contest the four seats which fell vacant. It proved to be a close fought election with honours evenly divided. Two long-standing members were defeated, J.W. Ford JP and Mr W. Nutter Barker, but Sir R.M. Stephenson retained his seat. Elected for the Ratepayers were Ebenezer Gibbons and Mr Fowell. James Meyer was again appointed chairman. The Board of twelve members met fortnightly to conduct

104. The Barracks, Pipers Yard, Clay Hill where the occupants had no water but the muddy pools at the bottom of the old course of the New River behind their houses. St Johns Terrace now occupies the site.

business.[31]

The Enfield Board had implemented the two principal recommendations of Dr Parsons's report; the appointment of a full-time inspector of nuisances and of a salaried medical officer of health. To the making of this latter appointment at an adequate salary it was perhaps persuaded by the offer of the Local Government Board to contribute half the cost out of a government grant. The choice for this last important office was a fortunate one, for it fell upon Dr J.J. Ridge, an ardent advocate of temperance and sanitation. Summonses followed the doctor's inspections. He condemned houses in Alma Road, in Meeting House Yard off Baker Street, and at the Barracks in Pipers Yard, Clay Hill where there was no water supply of any kind. Dr Ridge complained that the occupants there had to use the muddy, stagnant water from the old course of the New River behind the houses. Letchworth, the clerk, assured him that as soon as the mains were laid the Board would be able to force the landlord to connect, but Dr Ridge was not satisfied. 'The houses are unfit', he said 'and the landlord ought not to take the rent'. Mr Fowell, the newly elected representative of the Ratepayers, was outraged. 'It is a cruel thing for a medical officer to make such a remark...' he declared, 'should not the landlord provide a servant to wait on them as well?' Discussion was to be maintained at this elevated level whenever Mr Fowell was present at meetings of the Board. Complaints about these same premises, ten years earlier, by the then newly appointed surveyor H.T. Lewis, showed them to be, even then, in a poor condition. There was insufficient privy accommodation for the eleven families and in the principal building, the Barracks, the timber and bricks were so decayed that the walls were dangerous and the roof was giving way. Dr Ridge also reported houses in Andersons Yard off Baker Street which were totally without a water supply. Whatever water the occupants had was either doled out by the landlord or begged from neighbours. The difficulties facing the medical officer can be seen from the fact that he again had to inspect these same cottages in Andersons Yard after a case of diphtheria occurred there in 1889. In consequence of his earlier report most of the dwellings had been repaired, papered and whitewashed, but the first three houses were still unfit. In the four closets in the yard the cisterns were out of order and the smell was very bad; 'the houses', said the doctor, 'are more fit for pigs than human beings.'[32]

Water was supplied by May 1882 to 1,460 dwellings out of a total of 3,573, and plans had been approved to supply a further 500. The daily supply, 300,000 gallons, should have allowed for two hundred gallons to each house, but there was considerable wastage. The new houses near the Ridgeway, as also parts of the Old Park estate, lay so high that the pressure in the system was not sufficient to carry the water up to them; in order to raise this pressure Sir Roland Stephenson proposed to erect a water-tower, fifty feet high, with a small engine and pump, by the side of the reservoir at Holtwhites Hill. He also planned a new borehole next to the well in Alma Road where a more powerful engine and pump would be installed and a twelve-inch main laid to the reservoir. Sir Roland's plan to modernise the system faced strong opposition from the Ratepayers' Association. He pointed out in a letter that the present waterworks were not adequate to meet a growing demand. An increase of 2d or 3d on the rate would be necessary to pay for the proposed improvements. He feared however that the Ratepayers' Association would oppose a new loan to meet the expenditure. It was difficult, he complained, when you had unreasoning people to work for. He had considered seriously the idea that the waterworks should be sold to private enterprise, and this might well have solved some of the Board's difficulties, but Meyer was opposed, as was the Local Government Board, as well as the Ratepayers' Association.[33]

William Kitteringham outlined the difficulties in a report. Apart from the new pumping main, mains had to be laid to the new estates being developed. These lay at great distances one from another, and it would involve 30,000 yards of service mains, an extension equal to the existing service. The new estates would probably not be completed for about ten years, thus no early return, in the way of rates, could be expected on the outlay. Particularly costly were likely to be the new mains required along Lancaster Road and Browning Road for the Woodlands estate, and the extension along Brigadier Hill for the Cedars estate. Houses near the cemetery and those occupied on the Bridgen Hall estate still had no water supply.[34] Difficulties and uncertainties troubled the minds of those who endeavoured to plan for the future, but no such doubt ever restrained Ebenezer Marshall the secretary of the Enfield Ratepayers' Association. Marshall had an answer to every difficulty, an immediate and inexpensive solution to every technical problem. Fowell, his subaltern, was less inventive and mostly existed to acclaim the inspirations of Marshall. Between them they almost

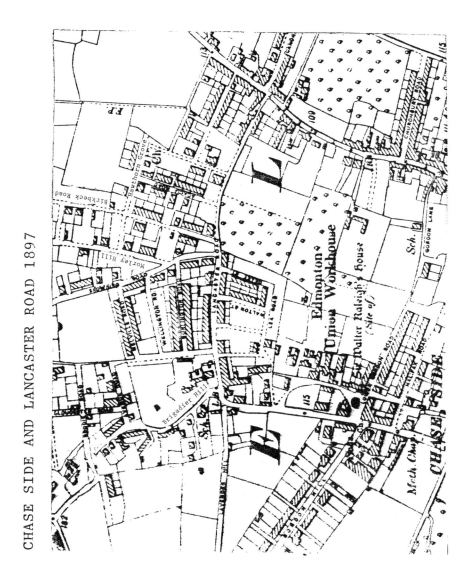

CHASE SIDE AND LANCASTER ROAD 1897

paralysed the Board. In response to the surveyor's painfully worked-out scheme, Marshall pronounced that there was no need to spend any money, all that was needed was to eliminate the wastage of water. The situation was made more critical when many of the wells in eastern Enfield went dry in the summer of 1882. The dearth of water was attributed to the deep well sunk by the New River Company in Goat Lane where powerful steam engines had been installed and were continuously at work.[35]

An epidemic of scarlet fever broke out in South Street in October 1882. Dr Ridge strongly advised the Board to provide a small hospital with rooms to isolate different infections. The Local Government Board urged at this time that urban sanitary authorities like Enfield, should provide such segregated accommodation in the ratio of one bed to a thousand population. The provision of an isolation hospital was also demanded by the chairman of the Guardians and supported by Sir R.M. Stephenson. The Ratepayers' representatives offered determined resistance. Ignoring the fact that eighty-four cases of scarlet fever had occurred by November 1882, of which eleven were dead, Mr Fowell summed up his views on the matter in another carefully worded statement. 'There's nothing like leather sir', he declared, 'here's an opportunity for going it and spending money'. Three more deaths occurred in Ponders End during the following month. Nevertheless the Enfield Board almost succumbed to the good doctor's pressure. A site at Cooks Hole (originally called Cooks Folly) belonging to the vestry, was proposed, but then it was rejected after a protest from the Lee Conservancy, because no sewers had been laid there. The Board resumed its apathetic search for a site, the chairman negotiating in a desultory fashion for a cottage and two acres in Goat Lane. Meanwhile Dr Ridge pursued his aim to clean up the parish, undeterred by the opposition of the Ratepayers. He discovered scarlet fever in Meads Cottages in Green Street where the privies were ruinous and overflowing into the gardens. 'It is a wretched place', he said. There were water-mains available but not connected to the houses. He suggested stand-pipes. Monro, the inspector of nuisances, drew the attention of the Board to property in Warwick Road where he was obliged to keep the tenants supplied with disinfectant because the stench coming up from the pumps was so abominable. Dr Ridge thought that a drain must be running into the well. Many of the six-roomed houses in Alma Road, some shared by two or three families, had no mains water; what was drawn up from the well contained an assortment of leeches and long worms,[36] although even this was perhaps reassuring, for at least they were alive.

The Metropolitan Asylums Board in January 1884 purchased, despite protests from the Southgate Local Board, thirty-six acres in Chaseville Park at Winchmore Hill, at £380 an acre, for a convalescent fever hospital. The foundation stone of the hospital, to be known as the Northern (re-named Highlands Hospital in 1948) was laid in May 1885. 'The main entrance of the administration department' reported the *Observer* 'is a fine specimen of masonry'. The patients (512 beds) were to be housed in seventeen pavilions. Local residents were not pleased. Nearby houses at Winchmore Hill, it was claimed, which had been let at £65 a year, now commanded no more than half that rent, and despite the fine elevated situation of the area people could no longer be persuaded to live there.[37]

Dr Ridge, concerned that he might not be able to contain any possible outbreak of smallpox, demanded from the Board clear instructions where he should isolate those suffering from the disease should an outbreak occur. Marshall and his followers treated the issue with clumsy frivolity, but the doctor continued to demand an answer. Marshall then told him, condescendingly though not convincingly, 'We will deal with it, we are not imbeciles, I will find out where to send them'. Ebenezer Gibbons, obviously affected by the doctor's concern, intervened to suggest that the Board should erect an iron hospital. To this Marshall responded with a guffaw, 'It's a pity we can't lift it up in a balloon and take it away'; this witticism was received with much merriment by his supporters. The Local Board at Edmonton was facing a similar problem and was

105. The foundation stone of the Northern Hospital (known as Highlands from 1948) was laid in May 1885. Thereupon rents of nearby properties tumbled to half their former value. This is the administrative block.

examining isolated cottages which might possibly be used. By February 1885, thirty cases had been moved from Enfield to the smallpox hospital at Highgate, but this was now full and the Enfield Board was obliged to leave patients in their own often overcrowded homes. From February to August 1885, 251 pauper patients had been admitted to the smallpox ward in the workhouse infirmary where fifty-one had died. The disease had now spread throughout the whole workhouse; fifty cases had occurred within the house for every one outside.[38]

The Enfield Ratepayers' Association again did well in the election of March 1883 after the number of working-class (artisan) voters had been greatly increased. Two of their candidates, John Josiah Wilson and Ebenezer Marshall, headed the poll and gathered more votes than James Meyer or Peter Rumney. It had been a hard fought campaign, the Town had been smothered with large posters urging the election of the Conservative candidates Meyer, Bosanquet, Rumney and Colonel Arbuthnot of the Small Arms Factory, while small shops all over Enfield displayed smaller notices promoting the candidature of the Ratepayers' representatives, Marshall, Wilson, Culloden Rowan and R.F. Pike. The confidence of the Ratepayers' Association representatives was so increased by their popularity with the electorate that they now felt able to treat professional advice from the Board's staff with contempt and the more gentlemanly members of the Board with open disrespect. The officers thus found themselves in difficulty. Mr Gilsenan, the conscientious road surveyor, urged that expenditure on the roads, which had amounted to £2,494 in the previous year, should not be reduced, for the roads would certainly deteriorate under the heavy traffic. Southbury Road suffered, he said, because of the large number of timber carts with narrow wheels which came that way late at night; he had seen seventeen in a line. He tried to persuade the Ratepayers' representatives that, over five years, granite would be cheaper than gravel and in any case the County

106.   Daniel Gilsenan the road surveyor. He lived in Raleigh Road and died in 1904.

would pay half the cost for granite and the Government one fourth, but the Ratepayers could see no further than the immediate expenditure. 'I drove this morning up Southbury Road,' declared Mr Pike, 'and I am persuaded that it does not require metalling'. Mr Gibbons concurred, for the cost of macadamising Southbury Road would have been £500. In October 1884 Marshall managed to overturn a decision taken by the roads committee to make up the main road in granite from Carterhatch Lane to the boundary with Cheshunt.[39]

The assertive ignorance of Ebenezer Marshall could only have been acceptable as a joke. In the face of technical opinion he devised his own crackpot schemes and persuaded his admirers on the Board to reject professionally considered advice. The proposed water-tower at Holtwhites Hill, he decided, was a waste of money. He could achieve the same result at a fraction of the cost by putting a standpipe on Windmill Hill. The laboriously calculated plans of the surveyor were dismissed as incompetent, the opinion of Sir Roland Stephenson was rejected with contempt. Marshall's standpipe theory was accepted by the Ratepayers' representatives with enthusiastic ignorance. Sanction had however already been granted to borrow the money to build the water-tower. Thus the Local Government Board had to send down a senior engineer, Samuel Joseph Smith, so that Ebenezer could explain to him why the scheme, which the engineer as inspector had already approved, was superfluous. The engineer expressed the opinion that Mr Marshall was talking nonsense; Mr Marshall became angry and accused the engineer of being unwilling, or unable, to understand his proposals. The Local Government Board however preferred the opinion of their engineer and refused to allow any change.[40] Thus the power of central government to withhold low-interest loans enabled it to restrain the ignorant opposition of some local authority members.

Sir Roland however could tolerate no more. In an open letter to James Meyer, printed in the *Observer* (14 July 1883) he wrote;

> 'In October 1881 you were a united Board striving to improve the condition of the parish with sound economy. You are now not only a divided Board ... time is wasted on prolix discussions of trivialities so that it is hopeless to expect members, whose time is of much value, to attend. Suggestions are put forward utterly impractical ... it is an insult to intelligent officers to ask them to answer such propositions. The recommendations of officers on scientific points are disregarded by members who are incompetent to form an opinion .... My term of office will soon expire, I shall not, under existing circumstances, renew it'.

Sir Roland finally resigned on moving out of the parish in November 1883. He died in December 1895.[41]

For some months Meyer was unable to attend meetings through illness. The *Observer* complained in July 1883 of the lack of respect shown to him and to Sir Roland by the Ratepayers. Mr Fowell was certainly not overmuch endowed with discretion. In August that year the *Observer* reported, with glee, a speech made by James Fowell in which he described the people he represented at Ponders End as filthy. 'They are as dirty a lot of people as you can find, they don't look fit to go within fifty yards of them ....' 'This language', said the editor, 'was not used towards them when their votes were required', adding that at that time Fowell had provided carts to carry them over to the polling booth at Enfield. Thus indignation was whipped up and a protest meeting was held on the cricket field adjoining the railway station in South Street; over a thousand people attended and Fowell hurriedly sent a letter of apology.[42]

Marshall and Fowell could not be polite even to each other; arguments lacking in substance constantly recurred between them. At a Board meeting towards the end of October 1883, Peter Rumney was ineffectually in the chair (Meyer being sick) and James Fowell was holding forth at great length to little purpose, when he was forcefully interrupted by Marshall. 'Will you rise sir?' Marshall demanded of the speaker. 'Yes, when you are chairman'. 'Then I shall rise myself because you are out of order'. 'But you are not chairman'. Marshall, throwing out his chest: 'I will take the lead then' Fowell: 'I want the chairman to ask me to rise, not you'. Marshall (with dignity): 'I am in possession of the chair'. Fowell ... 'Well go on then'. As was usual in such procedural discussions, Marshall emerged victorious. Meanwhile the chairman acted as a passive observer.[43]

When the half-yearly estimates were presented on behalf of Mr Letchworth the clerk at the end of October, Marshall made an immediate and apparently intuitive reduction of each item. Gilsenan, who worried about his roads, said that he did not know how he would be able to carry out the work. It would be the same as last year, he complained, and he would be forced to exceed the estimate. Fowell, Pike and Marshall were outraged at such interference from an officer and Fowell retaliated, delivering a lengthy diatribe concerning the poor state of the roads.[44]

Nevertheless the following April, at a time when other local boards in the area had increased their rates, Enfield was able to reduce the half-yearly rate by one

107.   Ebenezer Gibbons proposed lime trees along Silver Street and along the north side of the Town in 1884.

penny. This may of course have been due as much to the rising rateable value of property in the parish as to Marshall's economies. The Local Board had now set up committees to deal separately with the problems of finance, lighting, sewage farm, roads and waterworks. The Ratepayers' representatives, aggravated by constant attacks on them in the *Observer*, from time to time excluded reporters from Board meetings.[45]

A new crisis occurred in November 1883 when Marshall and his followers precipitously dismissed the rate collector and, despite a strong protest from the chairman James Meyer, at once appointed their own nominee, presenting him with a life interest in the office. Even on the question of a replacement for Sir Roland Stephenson, Marshall dissented. Meyer nominated Culloden Rowan (Ratepayers Association) as the candidate having the largest number of votes among those not elected at the previous election. In this matter however Marshall's opposition was not supported. In July 1884 Marshall made a strong attack upon Mr Kitteringham over the paving account. He ended however with some magnanimity, looking around for the usual applause, 'I do not like to condemn a man unheard, but it requires serious explanation'. When however the surveyor, who usually knew what he was talking about, dealt seriously with Marshall's attack in a detailed report, the Ratepayers voted that his explanation should be expunged from the records.[46]

It was Ebenezer Gibbons who proposed tree planting in the Town. The chairman, addressing the clerk, asked whether it could be done out of the rates. Before that officer could reply one member shouted 'No'. The clerk pointed out that it was done in Edmonton. Pike: 'They do anything there'. Marshall: 'I have received information that grave exception will be taken to planting; tradesmen like their shops to be seen, not hid. If we plant trees they will be destroyed'. The clerk enquired whether he meant naturally or by the tradesmen. Rumney: 'They will be murdered at once'. Marshall… 'It will be a murder of innocents'. This pertinent statement was followed by a prolonged discussion as to what Marshall meant by 'innocents', the trees, the shopkeepers, or the council's officers. At length the surveyor was asked to test public opinion on the matter and he came back two weeks later with a memorial in favour, signed by William Lock and twenty other shopkeepers around the Town. They proposed lime trees along Silver Street and along the north side of the Town. Not everyone was pleased. A correspondent from Ponders End wanted to know whether 'Gibbons and his money-saving friends had devised a scheme for saving the sum necessary'. On the previous Saturday, he said, Ponders End was in total darkness and the roads and paths were seas of mud and filth. There being a full moon he had taken the opportunity to walk to Enfield. Half way down Southbury Road he could see the lamps 'alight in Enfield Town and shining in every direction. We must have been asleep,' he concluded, 'when we voted for this gentleman and those associated with him'.[47]

The medical officer of health's report for the year 1885 shows a death rate of 17.5 and a birth rate of 37.86 per thousand. Nearly forty-eight per cent of the deaths were of children under the age of five, and the principal causes were epidemics, particularly measles and whooping cough; only one child had died of enteric fever. The condition of some of the rural property in the parish remained appalling. Dr Ridge, in October 1884, inspected four cottages in a lane leading from Old Road to Carterhatch Lane. The thatch was defective and let in the rain, they were very dirty and dilapidated, with no drainage and a single common privy which lay only a few feet from the cottages. There was no water supply. One woman living there had seven children and not a drop of water in the pump; she had no one to send and no one would give her any.[48]

The surveyor in July 1885 inspected St Patrick's Terrace behind the Plough beerhouse opposite St James Church. It comprised eight cottages, with a small strip of garden in front, forming a court, it was approached from the main road by a narrow passage. There was a well with a pump which had been out of action for months; the only water supply was from other cottages in the neighbourhood, but this was unreliable, yet the Board's water-main ran along the main road only a few yards from the houses. Mrs Mead, the owner, was given notice that the cottages must be connected. The surveyor also examined, in October 1886, houses being erected in Standard Road and found that the mortar being used consisted largely of vegetable mould with scarcely any lime. Notice under the by-laws was sent to Dean and Pullen the builders and to the Standard Freehold Land Society, but the surveyor insisted that the persons truly responsible were those who came down weekly and furnished money for the speculative builders to put up rotten buildings.[49]

What really concerned the respectable portion of the population however was that the splendid and highly-rated houses on the Ridgeway were still without water. The water-tower was now finished, it only remained to instal a gas-engine and pump to complete the work as planned, but then Marshall intervened again with a new technological inspiration. The gas-engine and pump were unnecessary, he explained, it could be done by using the pumps at Alma Road, three miles away. His admirers listened open-mouthed to this latest pronouncement

108.   The water-tower at Holtwhites Hill was built by 1885. It was needed to facilitate the flow of water from the reservoir there to the expensive properties being built high up on the Ridgeway.

of genius, and at once voted away the engine and pump. Meyer and the surveyor were dismayed. Mr Kitteringham pointed out that not only could Marshall's system not work, but that it would undoubtedly damage the whole water supply system. Marshall refused to be deterred by so biased and uncalled-for an intervention from an officer and brought the meeting to a close. Meyer had only one course open to him. He appealed to the Local Government Board which then intervened to insist upon the original scheme. The days when local gentry could expect deference had gone. Marshall, at the next meeting, attacked Meyer for his intervention so violently that a memorial was drawn up and circulated throughout the parish expressing sympathy for the chairman.[50]

6. Progress Resumed

Retribution was at hand for the Enfield Ratepayers' Association. At the Local Board elections in April 1885 their five candidates were heavily defeated, poor Fowell coming bottom of the poll. This still left Marshall, but he had lost his audience of admirers sure to applaud his every technological breakthrough. His opinions henceforth had to be expressed with more circumspection, in fact he began to act independently, disregarding more and more the non-spending precepts of the Ratepayers' Association. The authority of the chair was re-established and the advice of officers was now heard with respect. Following the elections, insinuations were made that certain property owners who were prominent members of the Ratepayers' Association had not returned for entry into the rate-books, the names of those tenants they had thought likely to vote Conservative; these had thereby been deprived of a vote. That there were landlords who believed that it was the duty of their tenants to vote for them is given credence by a letter in the *Observer* from C. Bitterlich of number two, Ebenezer Terrace. He had openly voted for the Conservative candidates. A week later he received notice to quit, delivered at his door by C.S. Whitbread, his landlord's nephew. Whitbread strongly denied any connection between elec-tion and eviction, claiming that a change of tenant had been decided about a month before. Why then, asked Bitterlich, had Mr Gibbons his landlord told him, only two weeks earlier, that he could get some wallpaper to make the place comfortable, reassuring him that the price would be allowed out of the rent? That was before the election, but after it was known that he had voted Conservative Mr Gibbons had told him that 'as I had voted against him, we should never agree and I had better look for a house elsewhere'. Character, especially when reconstructed from historical evidence can seldom be catego-rised as good or bad. There was much kindness in Ebenezer. We see it in April 1889 when, with a determination which would brook no denial, he collected from Enfield tradesmen and provided for the children of the workhouse school, 360 buns, 360 oranges and 360 packets of sweets. This became his annual treat.[51]

Without the Ratepayers' Association representatives the work of the Board went on more smoothly. An editorial in the *Observer* in March 1886 praised the work done in paving, lighting and road-making. It called for the paving of footpaths wherever there was a continuous line of houses, also near the railway stations. The *Observer*, having played a major role in the defeat of the Ratepayers' Association, remained highly influential in the parish. Enfield, it declared, was becoming pretty much a suburb of London and if tenants were to be found for the many empty houses, money must be spent on improvements. The rates of only a few residences such as those being erected on the Ridgeway, would suffice to meet the additional expenditure. The Local Board responded by promoting a scheme to pave and kerb all the principal streets of the parish over the ensuing three years. The immediate programme was the kerbing and brick-paving of Ponders End, the Highway, Ordnance Road, Parsonage Lane and Baker Street, one side of Church Street, and Windmill Hill as far as the railway and thence to Glebe Avenue. It was also intended to improve the water supply by sinking a new well 110 feet deep lined with iron cylinders, down to the chalk. The Board, to accomplish all this, applied to borrow £5,000, though £1,000 of this sum would be spent on the improvement of Glebe Avenue and would be recoverable from the owners of the houses.[52]

Dr Ridge's annual report for the year 1886 expressed his satisfaction. The death rate was down to 16.45 per thousand. 'We have a united Board', he wrote, 'vigilant and energetic officials, reasonably low rates, effective systems of sewage and refuse disposal, low death rates, and a steadily augmenting population'. There had been 371 deaths. No case of smallpox had been reported, but there had been an epidemic of diphtheria from which twenty-four had died. At the Local Board elections in March 1887 the four retiring Conservative members were returned. Two candidates, put up by the Ratepayers' Association, were heavily defeated.[53]

The death rate in 1888 went up from 16.34 to 19.25; this was attributed to the migration into the parish of poor people from the metropolis, also to the scourge of diphtheria, from which there had been forty-one deaths, and to whooping cough among the young. It was a bad year for Enfield, as can be seen by comparing these figures with a death rate of 20.3 in twenty-eight great conurbations in England and Wales. In Southgate, very middle-class and lately described as 'villadom', the death rate stood at only 11.7. The medical officer's report for 1889 shows that things in Enfield had returned to normal; there had been 1,010 births, 41.2 per thousand, and 376 deaths, a rate of 15.34 per thousand, but the 107 deaths of children under one year old remained a cause for grave concern.[54]

The Infectious Diseases Notification Act of 1889 placed upon the head of each household the responsibility to notify the medical officer of health of certain diseases. Dr Ridge reported that since the London Fever Hospital had declined to accept any further patients sent by him, he now had no place to isolate infected persons unless they were paupers and could be sent to the workhouse infirmary. The situation created a danger that infectious disease could spread rapidly. To remedy this state of affairs Enfield Local Board purchased nineteen acres known as Worlds End Farm, adjoining the Metropolitan Asylums Board Hospital. The land lay within Enfield, on the boundary with Southgate. The price was £2,000. Representatives from Edmonton, Enfield, Wood Green, Tottenham and Southgate were called together with the aim of setting up a joint hospital board, and the Guardians offered support. The Southgate Board however strongly objected. It rejected the invitation and immediately lodged an appeal to Parliament where it was ruled that the case should be heard before a parliamentary committee. Thus the proposal for a joint board was faced with indefinite delay and additional costs likely to amount to between £1,000 and £2,000. The interest of the remaining district councils in the project rapidly evaporated. Tottenham and Edmonton withdrew and the Enfield Board decided, as an alternative, to put up a temporary hospital on the site of an isolated house in Lincoln Road (where it is now traversed by the A10). The house stood in a former brickfield, currently used as a rubbish shoot, a hundred yards from the roadway. Protest meetings held in Bush Hill Park and Ponders End could be safely ignored.[55]

The temporary hospital opened at the beginning of December 1891. It had two wards each holding eight beds, a nurses' kitchen and a dispensary. It was made of iron with an inner skin of felt and lined with matchboarding. The patients, mostly children, would have to stay there for an average of six weeks. Dr Ridge made an appeal for toys, games, books and Bibles. The Board had been driven to act quickly by an outbreak of scarlet fever at the end of November. It had started in eastern Enfield and had spread to Bush Hill Park; there were 203 cases. Bush Hill Park at the same time was hit by an outbreak of enteric fever.[56] The cause of these outbreaks was investigated by Dr S. Monckton Copeman in January 1892. Despite the efforts of the Board, conditions in these poorer parts of the district remained unsatisfactory. Water closets had been installed, usually at the backs of the houses under the back bedroom. They were mostly of the long hopper type and in many instances were found to be filled to the brim, the occupiers having no water to flush them. Even when cisterns had been provided, they were either out of order or rendered useless by an insufficiency of water.

The ground level in the yards behind the houses was found to have been raised several inches by the deposit of refuse of all description, much of it ashes and cinders. The Local Board had recently supplied large galvanised iron tubs as refuse bins, but these appear to have been used for anything but their intended purpose, being ingeniously converted into wardrobes, rabbit hutches or dog kennels and the ashes being deposited as before.

He found that the sewers were adequate, except at times of heavy rain when they were liable to overflow, but they were badly ventilated. Many of the manholes had been sealed after complaints about the smells arising from them. Dr Ridge proposed that every house should have its own ventilator. The sewage farm had eight filter beds, each of about one and half acres, twelve acres in all. They were used when the sewage was not required on the rest of the farm, but Dr Copeman believed that most of the sewage still reached the subsoil.

Many cesspools had been replaced by water closets, according to Dr Ridge, but a number of those remaining were not watertight and sewage seeped into the gravel below. The Local Board had recently acquired a night-soil cart with a suction pump, so that the cesspools could be rapidly and effectively emptied. The officers of the Board had been struggling for years to cope with the insanitary condition of many houses, but nothing less than frequently repeated house to house inspections could solve the problem and this was impossible with the existing staff. The medical officer proposed the compulsory provision of approved closet pans and flushing apparatus, and urged that a certificate of proper sanitary condition be required before the occupation of new property was allowed.[57]

There had been 19,104 people living in Enfield at the time of the 1881 census, in 1891 there were 31,532, an increase of sixty-four per cent in ten years. There were 5,859 houses in 1891 and 6,184 families, an average of 5.4 persons in each house. The death rate, calculated on accurate population figures in 1891, was 13.84; the birth rate 33.91. One reason for this comparatively low birth rate might lie in a small advertisement appearing each week in the *Observer*, (eg 8 April 1892) discreetly tucked away in the bottom right hand corner of the front page; it offered to married people 'invaluable information on receipt of a stamped envelope'. Certainly by 1909 the county medical officer was prepared to endorse the view that the decrease in the birth rate (to 25.2) was due to the deliberate restriction of child bearing. The birth rate in Edmonton which was poorer, then stood at 32; in Southgate, which was better-off, it was 20.6.[58]

Mr Kitteringham had also been responsible for a much overdue reorganisation of the fire brigade. Following his appointment as surveyor it took only one more serious failure to persuade the Board that it was essential to make improvements; that failure had occurred in March 1880 when the Enfield engine had been unable to get to a fire at Mr Beadle's in Winchmore Hill for want of horses. They had gone to Mr Pepper, the jobmaster in Silver Street, as they usually did, but every suitable horse was on hire. They therefore sent to Mr Biscoe's in Church Street but he was unco-operative. They usually went to Pepper's, they were not going to make a convenience of him, he said. He refused. Other brigades arrived but not Enfield's. So serious was the humiliation that the Board felt impelled to take steps to prevent any recurrence of such a fiasco. The engine was forthwith placed in the capable hands of the new surveyor, who was directed to set up a volunteer fire brigade consisting of fifteen to twenty-five men, equipped with helmets, belts and hatchets, but no uniforms.

109.   Mr Pepper's stables. He was the jobmaster in Silver Street from whom the fire brigade hired its horses. The north end of the Inland Revenue office now occupies the site.

The Original Livery Stables--Established 60 Years.

ELEANOR PEPPER,
THE   ENFIELD   LIVERY   STABLES.
SILVER   STREET,   ENFIELD,   N.

WEDDING   CARRIAGES,   BROUGHAMS,   LANDAUS,   VICTORIAS,   DOG
CARTS, etc., supplied on the Shortest Notice and on the most Reasonable Terms

He was to ensure that secure arrangements were made for horsing when required.[59]

Kitteringham's reorganisation brought an element of efficiency first displayed when a fire occurred in September 1881 at Ponders End. The call had been received at a few minutes after midnight and the Enfield brigade was on the scene by twelve thirty, only alas to find that the fire had been extinguished by the engine from the crape factory, which thereby earned all the praise. Comments on the performance of the Ponders End brigade that night were unflattering, but this was not surprising. Mr Howell, their secretary, had not long before complained to the Board that his brigade had received three calls during August but, having no engine fit for use, they had been obliged to hire a trap to take the hose and standpipe to the fires. This revelation had been received with much hilarity by the representatives of the Ratepayers' Association who at that time dominated the Board, and when the Ponders End brigade asked for a new engine, the Ratepayers' members prevaricated until, at the end of January 1883, the brigade was curtly informed that the Board no longer recognised its existence. Ponders End brigade had by then been operating for

110. Both the fire station and the post office moved in 1883 into this new block built by Allen Fairhead in Southbury Road.

111. The Enfield Town fire brigade, in the years following the First World War, still retained the steamer which had been purchased in 1899. It was by then little used because two horses were required to pull it, and only one at a time was normally available. A motor engine was acquired in 1925. This photograph was taken outside the fire station in Little Park Gardens.

eleven years during which time the Board had regularly paid practice money to the firemen. It was 1891 before the Ponders End brigade was reformed. A fire station was then built and the Local Board agreed to purchase an engine and appliances.[60]

The engine house in St Andrew's churchyard was small and damp. The engine was old and the wheels displayed symptoms of dry rot, the hose was decayed. There was at this time (1882) an urgent need for a mortuary. Dead bodies when found had to be taken to the nearest public house and stored in a shed or an outhouse. In the event of a new home being provided for the fire engine, the building in the churchyard, it was thought, could serve as a mortuary. A temporary solution was presented in January 1883 when Joseph Pepper offered the use of part of his stable yard for the erection of an iron house for the engine. It was taken into consideration that, since Pepper's horses were likely to be hired, this arrangement would suit very well. However it lasted only until June when the Board accepted Allen Fairhead's terms to rent a fire station opposite the Great Eastern Railway station near the Town in Southbury Road. At the same time sanction was secured to borrow £400 to purchase a steam pump. The new steamer was tried out first at Cheshunt where, to the delight of the brigade, the force of water was so great that the chimney pots were knocked off the houses. The old engine was left forlorn in Pepper's yard. It was taken out in April 1903 and cleaned and polished for an exhibition at Earls Court. The old double-barrelled pump could still be made to throw a jet of water, though much of the woodwork was wormeaten. It survived at least until the early thirties when it was photographed on the Library Green, but no one seems to know what has since happened to this ancient relic. The brigade was further equipped in September 1884 with a Merryweather improved dog cart hose reel carrying 2,000 feet of canvas hose and 500 feet of leather hose.[61]

No amount of fire-fighting equipment however could work if there was a shortage of water and this frustrated the firemen's efforts time and again. A great fire broke out in June 1885 in Allen Fairhead's timber yard in Sydney Road. The Enfield steamer worked from London Road, the hose being carried through the Baptist chapel. The telegraph was used to summon all the neighbouring brigades, but so many engines arrived that there was not sufficient water for them all. The blaze spread to Patman's yard and engulfed the Duke of Abercorn: the flames could be seen from London Bridge. Another disastrous fire occurred at the end of March 1886 in a block of buildings known as the 'Old Curiosity Shop' in Baker Street. The alarm was raised at seven o'clock in the evening and the police station was alerted. Inspector Head called out the fire brigade and communicated with Mr Pike the turncock. Within a very short time the Enfield steam engine was on the scene, but the water could not be turned on. The Edmonton brigade arrived. Messengers were sent in every direction to get a supply of water but to no avail. The firemen could only stand and watch while flames engulfed the whole building and destroyed the contents. Two hours later, when the fire had almost burnt itself out, the first spray of water fell upon the flickering ruin. Once again it was pointed out that a telegraph line from the police station to the pumping station might have averted the disaster.[62]

From time to time the idea of a town hall was promoted by civic pride and rejected by parish parsimony. John Sawyer was the only attorney in Enfield in the 1850s. He was vestry clerk, clerk to the magistrates, clerk to the trustees of

112. A great fire consumed Allen Fairhead's yard in Sydney Road in June 1885 destroying also Patman's yard and the Duke of Abercorn. The flames could be seen from London Bridge. Note Mr Pike the turncock on duty.

various charities and subsequently to the Enfield Gas Company and when the Local Board was set up he became the clerk and general controller. All the business of the parish was conducted in the one-floor office belonging to Mr Sawyer, opposite Silverdale (ie opposite the Civic Centre; he lived at Redlingtons in Silver Street). The early building societies also met in his office. The Greyhound ceased to be a licensed house and fell vacant about 1860; a proposal was made soon afterwards for its demolition and the construction of a town hall on the site (the east side of the Market Place) with a public baths at the rear. The scheme fell through, but John Sawyer secured for the Board the remainder of the lease, and the Greyhound was converted for public offices. Sawyer died in 1860.

The idea of a town hall was revived in 1867 by the prospect of a new police and horse patrol station in London Road. An Enfield Town Hall Company was formed and certain gentlemen and tradesmen in the Town, it was said, had undertaken to buy shares to the value of £3,000, but again it all came to nothing. When the lease of the Greyhound was about to expire in 1887, the building was pronounced, by those who wished to destroy it, to be unsafe and unfit for future business. Its timbers, they said, were impregnated with dry rot. 'There is no doubt' declared the *Observer* (17 April 1886) 'that the ratepayers of Enfield will sanction the pulling down of the very old and dilapidated building'.[63]

These plans however were overtaken by a new proposal; that the Local Board should purchase Little Park in Gentleman's Row (the house now used as a Register Office). At this there was a storm of protest. Wrote one correspondent (5 August 1887):

'Little Park is part of the property purchased by Messrs Dixon, Ward,

Letchworth and Weld, with the 'white elephant' house thereon. If these gentlemen can ensure a ready purchaser for this, the least marketable portion of their estate... , the members of the Local Board, with their clerk-ruler (meaning Mr Letchworth) at their head... will materially deteriorate the character of the old Town of Enfield and deprive it of all dignity'.

Mr Letchworth, since 1860 clerk to the Local Board, was also one of the solicitors engaged in the sale, thus he stood awkwardly with a foot in each camp. The opposition convened a public meeting in the Sydney Road school where Captain Henry F. Bowles took the chair. It gave birth to the Town Preservation Association; yet before our living preservationists raise a cheer and rush belatedly to celebrate a centenary, I must point out that the object of this Association was not to restore Enfield's very handsome early seventeenth-century inn, but to pull it down and erect a town hall on the site.

Mr Letchworth demonstrated the very real advantages offered by Little Park. It was a fine house with plenty of space, and it could be purchased for £4,000. The acquisition of the grounds to the south would allow the Board to widen Church Street by twenty feet, and would at the same time provide a more adequate site for the fire station than the one in Southbury Road; it would moreover cost much less than the scheme to build new offices on the Grey-hound site. Despite an offer made by the 'preservationists' to finance the building of a new town hall, which they would then let to the Board at a modest rent, the decision was taken to move to Gentleman's Row.[64]

The scheme to provide Enfield with a town hall came to life once more early in the year 1894, after the London and Provincial Bank had reached an agreement to purchase the Greyhound. Supporters of the enterprise had promised £1,640; they proposed to persuade the trustees of Cox's charity to part with the Vestry House so that that too could be demolished, and the new town hall could thus be provided with an imposing frontage facing the Town. Mr Gilbee Scott, a local architect, drew up plans and sketches for a building to cost £14,000, and to incorporate a public library and shops on the ground floor. Dr Ridge was hopeful that the bank could be induced to relinquish its agreement to purchase. However the money required to buy the site could not be found, the dream of a town hall faded once more, the Greyhound was demolished and the bank was built. The London and Provincial was bought out by Barclay's in 1918.[65]

After Little Park became the council offices, its name was transferred to the house next door (5, Gentleman's Row). The accommodation sufficed for a time, but by 1900 the offices had become insufferably overcrowded. The surveyor with his staff of one assistant, two clerks, his road foreman, two building inspectors and the water inspector, occupied two rooms on the ground floor. The public library operated in two larger rooms, one was used for the storage and issue of books, the other served as the librarian's office and reference library and, for two days each week, was used for the collection of rates. The inspector of nuisances, with two assistants and two clerks, occupied another room, and there was a strong-room on the ground floor. On the first floor, the council chamber presented further difficulties, for it was too small to accommo-date all the members. The clerk with his three assistants had three rooms, and this was considered lavish provision. The council solicitor had one small room. The remaining rooms were occupied by the Burial Board, the vestry clerk, the registrar and the rate collectors. Things were at their worst however on the top

113.   The first bank to establish a branch in Enfield was the London and Provincial in 1875, with
premises on the east side of Enfield Town. Their fine building (shown in the illustration), now
Barclays Bank, on the near corner of the Market Place, was designed by the local architect W. Gilbee
Scott; it opened in 1898. Patman, a builder, had offices on the far corner.

114. James Meyer was chairman of the Local Board of Health from 1850 until his death in 1894. He was the great-nephew of the James Meyer who had purchased Forty Hall in 1799, and who had been a member of the Dutch Reformed Church. On the death of this James Meyer in 1826, the memorial service had been held in Baker Street chapel. The estate passed then to his brother Christian Paul Meyer and from him to his son, also named Christian Paul (1790-1857) who built Jesus Church. James, the chairman, was his second son.

floor. The School Board had two rooms with very low ceilings, and the surveyor's four draughtsmen were cooped up in one room seventeen feet square. One lavatory served the whole building. At this time the estate belonging to Chase Side House was being sold and the Urban District Council purchased the land now known as the Library Green, proposing, with apparently undiminished optimism, to build a town hall thereon.

James Meyer had been re-appointed chairman of the Local Board of Health for the fortieth time in April 1889. A ceremony had taken place at Little Park at which a portrait of the chairman by Sir Arthur Clay had been presented to the Board. James was the great-nephew of the James Meyer who had purchased Forty Hall, an estate of 280 acres, in 1799 for £11,940. James (the chairman) had begun to take an interest in parochial affairs soon after he left college in 1836. This fortieth anniversary had been the occasion for an unusually accurate prediction by the editor of the *Observer*. 'As at present constituted', he wrote, 'local boards are doomed and cannot be expected long to survive the revolution taking place in municipal and parochial institutions.' James Meyer did not live to see the end of the Board; he died in June 1894. John Josiah Wilson, who was elected in his place, was a market gardener and also a county councillor.[66]

Local government was fundamentally reorganised by the Act of 1894. The Enfield Local Board ceased to exist in November that year and elections were held on 17 December for the Enfield Urban District Council. In some places such as Southgate and Wood Green, the members of the old board were nominated without challenge as the new council, but Enfield had a contested election. Voting for the Urban District Council was by ward; polling was on a Monday from eight in the morning until eight at night. The Conservatives retained control. In the Ordnance ward three Ratepayer candidates defeated three working men put forward by the Co-operative Society. In the Green Street and Ponders End wards three Progressives suffered defeat, but two Progressives, Hugh Trenchard and James Warren, were returned in the Chase and Bulls Cross ward. J.J. Wilson was elected chairman. Committees were formed to deal with finance, the sewage farm, the isolation hospital, lighting and roads, water supply, the library, and general purposes.[67]

So it was that after nearly sixty years, the Enfield Local Board of Health came to an end. The very size of the parish (12,611 acres, larger than Edmonton, Southgate, Tottenham and Wood Green put together) had caused difficulties, many of which had never been surmounted. The recent rapid rise of the population had made matters worse: 450 houses, each requiring the expensive provision of services, had been built in the two years before the end of the Board. Nevertheless it had managed to keep its annual rate at only 3s 6d in the pound. During its last ten years the Board had spent £63,000 on public works of a permanent character, including a reservoir to hold one and a half million gallons, a water-tower, a new well, a vast extension of the water-mains and sewers, and the kerbing, channelling and paving of many roads. Improvements had been made at the sewage farm on which, in the previous year, a profit of £450 had been achieved. Surely, it was thought, this must be the only profitable sewage farm in the United Kingdom. Most of the money for these public works had been borrowed. The Board handed over to the new Council thirty-three miles of sewers, twenty-three miles of water-mains and sixty miles of public roads. Seventeen and a half miles of pathways had been kerbed and nine miles had been paved. Ten years earlier there had been 250 street lamps, there were now 530. It was forty years since the Board had taken to itself the responsibility to supply the inhabitants with water. Looking back, the chairman was doubtful whether it had been a wise policy, but water was now supplied to 4,500 houses. A public library had been opened, also two fire stations, a public baths, and a number of allotments had been provided.

The vestry, the organ of local government in pre-Victorian times, still survived. Although much diminished in its powers, it still appointed overseers and met twice a year to fix a poor rate.[68]

7. The Urban District Council

The most difficult problem transferred from the Local Board to the Urban District Council was the supply of water. Although it cost the ratepayers 1s 6d in the pound on the rates, and although thousands had been recently spent on a

115.   Enfield waterworks, the new engine house 1897, at Alma Road.

new well, the system remained so inefficient that the new Council was faced with the immediate need to borrow a further £11,000 in an effort to maintain an adequate supply. Before remedial action could be undertaken the Council had to know whether it was possible to secure an adequate supply of pure water within the parish, and if so what would be the best means of procuring and distributing it. Advice from the specialist firm, Messrs Taylor and Sons and Santo Crimp, maintained that there was an abundance of water in the chalk at Ponders End. A government enquiry in October 1895 examined the supply system in use in Enfield and declared that it was both ineffectual and costly. It advocated that instead of the existing three wells — Bycullah Park, which after having fallen into disuse had now been restored to working order, Alma Road and Eagle House — there should be four borings at Alma Road, and that a new engine house should be built there over the borings to house two sets of pumps, one to deliver the water to the high level reservoir, and the other to the low level reservoir. Work on this scheme was begun by February 1896. The *Observer* pointed out, somewhat late, that Enfield's possession of its own waterworks had proved an expensive privilege.[69] Work to cut off all surface water from the system was completed by October 1897 and two boreholes, two feet in diameter, had been sunk to a depth of 200 feet and connected to the existing well. The new engine house had been built and a pair of handsome and powerful beam engines had been installed. The new system however soon proved a disappointment. From the start water had to be denied to nurserymen and market gardeners and, after only two years, the new pumps failed. Constant complaints from householders of water shortage continued and many houses were cut off for days, roads could not be watered and throughout the summer the air was heavy with dust. The situation was aggravated by a prolonged drought in 1901, when application had to be made to the New River Company for 100,000 gallons a day, supplied into the mains at Ponders End at sixpence a thousand gallons.[70]

116.   The new well at Hadley Road at last solved Enfield's water problems, just as the whole system was about to be handed over to the Metropolitan Water Board in 1903.

A new source of water had urgently to be sought.

Experts were again consulted. This time a new well was advised on a site near Vicarage Farm in Hadley Road. Tenders for sinking the borehole there were submitted by the end of May 1901. It was to cost £40,000. The council that year had to supply 7,521 houses, while a further 1,051 houses were supplied by the New River Company, by the East Barnet Company, or by private wells.[71]

A Bill was presented to Parliament in January 1902 which aimed to consolidate the water companies and the local authority water undertakings in the London area under the newly constituted Metropolitan Water Board. Enfield Council was relieved to be informed in May that its district had been included within the scope of the new authority. All the existing plant was to be taken over at its true value, including the new Hadley Road well which had proved successful beyond expectation; some 12,000 gallons a day was being raised there. The Metropolitan Water Board held its first meeting in April 1903 and on 24 June 1904 the Enfield water supply system passed out of the hands of the Urban District Council.[72]

The East London Water Company, destined to be incorporated into the new authority, had announced in December 1898 an intention to construct 'two large lakes on the marshes in the Lea Valley'. One was to be of 462 acres and 2,926 yards long, lying north of the road from Ponders End to Chingford, the other of 384 acres and 2,754 yards long was to be constructed on the south side of that road. Thus the company aimed to acquire the whole of the Lea marshes between Cooks Ferry in Edmonton and Enfield Lock, a distance of nearly four miles. The MWB began work on the first of these reservoirs, north of the Lea Valley Road, in July 1907. The contract was worth £340,000, not including the new pumping station. A thousand men were employed there by 1910, fifteen and a half miles of railway track had been put down and twelve locomotives were in use.[73] The work was completed in 1913 and the new reservoir was opened on 15 March by King George V, the royal procession making its way to Chingford through the crowd-lined streets of the East End.

Despite such twentieth century projects, parts of the parish were still enduring pre-1850 conditions. The summer drought in 1911 had dried up the wells at Botany Bay and any water still to be found there was of poor quality. This hamlet, comprising thirty-six houses and 130 people, far out in the north-west of Enfield, lay remote from all civilised services (the name, like that of Worlds End, was probably invented by some Victorian humourist); it had no street lighting, water or sewerage. The Metropolitan Water Board formulated a plan to lay a water-main to the area and to erect a water-tower fifty feet high, 380 feet above sea level, to the north of the hamlet. The proposal drew a strong protest from an outraged W. Gundry at North Lodge, who felt that it would disfigure the neighbourhood and be needlessly expensive. Twenty-five workmen were engaged laying a water-main to Botany Bay in June 1913. The contract to build a water-tower there with a capacity of 30,000 gallons was given to Fairhead's, it was all but finished at the beginning of the First World War.[74]

Enfield still had two volunteer fire brigades, one at the Town and one at Ponders End, to protect its eleven thousand buildings against fire. The *Gazette* (6 March 1914) thought that progress had been remarkable since the establishment of the first volunteer brigade under Captain Tilley; it had then been financed entirely by public subscription, but public spending on it now, thought the *Gazette* had gone too far, for it took a whole penny rate to maintain the brigade. Concern was expressed about the high cost of equipment, the *Gazette* was not surprised that the Council had turned down a proposal to buy motor engines. The editor felt that more of the expense should be placed upon the insurance companies for it was these which benefited when a fire was put out; perhaps the brigades should concern themselves only with saving life and allow property to burn.[75]

Disposal of sewage was another problem facing the new Council. The Lea remained badly polluted; effluent from Enfield, Edmonton and Cheshunt was still discharged, almost untreated, into the river. Along the river bank for miles to the south of Enfield Lock lay great heaps of refuse which had been barged there from various parts of the metropolis, with foul sludge from the canal beds of London, waste lime from gas works and household refuse of all kinds. Vast quantities of manure were landed at Ponders End wharf.[76]

The sanitary engineer had set seriously to work to lay down a sewage farm following the failure of Mr Harrison's optimistic venture in 1875. A boiler with an engine house had been erected at Nightingale Hall Farm and was in operation by January 1877. The sewage at that time was treated on the irrigation principle, being distributed across the farm before it found its way into the Lee Navigation, but the population, which had then been only 18,000, by the end of the year 1904 stood at 49,000. Prosecutions against Enfield and Cheshunt for polluting the river were taken out in December 1904 and again in January 1906, on each occasion the Council asked for more time; it had sought permission to borrow £7,500 to improve sewage disposal. The machinery at the sewage farm was now twenty-seven years old and it was due for replacement. It was essential that the farm be extended, and the Council therefore acquired the adjoining Cuckoo Hall nursery of four acres. That year (1906) a scheme was submitted for using bacteriological treatment. A new engine house had to be built which could deal with 50,000 gallons an hour and adequate filter beds had to be constructed (four were in place by 1908). Only after this treatment would the effluent be allowed to pass over the farm before flowing into the Navigation near Angel Road, Edmonton.[77]

Enfield UDC had expended £30,000 on sewerage by 1911, but it had not proved possible to solve the difficulties of sewage disposal, any more than the problem of water supply, within the boundaries of one parish. The whole of the Lea Valley was affected. Southgate, where there had been a great increase in population, still discharged its effluent into the Edmonton sewers. Cheshunt had its sewage farm in Enfield, Enfield had its sewage farm in Edmonton. An elaborate scheme was evolved in 1911, in conjunction with the London County Council, to discharge all the Lea Valley sewage at the LCC outfall at Abbey Mills. The cost however would be £40,000, which would amount to sixpence on the rates. Edmonton, overwhelmed by sewage from Southgate, was enthusiastic. Even Southgate, not wishing to be entirely dependent on Edmonton was interested; the officers recommended the plan, but Enfield Council rejected it. It was to be half a century before a similar scheme, covering a wider area, was put into operation. Ponders End was not pleased. The value of property and the quality of life was diminished by the stench from the sewage farm and at times the place was plagued with mosquitos. Ponders End protests as usual went unheard.[78]

There had been, over the years, a stream of complaints against the private contractors who collected the refuse. The surveyor's report in March 1900 urged that the local authority could save £30 a year by doing the work itself. Thereupon the Council purchased three horses and three carts with the appropriate harness (from Mr Grout) and engaged three drivers at 24s a week and three younger men to help them at 18s. Much of the refuse at this time was sold to the London Brick Company (ashes being used in the making of yellow stock bricks) for a shilling a load. Unsold rubbish might be tipped in the most odd and unsuitable places. In October 1907 the Council received a deputation from the residents of Herewood Terrace on the north side of Southbury Road, west of the railway, asking for the removal of a dust shoot adjoining their houses, because swarms of flies were bred there which invaded their homes. Dr Ridge said that the sooner they had a dust destructor the better. Meantime house refuse continued to be taken away by the local authority, either to Council shoots, usually in former gravel pits, or to the brickmakers, but it was becoming ever more difficult to dispose of it in these ways.[79]

Negotiations were entered into in November 1909 for the purchase of the reservoir site in Southbury Road, with the land adjoining, to erect a dust destructor with a depot and cottages for the workmen, but sanction for a loan was not forthcoming. The refuse collected at Hadley Wood and Cockfosters was deposited in the woods by Camlet Way where the heaps became infested with rats. The Council decided (May 1913) that it should be taken to the main shoot in Carterhatch Lane; obviously it was thought that the people at Enfield Highway would be less susceptible to the nuisance.[80]

An outbreak of measles in the north-east part of the parish at the end of the year 1897 caused many deaths, mostly of infants and young children. There had been thirty-one deaths by January 1898 and between forty and fifty cases remained. It was difficult to keep a check on measles because it was not a notifiable disease, but the Council ordered that it should be made notifiable for

117.   Enfield's Isolation Hospital, opened in 1900 at Worlds End, replaced a temporary hospital at Lincoln Road. The brougham used as an ambulance was purchased in 1902; it opened at the back so that a stretcher could be put in.

118.   Patients could be isolated in one of a number of single-storey pavilions.

one month and sixty-nine cases were reported.[81]

The proposal to build a permanent isolation hospital at Worlds End had been revived and in October 1896 sanction was granted to borrow £29,669 for this purpose. Despite a prolonged industrial dispute, the hospital was nearing completion when it was visited by members of the Polytechnic Architectural and Engineering Society in May 1899. The visitors were impressed by 'the beauty of the entrance hall', also by the great care taken to ensure cleanliness by rounding the corners of the rooms. The hospital was opened on Saturday 10 February

1900; the public, invited in, found shining new furniture and cheerful fires burning. The patients were brought from the temporary hospital on the following Monday; they included a number from Edmonton for whom Edmonton Council paid one and a half guineas a week.[82]

A new ambulance, a brougham, was purchased in April 1902; it opened at the back to give access for a patient on a stretcher. There was a seat for a nurse by the patient's head and a cupboard for medicines. It had rubber tyres and finely tempered springs. Enfield and Edmonton in March 1905 became a united district to maintain the Isolation Hospital. During the diphtheria epidemic early in the year 1909, the hospital was found to be inadequate, and patients had to be sent to Walthamstow and Cheshunt at a cost of £579. The number of isolation hospital beds was a little over one to a thousand population. In August that year application was made to borrow £9,000 to build two new pavilions.[83]

There were alarming reports in September 1901 of smallpox in London; 163 cases had already been reported. In November Southgate Council took measures to protect its population against the epidemic and many people were re-vaccinated. The public vaccinator attended at Bush Hill Park School, Enfield in January to vaccinate those children whose parents had consented. A month later, the outbreak was widespread in the poorer parts of Edmonton. Some cases were in hospital, some at home, and many suspected cases wandered the streets. The first case in Enfield occurred at Ediswan's; the man was the foreman in the burnishing shop, which had to be closed and disinfected and all the workmen quarantined. The Council gave power to the medical officer to establish a temporary smallpox hospital; ten acres were taken at Crews Hill and tents were erected there. As the number of cases increased, an iron hospital was purchased which could accommodate thirteen patients. The epidemic continued into April; forty-three new cases were notified in the first fortnight of that month, mostly in eastern Enfield. The Council erected a third corrugated iron and matchboard block to house a further twenty smallpox patients, and two more tents were purchased for convalescents. It was deplorable, said the medical officer, that local authorities had no power to enforce isolation. By May only eight to ten new cases were being reported each week and the epidemic was over by September. There had been 102 cases in seventy-six houses in Enfield. Ponders End, lying nearest to Edmonton, had been the worst hit, sixty-eight cases had occurred there in fifty houses. There had been only nine deaths in Enfield, and the medical officer attributed the limited number to vaccination. The years 1904 to 1908 saw no further deaths from smallpox in the district. Enfield, as part of the Middlesex Joint Smallpox Hospital Board, had accepted by 1911 part of the responsibility for the smallpox hospital in South Mimms, but there had been no smallpox cases since the epidemic had finished in 1904 and it was now agreed that the hospital should accept tuberculosis cases.[84]

The year 1904 had brought a sharp increase in deaths among infants under one, to 158.3 per thousand live births, as against 113 in the previous year. This was thought to be due to the effect of the hot summer weather on milk, giving rise to an epidemic of diarrhoea. Nearly ten per cent of deaths each year were from tubercular diseases. Dr J.J. Ridge was of the opinion that facilities for the sterilisation of milk should be provided. There were fifty-six deaths from tuberculosis in 1907, which was nine per cent of all deaths; Dr Ridge described it as a preventable disease. In one or two places in the north of England, by 1906, milk was supplied in sealed bottles to ensure its purity (Donald Read. *England*

119. The hot summer of 1904 brought a calamitous rise in infant deaths, and primitive methods of milk production and distribution were blamed. Aluminium milk-bottle tops were first introduced by Stapleton's in October 1932.

1868-1914, Longman, 1979). From the beginning of the year 1909 a veterinary surgeon was employed in Enfield at a salary of £30 a year; he was required to examine every cow kept in Enfield, twice yearly. He examined 381 cows in December 1909 and found no trace of tubercle bacillus. The Council had decided upon the voluntary notification of tuberculosis in May that year. Some dairy farmers had already introduced their own precautions; Middleton's instituted a regular and systematic inspection of their Jersey herd at Home Farm by a bacteriologist. *The Sanitary Record* carried an article in 1913 by Dr W.P. Warren, who had replaced Dr Ridge as Medical Officer of Health for Enfield, describing a new plant to clean, cool and pasteurise milk, installed by H.W. Middleton at his dairy in Palace Parade. It rendered the milk, he said, entirely free of tuberculosis.[85]

The medical officer of health in Enfield, though now salaried, was still not a full-time appointment. Like Dr Ridge before him (who had died May 1908) Dr Warren held the offices of public vaccinator and police surgeon, and had a large private practice. The Enfield Public Welfare Association (self-appointed watchdogs over local government) continued to urge the appointment of a full-time medical officer but no such appointment was made until November 1926.

Infant mortality remained one of the worst problems in Enfield. As already stated, in 1904 it stood at 153.3 per thousand live births. The previous year it had been 113; in 1905 it was 117, in 1906 105.7 and in 1907 116. This last figure was worse than in any of the neighbouring parishes. Even in working-class Edmonton in 1907 infant mortality was 112, while in middle-class Southgate it was 72 and in the very select Wood Green it was a mere 69. The following year (1908) owing to the considerable reduction in epidemic diarrhoea, the figure in Enfield was down to ninety. Children were still put out to nurse in Enfield as they had been in the seventeenth century, though in the twentieth century the practice was a little more closely controlled. An inquest held in May 1909 tells something of the trade. George Poole Kane had been taken to nurse by Mrs Musson of Hawthorn Grove just before Christmas 1908, the child having been born in September. Mrs Musson was paid 5s a week. She had not notified the authorities as she ought to have done, but it was felt that there were mitigating circumstances, since the Act enforcing notification had only come into force on 1 April.[86]

The birth rate in 1909 was 24.36 which, the medical officer of health regretted to say, showed a serious diminution. Migration into Enfield had practically ceased by 1911 and over eight hundred houses stood empty. The birth rate was down to 23.14 (the figure for England and Wales was 24.4). 'It is regrettable' said the medical officer of health, 'to find the birth rate still diminishing. Probably', he went on, 'selfishness, love of luxury, the increased cost of living, and the unwillingness of married couples to undertake parental responsibility, account for the still greater paucity of children among the cultured classes'. The doctor reflected a national concern about what was felt to be the declining quality of the British race. Infant mortality in Enfield in 1911 was very high, at 140.79 (England and Wales, 130). It had been much lower in the years 1908 to 1910; 90.14, 111.42 and 83.15. The high figure was due to epidemic enteritis. 'Many mothers', said the medical officer, 'have a fixed idea that teething and infantile diarrhoea are connected, and they delay seeking advice; lives would be saved if they called in the doctor at once and would abide by his instructions. I fear', he went on, 'that not infrequently they exercise what they are pleased to term their own judgement and give the child items of diet which had been expressly forbidden'. The medical officer had been at a disadvantage in dealing with the crisis; eighty-one deaths from this infantile diarrhoea had occurred during the summer, but the first intimation of the illness received by the medical officer had been the death return.[87]

Local birth rates continued to decline. The number of births in Enfield in 1913 was 1,351, seventy less than in the previous year. The birth rate was 22.5 per thousand population. The middle classes were drastically cutting the size of their families. In residential sequestered Hadley Wood the birth rate was 8.49, in Enfield's Town ward, predominantly middle class, it was 13.71, in Ordnance ward, more well-to-do working class, it was 20.49, in Chase ward it was 23.92. In the part of Bush Hill Park east of the railway, among working-class commuters, it was 24.25 while in Ponders End it was 26.47. The Medical Officer of Health in December 1915 recommended the appointment of a health visitor and the building of four maternity centres.[88]

Notes to Chapter Five

1. MH 13. 69
2. *ibid,* William Ranger *Report to the General Board of Health ... Enfield* 1850
3. MH 13. 69, S.I. Richardson *Edmonton Poor Law Union 1837-1854 passim*
4. MH 13. 69
5. Enfield Surveyors' reports eg. 1D1865, MH13. 69, *Observer* Oct 1862
6. *ibid* N1866, 5 Ap 1879
7. MH 13.69, *Observer* S 1870
8. *ibid* Mr 1871, My 1872, S1874, 24 Ap, 5 Je, 3J1, 25D 1875, 8J1 1876
9. *ibid* J1 1871, J1 1870, Enfield Surveyors' reports 23S 1870, 3 Au 1866
10. *Observer* Ja 1871, J1, Au 1872
11. *ibid* F, Mr 1876, Enfield LBH minutes 5, 26 J1 1881
12. *Observer* 10F, 24F 1877, 25 Je 1881, Enfield LBH minutes, 11, 30 Oct 1879 27F 1880
13. MH 13. 69
14. *ibid*
15. HLG 1. 384, Census report 1901
16. *Observer* N 1873
17. *ibid* 1D 1874, 14 Au 1875, 19F 1876
18. *ibid* 16 Au 1895, 20 Ja 1899
19. HLG 25.10, *Observer* Mr 1864, J1 1868
20. *ibid* Au 1870, Au 1871
21. *ibid* My 1869
22. HLG 25.10
23. *Observer* 5 J1, 12 J1, 9 Au, 23 Au 1879
24. *ibid* 3 J1 1880
25. *ibid*
26. *ibid* 25 Je, 2 J1 1881
27. *ibid* 1 J1 1882, Dr Parsons's report quoted *Observer* 2 J1 1881
28. *ibid* 2 J1 1881
29. *ibid* 28 My 1881
30. *ibid* 17D 1881
31. *ibid* 15 Ap 1882
32. *ibid* 24 S, 15 X, 19 N 1881, 15 Mr 1889
33. *ibid* 6 My, 3 Je, 17 Je 1882
34. *ibid* 15 J1 1882
35. *ibid* 1 J1, 26 Au 1882
36. *ibid* 7X, 18N 1882, 24 Mr 1883, 13S, 15N 1884, 21 F 1885
37. *ibid* 21F 1884, 23 My 1885, 24X 1890
38. *ibid* 24 Je 1884, 21F 1885, 27N 1886
39. *ibid* 31 Mr 1883, 4X 1884
40. *ibid* 26 Au 1882, 14 J1 1883
41. *ibid* 14 J1, 1 D 1883, 6D 1895
42. *ibid* 28 J1, 18 Au, 25 Au 1883
43. *ibid* 27X 1883
44. *ibid* 3N 1883
45. *ibid* 12 Ap, 26 Ap, 10 My 1884
46. *ibid* 24N, 1D 1883, 12 J1 1884
47. *ibid* 20X, 1D, 15D, 22D 1883
48. *ibid* 20 Mr 1886, 4X 1884
49. *ibid* 11 J1 1885, 22X 1886
50. *ibid* 14 J1, 1S 1883, 20D 1884
51. *ibid* 11 Ap, 25 Ap, 9 My 1885, 26 Ap 1889
52. *ibid* 6 Mr 1886, 6 My, 30S 1887
53. *ibid* 11 Mr, 7 Ap 1887

54. *ibid* 12 Ap 1889, 28 Mr 1890
55. *ibid* 20S 1889, 6 Mr, 5 Je, 6N 1891
56. *ibid* 6N, 4D, 27N 1891
57. Enfield 614 (1893), '1892' Memorandum Dr S. Monckton Copeman and special report Dr J.J. Ridge
58. *Observer* 11 Mr, eg 8 Ap 1892, 20 Au 1909
59. *ibid* 13 Mr, 8 My 1880
60. *ibid* 17S 1881, 7X 1882
61. *ibid* 13 Ja, 2 Je 1883, 12 Ap, 27S 1884
62. *ibid* 13 Je 1885, 2 Ap 1886
63. *ibid* 17 Ap 1886
64. *ibid* 5 Au, 12 Au, 19 Au, 7X, 28X, 4N 1887
65. *ibid* 15 Je, 16 Jl 1894
66. *ibid* 4X 1889, 29 Je, 13 Jl 1894
67. *ibid* 16N, 23N, 30N, 21D 1894
68. *ibid* 5X 1894, eg 14X 1910
69. *ibid* 19 Ap, 26 Je, 2 Au, 18X 1895, 28F 1896
70. *ibid* 8X 1897, 31 Au, 14S 1900, 19 Jl, 30 Au 1901
71. *ibid* 11X 1901
72. *ibid* 12 My 1902
73. *ibid* 21 Je 1907, 29 Jl 1910
74. *ibid* 16 Je 1911, 27S 1912, 31X 1913, 4S 1914
75. *ibid* 6 Mr 1914
76. *ibid* 14 Au 1896
77. *ibid* 23D 1904, 25 Mr 1905, 16 Ja 1906, 4D 1903, 1 My 1908, 7 Je 1907
78. *ibid* 3F, 31 Mr 1911
79. *ibid* 16 Mr, 27 Ap 1900, 25X 1907
80. *ibid* 12N 1909, 11F 1910, 23 My 1913
81. *ibid* 21 Ja, 4 Mr 1898
82. *ibid* 30X 1896, 19 My 1899, 2F, 16F 1900
83. *ibid* 18 Ap 1902, 10 Mr 1905, 6 Au 1909
84. *ibid* 27S 1901, 3 Ja, 14 F, 21F, 28F, 4 Ap, 11 Ap, 23 My 1902, 14 Ap 1911
85. *ibid* 29X 1909, 10 Je 1910, 17 My 1905, 22 Mr 1907, 1 My 1908, 15 Ja, 24D, 14 My, 24N 1909, 6 Je 1913
86. *ibid* 1 My, 18S 1908, 14 My 1909
87. *ibid* 17 My 1912
88. MOH reports at Enfield

Chapter Six

Schools

1. Introduction

An examination of the community congregated around the crape works in South Street in 1841 demonstrates that respectable working-class people were aware of the importance of schooling and were willing to pay for it. Regularity of employment fostered an interest in education. Church and chapel competed to provide schools and Anglican clergymen even took to poaching infant scholars from the nonconformists. There was as much differentiation by class among those who worked in factories as there was in the more elevated levels of society. Sunday schools played a major role in raising self-respect by providing a rudimentary education for the children. Clergymen and ministers sought incessantly for bright, intelligent, moral young factory workers who might be willing to teach. The highest accolade which a minister could bestow upon a member of his congregation was that he or she would be suitable as a Sunday school teacher. Parents were not coerced, decent people wanted their children to learn to read and write.

Grammar schools throughout the country began to decline towards the end of the eighteenth century; usually the reason lay in the negligence of trustees. Enfield Grammar School abandoned the teaching of Latin and became an elementary school in 1825. Through the nineteenth century the ample endowment which had sustained the school since the fifteenth century was wasted away in the law courts. Meanwhile National and British schools were set up and these took over the original function of grammar schools in educating the poor. These circumstances left Enfield Grammar School both in need of a new role and a new source of income. It was transformed into a fee-paying, middle-class school, and as such it proceeded into the twentieth century when county grants opened its doors to the more ambitious and intelligent of the working class.

The role of providing elementary education in the early nineteenth century was taken over mainly by the Church of England with minor competition from the nonconformists. The 1870 Education Act made little difference in Enfield except that it forced Vicar Hodson to work more strenuously than ever to provide enough church schools to keep pace with the growing population. By his efforts Prebendary Hodson successfully prevented the setting up of a school board in Enfield for nearly a quarter of a century. It was established at last in 1894 but even then the vicar refused to accept defeat and managed to secure the chairmanship of the Enfield School Board, in which capacity he did his best to limit the money spent on board school education.

2. Secondary Education up to the First World War

Vestries were always well attended when something nasty was expected to happen. Twenty-three trustees of the Benfleet Charity, fifty-four named inhabitants, and many unnamed, were present on 24 September 1846 because notice had been served that the vestry had been called to consider the dismissal of James Emery, the schoolmaster at the Grammar School. He attended with a professional adviser and admitted the charge made against him, which was that he had marked scholars present in the register when they had been absent, but he denied fraudulent intent.

The motion for dismissal was proposed by Robert C.L. Bevan. There were one or two who argued that the charges against the schoolmaster were not of sufficient seriousness to warrant removal. He had served fifteen years during which time he had performed the duties of both master and usher without any increase of salary. He had promised to carry out whatever measures might be proposed by the trustees to improve the efficiency of the school. The vestry however remained adamant and the motion in favour of dismissal was carried by a show of hands. Emery's supporters demanded a poll, but it only confirmed the decision by forty-one votes to two.

Despite this overwhelming defeat, Mr Emery was not prepared to concede. His supporters raised the matter in time for the November vestry, held in the school. On this occasion they were defeated by ninety-one votes to sixty-three, but only by the use of plural voting, for the ninety-one votes were placed by forty parishioners. The defeated party protested in vain that their sixty-three votes represented forty-eight parishioners.

The December vestry considered three candidates to fill the post; Thomas Bowden, the Reverend William Flower and Charles Chambers. Chambers, being proposed by the all-powerful group of magistrates, James Meyer, Daniel Harrison and Robert C.L. Bevan, was elected by an overwhelming majority. In the light of later events their promotion of his candidature was ironic indeed. Mr Emery meanwhile sat tight and legal proceedings to eject him were begun in Chancery. The action failed and the trustees were ordered to pay £432 costs; they now found themselves at an impasse. It was at this juncture that John Sawyer (acting for his father Henry Sawyer, the vestry clerk) called upon Mr Chambers and made him a proposition (which of course he must in no way consider sanctioned by the gentlemen trustees). He might, the clerk insinuated, if he chose, pay Mr Emery something to induce him to move (the trustees themselves could not be seen to do this). Should he succeed, Mr Sawyer reassured him with confidence, anything he paid to Emery would be made up to him. Chambers, desperate to get the position, accepted. He had only £20 to his name, for he had spent £60 on the campaign to get himself elected. Therefore, relying upon the assurances of the parish clerk, he procured a short-term loan of £450 and paid the money to Emery, who was thereby persuaded to leave the school-house. The trustees, to Mr Chambers's dismay, now declined to recognise any responsibility for the offer. The good vicar, Mr Heath, seeing the new schoolmaster's predicament, set on foot a subscription, but the vicar was not presently popular in his parish, and only £78 was raised. Chambers, a highly efficient teacher by all accounts, was thus left drowning in an ocean of debt. He had been educated at Worcester College Oxford but had not taken a degree, nevertheless he had some knowledge of both Latin and Greek. Before his appointment at Enfield he had worked as a poorly-paid usher.

There were thirty boys when he took over the Enfield school and at that time, according to the vicar, the education there was no better than that provided at the National School. By his efforts he raised the numbers in ten years from thirty to seventy and considerably improved the standard of teaching. Meanwhile he managed to augment his salary by taking a few private pupils; in 1853 there were eight or nine, which constituted a private school. By 1857 he had seventeen boarders and five day scholars and some of the trustees themselves had sent their sons, grandsons or nephews to him privately. The private pupils were never instructed with the boys from the free school and never entered the school-house. The free boys were educated without charge, except that they paid a shilling a term for ink, and had to pay for their books which they purchased from Mr Chambers. There had been complaints by parents about the increased cost of these books. This had arisen because Mr Chambers had raised the standard of teaching above the elementary school level prescribed by the 1825 scheme. The books, which had formerly cost only 3s throughout the child's entire time at the school, now cost 14s 9d, and many of the parents regarded this as exorbitant.

School prizes were provided by the trustees, mostly for proficiency with a few for regular attendance at church, but the generosity of the trustees was cut off abruptly in 1855. The reason was that Charles Chambers had accepted the office of vicar's warden and had thus unwisely involved himself in the bitter feud between High Church and Low Church which continued to tear the parish asunder. It was at this time that the trustees first 'discovered' the schoolmaster's private school, to which many of them had formerly sent their children. The master claimed that the work involved did not interfere with his teaching at the free school, for he taught his paying pupils before nine, between twelve and two, and in the evenings. The remaining instruction was done by a French teacher and a teacher of English, paid by the master. The monitors reported that Mr Chambers would come into the free school at nine o'clock, he would read prayers and hear two or three classes, and would then walk around the school to see that the boys were in order and that they wrote correctly. Sometimes he left during the morning and sometimes he came back, but not always. In the afternoon he took classes in arithmetic and read prayers, then he left for half an hour, but he generally returned. The usher, Mr Crampin, however admitted that he had never worked at a school where there were so many half-day holidays.

Mr Chambers had hoped further to improve the standard of education. He pointed out in a memorial submitted in May 1857 that the number of schools in the parish had greatly increased since 1825. That was the year when the scheme under which the Grammar School then operated had come into force. At that time it had been the only school open to the inhabitants; now there were seven day schools and one night school affording 'ample provision for the poor', while the middle class for whom, in the master's opinion, the foundation ought to provide, had no suitable school. He felt that standards should be raised to the level of 'private, classical and commercial schools' and should provide an extended range of subjects suited to the needs of middle-class children. The master's salary was £147 10s, but only while the number of children in the school remained above sixty; on this same condition he was entitled to employ an usher, paid by the trustees at £50 a year, but if the numbers dropped below sixty, the usher would have to be discharged, and the master's salary cut by one-third.

Neither the schoolmaster's ability nor his record in office were of any relevance to the decision now taken by the trustees to dismiss him; he was an ally of the vicar and that was enough. Thus it was that John Sawyer, solicitor to the trustees, called at the offices of the Charity Commissioners on 31 May 1858 to lay a complaint against Mr Chambers and to seek the opinion of the Commissioners whether the trustees could remove him. Chambers's debts had increased and now amounted to £4,000 borrowed at rates of interest varying from five to ten per cent; £1,000 of it was said to be owed to local tradesmen. He had been forced to assign over his salary, in August 1857, to a scrivener from whom he had borrowed £730, and the scrivener had taken possession of his goods. A new charge was brought against him. He was accused that, having received as churchwarden money for lighting the church with gas, he had applied it to his own use and although he had since given power to the secretary of the trust to repay the money from his wages, these were found to be already assigned to meet another debt. Somehow the money had subsequently been repaid to the church. It was further alleged against him that he had induced a respectable tradesman of the Town to stand surety for his debts and this had resulted in the man's imprisonment and ruin.

Chambers had been forced to petition the Insolvent Debtors Court for relief. His insolvency, the trustees alleged, had interfered with his duties as schoolmaster and had caused him to be absent at intervals. Over the previous three weeks he had been forced to employ a substitute and this he had done without the sanction of his employers. The opinion was widespread in the parish, declared the trustees, that 'a person so acting in the eye of the public is quite unfit for the instruction of young children'. All this was laid before the Charity Commissioners who sent their inspector Mr Simons, to investigate.

There occurred yet another well attended vestry on 12 August 1858 when fifty-six vestrymen were present. Daniel Harrison was the principal speaker and he urged the dismissal of the schoolmaster. Mr Ford of Old Park then solemnly read aloud a motion which declared that the master, by his conduct, had totally forfeited the confidence of the parishioners and was not a fit and proper person to fill the office. J.R. Rignall defended the master persuasively, urging on the vestry the necessity to avoid further litigation. He pointed out that the last three law suits, against two former masters and against a tenant, had all been unsuccessful and had cost the trustees nearly £2,000. This argument was so obviously alarming the neutrals at the meeting, that Ford and Harrison raised points of order to prevent him speaking further. All this, they said, had been gone into when the matter had been examined by the inspector and it should not be repeated here. Mr Rignall urged in reply that his observations were in answer to attacks made on the schoolmaster by Mr Harrison at the present vestry, but Mr Harrison withdrew his allegations so that Mr Rignall was prevented from further presenting the schoolmaster's case.

This dispute was a renewed flare-up of the High Church, Low Church confrontation which had for some years disturbed the parish. Mr Chambers, by accepting the office of vicar's warden, had brought down upon his head the rancorous hostility of his former mentors, the magistrates James Meyer, Edward Ford and Daniel Harrison. The weak position in which his financial embarrassments had placed him had afforded them the opportunity to strike him down. According to Mr Rignall, Harrison had admitted that if Chambers had not identified himself with the vicar's cause, he would have been left alone. These great magistrates had packed the vestries, canvassing the support of publicans, beer-shop keepers, shopkeepers, small farmers and artisans, said Mr Rignall, all in pursuit of their vicious campaign against the vicar.

It was planned to confirm and execute the decision of the trustees to dismiss the schoolmaster at the September vestry. The vicar was present and took the chair. The motion to remove Chambers was moved by Edward Ford and was carried unanimously. But this resolution by no means ended the matter. Before the chairman was a letter in which the schoolmaster announced his refusal to recognise the authority of the vestry. 'I am advised' he wrote, and there can be little doubt that it was the vicar who advised him, 'that I have good legal grounds to dispute the validity of the proceedings'.

The vicar then protested that he had received no proper notification of the meeting of the trustees where the decision had been taken and, in consequence, he did not consider himself bound in any way by that resolution. Moreover he could not agree to any demand that Chambers should be forced to hand over possession of his house and of his office, to any person to whose authority he, the vicar, as a trustee, had not consented. The vicar's intervention made obvious the dubious legality of the resolution to dismiss Chambers. Despite this three trustees, Daniel Harrison, Richard Brailsford and Thomas Knight, conscious of the importance of their self-appointed task, left the meeting and strode across to the school-house. John Moore Heath, vacating the chair, followed closely behind. Rapping at the door, Harrison demanded of Charles Chambers the possession and the mastership of the school, declaring; 'Mr Charles Chambers, I attend here with other trustees to require you to give up possession of the school-house'. The vicar again intervened to insist that he did not recognise their authority. Upon which Chambers demanded, 'Have you any other authority?'. Harrison replied 'No other authority', whereupon Mr Chambers declined to surrender possession. The four men then returned to the vestry where Daniel Harrison proposed that legal action should be taken at once. The vicar was immediately on his feet to point out that no such action could legally be taken without the consent of all the trustees, and he certainly would not agree. The vestry, baffled, could only decide that the opinion of the Charity Commissioners must be sought.

Counsel engaged by the Commissioners was less than helpful. In an action of ejectment, he opined, all trustees must join and, since the vicar refused, this course of proceeding was not open. He advised the trustees to appoint a new schoolmaster and then to seek an injunction to restrain Chambers from performing the duties. But the trustees, he warned, must first get from the Charity Commissioners a certificate to authorise them to commence proceedings. Acting as best they could upon this unhelpful advice, a vestry was called in February 1859 to elect the new master. Its progress was marred however by a further intervention from the vicar who pointed out the legal weakness of the position being adopted. Some of those who had originally supported dismissal began to seek ways to defer the matter. A motion by Thomas Brading, seconded by John Tuff, suggested that it was undesirable and impolitic to proceed to the election... until a new scheme of school management had been prepared and approved by the vestry. Meanwhile the Charity Commissioners, becoming even less helpful, felt unable to sanction any legal action to secure the injunction against Chambers which they themselves had recommended. Their negative attitude was due in no small way to a letter from John Moore Heath in which the vicar carefully outlined the reasons why any resort to law by the trustees must end in failure and must inevitably involve trust property in enormous and unknown expense. Under these circumstances, he suggested, it was the duty of the Commissioners to consider what was the value to the school of obtaining a dismissal, and how far the trustees should be allowed to alienate the funds for the purpose of obtaining this result. Not too well concealed between the lines of the vicar's letter lay the inference that the impecunious schoolmaster could rely upon his support if the trustees did resort to law, and the vicar knew his law somewhat better than the lawyers employed by the Commissioners. He outlined the grounds likely to be adopted in the schoolmaster's defence. 'Mr Heath', he says, referring to himself in the third person, 'cannot refrain from expressing his astonishment that the Commissioners should have so easily satisfied themselves of the advantage it would be to the school to get rid of a tried and exceedingly good and successful master'.

The Charity Commissioners, offended and uncertain, wrote to reprove the vicar for his lack of respect and his refusal to co-operate with them. He replied coldly that since that august body had displayed no impartiality, and so little concern for the funds of the school, it ought not to expect to be resorted to as judge in the case. He attacked the decision of the Commissioners to exempt the trustees from personal responsibility for the costs of any litigation, thus leaving the charitable funds liable to be dissipated.

The trustees now found themselves in an untenable position. They had dismissed the master yet were unable to secure a certificate from the Charity Commission giving them sanction to enforce that dismissal through the courts. They now resorted to a course of action which was both unworthy and unwise. They ceased to pay the master's salary, thus laying themselves open to an action to enforce payment. They cut off from the school its supply of coal through the winter and refused to carry out even essential repairs to the building. Thus they courted the hostility of both parents and parishioners who saw Mr Chambers working on without pay and providing out of his own pocket (or the vicar's) whatever was necessary to keep the school going.

The following month saw a testimonial presented on behalf of the master from the parents of his former pupils. It thanked him for the quality of both his classical and commercial instruction which had enabled their sons to obtain situations of high responsibility. The list of signatures shows that many of the students had attended the school from as far away as Enfield Lock and Ponders End. A meeting of influential inhabitants in January 1860 unanimously urged the trustees to avoid resort to law. A motion was carried urging that no legal costs incurred by the trustees should be paid from the funds of the charity. Despite the fact that the trustees had withheld the services of an usher and had done their utmost to force the school to close, the numbers had increased and efficiency had improved. There were now eighty-two scholars. A second memorial, headed by John Tuff the local historian and chemist and carrying 304 signatures, offered the master new support. It roundly declared that the origin of the dispute lay in 'differences which unfortunately exist in the parish on ecclesiastical matters quite foreign to the school.'

Mr Chambers strengthened his position by his reasonableness. He offered to resign, though with compensation, in justice to himself and his family, to cover his expenses and two years salary. The blatant neglect with which the trustees were treating the ancient school entrusted to their care was daily diminishing their support within the parish. Broken windows had been left unrepaired and closets stopped-up. The school remained without water after the pipes had burst during the winter and these had to be repaired by the master himself. People were asking whether it was just, that Mr Chambers should be starved into submission.

Two meetings of the trustees called to consider the crisis were so ill-attended that no quorum could be found. The Charity Commissioners continued to give bad advice, urging that any action should be left to the schoolmaster. On 22 April 1862 his solicitor gave notice that he proposed to file a bill in Chancery. Still the trustees remained in a state of obdurate paralysis. A hastily called vestry deplored the fact that any attempt by the trustees to defend this action in Chancery must imperil the funds of the charity. An out of court settlement was urged and it was again demanded that any legal costs incurred should be borne by the trustees themselves. The Charity Commissioners continued to behave with unbending stupidity. Letters sent to them by the vicar in which he demonstrated the strength of the schoolmaster's case, in an endeavour to persuade the Commissioners to use their influence to arrive at a compromise, were passed over to the trustees' solicitor. Their reply to vicar Heath is quotable only for its extraordinary pomposity. 'In giving this necessary answer to your communication', their secretary wrote, 'I am to refrain from any discussion of the opinion expressed by you … '. Meanwhile the position of the trustees in the parish worsened, as did the condition of the school building.

Collections were now being made to pay the wages of a second master and to carry out the repairs necessary for the comfort and health of the children. The vestry, where opinion had completely changed, pleaded with the Charity Commission 'that the property of the school should not be sacrificed in the Court of Chancery to gain an end not desired by the parents of the boys or the parish in general'. Even the trustees themselves were now talking about compromise. At last in March 1863, somewhat too late, the Charity Commissioners instructed Mr Skirrow to report on the school. The weight of evidence taken before him strongly supported Mr Chambers's case, even from the four trustees who appeared. James Meyer spoke of his efficiency and good character and in this he was supported by Major General Richard Connop. Parents like William Ebben the baker, who had once been prominent in the campaign to eject the schoolmaster, admitted that two of his sons had been taught at the school since August 1858, and that he had never heard of any irregularities like 'getting into debt or intoxicated'.

Mr Skirrow in his report drew attention to the weakness of the trustees' defence against the master's claim, and proposed a settlement. The claims against the trust now amounted to £1,495. He suggested that the Charity Commissioners should authorise the raising of £650 by a mortgage on the charity estates. Slowly and reluctantly the trustees took steps to meet the claims against them. John Moore Heath left his vicarage and resigned from the trust in January 1866. 'I had foreseen from the commencement', he wrote, 'that they (the trustees) would inflict a great injustice on the schoolmaster and a serious injury to the interests of the school and the parish, but the Charity Commissioners, having decided that measures which involved the ruin of the school ought to be followed up, the school has been nearly ruined and the master burdened with £200 law costs which might otherwise have been paid to his creditors… '.[2]

The vestry which met in April 1866 protested yet again that the trustees, having expended nearly £1,000 on the late proceedings, had now effected, without consulting the vestry, a mortgage on the estate, despite an assurance given by certain trustees that no expense would fall upon the charity. A number of new trustees were appointed at this time including the Reverend William Douglas MacLagan, the new curate in charge at St Andrew's. The financial position of the school was now impossible. Insufficient income remained, after repayment of the mortgage and interest, to meet the salary of the schoolmaster. The school premises were so dilapidated that £600 or £700 would have to be spent on the building.[3]

The Endowed School Commission had now taken over the duties relating to education formerly exercised by the Charity Commissioners. For a few years the school stumbled on with insufficient funds to repay the mortgage or to repair the premises. In August 1872 the building was declared unfit for educational purposes and the trustees sought from the Endowed Schools Commission sanction to close it for a time. Sanction was refused. The trustees now however decided that they should end the delays and present new proposals to put the finances of the school on a firm footing. To this end the school did not reopen after the Christmas holidays. The trustees drew up a scheme of reorganisation to transform Enfield Grammar into a middle-class, fee-paying, self-financing establishment, providing 'a sound liberal education... for the children of that class of parishioner whose means entitled him to share with the charity the expense of his children's education', a school which might attract a better class of resident to rent property in the parish. Fees were to be not less than £4 and not more than £10 a year, the entrance fee not more than £1. Before admission, at the age of seven, applicants would sit an examination requiring the reading of a simple narrative, writing text hand, easy sums which involved the first two rules of arithmetic and multiplication tables. This test was never used to grade the applicants and few were ever rejected. Students at the age of thirteen were to be examined in reading, writing, arithmetic, English grammar, dictation and the elements of geography. Reading and spelling, writing, arithmetic, algebra and geometry, mensuration and land surveying, English grammar, composition and literature, history and geography, drawing and vocal music, Latin and French, and at least one branch of natural science, would be taught.

Mr Chambers resigned on a pension of £90 a year. Plans were now submitted to the Endowed Schools Commission for the restoration of the building. The Commission suggested one large room on the upper floor instead of the two smaller rooms and the demolition of the turret staircase. The changes were rejected by the trustees mainly on the grounds of cost, but also because the stair turret was architecturally important to the building. The school was reopened on 24 January 1876 under William MacDonald MA, with twenty-five pupils. MacDonald did not remain long and was replaced by W.S. Ridewood BA, BSc; he was to receive £120 a year and not less than £3 a year for each boy. Fees were £2 a term (drawing 6s 8d extra). Most of the boys were prepared for the Cambridge Local, but those especially proficient took the London Matriculation. There were three class masters, all former pupils, including the senior master George Brace, once a free boy, who had obtained a BA (first class) at London. There were also teachers of French, drawing and drill.[4]

Success did not come immediately. The Lord Mayor of London, at a prize giving before Christmas 1877, spoke of his regret 'that so useful an institution was not appreciated so fully as it deserved'. The large and commodious schoolroom was not half-filled. 'The people of Enfield', he said, 'had not given the school the encouragement warranted by the sound practical education imparted there'. He complained that parents no longer thought it their duty to pay for the education of their children. The trouble was that standards in state (ie board) schools were too high, so high indeed that few middle-class schools could over-top them in commercial education, and parents would not pay twopence for what they could get for a penny. The numbers grew only slowly;

1876	1877	1878	1879	1880	1881	1882	1884	1886	1887	1888	1889	1890
25	30	36	39	47	58	77	102	112	106	98	84	90

In 1876 only the ground floor was used for teaching but as the school grew the upper floors were appropriated and furnished. To provide access a stone staircase was put up outside the building. The playground was enlarged and some gymnastic apparatus was set up. There had been a slow increase in the number of students by 1884 but the parishioners remained unenthusiastic when asked to raise a thousand pounds for a scholarship. Few attended the meeting called, despite Edward Ford's generous offer to build a new house for the master so that the rooms occupied by him over the school could be released to accommodate a hundred more scholars. The house was completed by December that year, a stone tablet in the wall records that the building was erected 'in gentle memory of Elizabeth Hill Winchester Ford of Old Park.'

An inspection in 1890 describes a lower middle class school. The parents were shopkeepers, clerks, a few solicitors, one doctor and a general. Boys who failed to win the public examination scholarships often came as paying scholars. Many of the pupils stayed only about eighteen months and then were sent to schools in London, thus most of the boys were between twelve and fourteen. Where there were two brothers, one was often at the Grammar School and another at a National School. Circumstances like these impeded the improvement of educational standards in the higher classes. Forty-five of the boys in 1890 came from Enfield Town, ten from Ponders End and the Highway, five from the Ordnance factory, and thirty from beyond the parish boundaries; from Winchmore Hill, Palmers Green and Bowes Park. Fees were still £2 a term (drawing 6s 8d extra). There was little in the way of school activities. The trustees had hired a cricket ground during the previous summer, but the boys took little interest, preferring to go straight home after school. Some private schools by contrast made much of sport. The Palace School had long had its own playing ground and fielded both rugby football and cricket teams.

The teaching staff in 1890 consisted of Dr Ridewood the headmaster, paid £120 a year plus £3 a pupil, amounting to £390, George Brace BA at £120, Harold Smith, a student who had passed Inter BA, and was paid £65, and Albert Ely now matriculated and rewarded at £14 a year. A drawing master received a salary of £24, a drill instructor was paid 5s a session and a French teacher 6s, though French was taught only occasionally. In addition Harold Sage, one of the monitors, was paid £10 a year; the headmaster taught the monitors out of school hours. Latin took prime place in the curriculum, followed by scripture.[5]

The number of scholarship boys holding free places rose only slowly, from two in 1876, out of twenty-five, to four in 1884 out of 102, reaching six out of 98 in 1888. There was so little competition for scholarships that in some years not more than two boys were entered; the trustees of Enfield Charities even offered

120.   Enfield Grammar School boys and staff, 1883.

£10 as an incentive.

Poynettes Farm (see Vol. 1) was let at £60 a year in 1890, which was considered a very good rent, although it had fetched £100 in 1874. The Old Coffee House was much out of repair and the rent had to be reduced from £20 to £16. It was felt that if the school prospered it should be taken over for classrooms and a laboratory. The old master's house had been converted to classrooms although one upstairs room was retained as a study for the headmaster.

Standards at the Grammar slowly improved, new subjects were undertaken, trigonometry was taught and as well as Latin and French, German and Greek were offered, also physical science including practical chemistry. The Middlesex County Council, which had been set up in 1888, offered grants to public endowed schools where the standard of teaching had been approved; schools receiving such grants must be open to County Council scholarship boys. By this time (February 1893) Enfield Grammar had 120 scholars. 'The teaching appeared to be excellent', said a County report, and it went on to propose that the school would be suitable for scholarships for boys if the science teaching could be improved by the addition of a laboratory. To meet this condition the County offered to pay half the capital costs up to £500 and up to £200 a year towards the running costs.[6] Middlesex provided fifteen three-year technical scholarships for boys between eleven and thirteen throughout the county; they were valued at £20 a year each, plus up to £10 a year for maintenance. Among the leading pass marks in the first year were three Enfield boys, Ernest Knight, whose father was a bricklayer, Edward Hickford, the son of a sword-setter and Walter John Jeffery, the son of a carpenter. Young Walter was to bring further honours to the school when, in 1897, he went on to win a Middlesex County Council higher technical scholarship at the City and Guilds Institute College worth £100 over two years. It was only the second time that such a scholarship had been awarded by the County and both had been won by Enfield Grammar School boys. The school was now certainly held in higher regard. An Old Boys' organisation had been formed and its members presented a handsome sports challenge cup to commemorate sixty years of the Queen's reign. It was proudly displayed in Mr Beavan's shop in Silver Street. School sports at this time were held on the football ground at Cherry Orchard Lane.

At the prize-giving in December 1897 Sir John Gorst, vice-president of the Council on Education and founder of the Conservative Central Office, spoke of the growth and efficiency of the school. There were 150 scholars and three or four free places were offered by scholarship each year.[7] The school was financed very largely by fees, from which an income was derived of between £800-£900 a year. There were eight to ten free scholars. In March 1900 the County grant for technical education was increased to £300.

The 1902 Education Act was an important step towards the elimination of class distinctions in society. It created state responsibility for secondary education, providing, through the education committees of the county councils, further opportunities for lower middle class and upper working class children to obtain an education above the elementary level.[8]

The school by February 1904 had 160 scholars and was in urgent need of more classrooms and a larger playground. A year later there were 174 scholars and the governors had enabled the school to rent a field for cricket. A new scheme for the management of the Grammar School was formulated by the Board of Education in November 1905, under the 1902 Education Act. Governors were

121. A girls secondary school and technical institute was planned here in 1906 on a five-acre site in Holly Walk, secured from Sir Alfred Somerset at £900 an acre. The school opened in December 1909. The railings in the photograph belong to the Garden of Rest, the cows to dairyman Hawkins.

to be appointed, and Middlesex County Council took over financial responsibility. It was to be a public secondary school for boys, for day scholars only between the ages of eight and eighteen. Entrance was to be by examination, and tuition fees were to range between £4 and £10 a term. Scholarships valued at up to £40 a year were to be offered to Enfield boys. Plans greatly to extend the school were formulated jointly by Enfield Council and the County in June 1907. Land had been purchased and it was proposed to build five additional classrooms, a hall, cloakroom, common room, changing room and lavatories. The old school hall was to be used as a dining hall, and there would be accommodation for 230 pupils. By the end of that year the County Council was responsible for five secondary schools including Enfield Grammar, Tottenham Grammar and Southgate County. It maintained a further four secondary schools including Latymer Edmonton. In September 1908 Dr Ridewood advised the governors of his intention to retire; Edwin M. Eagles was appointed at the following meeting and took over in January 1909. The estimated annual income of the school at this time was £2,296, the cost per pupil was £14 7s, the highest of any secondary school run by the County. The extensions were completed in September 1909. A handsomely decorated assembly hall had been provided and an ample playing field near the school. The age of entry was raised from eight to ten.[9]

The County had co-operated with the Urban District Council in 1906 to plan and build a girls' secondary school and technical institute. A five-acre site in Holly Walk was secured from Sir Alfred Somerset at £900 an acre. The foundation stone of the new school was laid in November 1908 and it opened in December 1909. Miss E.R. Broome MA was the first headmistress. Fees per

122.   Edith Clutten was trained through the pupil-teacher system; she taught in Enfield for forty years.

term in 1910 were £2 2s 6d, which covered the use of books and stationery, and equipment for hockey and tennis. The school could accommodate 220 pupils; it had eight classrooms, a cookery room and two laboratories which were made available to boys from the Grammar School.[10]

The new school was also to house the girls from the pupil-teacher centre. This provided an opportunity for both boys and girls, of sixteen and over, who wished to train as elementary school teachers. It had sixty-two students at this time, the male students were to be housed in the Grammar School. Under the pupil-teacher system of training, the County submitted to the local education committee the names of candidates who would be nominated for bursarships (£10 for girls, £12 for boys) to enable them to continue their education at secondary school for a further year. At the end of this time they had to pass an examination to obtain their student teachership and this brought a grant amounting to £30 for boys and £26 for girls. They then worked as student-teachers for a year in the schools. The pupil-teacher system thus provided a rope up which a child of quite poor parents could, with application and determination, haul herself (even himself) up into the teaching profession. The career of Edith Mary Clutten perhaps typifies the process. She was first a scholar, then a pupil-teacher, at a National school in Southwold where, by 1901, and at the age of twenty, she had completed her training. That school however was too small to offer her any advancement since it employed only a headmistress, an assistant mistress and two pupil-teachers. She therefore, warmly recommended, obtained a position as an assistant mistress at a National School in Norwich where she proved a conscientious teacher and gained considerable credit by being a regular communicant at the local church. She remained there for two years until she left to obtain a teaching certificate at the Norwich Training College. From there she was appointed to St Andrew's Girls School in Enfield in October 1905, her teaching certificate being duly forwarded to her in March 1907. She seems not to have particularly distinguished herself in any subject but needle-work, but she was spoken of as 'industrious, caring, a good disciplinarian and scarcely ever absent'. Owing to falling numbers at the National School she was transferred to the new Lavender School, in the girls' department, in 1910, where she was to take charge of the needlework. Her salary in 1912 amounted to £8 11s a month. She moved in 1921 to Eastfield Mixed School which was generally regarded as difficult, and in 1924 to Bush Hill Park Senior Girls. She was admired as an excellent teacher, 'her reputation as a class teacher', said one headmaster, 'was made before she came here'. Her last post was a move back to Eastfield in 1935 from where she retired, well respected, eleven years later after forty-one years service in Enfield schools. She died at the age of ninety in the year 1978.

The number of free places grew slowly. The County offered fourteen schol-arships at the Grammar School in 1910 and sixteen were offered at the Girls' County School. A new scholarship scheme was set up early in 1911; it provided free places for four years at the Grammar School, at Latymer Edmonton, at Enfield County School and at the Southgate County School. Applicants had to be under thirteen and had to contract to stay for a least three years, admission was by examination in arithmetic and in English, both written and oral. The slow expansion of free secondary education continued through the war. In 1917 the County Council provided 437 free places, including twenty boys at the Grammar School, ten at Southgate County and six at Latymer. It also provided sixteen places for girls at Enfield County, six at Latymer and ten at Southgate County.[11]

St Andrew's Upper Grade School opened in the old National school building in London Road in 1891; it moved to Cecil Road in 1895. Scholars were charged 6d and 9d a week. It took boys and girls between five and eight and girls over eight. The curriculum covered all subjects taught in public elementary schools up to standard six and girls were prepared for entry into the County School. It largely recruited its pupils on social rather than educational grounds. The children came from a broad catchment area, from Palmers Green, Southgate and Edmonton as well as from Enfield.

3. Private and Technical Education

Many private schools, large or small, cheap or expensive, existed for the education of those whose parents could afford to pay. At the Hill School, possibly in Gothic Hall at the north end of Baker Street, in 1867, the Reverend J.H. Walker prepared boys for the public schools 'at moderate terms'. M. Smith, who had recently opened his school (May 1872) at Rose House in Baker Street, 'was ready to receive a few more boys' at 1s 6d a week. A.T. Cuffley, in July 1872, announced that he proposed to open 'a good middle-class day school' in Enfield. There was a preparatory school for boys and girls under the age of nine at Gordon Lodge in Chase Side in December 1872, run by Mrs Dillon with the assistance of a tutor and a governess. Children were taught English, French, drawing, music and drill, the terms were a guinea and a half a quarter, raised in 1874 to eight guineas a year. In the same house Mr Dillon prepared students for the universities, the civil service and the public school preliminary examina-tions. At Elm House in Gentleman's Row there was a girls boarding and day

123.   *The North Middlesex High School for Girls moved from Fortescue Villas Gentleman's Row, in 1901, to a new school in Waverley Road.*

124.   *The Misses Garrard ran a day school at Percy House on the north side of Church Street. The house was demolished in 1907.*

school where were offered English, science, drawing, the theory of music, and classics, with French taught by a resident French lady. The West Enfield High School for Girls, in Glebe Avenue, charged three to five guineas a term, in

125.   *Shirley Lodge stood on the south side of Windmill Hill (east of the railway station) and Misses Edith and Louisa Chambers ran a school there. They were the daughters of Charles Chambers, one of Enfield's most controversial Grammar School headmasters. The house was demolished around 1925.*

advance.[13]

The most important of the girls private schools in the area was the North Middlesex High School for Girls at High Road, Tottenham and, from 1892, at Fortescue Villas, Gentleman's Row, Enfield. The headmistress, Miss Woolley, had formerly worked under Frances Buss the outstanding headmistress of the North London Collegiate School. The North Middlesex School, founded in 1884, was a pioneer in the provision of higher education for girls in this area. It boasted a record of almost two thousand public honours and successes by the end of the year 1898, an average of 185 a year over the previous ten years. Students were prepared for the London Matriculation, the Oxford Locals, the Royal Academy of Music and the Royal College of Music examinations. The school aimed to provide education for those girls who would otherwise be educated at home. Fees were four to five guineas a term in 1898, raised to six guineas in 1911. Pupils were prepared for Girton, Newnham and Oxford Halls. There were thirty girls when the school was taken over in 1899 by the Misses Webster and Miller, but by 1901 the numbers had greatly increased and a new school was built in Waverley Road. A kindergarten and preparatory school was opened in 1910 at Grange Park to serve the new middle-class estate there.[14]

The Misses Garrard ran a day school in 1894 for girls and boys at Percy House in Church Street, while that same year, at Shirley Lodge on Windmill Hill, the Misses Chambers (the daughters of the before mentioned Charles Chambers) taught English, French, Latin, music, callisthenics and drill to prepare their students for the public schools. The Claysmore School at Clay Hill opened at Claysmore in 1896, and school buildings were erected in the grounds. 'The reputation for hospitality at Claysmore during the residence of Colonel and Mrs Bosanquet', said the *Observer* (17 July 1896) 'has been revived by Mr Alexander Devine, the principal, who invites parties to the house on Saturday afternoons'. These included members of the Young People's Guild at Bow and members of the Mildmay working men's club with their wives. They watched school cricket and partook of tea at tables on the cricket field, being waited on by the pupils; music was provided by the band of the Chase Farm School. The entertainment culminated in an evening concert in the Oak Room. A junior boarding school was added there in March 1900. Alexander Devine had begun his working life as a clerk, but he did a great deal of work in the management of boys clubs. He was one of the pioneers of the modern public school, encouraging manual labour and hobbies as well as sport. Claysmore was an estate of a hundred and fifty acres, formerly owned by the Bosanquets and before them (until 1847) by Edward Harman who had enlarged and improved the mansion. He had added a gallery, sixty feet long and panelled, with a carved oak screen and costly stained glass windows set in copper which contained thirteenth century work. Devine aimed to eliminate certain features which he regarded as undesirable in the old public schools, and his boys were required to maintain the school by their own labours. The students were mostly of wealthy parentage including foreign royalty and the sons of peers and baronets, but all social distinctions were in abeyance. The boys built their own rifle range and kennels and visits were organised to local factories. There were no competitive examinations. The school moved to Pangbourne in Berkshire in 1902 and to Winchester about 1905.[15]

Middlesex County Council began tentative efforts to provide technical education in the 1890s with evening classes in woodwork, ambulance work, laundry work, dressmaking, cookery, nursing, shorthand and book-keeping. More technical subjects were added including engineering and electrical engineering. A large proportion of those registering for the technical courses came from the Royal Small Arms Factory, so much so that the start of the classes in the year 1898 had to be delayed because overtime was being worked at the factory. Major Bowles urged the need for a centre from which technical education in Enfield could be organised and, in September 1905, the County purchased the former Ediswan Institute at Ponders End for £800 and spent £150 to repair and equip it for the ensuing session, the local authority contributing £300. Special classes were provided on electric lighting and power transmission. Evening classes were attended by 1,213 students in February 1909. The demand for technical education from trainees at the RSAF and the gunpowder factory gave rise to a question in the House of Commons that year and elicited an offer from the War Office to contribute £500 to build and equip a technical institute at Ponders End to replace the Ediswan Institute. The County agreed to provide £4,400 and the Urban District Council £1,700.[16]

The new Technical Institute at Ponders End co-operated closely with the local electrical and gas industries and with the Royal Small Arms Factory where the apprentices were put through a thorough course in the workshops, each under the instruction of a skilled workman. They sat their examinations at the Institute, competing for the Whitworth scholarships. Training particularly emphasised the role of costs in production; 1,485 enrolled for classes in October

1913. The building housed a large electrical testing laboratory and a photometric and optical room. It was also home to an intermediate technical school for boys between fourteen and sixteen. Technical education, with the decline of apprenticeships in the area, had become essential to the supply of skilled labour for local industries. It offered preliminary education in basic subjects as a prerequisite to the study of machine construction, applied mechanics and electrical engineering. Boys could enter free of charge straight from elementary school. They were required to take a first year course which comprised practical mathematics, English, mechanical drawing and metal work. They could select more specialised subjects in their second year, like machine construction, mechanics, magnetism and electricity, or building construction. Scholarships were available to those who made good progress. Senior trade courses were provided for students over sixteen at moderate fees. The technical institute in the Girls County School at Holly Walk concentrated largely on commercial subjects. Technical education remained the responsibility of the County, but there was an influential local committee chaired by Colonel Bowles.[17]

4. Vicar Hodson and the Voluntary Schools

The Grammar School remained the only establishment for the education of the poor in Enfield until 1800 when the Girls School of Industry was established by the Church of England in the Old Coffee House behind the King's Head. Girls aged from nine to fifteen were instructed in needlework, knitting, laundry, plain cooking and household work as a preparation for a career in domestic service. Practical experience in plain cooking was acquired by work in a kitchen which provided dinners for the sick and aged poor in their own homes. The school remained in the Old Coffee House until given notice to quit in July 1874; an appeal was then made to raise a fund to build a new school. A site was found opposite the Vicarage where a fire in June 1868 had destroyed nine houses. The foundation stone was laid on 28 October 1875 by Gwendoline Somerset, one of the daughters at Enfield Court, in the presence of the charity girls who had marched over from the old school in their new uniforms. The new building was to incorporate a kitchen to prepare meals for the aged poor. The school closed in 1909. The premises were subsequently used partly as a home for nurses, partly as a preparatory school. The building was totally reconstructed in 1987 behind the original facade. The Nonconformist Girls School of Industry in Baker Street has been described in volume one. The Congregationalists in 1830 had set up an infants school at Ponders End with a schoolmistress's house attached. The mistress, Mary Ann Blythe lived there for fifty-one years. She retired in 1855 but retained the house until her death in 1881 at the age of ninety-two.[18]

The founding of the National Society in 1811 saw the beginning of the involvement of the Church of England in elementary education. The British and Foreign School Society was the Nonconformist response, although it was claimed that its schools were undenominational. Parliament authorised its first grants in aid of education in 1833. The grants were dispensed through these two societies and, soon afterwards, local churchmen and dissenters embarked on the provision and maintenance of rival schools for the education of the poor in Enfield. Only those schools which qualified by the approval of the inspectors of

126.   The Old Coffee House, later the Enfield Assembly Rooms, was used to house the Girls School of Industry from 1800-1875. It later became a science laboratory for the Grammar School. It was demolished in 1938.

the Department of Education could receive grants. The Church of England was in a much stronger financial position to build and maintain schools, thus it was that between 1839 and 1850, eighty per cent of all government grants for elementary education went to the National Society. From 1862 government grants to schools were replaced by an annual capitation grant of 12s a child; 4s of this was dependent upon regular attendance, the remainder upon an annual examination in the 'three Rs' conducted by HMI.

St James National School at Enfield Highway was established in July 1834. A National school in South Street was opened in 1838, next to the site where St Matthew's was later built. In November that year the British Society opened their school in Chase Side. A committee of nonconformists had been set up and, when £350 had been raised, application was made to the Lords of the Treasury for a grant of £250; £200 was forthcoming. The school-house comprised two classrooms, each forty feet by thirty, one for boys, one for girls. Handbills announcing the opening were distributed in the neighbourhood and on the first day eighty boys and thirty girls were admitted. The children were taught reading, writing, arithmetic, grammar, history, geography, musical notation and singing. The boys practised mental arithmetic, the girls were taught needlework; scripture was given a high priority. No child was refused admission on account of religious beliefs. Alec Woodfield started there in 1848. He had been born in Chase Side in 1840 and he received his earliest education at an infant school in Baker Street. Chase Side School, he recalled, had an examination once a year presided over by three important local gentlemen, Colonel Dixon (of the RSAF), Sir John Lawrence (of Southgate House) and Edward Ford JP; the children had to present their copybooks before them for inspec-

127, 128.   The former British School, Chase Side, 1838-1901, first converted to a milk depot, now 1991 heavily disguised as 'The Moon Under Water', winning a well deserved award in an Enfield in Bloom competition.

tion. Once a year there was a school treat, the scholars would march to Alderman Challis's house, 'Woodfield' in Baker Street, (earlier the home of Dr Abernethy) to partake of a splendid dinner of roast beef and plum pudding. 'When writing lessons were in progress', he recalled, 'boys were told off to supply us with ink, one for each row of desks. Each boy carried an ink bottle with a handle, he would walk up and down, and when we wanted some ink, very often in the middle of a copy... we used to have to dip in his pot'. The school had no playground.[19]

The National School in London Road opened in March 1840. It consisted of two schoolrooms, each forty feet by eighteen. A room for infants was added in

129.   The National School, London Road, was opened in 1840 and closed by 1911.

130.   The Protestant school formerly run by J. W. Bosanquet in Flash Lane.

January 1865. A school at the Royal Small Arms Factory opened in 1846; it was financed entirely by the War Department until 1855 when it was taken over by the National Society. A room for infants was added in 1856. The educational requirements of the scattered population around Forty Hill was met by the building of a National School there in 1849. The Holly Bush School (later St Michael's) in Chase Side was established by vicar Heath in 1864 and in June 1869 an infant school was opened in the former Girls School of Industry in Baker Street. The needs of the area around St John's, Clay Hill, were met, somewhat precariously, by the existence of J.W. Bosanquet's Protestant School in Flash Lane. The National Society opened a school there in 1859 and about the same time they established a school for boys at Trent.

Thus by the year of the Education Act 1870, the Church of England, supported by the State, had made considerable progress in the provision of education for the poor in Enfield; the nonconformists had achieved much less. The education of the poor was taken seriously by the government. In many areas the rapid expansion of the population had imposed an insupportable burden upon the voluntary bodies. The Education Act passed by the Liberal Government in 1870 in response to this difficulty, allowed for the establishment of elected school boards in places where voluntary school provision was found to be inadequate; such school boards would then have a duty to set up rate-supported schools. No school board was required to be set up in those districts which were adjudged to have sufficient voluntary school places. This, to the relief and gratification of the vicar and a majority of the ratepayers, was declared to be the situation in Enfield.

The calculations necessary to arrive at this decision had been made by the poet Matthew Arnold, as inspector. Sylvia Collicott, in a well researched paper on the Enfield School Board, challenges Arnold's returns which show 2,048 children in officially recognised schools and the deficiency of school places, at less than five hundred, to be insignificant. The enumerators' schedules of the 1871 census, says Miss Collicott, reveal that forty-five per cent of children between five and nine were not at school. Arnold's figure, she points out, included moreover three schools which were not recognised by the Department as being of a sufficient standard to warrant a grant. The first was the little Baker Street infant school with sixty boys and girls in the building later called Kingdom Hall, the second was the Loves Row infant school, held in a rented room which had formerly been a Dissenters' meeting house, where an uncertificated mistress taught the children of local labourers, the third was the Trent girls and infants school. By the elimination of these, she says, Arnold's figure should be reduced from 2,048 to 1,825. Certainly by the time a school board was set up in 1894 there was a large number of children not registered at any school.

The population in 1871 was 16,053 of whom 12,398 were adjudged by Arnold to belong to families of a class whose children would be expected to attend elementary schools. Taking children of school age to be one-fifth of this number, he gave a figure of 2,479 school places required; the deficiency therefore amounted to 431. This shortage of places, Arnold found, was entirely in the eastern part of the parish and the problem there might at any time be aggravated or ameliorated by fluctuations in the level of population dependent upon the availability of employment in the factories, especially at the Royal Small Arms Factory. He further pointed out that Mr Harman, the vicar at St James at Enfield Highway, was building a new school which, it was hoped, would

Photo by R. B. Lodge]   [Enfield

THE REV. PREBENDARY G. H. HODSON

131.   The Reverend Prebendary G. H. Hodson.

reduce the deficiency from 431 (according to the inspector) to 300.[20]

Enfield most certainly had a shortage of school places in 1870 and it was probably greater than the figure calculated. During the twenty years up to 1891 the population increased from 16,053 to 31,799, nearly a hundred per cent, yet no school board was called in Enfield until 1894. Every deficiency of school places, as it was brought to notice throughout these years, was either met, or obscured from view, by the unremitting efforts of the vicar George Hodson. Prebendary Hodson was aware that school boards could choose to provide no religious teaching, or, what to him was equally evil, to provide undenominational religious instruction. He was an evangelical and an ardent advocate of Church education. He believed that Anglican religious instruction was a vital weapon in the battle to defend the Church of England against encroachment from dissent, or decomposition through apathy. He was a bachelor and came to Enfield at the age of fifty-three in the very year of the Education Act. He had taken a degree at Trinity College Cambridge, gaining a first class in the Classical Tripos. He became a missionary priest in the slums of Oxford, ever eager to spread education (particularly religious and according with the teachings of the established Church) among the poor. Subsequently he was appointed to the living at Cookham Deane near Maidenhead in Buckinghamshire where he set up a school. He remained there for twenty-six years until he came to Enfield. He was a man whose convictions never wavered, whose courage never failed, warm hearted and generous to his fellow churchmen, harsh and hostile towards Dissenters. He was the second son of George Hodson, archdeacon of Stafford. His elder brother James had been rector of Edinburgh Academy, his younger brother was the famous (or infamous) Major Hodson of Hodson's Horse, attacks on whose reputation in Smith's *Life of Lord Lawrence* published in 1883, were to cause the vicar so much distress that he at once wrote a biography in defence of his brother's memory.[21]

It was the vicar's energy and drive, often bringing him to the point of exhaustion and illness, which raised the sums of money repeatedly needed to maintain and expand the church schools. These were financed by subscriptions, by government grants, and by the pence collected from the children. The income scarcely maintained the schools and left little over for new building. He therefore had to spend much time and ingenuity in an endeavour to whittle down each estimate made by the inspectors of the number of school places deficient. Faced with an initial shortage in eastern Enfield, he argued that there were vacancies in the schools near Enfield Town which, he asserted, were well within reach of children living at Enfield Wash and Ponders End, although it was a two to three mile walk each way. Further he announced that a new infant school had been built to take the place of the one in Baker Street condemned by the inspector. He claimed that the Girls' School of Industry (C of E) still housed in the Old Coffee House, which had been without desks, books, decent drains or a certified teacher, was to be put on a new footing from the ensuing Christmas. Also he pronounced that a school was to be provided at the Jute Factory for the part-time education of sixty children employed there. This number, he said, was likely to be much increased, as the works were expanding; the school would be under the inspection of the factory inspectors.[22]

He had the Holly Bush School rebuilt and reopened as St Michael's School behind the church, and he submitted plans for a school in Fighting Cocks Lane (Gordon Road). The new school promised at Enfield Wash had still not opened in August 1874, partly from want of funds, partly from want of children to fill it, but mostly because Prebendary Hodson had been ill with rheumatic fever. Immediately upon his return to health, he again assumed command of the campaign to prevent the imposition of a school board. He urged that there were 150 vacant places at the British School in Chase Side which could be used to meet the deficiency which existed in eastern Enfield. He argued that this deficiency had already been reduced because nine hundred hands had been discharged from the Royal Small Arms Factory before Christmas 1873. He wrote telling the Department of Education that a dissenting school had opened recently in Totteridge Road.

The vicar seized upon and reported to the Department every scrap of information about new schools planned and school improvements, projected or imagined, which might prolong the control of elementary education by his Church. A new school for a hundred infants had been built at the Royal Small Arms Factory in 1875, and the removal of the infants made room for eighty extra places in the boys school there. The Jute Works, the vicar claimed, was carrying off many of the older girls from the neighbourhood and that factory had its own school. He was of the opinion that the Girls School of Industry would now be able to satisfy the requirements of the inspector. He endeavoured to persuade

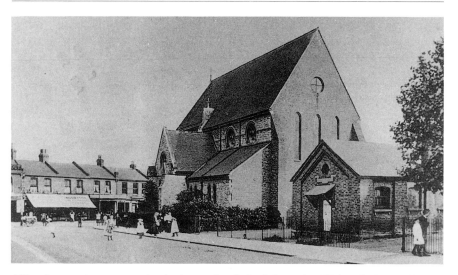

132.   In an endeavour to maintain the number of school places vicar Hodson had the Holly Bush
School rebuilt as St Michael's School, behind the church in Chase Side. It was moved to Brigadier
Hill in 1881.

James W. Bosanquet to restore his Protestant school in Flash Lane, but the vicar
got no help from him. 'It is not my intention', wrote Bosanquet 'to carry on that
school which I have maintained for twenty years. I think it is for the best interest
of Enfield ... that a school board, as soon as may be, be introduced, and any
course which may ultimately lead to this object, it would be my wish to promote'.

Thus James Whatman Bosanquet closed his Protestant school. The vicar, to
compensate, built another schoolroom at St John's, enlarged St Michael's
Chase Side and took measures to bring it up to the standard of a 'public
elementary school'. The 1876 Education Act required the setting up of a school
attendance committee in every district. It also rendered it possible, though not
mandatory, for local by-laws to be passed making elementary education compulsory between the ages of five and ten, and it required boards of guardians to pay
the fees of very poor children. School boards were formed that year in both
Tottenham and Edmonton (including Southgate); one was already in existence
at Waltham Abbey. In Enfield the Local Board of Health set up a school
attendance committee but it adopted no by-law to compel attendance at school,
for to have done so would have resulted in applications for non-existent school
places. The vicar's only real triumph at this time was the opening of a new
National school in June 1879 at the junction of Cecil Road and Sydney Road.
The ceremony was performed by Dr Maclagan, formerly curate in charge at
Enfield, by this time Bishop of Lichfield. It had been built by Allen Fairhead for
£1,209.

School attendance between the ages of five and ten was finally enforced by
Mundella's Act of 1880;[23] this, with the 1876 Act, brought the impending school
board closer. The vicar's problems lay, as always, in eastern Enfield. St James
National School cost £600 a year to maintain, the government grant was £230,
the money paid by the children brought in £165, £5 was raised by church
offerings and about £35 from other sources. This left £150 a year to be found

133.   The National School at the junction of Cecil and Sydney Roads was opened June 1879, closed 1971. Photograph 1898.

by voluntary contributions, and the inhabitants, especially those in Ponders End, were far from wealthy. The local press was solidly behind the vicar in his efforts to defend the voluntary system. School boards were repeatedly criticised for providing too high a standard of teaching. 'Nowadays, to gain a good position', complained *Meyers Observer* (23 December 1880) 'a young man must pass a competitive examination. The so-called elementary schools are bringing up their educational requirements to such a high pitch, soon to be equal to Harrow or Eton'. It predicted, with apprehension, that middle-class schools would eventually be swallowed up by the board school system.[24]

The vicar's laboriously devised but ramshackle defences were seriously threatened by the impending closure of the jute works in 1882. The lease of the school there, known as the Ponders End mixed boys and girls, and originally set up to meet the needs of half-time child workers at the factory, would expire at Christmas and the Commission of Bankruptcy would only allow the school to continue until then. To add to the difficulties, Mr Cotton, the Baptist minister, announced the closure of the Totteridge Road School, though this had never been inspected and approved. The vicar, ever an opportunist, at once took over the premises to open it as a school for ninety girls and infants. Prebendary Hodson was having to use all his ingenuity to provide further accommodation before the jute factory finally closed.[25]

The Nonconformists, adhering in general to the Liberal Party, advocated the formation of a school board. Many Nonconformists resented having to send their children to National schools where the creed was a central part of the curriculum. The managers of the British School in Chase Side had declared themselves in favour of a school board in 1876 and for this reason had taken no steps to expand their school. Henry Storer Toms, the Liberal pastor at Christ Church, had called a public meeting in 1878 to press for a school board.

134.   The Nonconformists objected strongly in 1881 because the vicar proposed to build a school at Brigadier Hill, for he planned to use land which belonged to the parish. Their protests were overridden and St Michael's School was built and opened in January 1882.

The Nonconformists objected strongly in April 1881 when the vestry proposed to offer parish land at Brigadier Hill to build a National school. The vicar offered similar land to them, but they told him that they wanted a school board, and were not disposed to erect fresh schools on the voluntary principle. Despite their protests the vestry went ahead and St Michael's School opened in January 1882. The Nonconformists were in a difficult position. One of them, complaining in August 1882 of the shortage of schools at Ponders End, related how he had sent his children to a Church of England school where a 'lady teacher' had told them 'Dissenters' children are a nuisance'. The uncertainty about the future prevented Nonconformists and others from setting up private schools (charging say 9d a week) for fear that they would be rendered uneconomic by the advent of a school board.[26]

A new district of working-class housing had been growing up at Bush Hill Park (east of the line) since the opening of the station there in 1880. The vicar, perceiving the danger, went swiftly into action and by November 1882 he had managed to set up and open a new school (now a branch library) about a quarter of a mile from the station. He had engaged as mistress Miss Griffiths, certificated and lately in charge of a school at Aberdare. The inspector visited the area. 'Multitudes of not very large houses have, within the last few years, sprung up near Bush Hill Park station', he wrote. 'From what I hear and see in this neighbourhood the population is wonderfully shifting. The school for infants and girls is intended for the children of the poor'. He had no regrets about the closing of the jute factory school, the premises he said 'are utterly bad'; a good boys school in Ponders End was required whether or not there was a deficiency of places. He felt that there certainly was a shortfall, but much depended on the state of work at the factories; if some were to close, many families would have to move away in search of work.

135. Parents were reluctant to send their children to the Royal Small Arms Factory School, although it had an excellent reputation, because Ordnance Road was so frequently flooded.

A number of boys from Ponders End went to St James School which, though it had accommodation for 162, now had 238 on the register, the average attendance however was only 168. The inspector thought that the boys school ought to be enlarged. There was no pressure on the girls and infants schools. A certain amount of accommodation was available at the Royal Small Arms Factory School, but he felt that this was too far from Ponders End and most parents in eastern Enfield preferred to send their children to St James because the lower end of Ordnance Road was so often flooded. In May 1883 the inspector reported that the Jute Works remained closed and the school there stood empty.

The deficiency of school places was always at its worst in Ponders End. The Baptist minister, the Reverend A.F. Cotton, as part of his campaign for a school board, made a house to house investigation in the area. Many of the parents expressed their dissatisfaction at having to send their children long distances. Within the previous day or two (June 1883) school fees had been raised. Parents complained bitterly and threatened that they would refuse to pay. The attendance committee would then be obliged to resort to the courts to enforce payment. 'What they have done already in this way', Mr Cotton went on, 'has much embittered parents' feelings'.

Following the closure of the jute factory in 1882 a second inspector made a survey in the Ponders End area. He counted 714 houses, a hundred at least of which were unoccupied. Three-quarters of the families in the area were of the 'elementary school class'. St James, within a mile and a quarter, took ninety boys from Ponders End. St Andrew's National School, over two miles away, had room for sixty or seventy boys, and about ten were already there. Many of the boys went to the British School, nearly three miles distant; therefore, this inspector concluded, 'there is no necessity to establish a new boys school at Ponders End'. This verdict suited the vicar, who seems to have secured the inspector safely in his pocket.[27]

There did remain a residuary problem, not considered by the inspector, of some twenty-six Ponders End boys who never attended any school. Mr Cotton set off to investigate. Harry Hitzell at number fourteen Northampton Road was twelve years old and subject to fits. William Wright, at number twenty-eight, was the eleven-year-old son of a labourer; he had been sent home because he had fleas, and remained at home because he had no shoes. At number thirty-two, Michael and Robert, the sons of James Davis an out-of-work dyer, had no shoes and no money for school fees. In Napier Road he found William Green, eight years old. Both his parents were out and he and the other children there were very neglected. Herbert Baker, ten years old, the son of a printer, parents out, could offer no adequate reason for not going to school. Alfred and George Dukes had been sent home three weeks earlier because they had been unable to pay the school fees. Some would not send their children because of the distance, some promised to send them next week and some attended dame schools. John Atkins a bricklayer of Suez Road was out of work and could provide no money for school fees. William Wing, an out-of-work navvy, could not finance young George's education for the same reason. Joseph Webb, in Alma Road, the seven-year-old son of a labourer, had no clothes fit for school and had been sent back for fees, so had George William Jones, son of an out-of-work grinder. The brothers Fred, Benjamin and Harry Rawlings had no money for fees because their father, a labourer, was out of work, so too with George the son of another out-of-work labourer; all came from Alma Road.[28]

Enfield thus remained without a school board long after boards had been set up in the neighbouring parishes. The vicar and his friends still stood resolute to protect their Church schools, though at a considerable cost to themselves in time, health and money. An appeal was made by the Enfield Church Schools Committee, in February 1886, for funds to liquidate its debts; the response was disappointing, £220 was raised against a target of £350. But Mrs Twells paid the cost of a new classroom at Sydney Road, and an infant school was opened at St Michael's. On the debit side, the old dissenting school at Baker Street closed, rendering it necessary to find room for fifty children by enlarging the Gordon Lane school at a cost of £150. The vicar's policy still had the approval of a majority of ratepayers. Public education was costing them nothing, while in Tottenham, with its school board, people such as themselves would soon be paying 1s 5d in the pound. Many of these ratepayers sent their offspring to private schools, thus they had every reason to prefer the status quo.[29]

The Reverend A.F. Cotton knew the poorer areas of Ponders End better than most, through his struggle to provide meals for the children of the unemployed there. Throughout the winter of 1886/7 he had fed an average of a hundred at table. 'How is it', he asked, 'that a large proportion of these children tell me that they go to no day school?'. Every week when he canvassed the district by the Ediswan electric factory to list the children who needed to come to dinners, he found a score of urchins at his heels who ought to have been in school, as ought many others who answered the doors. 'Would this be so if we had a school board?' he demanded.[30]

Enfield now employed two school attendance officers. Their duties were important, for upon the average attendance depended each school's income from the State. Their salaries were raised in July 1889 from £130 to £143 a year, with expenses, and the senior officer was provided with a horse and trap. Undoubtedly there were many families too poor or too inadequate, to pay school fees. In Enfield, where the voluntary system still prevailed, out of 4,700 pupils only seventeen were paid for by the Edmonton Union, whereas in Tottenham, where poor children had their fees paid from the education rate, 1,100 children out of 11,000 received help.

The vicar raised this problem as a member of the Board of Guardians in November 1889. He proposed that the parents of children who did not attend school should be examined as to their ability to pay, then the attendance officer, on behalf of those adjudged too poor, should bring the matter before the Guardians, and the Edmonton Union should pay the school fees. He no doubt was aware that the parents themselves would never apply to the Guardians, because of the stigma attached to the poor law. The new proposal, he hoped, would transfer to the school attendance officer the responsibility for making the application. But neither directly nor indirectly could parents be persuaded to turn themselves into paupers. Thus it was that, if the children attended school, the school managers had to remit the fees and were themselves the losers.[31]

Within the previous ten years, said the *Observer* (11 July 1890) there had been a large increase of school accommodation, but there were now so many children in the urban district, the editor went on, that were all of them to apply to the schools for admittance it would be impossible to find places. This stark reality, however, did not lead the editor to urge the creation of a school board, but merely to appeal to his readers to find more funds 'to maintain our present system with its record of excellent teaching results'. Further difficulties for the vicar and his allies resulted from the muddled terms of the 1891 Free Education Act which provided that, after one year's grace, a school board could be instituted if a deficiency of free places was established. At the same time the Act offered to school managers a Treasury grant of 3d per child each week; this for an average attendance would amount to 10s a year per child. It was intended that this grant would be in lieu of school fees, but if the existing fee was more than 10s, then the school could continue to charge the difference. The school boards for Edmonton and Tottenham decided that all their schools should now be free. In Enfield it was agreed that the grant should be accepted for all the National schools, but the vicar was unwilling to forgo those fees in excess of 10s.

The Liberals in Enfield continued to campaign vigorously. They held a meeting in the Lecture Hall in Chase Side in December 1891, where A.G. Kitching JP, chairman of the Enfield Liberal Association, urged the immediate formation of a school board, 'while not interfering with existing voluntary schools'. The vicar must have been aware that his position might be overrun before long, but he was determined to resist to the end. He opened a new

National infant school in Sydney Road in 1891. He wrote to the Department of Education in February 1892, claiming that he was now in a position to provide a new school which would accommodate 400 children; it would cost £2,000. He produced further plans for enlargements and extensions all over the parish, but the prospect of raising the money to carry out these plans was becoming ever more remote.

A branch of the Free and Popular Education League had been set up in Enfield; W. Richards was the secretary. This organisation began to exert pressure on the Department. Richards expressed an intention to write to the vice-president of the Council and to Mr Gladstone, and he warned that questions would be asked in the House of Commons. 'Enfield is now so growing in population', he went on, 'that nothing but a school board can provide for the demand'. The managers of the British School expressed an eagerness to hand over to a school board. Prebendary Hodson, still campaigning to prevent the impending change, complained that Her Majesty's Inspectorate was beginning to demand luxuries, such as improvements in lighting and ventilation.[32]

The vicar's situation became more and more desperate. He summoned his supporters to a meeting, urging that there was still time to avert the necessity for a school board, but only eighty-nine people attended and many of them proved to be opponents of voluntary education. 'The education question in Enfield' said the *Weekly Herald*, reporting on this meeting held in August 1893, 'has reached an acute stage'. According to the Education Department, Enfield was 519 free school places short. The vicar claimed that the number was only 250. A 3d rate, he suggested, would raise £1,200, enough to provide accommodation for 300 children and enable them 'to carry on the schools in their present efficient condition.' The *Herald* warned that, with a school board, the rates would go up by leaps and bounds, 'until it stops little short of those in Tottenham'. Vicar Hodson, addressing the meeting, pointed out that 5,200 school places were provided by the Church, 1,350 by the Nonconformists, and 150 by the Roman Catholics. He was critical of the Nonconformists for not making a more equitable contribution. He complained that the Department had become hostile to voluntary education and declared roundly that those who wished to avoid having a school board must put their hands into their pockets. Ebenezer Gibbons, though a Baptist, rose to support the vicar. He claimed that he came as a representative of the struggling classes — the ratepayers of Enfield. Himself a Nonconformist to the backbone, he was ashamed of his brethren for not putting their shoulders to the wheel. He hoped that, if a school board was established, they would not put any wasters on it. They did not want palaces to teach their children in. Let them select men who would study economy as well as efficiency. After several rousing speeches in this vein, the organisers were somewhat disconcerted to find themselves facing a motion advocating the formation of a school board. Mr Fitch, a Liberal, pointed out that those who subscribed more than half a guinea a year for the support of the voluntary schools numbered less than a hundred persons; why should the rest of the ratepayers go scot-free?. 'Many who do not assist the voluntary schools at all would like the present happy state of things to continue.' Another advocate of a school board was Solomon Kauffman, a radical who had to speak through considerable barracking. He was glad that the times were fast passing 'when one's being a large ratepayer afforded the exclusive privilege of ruling the roost.' Every penny spent on education was a penny saved on prison and workhouse expenses.

Mr Murphy, described as a working man, spoke of the working population of Bush Hill Park where there were 1,170 children, 769 of them between the ages of five and thirteen. School accommodation in that area was insufficient, it was wrong that parents should have to send their children over a railway crossing. Another speaker demanded to know why the meeting had not been publicised in the eastern half of Enfield; that was where the shortage of school places existed, the Highway school was crammed to suffocation. Another 'working man' complained that his children had been sent away from the Highway school three times because there was no room. All the leading Liberal advocates of a school board were present and spoke. They included George Spicer, a leading Congregationalist and paper manufacturer who lived on the Ridgeway, and Dr J.J. Ridge the medical officer of health in Enfield. Though the meeting voted narrowly in favour of the continuance of the voluntary system, the bastion, so long defended, fell at last, overcome in the end by an announcement from the War Office that the school at the Royal Small Arms Factory must close. Notice ordering the election of the Enfield School Board was issued 29 January 1894, polling was to be on Saturday 10 March.[33]

The vicar comforted himself in the knowledge that although the Edmonton School Board had been in existence many years, Church schools there still educated two-fifths of the children. He feared nevertheless that the Board schools would draw away subscriptions. An attempt was made, between church and chapel, to contrive the composition of the School Board prior to the election by arranging the appointment of five churchmen and four nonconformists, but people were divided less now by religion and the effort was thwarted by those, led by Dr Ridge, who were truly concerned with education.[34]

5. The School Board

Fourteen candidates were nominated to contest the nine seats. There were four polling stations: Sydney Road, South Street, Ordnance Road and Cockfosters. Each elector had nine votes which he could bestow upon one, or distribute among a number of candidates. Fifty-three per cent of the electorate voted. The resulting Board comprised the Church party with three representatives, Dr Ridge's Progressives with three, and the Independents (ie Nonconformists) with three. The Independents voted in such a way that most issues went in favour of the Progressives. Nevertheless George Hodson was elected chairman. The Board had to work within the terms of the 1870 Act, building Board schools only where necessary to supplement the number of places provided by Church schools. The Church party however feared that Church schools would be unable to compete on equal terms with the new Board school buildings which, the Progressives urged, should be built to a high standard. During the time of this first Board, three previously existing schools came under its control; the British School in Chase Side, the former Government School at Enfield Lock and the school at Botany Bay. The former British School was transferred to the Board, with its existing staff, on 1 February 1895 but, following an adverse report by H.M. Inspector who complained of overcrowding, the Government grant was suspended and the Board was forced to consider a new building. Plans were

136. The high cost of building Bush Hill Park School aroused bitter controversy for it cost £18 10s a pupil. Doncaster could build schools, it was said, for £8 a pupil. It was the first Board school in Enfield and opened in June 1896.

137. A class at Bush Hill Park School about 1909.

initiated for three new Board schools, two of which, Bush Hill Park and Chesterfield, opened before the election of the second School Board in 1897.[35] Alma Road was begun soon afterwards. The management of the Roman Catholic school in Alma Road, hearing that a new Board school was projected nearby, offered to transfer their premises to the Board, but the building was not considered suitable, for it had accommodation for only 131 children, whereas the projected Board school planned there was for 400 boys and 250 infants.[36]

Bush Hill Park was the first Board school to be completed. It was needed urgently for the population in the area had doubled in the seven years up to 1894 and this rapid growth looked likely to continue. Within the previous eighteen months two new roads had been laid out there and ninety-nine houses erected on them. There were now six hundred houses in the streets east of the railway. The school aroused bitter controversy from the moment of its conception, mainly because the Progressives demanded the provision of a school hall, which Hodson and his allies held to be an extravagance. The foundation stone was laid in September 1895. G.E.T. Laurence was the architect, Allen Fairhead was the contractor, the estimated cost was £11,115, or £18 10s for each pupil. George Spicer, speaking at the opening ceremony, felt called upon to defend the expenditure. The vicar, of course, was unreservedly critical. He declared that a great deal of unnecessary work was being done, (the reader may have observed the handsome terracotta in the gables) building costs, he said, ought to be limited to £10 a pupil, and he cited Doncaster where the costs per head were £8. The *Observer* supported the vicar, running a virulent campaign against the Progressives and accusing them of aiming at the extinction of Church schools. This charge was given unfortunate credibility for, when the school opened in June 1896, of the 481 children who enrolled, 468 were taken from voluntary schools. The vicar was bitter. 'You have succeeded so far', he told the School Board, 'only in wresting 468 children from denominational teaching'.[37]

The high cost of school buildings aroused considerable dissatisfaction among the ratepayers; no less than four deputations attended at the Board meetings to protest. The protests were so far effective that the projected expenditure on Chesterfield School was somewhat lower. It was built by C.H. Hunt of High Wycombe at a total cost of £15,091, £12 12s 9d a scholar. This school opened on 11 January 1897 and the teachers and children transferred from the former War Department buildings. At the end of the first week 456 boys, 388 girls and 301 infants had been enrolled. School football among the elementary schools was first organised at this time. Chesterfield's team was set up in December 1896, before the new school buildings opened, and the headmaster appealed for the donation of equipment. By January, seven elementary schools had joined the Enfield School Sports Association for football. A junior mixed school was added at Chesterfield in June 1897.[38]

As the second School Board election approached in March 1897, interest mounted and for a month before polling day the parish was deluged with electioneering material. In January 1895 there had been 5,900 children on the books, now there were 6,900. Twelve candidates offered themselves for the nine seats, among them J.H. Matthews, a workman at the Royal Small Arms Factory. His candidature was commended to the working class by Henry Barrass and with the support given to him by the artisans at the factory, he came second from the top of the poll. In the Ordnance ward, where the factory was situated, 1,336 voted out of a possible 2,050. The resulting Board contained three moderates (Church party), four Progressives and two Independents (Nonconformists); both the Independents were expected to vote with the Progressives. Hodson's claim to be re-appointed chairman was not recognised and he was replaced by George Spicer. Hodson was elected vice-chairman, although he declared

138.   Dunraven, the home of the Spicer family.

139.   The Spicer family at Dunraven. George Spicer is standing with his back to the window.

himself to be reluctant; he would, he said, have preferred not to accept, but he accepted. George Spicer was to retain the office of chairman until the Board was disbanded in 1903. He was a leading member of the Radical Liberal Association in Enfield and a deacon at Christ Church, Chase Side. He came to live at Dunraven on the Ridgeway in 1882. He died in 1911.[39]

140. Alma Road School 1907/8, a remarkably well disciplined and respectable looking bunch of boys.

Tenders for the building of Alma Road School were submitted in June 1896 and that of Allen Fairhead was accepted. The school was opened on 31 May 1897. Like its two predecessors it was designed by E.T. Laurence and built at a similar cost to Chesterfield. At the end of the first week 290 boys and 145 infants had been enrolled. When the school was inspected in June 1898 the report was so good that a government grant of 22s 3d a child was awarded. Discipline was described as excellent in all classes, the only criticism was of the reading. It was proposed in June 1898 that a school for three hundred girls should be added there and, although strongly opposed by Hodson, the proposal was agreed by the Board.

That same month Laurence was commissioned to prepare plans for a new school at Chase Side for a shortage of school places had been found to exist in that area. The former British school, described as unsatisfactory by the Department of Education, had accommodation for 345 and had 401 on its books; it would be closed when the new school opened, and the children would then be transferred. St Michael's, built for 626, had 724 on the books, and St Andrew's in Gordon Road, built to accommodate 150, had 156. It was pointed out that 205 houses had recently been built in the Town ward, and this took no account of the Orchard estate which was being developed in Lancaster Road. The new Chase Side School would take 1,160 pupils; the vicar demanded that it should be much smaller, but his motion to that effect failed to find a seconder. The old British school closed 29 March 1901 and teaching was resumed in the new school on 15 April. The approach was by a newly constructed road to be known as Trinity Street.[40]

When the Enfield School Board had been set up in December 1894 there had been a deficiency of school places amounting to 968. Three thousand places had been added in the ensuing four years yet the deficiency had hardly diminished; it stood in September 1898 at 901. Enfield was growing faster than ever. An innovation at this time was the plan to build a school for deaf children at Bush Hill Park; the vicar alone opposed the proposal. A sub-committee, set up to look into the matter, visited a college where teachers of deaf children were trained; they reported that a specialist teacher could be obtained for between £80 and £90 per annum.

The Church schools were still struggling to clear an accumulated debt of £1,120. An appeal was launched in June 1896 and £800 had been collected by July, but the National schools remained severely handicapped by a want of funds. Somehow they managed to hold their own. In July 1899 more than half the children in Enfield still attended Church schools, 4,625 as against 3,482 in Board schools. It was not until September 1900 that Board school numbers surpassed those in Church schools; the Church schools however compared most unfavourably in respect of the quality of buildings and equipment.[41]

6. Edwardian Elementary Education

The Education Act 1902 gave power to urban districts with a population of more than 20,000 to become the authority for primary education and to take over both the voluntary and the rate-erected schools. Enfield Urban District Council at once formulated a scheme to administer the new Act. The education committee would be made up of eight council members representing the four wards, and seven co-opted members. Those to be co-opted were the Reverends Hodson, Kempe and Toms, with Silas Beaven, W.F. Field, George Spicer and Mrs Warren. The School Board was to be wound up by 1 May 1903.[42]

Enfield education committee took over five Board schools with fifteen departments, one deaf centre and four cookery instruction centres. It also took over all the voluntary schools including the recently opened Roman Catholic school in Cecil Road. There was accommodation for 5,234 pupils in the Board schools and 4,088 in the voluntary schools. The education committee would take into its employment 265 teachers, 144 from the Board schools and 121 from the voluntary schools. School attendance had risen from an average of seventy-seven per cent in 1895, to eighty-six per cent in 1902. George Spicer was elected chairman and was re-appointed after the election of 1906.

Thus the voluntary schools (almost entirely Church of England) became rate-provided yet retained their independence. The Nonconformists objected and set up the Citizen's League to urge that their supporters refuse to pay the education rate. It was argued that parents might be forced to send their children to Church schools. Dr J.J. Ridge urged passive resistance by withholding a proportion of the rate. Thirty-one people including Dr Ridge and the Reverend Storer Toms were prosecuted in July 1904 in the Enfield Police Court; their jewelry plate and furniture were distrained by the official broker and sold by auction. This completely hopeless campaign was pursued for an incredible time. In September 1912 the Reverend A.W. Welch of the Totteridge Road Baptist chapel and J.G. Hunt a draper, being prosecuted for the non-payment of rates, protested against being forced to pay for the teaching of Roman Catholic doctrines, but by this time the campaign had become an anachronism. The struggle was over, the Church schools had at last found a safe haven sheltered from the cold winds of financial shortage. Some Church school buildings remained sub-standard. All the children at St George's Roman Catholic school were taught in one room and the head teacher was charged with all instruction above standard one. Vicar George Hodson died in July 1904, and the *Enfield Observer* paid tribute with a six-column obituary. The induction of R. Howel Brown took place on 2 February 1905.[43]

George Spicer retired as chairman of the education committee in April 1907. He had been a member of the School Board from the beginning and had been elected chairman after three years. Alfred Bowyer now replaced him. The new chairman was concerned that there were many children in the district who had never been registered for school. The two school attendance officers had only time to check the absentees who were on the books, for there were 1,200 of these every day, they had no time to investigate those who had never been entered on the registers. Bowyer prophesied that if all these children were brought into the education system, the schools would quickly become overcrowded and that in consequence two or more new schools would have to be built. Bowyer's forebodings were based upon the assumption that the population would continue to grow, but this did not happen, indeed the building of houses for the working class, for whom elementary education was largely provided, virtually ceased in Enfield from 1907 until the mid-twenties. This circumstance led for a time to an over-provision of elementary schools.

On becoming chairman Bowyer asked for the appointment of an additional school attendance officer to prepare trustworthy information on the total number of children of school age in the district. This drive to include all children of school age, who were not taught privately, in the elementary education system seems to have succeeded, although up to the First World War half these children left school before they reached the age of fourteen.[44] Average school attendance in 1895, in council (ie Board) schools, had been eighty-two per cent, in non-provided schools seventy-six per cent; in 1908 the respective percentages were ninety and eighty-seven. What was even more striking was that while the population from 1895 to 1908 had increased by forty-two per cent, the average number in school, in the same period, had risen by a hundred per cent. This suggests that in 1895 there had been a very large number of children not registered at any school.[45]

Many children in the poorer parts of the parish left school early by means of exemption certificates. In the last week in September 1912, for instance, 117 applications came before the committee from the poorer eastern side of the parish, against thirty-five from the western side. Most labourers wanted their children to become bread-winners as soon as possible. Members of the education committee grew concerned as the number of applications to leave early increased. Some parents, they said, were taking unfair advantage of the system. It was urged that school attendance officers should find out the fathers' wages before certificates were granted and should ensure that all the conditions required had been fulfilled. The child had to be thirteen and must have made not less than 350 school attendances out of 420 in each of the previous five years. The parents had to show that the child would be beneficially employed. J.H. Matthews claimed that firms were taking advantage of the system; he knew of one lad who had worked at a large factory for over two years at the same wage. Such factories, he said, were overrun with thirteen-year-olds. The committee allowed many to leave who, it was thought, would make no further progress at

141.   Southbury Road School soon after it opened in October 1905.

school and would be unable to get into the seventh standard. The chairman, defending the system, said that boys could often get jobs at thirteen which would be gone if they waited until they were fourteen, 'if they have had ten years at school', he thought, 'that is quite enough'.[46]

A new school had been proposed in September 1906 on a site in Eastfield Road, for 400 boys and 400 girls. It was opened in January 1909. An application was made in the following month to borrow £18,000 to build Lavender Road School. There were, by September that year, 11,480 children on the books, taught by 237 certificated teachers, fifty-three uncertificated, and eight others. Thus there were forty-eight children to each certificated teacher. Lavender Road School was opened in June 1910 and the temporary school, in the former British School, was closed. The George Spicer School opened on 27 January 1912 for 1,340 boys, girls and infants. A new scheme of elementary education, adopted in March 1912, limited classes to fifty and allowed the brighter children to move up three standards in two years. Before this time the population in Enfield had ceased to grow, and the 1911 census showed it to be substantially lower than had been estimated. The district had 11,751 elementary schoolchildren on the books (average attendance 10,500) in September 1911; it had accommodation for 13,167. The George Spicer School, moreover, would add a further 1,200 places.[47] The numbers were to remain static for some years. In 1915 there were still only 11,518 on the registers.

School health services were provided under the Education Act 1907. One ineradicable problem was the number of children sent to school in a verminous condition; they were excluded from the classroom after warnings, and the parents were threatened with prosecution. Their houses, clothes and bedding were disinfested. In 1913, 476 verminous children had to be excluded, some repeatedly, but such measures seldom resulted in permanent improvement. The school medical officer proposed that a cleansing station should be set up at the Southbury Road School clinic. Any child found to be badly undernourished by the school medical officer or the school nurses, was reported to the head teacher and added to the dinner list. Meals were provided from charitable sources. As a whole, the physique of Enfield children was described as good. Their condition had much improved over the last few years; only thirty-six had been reported as undernourished through the year 1911. So great was the degradation still associated with the label 'pauper' however, that most parents preferred to see their children hungry rather than allow them to accept free meals. Distress in 1911 had not been widespread, indeed the provision of books was a more serious problem in schools than the provision of meals.[48]

Dr Catherine Boyd, the school medical officer, lamented the amount of preventable suffering caused by lack of infant care. She suggested the better teaching of hygiene in schools, particularly dental hygiene. A thorough and systematic examination of eyes, teeth and ears was carried out at the Southbury Road School clinic, but many of the notifications of physical defects made by Dr Catherine Boyd were disregarded by parents. Forms had been sent out in respect of three hundred children in the previous twelve months (1912), of these 181 remained untreated and twenty-two had left the district. Even with financial assistance available for spectacles, only sixty-three had been treated out of 174. Fifteen cases.of deafness had been reported to parents, not one of them had accepted treatment for their child.[49]

Empire day had been honoured for some years at the Grammar School. In 1913 a thousand scholars from the voluntary schools also took part in ceremonies, saluting the flag and singing patriotic songs, but the eleven thousand who attended council schools took no part.

Central government, by 1914, intervened increasingly in elementary education. Originally £200,000 had been shared out by those authorities whose education rate was more than 18d. The sum had lately been increased to £350,000. Enfield, in the year 1914, claimed £13,000 and received a grant of £9,000. There were by then five women on the education committee.[50]

Notes to Chapter Six

1. Ed 27. 3434, 3435
2. Ed 27. 3437
3. Ed 27. 3439
4. Ed 27. 3440
5. *Observer* 29D 1877, Ed 27. 3441
6. *Observer* 13 My 1892, 24 F 1893, 3 N 1893
7. *ibid* 7 My 1897, 21 My 1897, 18 Je 1897, 24 D 1897
8. *ibid* 23 Mr 1900
9. *ibid* 19 F 1904, 24 F 1905, 24 N 1905, 22 D 1905, 6 Jl 1906, 27 D 1907, 2 X 1908, 8 Ja 1909, 12 F 1909, 24 S 1909, 4 N 1910
10. *ibid* 6 Jl 1906, 8 D 1905, 30 Jl 1909, 24 S 1909, 7, 21 Ja 1910, 2 Je 1907
11. *ibid* 7 Ja 1910, 10 N 1916
12. *ibid* 24 F 1911, ED 99.81
13. *Observer* 5 Au 1892
14. *ibid* 2 D 1898, 24 F 1911, 17 Ap 1925
15. *ibid* 19 Ja 1894
16. *ibid* 7 Ja 1898, 8S, 2D 1905, 24 D 1909
17. *ibid* 12 D 1913, 12S, 26 S 1913
18. *ibid* 1S 1874, 23 Oct 1875, VCH Middlesex 5. 253, *Observer* 28 My 1881
19. Taylor, R.W. *A History of a School* 1968, Ed 7.88 *Observer* 12 F 1926
20. S. Collicott *The Enfield School Board*, Ed 16. 209
21. S. Collicott *op cit Observer* Ja 1870, 26 My 1883, 8 Mr 1901, Donald Leinster-Mackay. *The Rise of the English Preparatory School* 1984
22. Ed 16. 209 (26S, 5 Oct 1872)
23. Ed 16. 209 (1874-1877) *Observer* 1 Mr 1879
24. *Observer* 10 Jl 1880
25. Ed 16. 209 (N 1882) *Observer* 12 Au 1882
26. *ibid* 21 Mr 1891, 2 Ap, 14 My 1881, 14 Ja, 26 Au 1882
27. Ed16. 209
28. *ibid*
29. *Observer* 20F, 31 Jl 1886, 23 S 1887, *Weekly Herald* 25 Au 1893
30. *Observer* 31 D 1886, 17 Mr 1887
31. *ibid* 12 Jl, 15N 1889, 31 Ja 1891
32. *ibid* 29 Au, 29 My 1891, Ed 16. 209
33. *Weekly Herald* 25 Au 1893, Ed 16. 209, *Observer* 4 Au 1893
34. *Observer* 15 S 1893, 26 Ja 1894
35. *ibid* 16 Mr, 30 Mr, 4 My, 14S, 23N, 16N 1894, 20S, 27S 1895, 18 Je 1896
36. *ibid* 5 Au 1898, 4 Ja 1895
37. *ibid* 4 My 1894, 27S, 18 Oct 1895, 12 Je 1896
38. *ibid* 22N 1895, 15 Ja 1897, 18 D 1896, 1 Ja 1897, 3 Jl 1896
39. *ibid* 26F, 5 Mr, 19 Mr 1897, S. Collicott *op cit, Gazette* 10 Mr 1911
40. *ibid* 3 Jl 1896, 4 Je 1897, 10 Je, 24 Je 1898, 22 Mr 1901
41. *ibid* 9 S, 30 D 1898, 29 N 1901
42. *ibid* 22 Mr 1902, 13F, 3 Ap
43. *ibid* 15 My 1903, 8 Jl 1904, 19 My 1905, 29 Jl 1904
44. *ibid* 5 Jl, 12 Ap, 19 Ap 1907
45. *ibid* 29 Ja 1909
46. *ibid* 8 Mr 1912
47. *ibid* 15 Ja, 24 S 1909, 3 Je 1910, 8 S 1911
48. *ibid* 22 My 1914, 20 Oct, 3 N 1911
49. *ibid* 31 My 1912, 6 My, 19 S 1913
50. *ibid* 30 My 1913, 8 My 1914

Chapter Seven
Out-and-Out Christians

1. Introduction: Churches and Chapels

'He's a rum dog. Don't he look fierce at any strange cove that laughs or sings when he's in company!', pursued the Dodger. 'Won't he growl at all when he hears a fiddle playing! And don't he hate other dogs as ain't of his breed! Oh no!' "He's an out-and-out Christian" said Charley.

This was merely intended as a tribute to the animal's abilities, but it was an appropriate remark in another sense, if Master Bates had only known it, for there are a good many ladies and gentlemen claiming to be out-and-out Christians, between whom and Mr Sikes' dog there exists strong and singular points of resemblance. (*Oliver Twist*)

No local historian can ignore religion when discussing the nineteenth century. Matters of religion were reported in the local press with that same close attention with which such papers now present the assaults, violent or indecent, of each passing week. The religious census taken on 30 March 1851 is said to have shocked the country; out of a population of eighteen million only seven and a quarter million had attended a service that Sunday, not more than forty per cent. Even having allowed for the very young and the sick, and those who had to look after them, it left more than five million people who could have gone to church or chapel, but did not. Church services in Enfield on that Sunday were attended by 4,619 worshippers, out of a population numbering (1851) 9,453. During the first fifty years of Victoria's reign, seven churches and eleven chapels were built in Enfield.

St Andrew's Church remained the most popular place of worship; 1,413 people, including 744 school children, attended morning and afternoon services there on Sunday 30 March 1851, the day of the National Religious Census. With its galleries on three sides, St Andrew's could accommodate 1,200 worshippers. The Clay Hill area was served by J.W. Bosanquet's little Protestant church in Flash Lane, used throughout the week as a school. St James at the Highway had been erected in 1831, at a cost of £6,000. It could seat 695 and it drew 290 worshippers on that Sunday. Jesus Church, built at the expense of Paul Christian Meyer of Forty Hall, had been consecrated in 1835. It could seat 300 and a total of 234 came to the two services. The minister was Charles William Bollaerts. The Small Arms Factory church at Enfield Lock belonged to the Board of Ordnance, and had been licenced for services since 1846; a congregation of seventy attended that Sunday afternoon.

There was a Wesleyan Methodist church at Ponders End, built in 1849; it

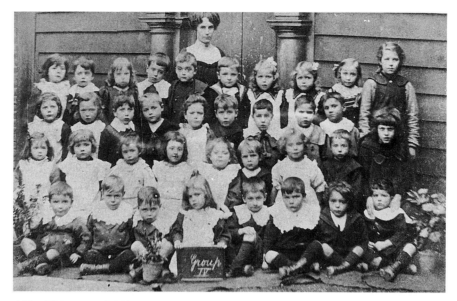

142.   This group of children was taken in 1905 outside the first wooden chapel of the Wesleyans. Formerly in Gordon Road, it had been re-erected behind the 1864 brick chapel in the south-east corner of the junction of Sydney and Cecil Roads.

seated ninety and drew forty-four adults and seventy-six children to the Sunday services. It had closed by August 1860 and the building was converted, at the expense of Alderman Abbiss, into a mechanics institute, incorporating a school, a reading room and a lecture hall, all for the benefit of the working classes. There was another little Wesleyan Methodist church erected in 1845 behind Lyne's the grocers at the corner of Fighting Cocks Lane (now Gordon Road) and Baker Street, a small wooden building where Henry Cave the grocer was the chapel steward. This attracted 184 people, including thirty-four school children, to its Sunday services. A new Wesleyan chapel was built in brick in July 1864 at the junction of Cecil Road and Sydney Road, and the old wooden chapel was taken down and re-erected behind it. Thomas Fielding was the minister at the Enfield Highway Independent chapel, put up in 1820; it held only 130 worshippers. It was full for the morning service that Sunday and in the evening no fewer than 170 squeezed through the doors.

The two Independent chapels, as yet unreconciled, still stood cheek by jowl on Chase Side. John Stribling was the minister at Chase Side Chapel. It was then known as a Countess of Huntingdon's chapel, having always been supplied with ministers from Cheshunt College, nevertheless it remained strictly Independent. It could hold 220, and 200 came to the evening service. Next door, in the Zion Chapel, George Wilkinson was the minister. This was the original chapel built in 1780. It had sittings for 350 adults and 120 children; 320 attended the evening service there. The oldest Nonconformist building in the parish was the meeting house in Baker Street. The minister was Samuel Joseph Smith. It had 140 free sittings and 160 reserved for those who paid for their seats. People paid in all the Nonconformist chapels for, unlike the churches, they were not financed by a church rate. This, the Dissenters held, was a gross injustice and they opposed every church rate in vestry. A threepenny rate had been proposed in 1849 and the vote had been carried by a show of hands. The Nonconformists thereupon demanded a poll which was held on the following day; it was open from eight-thirty until ten in the morning and from twelve noon until four. The result was 185 votes in support of the rate, and sixty-eight against. Church rates were made voluntary in 1853 and were abolished in 1868. Ponders End Independent Chapel had 400 paid seats, 200 free and standing room for forty poor folk. The two services there that Sunday were attended by 600 people. Out on the Chase, at Holly Hill, was the Lady Huntingdon's Chapel, a small building used for Sunday evening lectures given by students of Cheshunt College and attended by the poor of the neighbourhood.[2] The Countess of Huntingdon's Connection was a sect which had seceded from the Church of England in 1790: its beliefs lay somewhere between Low Church and Congregationalism.

2. The Vicar Against the Parish

The Tractarian movement sought to introduce beauty and reverence into public worship around the middle of the century. The high pews, behind which the well-to-do had long been allowed to doze through lengthy sermons, were everywhere being destroyed by High Church ministers. They introduced crosses, flowers and candles. The role of the priest was exalted, the Eucharist became the chief act of worship, strange vestments and rites were brought into use which a Low Church laity might consider as tending towards a Roman Catholic form of worship. The smouldering resentment of the laity was finally fanned into flame by a papal brief of 1850 announcing the re-establishment of the Roman hierarchy in England. It seemed that there must be a plot to reconvert this country to Roman Catholicism.

Dr Daniel Cresswell, the vicar of Enfield, died in 1844. He had been a well-loved, widely accepted figure in the parish since 1823, a friend of Charles Lamb and a mathematician of some repute. His successor, John Moore Heath, was of the family of Sir John Moore of Peninsular War fame. He married the daughter of Edward Harman who lived at Claysmore until he had the misfortune to become bankrupt. The house was then taken over by James Bosanquet. It is possible that the rabid hostility which developed between the vicar and the Bosanquets might have, in part, resulted from this circumstance. The Heaths were a brilliant, if somewhat disputatious family, closely involved with the law. It is said that John Moore Heath himself had hoped to enter the legal profession but he was barred by his deafness. His gift for incisive and devastating legal argument which was so to upset the Charity Commissioners, suggests that he might have made a most formidable barrister. His father was George Heath, sergeant-at-law. One brother, Douglas Denon Heath, was a brilliant classical and mathematical scholar who became a county court judge. Another brother was Dunbar Isadore Heath. He, like John, entered the Church, and he also brought down upon his head a similar narrow-minded hostility. He was deprived of the vicarage of Brading in the Isle of Wight in 1860, for an attack upon the Thirty-nine Articles in his published *Sermons on Important Subjects*. John Moore Heath played an active role in setting up the Enfield Local Board of Health in 1850 and was elected to the Board that same year. He was also

143.   John Moore Heath, the very controversial vicar of Enfield, was related to Sir John Moore of Peninsular War fame.

treasurer of the Enfield Savings Bank. The census of 1851 describes the household at the vicarage; he lived there with his wife, two young daughters, a cook, a nurse and a housemaid. Those who in their childhood memories recalled the vicar, described him as 'a tall dark man who always rode a handsome black horse', 'very deaf and used an ear trumpet'. He was interested in meteorology and kept a rain gauge at the vicarage. He gathered together a fine collection of Dutch and German oil paintings and was an active member of the London and Middlesex Archaeological Society. His opinions were strongly held and inclined towards the High Church party. He was a man not at all averse to controversy. As soon as he arrived in Enfield he fell out with his wealthiest parishioner and a leading member of the vestry, James Meyer, over the setting up of a separate parish at Jesus Church. His relations with Meyer were to grow worse, and his High-Church views alienated the richest and most powerful members of his congregation.

It was not until 1853 however that the dispute arose which was to disrupt the peace of the parish. Mr Heath was determined to remove the old box pews from St Andrew's Church; many of them were privately owned. His plan was highly offensive to the Low-Church majority, which included most of the thirty-five pew owners whose property the vicar proposed to destroy. A letter signed by a number of local magistrates, including Edward Ford of Old Park, James Meyer of Forty Hall, Daniel Harrison of Chase Hill House and R.C.L. Bevan of Trent Park, expressed strong opposition to the proposal. Nevertheless that summer the vicar engaged the architect John Piers St Aubyn to draw up plans for the re-pewing of the church. The work was to be financed by a public subscription, thus he was not obliged to bring the matter before the vestry, and he sought no faculty from the diocese.

144.   Chase Hill House, the home of Daniel Harrison, one of Vicar Heath's most uncompromising opponents, lay on Chase Hill off Chase Green.

He aimed to achieve his objective backed only by a small party of supporters. Among them stood the formidable figure of David Waddington, a man of the railways, hardened by many a confrontation with angry and disappointed shareholders, a friend and associate of George Hudson the 'railway king'. Waddington had come to live at Adelaide House, Forty Hill around 1847, and had been appointed vicar's churchwarden. He had made his first appearance at the vestry in June 1853. Seeing the opposition in the parish growing daily more powerful, the vicar and the railway director decided upon immediate, drastic and decisive action.

In the early hours of 12 October 1853 a gang of workmen from Norwich was brought by train to Ponders End station and thence conveyed to St Andrew's Church. There every pew was ripped out, broken up and dumped in the churchyard, leaving only Meyer's pew in dignified isolation. The labourers were back on the train and on their way home by six-thirty that morning. For years afterwards the old pews lay in the churchyard, a symbol of the vicar's Pyrrhic victory. Ebenezer Gibbons, writing of his childhood, recalled the games the boys had played there over the stacks of old timber.[3]

Too late, the opposition mustered its forces to pack the vestry of 20 October. Meyer put forward a strongly worded resolution deeply regretting the conduct of the vicar, which he described as 'contrary to the known and expressed wishes of the majority of the parishioners'. He demanded that the matter be submitted to the Lord Bishop and that proceedings be taken at once for the restoration of the pews. But the vestry, seeing outside the windows the impossibility of carrying out this plan, replaced Meyer's strong resolution with a tame proposal to set up a committee. It was to include the joint perpetrators of the offence, the vicar and David Waddington. The vicar's opponents were seething with anger but could find no way to restore what had been destroyed and the committee became enmeshed in a tedious argument about the precise height of the new pews and, being unable to agree even on this, a poll was demanded. Unfortunately the poll provided an opportunity for the vicar's more vociferous adversaries to stir up trouble. Held in the assembly rooms at the King's Head, it resulted in a crushing defeat for the vicar's supporters by 281 votes to ninety-two. The poll remained open all day and towards evening the attendant crowds, through the dangerous conjunction of drink and religion, became so threatening that Heath and his curates found it necessary to withdraw by way of the window; they fled across the bowling green and sought sanctuary in the Grammar School. The Church's sad loss of dignity rendered the situation pregnant with possibilities for a local versifier and wit:

> The eye of the vicar waxed deadly and chill
> As it gazed in despair on the far window sill,
> Some roguish hand beckoned and hinted a flight
> And forth through the window he fled in a fright,
> And loud was the laughter and great the amazement
> That the Church's annointed should go out through the casement.

Graham Dalling, in his delightful paper on the controversy has found evidence that the no-popery brigade, including some of the more pugilistic of the Nonconformist community, had been involved in the trouble. Three days after the poll the Reverend John Fuller Russell, the High-Church vicar at St James, sent a letter to Thomas Brading, a Nonconformist grocer from Ponders End, announcing that he would henceforth cease to patronise Brading's shop,

> 'Because in a matter with which you, as a dissenter, had no business whatever ... you chose to act the dishonest and disgraceful part of ring-leader among the vilest ruffianism... and ribald profanity of the neighbourhood, for the purpose of insulting and abusing ... persons of the clergy ... of this parish'.

The poll book shows that in Enfield Town there was only a marginal majority against the vicar, whereas the more plebeian Ponders End and Enfield Wash were almost totally opposed, as were the important gentry of the parish. A special resentment was reserved for David Waddington:

> 'Where was the Manchester upstart so loud
> So skilled to cajole and bully the crowd'.

All that concerned him was that his objective had been achieved. That feelings continued to run high is revealed in an exchange of correspondence between Waddington and Daniel Harrison, who wrote:

> 'I much regret that I should have been caused by the offensive epithet [blackguard] which you used towards me, to so lose my temper as to strike you in the church. I hereby tender you an apology'.

The 'apology' was rejected.

> 'You seem to have forgotten', wrote Waddington, 'that the expression applied to you was caused by your previous offensive conduct towards myself. If you think it proper to make an unconditional apology, I shall take the same into consideration, if not I shall adopt such a course as I may be advised'.

Under this thinly veiled threat of legal action, Harrison hastened to make an unconditional apology. Waddington thereupon humiliated him further by having the correspondence printed and published. The mob continued to express itself in its own way, and that November an effigy of the vicar was burned

145. *James Whatman Bosanquet, the founder and treasurer of the Protestant Association, lived at Claysmore on Clay Hill.*

146. *The drawing room at Wildwoods, the home of Admiral Bosanquet, 1843. (Ashmolean Museum, Oxford)*

in the Market Place.

The flames of controversy slowly subsided, though the embers continued to smoulder and it was not long before the flames burst forth once more. It was the vicar who again stirred the fire. Clay Hill was the heart of the Protestant Association. This organisation of worthy gentlemen had been set up by the

Bosanquets. James Whatman Bosanquet was the founder and treasurer. He was a retired banker who had earned a considerable reputation as a writer on Biblical and Assyrian chronology. He died in December 1877, having lived at Claysmore for thirty years. Gentlemen who subscribed £2 to the Protestant cause could join the committee. Ladies subscribing 10s might elect a ladies committee, others who felt strongly could subscribe 5s and become members. The cantankerous Captain (later Admiral) Charles John Bosanquet lived at Wildwoods; it was he who built the lake there. The Bosanquets had their Protestant school in Flash Lane; it was used on Sundays to provide Low-Church lectures for the labouring classes. Within this Low-Church stronghold the vicar proposed, in 1857, to build a new chapel on land of which he owned the freehold, and to provide High-Church services there. Again he employed the architect Piers St Aubyn, whose delightful little building in multi-coloured brick (St John's at Clay Hill) stands peacefully now among the trees, having long forgotten the controversy which raged around its birth and early years. The chapel opened for worship on 10 November 1858 and immediately came under attack, not merely verbal, from Captain Bosanquet, who removed the ornaments from the altar, interrupted the services and brawled with and assaulted the curate. The chapel was forced to close on 12 June 1859. The protection of the law could not be depended upon, for the magistrates joined with the Protestant Association to present the Captain with a handsome testimonial of their approbation. A petition was raised against what the Protestants called 'this new strange form of worship' introduced at St John's.[4]

A commission of the Bishop of London, Archibald Campbell Tait, had sat at the court house in Enfield on 14 April 1859 to determine what the Bishop considered to be the causes of the dissension which had arisen in the parish. His alleged object was to re-establish peace in Enfield. Since however the Bishop himself was a strong supporter of the Low Church party, his report could hardly be an unbiased adjudication. Quarrels and disagreements broke out at every vestry whenever the vicar was present. In May 1859 the vicar's nomination of John Riley Rignall as his churchwarden was met with sullen silence; the nomination as churchwarden of Captain Bosanquet, which followed, was greeted with applause in the vestry. The vicar then named William Smith Mead as parish clerk. His right to make the appointment was immediately questioned, but the vicar pointed out that since there were now no church rates, it was he who paid the clerk's salary. Frustrated, the opposition, in the person of Mr Drummond, proposed the appointment of a Sunday afternoon lecturer. The vicar was equal to the challenge. The remuneration, he said, was by an ancient gift now reduced to insignificance by centuries of inflation; this was the reason why the office had been vacant for such a long time. Mr Heath admitted that the parish certainly had the right to make the appointment. Perhaps, he went on, allowing his dislike to get the better of his discretion, Mr Drummond, or one of his friends, might wish to subscribe a goodly sum for the salary, though, he added, he would allow no one to enter his pulpit unless it was with his approval. The vicar's taunt brought Mr Drummond red-faced to his feet. 'I would undertake', he shouted, 'to subscribe as goodly a sum for a good pious man as lecturer as you did to stop the law proceedings of the trustees against Mr Chambers'. This reference to the calamitous dispute between the parish and the Grammar School master brought the meeting to a tumultuous conclusion.[5]

Next came the macabre incident of the burial of the boy Michael Parish. The

147. Much of the trouble in the parish centred around St John's Clay Hill, a delightful little church in multi-coloured brick which stands peacefully now among the trees, having forgotten the controversies of its early days.

lad had never been christened, and his parents were Baptists. Those in charge at St Andrew's decided that they should adhere strictly to the articles of the Church of England, therefore there could be no burial service. The senior curate, the Reverend Mr LaBarte, had met the mourning party and the coffin had been taken to the grave and lowered in. At this tragic moment there appeared on the edge of the churchyard, standing upon Holly Walk, the figure of Mr Fox of the City Mission. Reading loudly from the Bible he gathered the mourners about him. The curate ordered him to be silent and was ignored. The curate became angry, shook his fist in the face of the missionary and, when this too was ignored, he ordered the grave to be filled in at once. Now the clatter of stones upon the coffin of their dear dead son broke in upon the prayers of the grieving parents. Mr Fox made the most of the situation to attack the High-Church proclivities of the clergy. He accused them, somewhat irrelevantly, (in the *Enfield Observer*) of turning their backs upon the congregation during the celebration of communion, of covering the communion table with a white cloth, and other heinous crimes against God, and with growing fervour evoked the spirits of certain saints of his own persuasion to protect him from such superstitious Roman Catholic practices.

Oh for an hour of Luther now
Oh for a frown of Knox's brow.

But the reader may feel he is able to do without such luxuries.[6]

As already mentioned, Captain Bosanquet had been causing trouble at St

148.   John Riley Rignall in his old age. He had been a loyal supporter of vicar Heath.

John's where on 5 June 1859 he brought the service to a sudden and unseemly end. On the following Sunday a vast concourse, mostly sightseers, hearing that something sensational might occur and not wishing to miss it for the world, streamed out to Clay Hill. They were disappointed. The Church door was shut, and pinned thereon was a paper, signed by the vicar, announcing closure until further notice. Proceedings in the ecclesiastical courts were begun against the brave Captain.

Things could hardly grow worse, but they did. A fight broke out in the vestry at St Andrew's between the two new wardens, Bosanquet and Rignall (the vicar's warden) over which of them was to take charge of the offertory. Rignall was brought before the magistrates on a charge of assault. The Enfield magistrates were hardly without prejudice in this case, Edward Ford and Daniel Harrison being among the vicar's leading antagonists. It was because of this that Edward Busk was brought in from Edmonton to add an air of impartiality. Rignall, citing the disturbed state of the parish, demanded to be heard before a higher court. Busk ruled that this was not possible without a preliminary hearing, but he managed to procure a deferment. Finally a settlement was reached which left the offertory in the custody of the vicar, who agreed to drop proceedings against the Captain, who in turn withdrew the charges against Rignall, who apologised for his violence. Thus an uneasy peace was restored, but not for long.[7]

It was announced that St John's would re-open on Christmas day 1859. Anticipating excitement, many people rose early and walked or rode out to Clay Hill. It was the season of good will and peace on earth. The church bells were ringing and the sun was shining when Captain Bosanquet entered the chapel. He made his way straight to the communion table, removed from thence the super altar and carried it out to the porch, but finding that there was a valuable cover he carried this back and thrust it under his seat. He then returned to the communion table, which was covered by a cloth with broad fringes. These he folded back out of sight so that the congregation could see the table, as God obviously intended and, satisfied that the service could now proceed in peace, he returned to his seat. The vicar arrived soon afterwards and fell into a fury. He demanded of Bosanquet whether he had taken anything from the communion table. The Captain replied with dignity that, as churchwarden, he had had to remove the super altar. Thereupon the vicar dragged the Captain from his seat in an endeavour to eject him from the chapel, but not succeeding, he ordered the church doors to be closed and retired into the vestry. Bosanquet followed behind and when he attempted to push past the vicar a scuffle ensued during which the Captain's hat was crushed against the wall.[8]

On the following Sunday, 1 January, hearing the church bells ring, the good Captain proceeded again to the chapel. Finding the doors locked, he went round to the vestry but found Rignall and several other men on guard there. He gained entry at last when the main doors were opened at ten to eleven, but there were eight or ten 'powerful men' standing before the communion table. Depositing his umbrella, the intrepid Captain advanced towards them. Rignall barred his way. 'If you come here', he warned, 'you will be put out'. Mr England stepped forward to emphasise the point with 'If you approach this table you will be turned neck and crop out of the chapel'. The Captain retreated, strategically. Seeking a softer target, he made his way to the organ loft and succeeded in expelling Miss Evans the organist and another young lady. He then locked the door, determined that no music should disturb the communion service, even if he did, for music had been expressly forbidden by the Bishop. He sat throughout the service watching with anger the performance of 'heathenish Roman rites' and, the moment it was over, he made his way into the vestry 'to see the collection counted', he said, though more likely it was in the hope that his presence might provoke the vicar. It did. A skirmish ensued and on hearing Heath crying loudly for help, England and others rushed in calling out 'You cowardly blackguard', and 'Turn him out and kick him'. Other witnesses described the ejectment, which only got half way down the nave, as somewhat more restrained, claiming that no more force was used than was necessary. Charges and counter-charges were laid before the magistrates, and Mr Busk, bewildered, could only refer the matter to a higher court where it was examined before more learned judges for nearly three years, Bosanquet versus Heath, and Heath versus Bosanquet, until at last the vicar emerged victorious in October 1862. It was a hollow victory, for both plaintiff and defendant were to bear their own costs.[9]

Meanwhile the campaign against the vicar continued in an open letter addressed to R.C.L. Bevan of Trent Park and signed by the more important personages in the parish. It bore the names of James Meyer of Forty Hall, all the Bosanquets of course, Edward Ford of Old Park, Richard Connop of Durants, Henry C.B. Bowles of Myddelton House, A.P. Somerset of Enfield Court and others whose degree of importance must have been apparent to lesser mortals at the time. The letter proposed a petition to Parliament against those clergymen who introduced into the Church of England 'forms of ceremonies suitable to a popish place of worship'. Bevan presided over a public meeting at the King's Head where the petition was initiated. It was presented to Parliament bearing a thousand signatures in April 1860. The Dissenters, feeling that they must lend their assistance to combat evil and persecute the vicar, invited Lord Shaftsbury to attend a meeting at the British School in Chase Side. There the London City Mission made known its intention to send missionaries to Enfield; perhaps it was felt that the needs of the people here had become more pressing than those of the unfortunate natives in Africa.[10]

The war in the parish dragged on in a desultory fashion over the next five years. The Bosanquets did their best to keep it going with long and involved letters to the *Observer* which I will refrain from quoting since public taste for such polemics is no longer what it was. At last the editor declined to receive further correspondence from the antagonists. Interest, even then, was apparently waning. Meanwhile the state of St Andrew's church continued to be disregarded. The walls were disfigured with damp stains, strange fungi grew in the pews. 'The organ has a cold and is mute. The Lord's house is the shabbiest in the parish'. The vicar at last left his church (December 1864). The freehold of St John's was transferred from the vicar to the Ecclesiastical Commissioners in the following August, and soon afterwards the little church was consecrated by the Bishop. 'We must all regret' said that dignitary with doubtful sincerity, 'the physical infirmity of the vicar which has caused his separation from his parishioners'. His duties completed, the Bishop returned to Claysmore and the hospitality of the Bosanquets. The following month the Reverend W.D. MacLagan entered upon his duties at Enfield as curate in charge.[11]

It was his exertions which brought about the somewhat too wholesale restoration of St Andrew's in 1866-7. More than £4,000 had been raised by voluntary subscriptions. The roofs of the nave, chancel and aisles were replaced, though it was thought that it would have cost little more to have repaired the original ones. The south chancel chapel until this time had been enclosed and used as a vestry. The screen which had separated it from the church was needlessly destroyed and the present vestry was built. New floors were constructed throughout the church which, within six or seven years, were destroyed by dry rot. The oak galleries were replaced, and a stone pulpit and a brass eagle were presented by Colonel Somerset of Enfield Court. This new stone pulpit aroused so much antipathy that F.G. Widdowes, the architect in charge, hastened to dissociate himself with both the design and the execution of the object. During the six or seven months required for the restoration, the church remained unusable and the services were held in the Riding House at Enfield Court. The beautiful arched monument in the north chancel chapel, probably built to honour Isabel Lady Lovell around 1530, was restored and partially decorated at this time at the expense of the Duke of Rutland, by Messrs Earp, monumental sculptors and Mr Pulling an ecclesiastical decorator.[12]

John Moore Heath had retired to Milland, near Haslemere, but he remained vicar of Enfield until 1870 when George Hodson was appointed. As Graham Dalling says, 'Hodson was a good choice for Enfield, his Low Churchmanship and reactionary political views earned him the love and respect that had been denied to his predecessor'. Heath died in 1882, in his seventy-fourth year. He was buried in St Andrew's churchyard next to Daniel Cresswell. On his tomb is carved an appropriate text: 'Lord now lettest Thy servant depart in peace'.

3. God's Church and the Devil's Chapel

The Reverend W.D. MacLagan, who later was to become Archbishop of York, proved less malleable than the important parishioners might have hoped. Within a year or two they had cause to complain against further innovations. An angry letter was dispatched to the Bishop of London (and printed in the

Observer) in February 1868, demanding the withdrawal of changes introduced, notably the use of a purple altar cloth with the letters IHS embroidered in white. This, it was claimed, was preventing parishioners from taking communion in the parish church. The letter was signed by all the leading gentry: James Meyer of Forty Hall, J.W. Bosanquet of Claysmore, Edward Ford of Old Park, Philip Twells of Chase Side House, Henry Bowles of Myddelton House, Edward Fox of the London Missionary Society, W. Nutter Barker of the Palace School, and others. Nevertheless MacLagan stood his ground. In an open letter addressed to the memorialists he pointed out, with judicious sarcasm, that their request was founded on a complete misapprehension, quite excusable on the part of several of the memorialists 'who are not in the habit of attending services in the parish church. So far from there being any diminution', he goes on, 'in the number of those who attend communion service, it will, I am sure, relieve your minds, but gratify you to know, that the communions on the last three Sundays have been more numerously attended than at any time since I came to the parish'. The Bishop upheld his curate-in-charge.[14]

One would have thought that Hodson at least would have escaped attack by the wealthy gentry, nevertheless he too transgressed the over-extended boundaries of their self-esteem. Vestries had always started half an hour later than the time announced to ensure that everybody waited upon the arrival of Meyer and Bowles. Hodson, whose entire time was devoted to his self-imposed duties in the fields of religion and education, decided that vestries must commence on time. Thus, when Meyer and Bowles made their entrance, proceedings were well under way and the vestry was discussing, without their acquiescence, the appointment of six sidesmen. Meyer, after protesting against the chairman (Hodson) presuming to proceed in the absence of himself and his neighbour, declared that he was not ready to assent to the introduction of any new-fangled notion, he preferred keeping to the good old customs, preferred to stop any innovation immediately it presented itself. The vicar replied, without too much deference, that those who attended the parish church (Bowles and Meyer went to Jesus Church) must be the best judges of what was required there. The sidesmen were needed to keep order. 'In the galleries, and on Sundays more particularly, might be witnessed many disorderly people'. He had frequently been annoyed to see persons left standing about in the aisles; it would be the responsibility of the sidesmen politely to convey them to spare seats. Mr Whitaker* (of Whitaker's *Almanac* fame, who lived at White Lodge in Silver Street) agreed; his daughters often complained to him of the excessive rudeness of persons sitting in the gallery. The unusual outcome was that Meyer and Bowles were overruled and the six sidesmen were appointed.[15]

Pews were still causing problems. They were allotted to heads of families and there were not enough to go round. One gentleman complained that he had applied for a pew three years since and no notice had been taken. Many like himself, he said, living near the Town, had no seats, while pews were granted to people from Forty Hill. Pews intended for five or six persons were occupied each

---

* Joseph Whitaker began the *Almanac* in 1869; he had come to live at White Lodge in 1862. He also set up the *Bookseller*. He died in May 1895 and the family left White Lodge and Enfield. His son Cuthbert was to return and to write a history of Enfield published in 1911.

Sunday by only two or three from the family. Offertories by Church of England congregations, even at St Andrew's, were never sufficient to meet requirements. The vicar complained that the Dissenters contributed ten times as much towards their chapels as churchmen to their churches. Both the Baptists and Congregationalists were steadily reducing the debts resulting from their new buildings. The Compulsory Church Rate Abolition Act (1868) left the churches much more dependent on collections. Long before this many Nonconformists had refused to pay, but the Church had been unwilling to resort to law because it would have made matters worse. It was now suggested by the churchwardens that seat-holders should contribute 12s to 15s for each seat (£3 to £4 a pew) but even when paid for, a seat could be considered as reserved only for the Sunday morning service, on all other occasions seats were free and unappropriated.[16]

It was recognised by the autumn of 1872 that a new church would be required to meet the needs of the growing population on the Gordon estate. Mr Batters of Brigadier House offered £2,000 on condition that an equal sum was raised by subscription. Vicar Hodson agreed to provide the endowment and St Michael's was consecrated 16 May 1874. St Matthew's Church in South Street was built in 1878; the population of Ponders End at the time was about 3,000. An ecclesiastical parish was formed in the area.[17]

The working-class estate east of the railway station at Bush Hill Park continued to grow. A schoolroom had opened there in 1883 and in January 1885 Vicar Hodson appealed for £230 to erect an iron church. His appeal was so successful that a permanent church could soon be considered. The foundation stone of St Mark's was laid in November 1890. An iron church to serve the expanding population on the Birkbeck, Cedar and Laurel Bank estates had been set up about 1886. Ten years later Mr Macy, who had already provided St Luke's Institute, proposed the building of 'a noble and spacious church'. The fund increased steadily. The design for the new church, by James Brooks, was accepted for exhibition at the Royal Academy. No part of Enfield, except Bush Hill Park, had developed more rapidly between 1886 and 1896 than the areas north and south of Lancaster Road. There were six ecclesiastical parishes and ten churches in Enfield by August 1899. St George's was consecrated September 1900, St Stephen's, Bush Hill Park in 1907.[18]

'To the number of religious bodies already in Enfield, Episcopalians, Congregationalists, Wesleyans and Primitive Methodists', declared the *Enfield Observer* (April 1867) 'we are to add the Baptists'. On Tuesday 19 March a service to inaugurate a Baptist church was held at the Wesleyan chapel in the New Town, with a sermon by the Reverend T. Attwell of Camberwell; there was a good attendance. As a temporary measure Sunday evening services were at first held in Mr Biscoe's assembly room at the Rising Sun in Church Street. It was always the intention of the Baptists to build a church and, by November that year, an iron chapel was being put up in London Road. Within eight years it had been taken down and sold and they had embarked upon the construction of a new tabernacle designed by the architect Lewis Banks. This was completed within eight months at a cost of £2,350 of which £1,350 had been subscribed before the building was finished. While the new chapel was being built services were held in the large room at the Palace School, by the invitation of Nutter Barker. The tabernacle flourished, in 1884 it was so crowded on Sunday evenings that at times people had to be sent away for want of room, even to stand. The Baptists also opened a chapel in Totteridge Road in March 1872. A Strict Baptist chapel,

149. The Baptist tabernacle London Road, erected 1875 and converted by Woolworth's into a shop in 1925.

150. The Chapel on the south side of South Street was built by the Alma Road Baptists in 1889, but had to be sold to the Methodists in 1896, following the decline of the Baptists consequent upon the closure of the crape works.

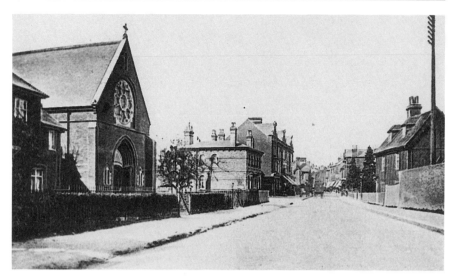

151.   The foundation stone for a new Roman Catholic church at the corner of Cecil Road and London Road was laid in September 1900; services began in April 1901. On the east side of London Road, opposite the police station, stood the Patrol Cottages where there formerly lived patrolman Watkins, a Waterloo man, who became part of the Metropolitan Police force in 1836.

which had met since 1873 in a room in Ordnance Road, obtained a freehold site in Putney Road in October 1875; there they put up a small plain brick building capable of holding more than one hundred persons. It cost only £276, for the minister, Mr Alfrey, had laboured with his own hands in order to reduce the outlay. The church was to admit no one to the Lord's table who had not been baptised by immersion. Infant baptism they considered to be an innovation.[19]

The little Alma Road Baptist chapel was in the poorest part of the parish, yet it had an average attendance each Sunday of 110 and the Sunday school was attended by 124 children. The congregation decided to move from Alma Road in 1889 to a more accessible site in South Street. There the services attracted so many worshippers that they resolved to rebuild at a cost of £3,000, and raised a mortgage of £1,400, but their fortunes now faded with the decline of the crape factory, followed by its closure at the beginning of the year 1894. Many of the congregation moved away, others were impoverished and subscriptions fell. The chapel could no longer meet its repayments and, threatened with foreclosure, they sold the building to the Methodists.

The editor of the *Enfield Observer* might also have mentioned, among the religious bodies in Enfield in 1867, the Roman Catholics. The expansion of the Ordnance Factory in 1854, according to John O'Halloran*, had attracted a large number of workers into the area including many Roman Catholics. A mission had already been set up at Waltham Cross by Father George Bampfield who, in June 1862, wrote to the *Tablet* appealing for funds to build a chapel and schoolroom at Enfield. The appeal was met by J.S. Moorat, the owner of Bush Hill Park (The Clock House) who built a small chapel on his estate at the corner

* *The Revival of the Old Faith in Enfield*

152.   *The Jute estate, taken from the top of the gas holder. Alma Road stretches northward, Enfield waterworks can be seen on the right and the school on the left. Stanley Street lies parallel, then New Road (out of the picture), an estate of six-roomed Jute cottages with shops on the South Street frontage.*

of London Road and Cecil Road, though this was a distance of some four miles from the factory. He settled £20 a year to enable the priest at Waltham Cross to serve the mission, which opened on 10 May 1863. The foundation stone for a new Roman Catholic church on the same site was laid in September 1900, the opening service was held there in April 1901. This building was destroyed by the land-mine which fell in London Road on 15 November 1940; in 1956 it was replaced by a fine new church on an adjacent site. The workers from Dundee who came down when the Jute Works was opened about 1865 included a number of Roman Catholic families. They formed a congregation and gathered for worship in one of the small cottages on the Jute estate. It was looked after for a time by Father Hickey from Waltham Cross, until Father Bronsgreest came and secured a cottage in Stanley Street. He used the downstairs room as a school; the larger bedroom had to serve as a church, the smaller as a confessional. Subsequently a corrugated iron building was erected in Alma Road. Services were held there for some years until a new church was built in Nags Head Road; the iron church was then taken down. Behind the site in Alma Road they had built a school. The foundation stone of the present Roman Catholic church in Ponders End was laid in September 1921.[20]

The Ponders End Congregational chapel was said to have been founded in the house of Lady Collatt, a descendant of Oliver Cromwell; the first chapel was built in 1757. A Sunday school was opened in 1800 and an infant day school in 1830. The chapel was renovated and reseated in 1865 at a cost of £600. Litigation over the freehold in 1876 found against the trustees and cost them £1,500; further litigation in 1894 cost the church £594. It was decided in 1868 to rebuild the Lady Huntingdon chapel at Whitewebbs; it had formerly been at Holly Hill. The chapel continued to be serviced by the students at Cheshunt College, and a foundation stone was laid by J.B.Howat of Bridgenhall.[21]

153.   The Congregational chapel opened at Ponders End in 1757 and was demolished after being bomb-damaged during the Second World War.

The building of the Wesleyan Methodist church on the corner of Church Street near the New River (part of the Little Park estate) was begun in August 1889 and a memorial stone was laid two months later; it opened for worship in May 1890. A schoolroom was provided below the chapel for 350 children. Fairhead was the builder, the architect was F. Boreham. The Methodists also secured, at the beginning of the year 1896, what was described as 'a fine building in South Street, recently given up by the Baptists'. July 1904 saw the laying of a foundation stone for a new Methodist church in Ordnance Road to replace the iron chapel which had been used there for twenty-five years.[22]

In the year 1904 there died one Edward Robinson, a market gardener of Bulls Cross, who had lived in his early years in the ancient wooden house in Chase Side known as Raleigh's Cottage. This man had been one of the pioneers of Primitive Methodism in Enfield. The sect, all poor industrious people, began worship in a barn next to Raleigh's Cottage following the visit to Enfield of some of their early preachers. Subsequently they built a little chapel next to the site later occupied by the Cottage Hospital. The foundation stone of their more imposing chapel in Chase Side, which is now almost obliterated by a conversion, was laid in 1894. Another group of Primitive Methodists worshipped at a house in Wellington Road. A church and an assembly hall were begun in August 1905 at the corner of Edenbridge and Wellington roads. The Enfield circuit by 1906 had 245 members.[23]

A missionary spirit abroad in the 1860s led to the Reverend Storer Toms to preach a series of sermons on Chase Green, on the need for the gospel. The two chapels on Chase Side reunited at last on 7 December 1871, after eighty years separation. The health of Mr Stribling at the Zion Chapel had begun to fail, on account of this he was given a pension for life and Storer Toms was appointed minister of the reunited congregations. The Zion Chapel was demolished to make way for a church to be built by the architects Tarring and Company, at a cost of £5,000. The new building rose gracefully, its fine steeple pointing

154. *The new Christ Church, Chase Side rose gracefully, its beautiful spire pointing inspirationally towards heaven. It was greeted by Prebendary Hodson, in November 1875, with an article entitled* 'Where God has His Church the Devil will have his Chapel'. *Beyond the church can be seen the former Chase Side chapel.*

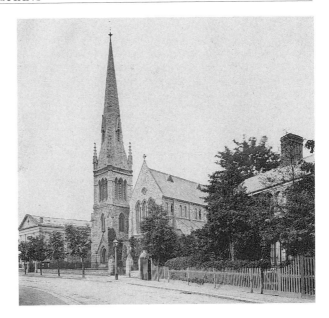

155. *The Reverend Henry Storer Toms, minister at Christ Church.*

inspirationally towards heaven. It was greeted by the vicar, in the parish magazine, with an article entitled *'Where God has His Church, the Devil will have his Chapel'*. His bigotry raised an outcry, and the vicar retreated. He needed at least the neutrality of the Nonconformists in his struggle to prevent a school board. He claimed, somewhat absurdly, that by 'devil's chapel' he had meant the public house, on which subject his references to 'handsome seats, rare music, fine preachers', followed by a tirade on baptism, regeneration and the holy communion, could scarcely have appeared apposite. The church of Christ remained divided even after death and in the new cemetery a broad gravel path separated Nonconformists from members of the Church of England. The Congregationalists were also busy in eastern Enfield where the foundation stone was laid for a new chapel in January 1874.[24]

Many itinerant labourers came to Enfield for the haymaking, from Cambridgeshire and elsewhere. Mr Walker of Green Street allowed a hundred and fifty of them to sleep in his barns, and other farmers did likewise. Each Sunday during the season about a hundred of them would attend services in a meeting room in Logsdon's yard behind the Vestry House in the Town. After the meeting they would bring the forms into the yard where Mr and Mrs Ebenezer Gibbons laid on a substantial tea. Mrs Logsdon, the wife of the coach-builder whose premises occupied three sides of the yard, took an active part in the provision of comforts. The meeting house was a long building in brick and flint with a wash-house, coach-house and stables on the ground floor. The meeting room on the upper floor, with its distempered walls and low unpretentious pulpit, was lit by two circular windows on the east end. It was reached by a staircase at the entrance to the yard. Services were held there as late as 1864, indeed the building was not demolished until 1923; in later years it was used by Mr White a basket maker.[25]

Dissent inevitably gave rise to those who would devise their own approach to the Almighty. At Winchmore Hill the Providence chapel was set up, devoted to the teachings of William Huntingdon SS (Sinner Saved). It was a congregation of Calvinistic Independents who eschewed water baptism in every form. Huntingdon had been illiterate and poor, but he had married money and with it he built a large chapel in Grays Inn Road. The members looked upon him as the apostle of modern times. The Providence, Winchmore Hill was capable of seating about fifty persons. An *Observer* correspondent (5 June 1875) who set out to find it, was directed across the railway bridge 'where he would come upon the little temple'. About 1890 William Sheppard set up a small mission for working people in a barn on a field at Brigadier Hill. Soon afterwards an iron hall was erected. Sheppard left the area at the beginning of the year 1908 and the mission declined. New trustees however, appointed in 1909, brought about a revival.[26]

The Reorganised Church of Jesus Christ of Latter Day Saints in Enfield was set up in the late 1870s by the efforts of Mary Matilda Kemp who heard of the church and its teaching from a cousin living in Hackney. She was the wife of Alfred Kemp, harness maker and postman of Baker Street. The congregation met alternately in the Kemp home and in the home of David Oakman in High Street, Ponders End. A room was taken at Bush Hill Park in the 1880s but the branch disbanded towards the end of the century. In 1900 Joseph Kemp, son of Matilda, opened his home in Enfield for meetings until, in 1903, the church moved to premises above a shop at the corner of Churchbury Road. A larger meeting hall was taken in 1912 at 317 Baker Street. The present church in Lancaster Road was built in 1929.[27]

4. Late Victorian Respectability and Its Decline

Public behaviour was improving and the number of arrests for drunkenness was decreasing. Alderman Abbiss JP was able to announce with some pleasure in 1875 that for the first time since he had sat on the bench not a single case of drunk and disorderly had been brought before him. Even Bank Holiday Mondays in Enfield had gone quiet. Two thousand people had come to Enfield for the day in August that year, by the Great Eastern Railway alone, yet a correspondent for the *Observer*, returning home at half past ten that night, found the place peaceful. 'Only a few- a very few- singing out of tune, merry but not inebriated'. The George was quiet, as were the Nag's Head and the King's Head. The Holly Bush was full, but everyone was sober and orderly; the Hop Poles was shut.[28]

Eastern Enfield too appears to have become a more sober and law-abiding place. A correspondent in the *Observer* (7 January 1882) boasted that:

'no respectable woman fears molestation in the streets at any time. Sunday' he goes on, 'is generally a quiet day ... few are seen out besides the regular attendants at places of worship, though in summer the calm is broken by excursionists from east London, also by the opening of a place of amusement known as the Bell gardens ... but anything like revelry or excessive drunkenness is rare'.

Mostly, he asserted, the people were indifferent to religion; a religious census, he thought, would reveal a very small percentage attending church or chapel. Despite this there was an observance of Sunday as a day of quiet. In this respect things had much improved and obviously it was not due to religion. The correspondent attributed the improvement to the progress of education, especially over the last ten years. As many children, he claimed, attended Sunday school as day school, and he gave much credit to the work of the temperance movement in the area.[29]

The temperance movement had been working in Enfield since 1851. Early meetings were held in Mr Monro's barn in Nags Head Lane (Southbury Road) and it was that gentleman's generosity which maintained the movement for some years. A new hall was opened in Brigadier Hill on Easter Monday 1859, built at the expense of Mr Betts the baker; the Band of Hope sang temperance melodies to mark the occasion. The temperance movement subsequently declined, 'dormant for a time but never dead', until it was revived in the early seventies when, to quote one enthusiast, 'a missionary came amongst us'. That missionary was Dr J.J. Ridge. He infused new life into the old cause. Meetings became frequent and the Band of Hope was re-established. Premises in Baker Street, owned by the good doctor, were opened as a coffee tavern, known as the British Workman. The Enfield Coffee Tavern Company was formed in July 1879 to take over the establishment. The company was inter-denominational, James Warren of Capel House became chairman and the directors were Major B.T. Bosanquet of Forty Hill, J.S. Law of South Lodge, E.C. Nepean of Portcullis

156.   The Church School of Industry (1875) and the Duke of Lancaster Temperance Coffee Tavern (opened 1881) on the east side of Silver Street opposite the vicarage. The space between the two buildings was subsequently occupied by a cinema. The Enfield Gazette took over the former coffee tavern in 1893. These buildings were reconstructed in 1987 behind the original façades.

Lodge, Dr J.J. Ridge of Carlton House and F. Searle of London Road.[30]

The company aimed to establish further taverns where coffee, tea and cocoa would be sold instead of alcoholic drinks. The British Workman proved to be too small for economic management; already it was overcrowded in the evenings. The company had the good fortune to have been presented by Miss Adams with a valuable site in Silver Street opposite the Vicarage, where a great fire had occurred in 1868. Here the directors proposed to build a larger tavern with sleeping accommodation for working men at a cost of £1,300. Named the Duke of Lancaster Coffee Tavern, it opened in January 1881 with a performance by the Enfield Star Minstrels who appeared with faces blackened in true minstrel style. The dining room had marble-topped tables on which a substantial dinner could be provided for sixpence. There were twelve bedrooms with spacious lavatories on each floor, a kitchen, and a bagatelle room. The establishment survived a considerable setback that summer when the manager made off with the cash box; nevertheless a public hall at the back was built the following year at a cost of £500. The shareholders, carefully considering their policy for letting the hall, opted for caution; 'It may be well to draw the line at noisy William Boothites, misnamed Salvationists', they said, 'who disturb their neighbours and create a nuisance wherever they go'. There was never any profit arising from the activities of the company. In 1887 for instance, there was a loss on both houses; at Baker Street £77 and at the Duke of Lancaster £30 and, within a year or two, the coffee tavern was offered for sale; it was taken over by its manager.[31]

The Salvation Army had become very active in eastern Enfield by 1885, but the drunks and rowdies on the increase once more, made life difficult for these devoted souls. That July, police sergeant Griffin was called to the Salvation Army fort at Enfield Wash to remove John Shepherd who stood drunk and defiant in the doorway, refusing to go. The sergeant arrested him, whereupon he hit the sergeant in the mouth and pulled his whiskers. His mates, encouraged by his apparent triumph, attempted a rescue. Shepherd got a month with hard labour despite a plea made by his solicitor, Mr Negus, that the man had been provoked by the Salvation Army, which had been parading the streets, beating drums and carrying flags. On the following Sunday there were further disturbances at the 'fort'. Time and time again Salvation Army officers suffered assault, both at the Wash and at the hall in Ponders End; charges brought against their assailants were often dismissed by the magistrates. Nevertheless the message of the Salvationists seemed to be getting somewhere. That October, (1885) the Reverend Hugh McSorley of the Board of Guardians (vicar at St Paul's, Tottenham) angrily demanded that a committee be set up to enquire into services said to have recently taken place in the workhouse. He had been told that the inmates were marching about the yard, after the mode of the Salvation Army, to music from empty tinned meat cans. The master reassured the vicar however that there had been no sudden subversion of the doctrines of the established Church. There was a petition against the activities of the Salvation Army in 1866; it bore seventy names collected in the poverty-stricken area around Alma Road.[32]

The Town in 1894 provided plenty of entertainment for the lower orders. Every Saturday night the Social Democratic Federation took possession of the fountain and harangued the crowd from the steps. Opposition in the form of the Salvation Army would arrive at eight o'clock, armed with a brass band, to take up position nearby. The 'socialistic speakers', no longer able to make themselves heard, were forced to wait for the Salvationists to finish at nine, but by that time, through a too-potent mixture of drink and religious exhortation, the crowd had become over-excited, and the socialists were met by hooting and pushing. Police Inspector Dowty, always 'anticipating worse disorder', would then bring the meeting to a close and escort the Social Democratic Federation back to the Great Eastern railway station, followed by a hostile crowd. This was quite a usual Saturday night programme in the Town.[33]

Standards of behaviour continued to worsen as the old century waned. Rival gangs of hooligans from Ponders End and the Highway were making life unpleasant for respectable folk. The conduct of excursion parties in the parish was causing concern; there were disgraceful orgies, according to the *Observer*.

'We see' said that paper (23 August 1901) 'quite young girls, sometimes in disordered attire, dancing around their conveyance, assisted by male companions, to scream out all manner of comic songs, accompanied by ribald jest, made more hideous by some *musical* instrument'.

Gambling was on the increase; men and boys gathered at street corners to play banker or pitch and toss. 'Rowdyism', said the *Observer* (31 August 1906) 'has become prevalent on the streets of Enfield'. The paper complained of disturbances caused by children at band concerts on Chase Green. Corner boys and hooligans gathered after the pubs turned out on Saturday nights, in the lane by the Grammar School, 'howling songs in wilful discordance and overflown with insolence and mixed drinks'. The previous Saturday, complained Dr Ridewood, they had torn off the gas jet over the church door, broken the iron work on Miss Boswell's gate (Uvedale House) and pushed a firework through the headmaster's letter-box. Dr Ridewood, seething with indignation, had chased them across the Market Place.

Sir Frederick Orr Lewis found his Whitewebbs property pestered by hooliganism and petty theft every time the drunks were turned out of the King and Tinker on Saturday nights and at Sunday dinner-time. They would go lurching across the park, right up to the house, shouting and singing bawdy songs. Greenhouses were broken into and vegetables were stolen from the gardens. One fine weekend, not long before the First World War, Lady Orr Lewis arranged a house party and the younger guests were enjoying themselves in the beautiful gardens and tennis courts around the mansion. The young ladies, wearing the latest daring fashions and showing an unusual amount of calf and ankle to the delight of the gentlemen, young and old, were distressed to find their admirers augmented by a crowd of jeering drunks recently turned out of the King and Tinker. The butler, dispatched to send them away, was met by a barrage of insult and abuse. The gentlefolk were forced to retreat behind doors, the young ladies were in tears, the police had to be called.

Sir Frederick consulted with Colonel Bowles, whose estate adjoined. He also suffered poaching, pilfering and vandalism. Much of the trouble, the two gentlemen said, was caused by a public footpath which ran close to Whitewebbs mansion. They applied to have it closed so that the public could be excluded from their parks, or at least diverted away from the mansion. Both proposals aroused considerable opposition at all levels; by Dugdale Sykes a solicitor, by Cuthbert Whitaker a local historian and by other conservationists, and also by the Labour Party which organised a protest meeting in Church Street where W.E. Williams, described in the *Gazette* as a 'mob orator', stirred up the crowd against the hunting, land-owning classes. Despite the opposition a diversion was allowed by the magistrates J.W. Ford and Sir Alfred Somerset, themselves considerable landowners. The campaign was nevertheless pursued by the socialists with considerable animation. Small groups of demonstrators hung about the gates at Whitewebbs shouting slogans like 'Foreigners go home' (Sir Frederick was a Canadian) and 'Burn down the mansions and give our children bread'. Messages about 'grinding the face of the poor' were chalked up on the lodge walls, stones were thrown at cars leaving the park, a groom was waylaid at night and beaten up, a row of young trees planted as a windbreak was sawn down. Sir Frederick even bought revolvers to protect himself and his valet. The troubles subsided only upon the outbreak of the First World War.[34]

The evangelical movement remained active into the new century. A series of evangelical services was held in the 'Great Tent' in Baker Street with the band of Chase Farm School in attendance. The Workmen's Train Mission, in 1909, held meetings on six trains every morning on the Great Eastern railway. The Enfield Town Christian Mission had been set up in 1897 and E.S. Gibbons became secretary. He was to hold that office until 1932 when the congregations at the mission averaged four or five hundred. Yet the new century saw a decline in the importance of religion in Enfield, as throughout the country. The *Daily News* religious census, taken on Sunday 18 October 1903, showed that services in Enfield had been attended by 15,015 worshippers. Church-going remained more a custom in the western part of the parish; of the 15,015 attenders at

157. The notice announces that St Paul's Presbyterian Church in Church Street Enfield 'will be opened on Wednesday 26 September 1906'. On the extreme right are the gates of Chase Park, Windmill Hill.

church or chapel 8,738 were from the western and 6,277 from the eastern part. The numbers attending were:

Established church	7,719
Nonconformist	6,140
Roman Catholic	404
Other services	752

When a deduction was made for those who attended more than once that day, the number of worshippers arrived at was 9,610 or 22.84 per cent, which was roughly in line with the percentage in the whole area surveyed. Out of six million people covered by the census, one person in five attended a service.[35]

The Presbyterians, in 1906, decided to build a new church. They had worshipped for some years in a building off Chase Green, which had also been used as a school and a hall. Recently, owing to growing numbers, they had had to hire the new drill hall opposite for their services. The new church was planned to seat six hundred worshippers; it would cost £6,000.[36]

St Andrew's Church by 1908 was once more in need of repair; the architect, J. Oldrid Scott, estimated that the work would cost £1,800. The High Church, Low Church controversy had died down. Certainly the general public had lost interest, but within the Church it was not dead and the plans for restoration drew forth shrill accusations of ritualism. The loss of 178 seats was also a cause of complaint. Mr Bowles reassured the critics that they would be lost mostly from the gallery; they were seats which were not used, because people sitting there were unable to hear the service, moreover children played about in the gallery during worship. The interior plaster was stripped off to reveal a great deal of the brickwork by the side of and above the chancel arch which had been done two hundred years earlier. The east window was raised three feet, the organ was removed from the east end of the south aisle, and a new oak screen was placed there. The former doorway to the rood loft was reopened to give access to the organ loft. The north and south aisle galleries were shortened at their eastern ends. During the restoration, services were again held in the Riding House. The cement was removed from the south and west fronts of the tower in 1910 and a new clock was installed. At the east end of the south aisle, where the organ had formerly stood, St John's chapel had taken shape.[37]

Notes to Chapter Seven

1.   HO 129, 137 (1851 Religious Census)
2.   *Observer* Au 1860, Jl 1864, Enfield. Minutes of the select vestry.
3.   Graham Dalling *Enfield's Railway King* EHHS 1978, *Recollections of Old Enfield* p83 reprinted EHHS 1983.
4.   *Observer* F 1859
5.   *ibid* My 1859
6.   *ibid* X 1859
7.   *ibid* Jl 1859
8.   *ibid* Ja 1860, F 1860
9.   *ibid* F 1860, X 1860
10. *ibid* Mr 1860, Ap 1860
11. *ibid* S 1864, D 1864, Au 1865, S 1865, X 1865
12. *ibid* Je 1866, Ja 1867, F 1867, Ap 1867
13. G. Dalling *op cit* p9
14. *Observer* F 1868, Mr 1868, Je 1868
15. *ibid* My 1871
16. *ibid* My 1873, Au 1867, 25N 1876, 26 Jl 1879
17. *ibid* X 1872, My 1874, Graham Dalling *Parish Church of St Matthew Ponders End 1878-1978*
18. *Observer* 24 Ja 1885, 14N 1890, 16X 1896, 26X 1906, 14S 1900
19. *ibid* N 1867, 20 Mr, 18S 1875, 28 Je 1884, Mr 1872, 5 Je 1875, 9X 1875
20. *ibid* 30S 1921
21. *ibid* 23F 1894, 10 Ja 1896
22. *ibid* 11X 1889, 23 My 1890, 10 Ja 1896, 29 Jl 1904
23. *ibid* 2S 1904, 29 Je 1894, 11 Au 1905, 26X 1906
24. *ibid* Je 1867, Geoffrey Knight *Nonconformist Churches in Enfield* p6 EHHS 1973, *Observer* 27N 1875, 4D 1875, Ja 1874
25. *ibid* 22 Je 1923
26. *ibid* 4 Je 1909
27. information Miss L.E.A. Oakman.
28. *Observer* 7 Au 1875
29. *ibid* 22 Mr 1884
30. *ibid* 29 Ja 1876
31. *ibid* 12Jl 1879, 1 My 1880, 29 Ja 1881, 9 Ap 1881, 8D 1883, 18 F 1887, 31X 1890
32. *ibid* 25 Jl 1885, 17X 1885, 13 Au 1886
33. e.g. *ibid* 28 S 1894
34. *ibid* 16N 1906, Smith, Nina S. *George* Cape 1984, *Gazette* 17S 1971
35. *ibid* 17 Au 1900, 12N 1909, 25 Mr 1932, 12 F 1904
36. *ibid* 21 S 1900, 19 Ap 1901, 20X 1906
37. *ibid* 28N 1908, 8 Ja 1909, 23 D 1910

Chapter Eight

Leisure, Pleasure and Politics

1. Introduction

The local agricultural labourers in the 1830s toiled Monday to Saturday yet were scarcely able to put bread in the mouths of their children. On the seventh day they would be released to enjoy the delights of Enfield. Charles Lamb, who was no lover of the labouring classes, deplored their Sunday idleness.

'The weekdays would be intolerable', he complained, 'but for the superior invention which they show here in making Sundays worse. Clowns stand about in what was the Market Place and spit minutely to relieve ennui. Clowns to whom Enfield tradespeople are gentle people. Inland clowns, clods and things below cows. They assemble to infect the air with dullness from Waltham marshes. They clear off on Monday mornings like other fogs.'

The Victorian period was to see a slow improvement in the happiness and behaviour of the poor. More leisure time was provided by the gradual introduction of a five and a half day week from the 1860s; at the same time facilities for the more pleasurable use of leisure became available. Working men took an active role in organisations. Some joined the Volunteers both in Enfield Town and at the Lock, and brass bands were formed which were to be an admirable feature of working-class culture up to the First World War and beyond. Cricket flourished, in the 1860s many local teams were formed which played against each other and against teams from the private schools. Enfield had a rugby team in the 1870s. The Victoria Swimming Club taught many boys to swim and organised races along the River Lea to Waltham Abbey. Cycling became very popular with the advent of the safety bicycle in the 1880s. The railways widened horizons; there were excursions by train on bank holidays to popular east coast resorts. Many excursionists came to Enfield and a 'retreat' was set up at Holtwhites Hill for their entertainment. A small theatre opened in 1885. Public houses provided facilities for billiards, quoits and bowls. Occasionally prize fights were staged, though illegal. Football became popular in the 1890s; Cherry Orchard Lane was the important venue in Enfield. Spurs became a professional team in 1895, and in the following year the Enfield Football League was set up. Much popular entertainment and mutual self-help was provided by the PSA. Little music halls opened and occasionally there came a circus or a menagerie; the first permanent cinema opened in Enfield in 1910.

Many working men, up to the First World War, continued to find their pleasures in the pub but, in the mid-Victorian period, Enfield seems to have become a sober and orderly place. Even on a bank holiday Monday in 1875 a correspondent found the public houses 'peaceful'. Another correspondent, about that same time, claimed that excessive drunkenness in Enfield was rare; this he attributed not to religion, but to education and the work of the temperance movement.

My more critical readers may be surprised at the apparently incompatible marriage in the title of this chapter between pleasure and politics. To tell the truth, it is a marriage of convenience. Yet in pre-television days there was some pleasure in politics. Saturday nights in the Town were full of fun, of a sort. Speakers from the Social Democratic Federation racked their throats to be heard above the Salvation Army band; inevitably they had to withdraw from the unequal contest until the bandsmen headed back to their citadel at nine o'clock. By that time however, the crowd had become belligerent and the police would call a halt to proceedings and escort the speakers to Enfield Town railway station, followed, according to the conservative *Observer*, by a hostile mob. Drunkenness, rowdyism and street gambling seemed to increase in the 1890s in all parts of the parish, and church attendance declined.

There was an air of seriousness about the suburban middle class in the mid-Victorian period. They attended lectures on such abstruse subjects as Cardinal Richelieu and Thomas Hood, they went to concerts and oratorios and read books. Music societies were formed, not merely for appreciation, but for performance. To what extent this seriousness extended to the upper levels of the working class it is hard to discern; some may have used the libraries at the mechanics institutes or attended lectures there and many would have enjoyed the penny readings at the British School in Chase Side. Some purchased pianos for the parlour (like Mr Pooter in *Diary of a Nobody*) and later, gramophones. Few would have been able to subscribe to Meyers's circulating library, and few could have afforded the concerts and oratorios at the Riding House or the Athenaeum. Many local artists and craftsmen of some talent were revealed in Arthur Mackmurdo's fine exhibition at the Athenaeum in 1883. A public library was opened in 1894 with a branch in the Town and one in eastern Enfield, but they were mostly used by the middle class.

Traditional forms of entertainment survived through much of the Victorian period. The Enfield fair flourished until 1869 when it was killed off in its prime by nonconformist and evangelical zeal. Bonfire night continued to be celebrated in the old way. A maypole was set up on Chase Green on May Day and sweeps exchanged clothes with their wives to celebrate.

The Enfield electorate expanded through the century as the population grew and the franchise was broadened. Many working-class men were given the vote for the first time by the Act of 1884. The following year a parliamentary constituency under the name of Enfield, but incorporating both Edmonton and Southgate, was created. These developments gave rise to a new interest in parliamentary democracy. A mock 'house of commons' was formed where each 'member' represented a 'constituency' and current political issues were earnestly debated. The new interest, and the decline of deference, gave rise to heckling and disorder at political meetings of the established parties. Enfield remained staunchly Conservative until the 1906 election when the Liberal candidate was returned. This election, for the first time in this area, saw the intervention of the new left. The member for Enfield, by 1914, represented nearly thirty-three thousand electors.

2. Culture — Mostly Middle-Class

Artists and philosophers sometimes set, or perhaps interpret, the tone of a period of national history. Locally that duty was often assumed by the proprietor of the local newspaper. If any one man shaped the minds and moved the consciences of the middle class in late Victorian Enfield, that man was J.H. Meyers, the owner of *Meyers's Enfield Observer* (now the *Gazette*). James Meyers began printing his paper in 1859 (1855 had seen the repeal of stamp duty on newspapers) in two rooms over Mr Glover's grocery shop, number two Silver Street. There was little required in the way of printing at this time and he would go around seeking out work and collecting items of news. His newspaper, for the first ten years, came out once a month. He lodged at Mr Boultwood's house, on the west side of the Market Place (the site now occupied by the Bradford and Bingley) and he married Mr Boultwood's daughter. Subsequently he moved to a shop next to the Nag's Head, on the east side of the Town, and later to the premises next to the George. There he opened his subscription library with a thousand or so volumes, backed by the stock of Mudie's Circulating Library in Oxford Street whose books could be obtained, two volumes at a time, for 25s a year. In December 1882 he announced the publication of a new journal, the *Enfield Magazine*. J.H. Meyers retired in 1887 and died five years later (*Observer* 10 June 1892). In September the following year the firm transferred to larger premises in Silver Street (*Observer* 15 September 1893) which had formerly been the Duke of Lancaster Coffee Tavern. It retained these premises until 1984.

The parish in 1859 was becoming culture conscious. The Enfield Literary and Mutual Improvement Institution held regular monthly meetings at the Lecture Hall in Chase Side. Cardinal Richelieu was the subject in January 1860, and in April there was a talk on Thomas Hood. Musical evenings were held and a music society was established in the Town, not merely for musical appreciation but also to purchase musical instruments, set up an orchestra and to rehearse. It had fifty-five working members in the early sixties; H.M. Jenkins was the conductor and total subscriptions amounted to £66. Meyers's public library opened a music circulating library in December 1869. The penny readings at the British School in Chase Side were another attraction; Thackeray, *Oliver Twist*, Hood's *Tale of a Trumpet* and Gilmore's *Ramsgate Lifeboat*, all drew good audiences. A horticultural society was set up and held its first show on 21 June 1867 at Old Park.

In Ponders End Alderman Abbiss purchased the building formerly occupied as a Wesleyan chapel and established a mechanics institute there in 1860, with a schoolroom, reading room, and lectures for the benefit of the working classes. Both the Highway and Enfield Lock had their philharmonic societies. Ponders End had a cricket club by 1862, also a mutual improvement society and, last but not least, it had a brass band.

Arthur Mackmurdo (1851-1942) the architect, was a key figure in the Arts and Crafts movement and a founder of the Century Guild. He was born in Church Street, Edmonton and lived at Halcyon House which he had built in Private Road. He drew attention in 1883 to the quantity and quality of the work produced in Enfield by local artists. Much of it, he said, remained unknown even to neighbours, it being exhibited in London and in the West End. He thought a creditable exhibition might be drawn together, and perhaps enriched by loans from local art collections. Music too should play a part, but the musicians should

158.   *It was in the building next to the George that J. H. Meyers, the proprietor of the* Gazette *and* Observer, *opened his subscription library backed by Mudie's of Oxford Street. Next door was the photographic studio belonging to his son Milton Meyers.*

J. H. MEYERS

Is now showing a

CHOICE & VARIED ASSORTMENT OF

EASTER CARDS.

PLAIN AND FANCY STATIONER,

BOOKSELLER AND BOOKBINDER,

ENFIELD TOWN.

be sought beyond the bounds of the parish, 'since music, the most social of the arts, is least local in character'. Mr Rowan offered the use of the Athenaeum (*Observer* 10 November 1883).

The exhibition took more than a year in preparation and was presented in spring 1885. Two artists were picked out as of special interest in the *Observer* (16 May 1885); Mrs Nina Forbes of Southbury Road, an art teacher who exhibited paintings of the Lake District, and Walter Reynolds who lived for six years at Beechcroft, Bush Hill Park, who had entered a number of water-colours, some depicting local scenes; *'The lake at Bush Hill Park'*, several views in Trent Park, *'Winchmore Hill from the Ridgeway', Chase Side, Enfield from the fields with a view of Christ Church*, and a painting of the King and Tinker.

Preparations were going ahead in 1892 for a poll on the adoption of the Public Libraries Acts. It was held at the end of March that year and it resulted in a vote in favour, 1,576 for, 1,194 against, with 1,457 spoiled returns. Nearly a year later the opening of a free library in Edmonton reminded library advocates in Enfield that their Board had as yet taken no action except the imposition of a library rate. Another year drifted by before it was observed that the Local Board would soon have in hand the proceeds of that library rate and ought to be thinking about the appointment of a library committee. One reader suggested, in the *Observer* (9 June 1893) that a library should be established in Enfield Town and that the libraries in the mechanics institutes at the Royal Small Arms Factory and at Ponders End should be linked with the public library service. The Board however undertook a less elaborate scheme and proposed to use the scullery at the court-house in Little Park. It was decided not to co-opt non-Board members to a library committee.[1] Steps were now taken to install a woodblock floor, a window, a chimney-piece and a grate in the scullery, in preparation for the launch of the library service. The budget for the first half-year showed an expected expenditure of £546; £300 on books, the salary of a librarian would be £37 10s, the wages of a clerk £7 10s, and library fittings would cost £120. There were to be reading rooms and circulating libraries (ie lending libraries) in the Town, at Ponders End fire station, and in the schoolroom at Ordnance Road. The library was nearly ready by February 1894, some 3,000 books had been classified, catalogued and arranged. Those who had books to donate were urged by the local press to do so at once, before the catalogue was published. Copies of this catalogue, compiled by C. Frederick Harrison the librarian, survive. It was an excellent piece of work, carried out in the shortest possible time. The library was opened at Little Park by F.A. Bevan of Trent Park on 27 July 1894. By March 1895, 2,537 borrowers had enrolled and 1,321 books had been borrowed, mostly fiction (858); the most popular classes among the non-fiction were history, travel and religion. The chairman of the library committee

*159.   The architect Arthur Mackmurdo lived at Halcyon House (left) which he built in Private
Road. He also built Brooklyn, number 8 Private Road (right), which still stands.*

was Hugh Trenchard of The Firs, Clay Hill.[2]

A grant of £4,000, proffered by Andrew Carnegie to build a branch library in
eastern Enfield, caused consternation in the Council. The rate available for the
library service was restricted by the Libraries Acts to a penny in the pound. It
produced only £785 a year, and it would be impossible to maintain two libraries

on such a budget. The money was hurriedly put away in the bank while the council considered the sad predicament in which it had been trapped. It was thought at first that permission might be granted to spend the money on a new central library as part of a town hall, but this proved unacceptable to the donor. The Council therefore decided to build the library at Enfield Highway and it was opened in 1910. Meanwhile the library accommodation at Gentleman's Row had become so full that it was impossible to find room for new books. The Council therefore sought from the Carnegie Trust the means to provide an improved service at Enfield Town, where there were now 4,000 borrowers. It was in November 1910 that the committee entered into negotiations with Carnegie for a further £4,000 to build a new library on the site now known as the Library Green, a museum was included in the plans but the donor would not approve this as part of his gift. Since the building of a town hall was still vaguely contemplated, the library building was begun right at the back of the site and facing the wrong way so that space might be left, but within a few months the town hall project had again been relegated to a more indistinct future. The unsightly wooden screen which had been put up around the site was taken down and a pleasant little green (Library Green) was laid out surrounded by trees and shrubs. The new library opened in July 1912. The reading room was made available to the public between the hours of 10am and 10pm, the lending library closed at 9pm daily except Wednesday when it closed at 1pm. A reference library of 2,300 volumes opened there in October 1913.[3]

3. The Pleasures of the People

Throughout the eighteenth century public meetings, dances and entertainments, for the best people, had taken place in the Assembly Rooms behind the King's Head, but for some years now the more important public functions had been held in the Riding House in the grounds of Enfield Court. This was a large circular building erected in 1858 and greatly improved in 1863. It was used for riding and exercising Colonel Somerset's fine stud of horses. The original floor was of tan (the residue from local tan-pits). This was covered for functions by a sectional boarded floor sixty-three feet in diameter, rendering the hall capable of seating five or six hundred people. Hard by were the stables and the coach house where the 'Hirondelle', the Colonel's famous coach, was housed. The coach-house too could be converted for smaller gatherings. Following the improvements of 1863, a band concert was held at the Riding House with an invited audience described as 'numerous and select'. The grounds subsequently remained open and dances were held there throughout July and August. The entertainment achieved perhaps its highest degree of elegance in January 1873 when a subscription ball was presented and music was provided by the band of the Royal Italian Opera from Covent Garden. Three guineas entitled a subscriber to six tickets, non-subscribers paid 12s 6d, supper and refreshments were included.[4]

The Bycullah Athenaeum, built in 1881, stood where there is now a petrol station on Windmill Hill. It burned down one windy night in December 1931. Handel's 'Messiah' was performed there before Christmas 1883; oratorios were much loved by the Victorians. The programme for one evening in February 1887 provides an example of what was usually presented. The main feature was a 'Dioramic Dissolving View Entertainment' with seventy views of a train journey from Euston to Harlech. The apparatus was described by a reporter from the *Observer* as a 'powerful triple oxy-hydrogen lantern'. Miss L. Pyne occupied the piano stool from where she provided incidental music. A concert by the Carl Rosa Opera Company followed. Seats were at 6d and 1s, the proceeds were contributed to the Enfield Cottage Hospital. Following the bankruptcy of Culloden Rowan, the Athenaeum was taken over in 1892 by the Bycullah

161. The Eeles family forge had stood in Ponders End High Street for nearly 200 years until it was wrecked by Hitler's bombs one Saturday night in 1940. Around 1910 they had six men working there at two forges; they began at 5.30am and before breakfast forty shoes had been fashioned and fitted. There were plenty of horses in the area; over a hundred were used in the construction of the King George V reservoir and David Heath had about two hundred. The man without a cap is Albert Eeles.

Athenaeum Company which purchased the building for £1,130, which was less than it had cost to build. Improvements cost £640, but little profit resulted, and no dividend was paid from 1899 to 1914. With the outbreak of war the dramatic company ceased to function and dances were no longer held. The premises were taken over by Klinger's for war work.[5]

A theatre opened briefly in April 1885 near Enfield Town railway station. It was called the 'Excelsior'; seats were priced at 1s, 6d and 3d. A different play was put on almost every night; on Monday and Tuesday, for instance, they presented C.A. Spalding's *'Called Back'*, on Wednesday *'Blow for Blow'*, on Thursday *'Joe the Fireman'*, and so on. Music was provided by the Enfield Brass Band. The Sun music-hall in Church Street opened in March 1886 and for a short time presented variety 'by a company of talented artistes' on Mondays and Saturdays. Admission was 3d and 6d; lads were not admitted unaccompanied.

The Foresters music-hall was licensed by the Middlesex County Council in 1891; it was presented in a corrugated iron hall with a matchboard interior behind the Railway Hotel in South Street. It seated between 250 and 300 people. Performances, 'free from vulgarity', were given on Saturday and Monday evenings, admission was inexpensive, Professor Dalziel, a well-known local entertainer, was the general manager. After closing for the summer months, it reopened in October with a bill headed by Chirgwin 'the white-eyed Kaffir', supported by comedians, dancers, acrobats, chair-vaulters, ballad singers and

*162.   Church Street, 1902.
William Brand the hairdresser
can be seen standing at his
door, Fountains the coach
builders is next door, then the
Rising Sun and beyond the
entrance into Welch's livery
stables lies Graham's cycle
manufactory.*

negro minstrels. It was still flourishing in the winter of 1894/5; G. Hollingberry
was then the proprietor. There is evidence of the existence of a concert room
in a beer-house at Ponders End long before this. The surveyor, examining an
old chimney at Mr Eeles's forge in June 1868, relates quite gratuitously that the
premises had formerly been a brewery and afterwards a beer-house, and the
room over the smithy had been the concert room. (Surveyor's report). Music-
hall was becoming very popular by the turn of the century; Fred Karno and his
'Jail Birds' were at the Holloway Empire. The Edmonton Empire opened as a
music-hall on Boxing night 1908.[6]

Lord George Sanger's circus came to Enfield on 12 September 1892 with
three hundred horses, two herds of elephants, a troupe of camels and performing lions. Public houses continued to provide entertainment; at the Rising Sun
in Church Street Mr Biscoe informed the world that he had fitted up, at great
expense, a first-rate billiard room. Quoits became popular in the public houses
and in clubs, in a match played at the Forty Hill Club against the Ponders End
Radical Club in July 1891 the home side lost by ninety-three to seventy-six.
Bostock and Wombwell's menagerie was here before Christmas 1907, setting up
on the old fête ground at the top of Baker Street. 'Cecil, the largest lion in the
world', was the star of the show.[7]

The Enfield fair was held each year for three days during the last week in
September. The Town from the corner of Silver Street to the Market Place was
crowded with stalls which sold oysters, mussels, cookies and sandwiches. There
were toy and gingerbread stalls, stalls for skittles, nut shooting and wheels of
fortune. Beyond these were exhibition shows, legerdemain tricks and feats of
strength, a steam roundabout and swings. The Market Place, from the parish
pump to the church rails, complained one high-minded correspondent with
some indignation, 'was filled with a monster booth of which the least said the
better, we will merely remark that persons least expected in such places were
seen sitting in the entrance, and young children, late at night, sleeping through
scenes of revelry that morality shudders to witness'. At the fair in September

163. The quoits team at the Wheatsheaf. In the back row in the straw hat, Freddy Frost the licensee.

164.   The Enfield fair was held each year for three days during the last week in September. The Town
from Silver Street to the Market Place was crowded with stalls. (From a painting by George Forster,
1848)

1868 two men from the parish of St Giles were taken into custody for singing and selling printed songs 'of an indecent tendency'. They were fined £20. 'Enfield', declared Mr Sykes, 'was inundated with a crowd of the lowest classes of the population of London... for three days business was almost brought to a standstill, there were such disgraceful scenes of debauchery and drunkenness that the leading residents and tradesmen of the Town were almost unanimous in urging suppression'. Those most prominent in demanding the abolition of the fair were the two Nonconformist grocers, Mr Cave at the corner of Sydney Road, and John Stribling in Chase Side. Edward Ford, the chairman of the magistrates, was approached and willingly took up the matter. A petition to the Home Secretary and to the Commissioner of Police was signed by nine magistrates, nearly all the ministers and some ninety of the principle inhabitants. Thus the Enfield fair was killed off, while it was still at the height of its popularity, by a holy alliance of nonconformist and evangelical zeal.[8]

There was resistance, and a protest meeting was held at the King's Head Assembly Rooms. Those who opposed suppression were much looked down upon by the respectable members of the community, especial emphasis being laid, in *Meyers's Observer*, upon the presumed illegitimacy of a certain gentleman present by the name of James Door, allegedly so named because he had been discovered as an infant upon a doorstep, a circumstance which obviously rendered it impossible to take his opinions seriously. The opposition, such as it was, was overborne, and the magistrates issued an order suppressing the fair.[9]

It was therefore with some amazement, indeed indignation, that the respectable citizens of Enfield, on 22 September 1869, beheld a caravan enter the Town and draw up opposite the George. More vans approached and halted. The booth people got out and stood around undecided what to do. They conferred and at length a delegation was despatched to the police station. The police could offer no advice, they must wait until the inspector arrived back at six o'clock. The six o'clock train bore no inspector. A rumour ran through the crowd that he was on his way by horse. At last he arrived, dismounted and entered the police station. Everyone awaited his decision, then the inspector emerged, remounted and rode off, apparently as ill-informed about the rights of the matter as all the others.

It was William Hubbard of Baker Street, the celebrated manufacturer of gingerbread, who broke the stalemate (though stalemate seems to be an ill-chosen word when talking about Mr Hubbard). He stepped forward and set up his stall. The others followed suit. Nevertheless the magistrates' order had frightened away the chief attractions; the whole affair proved dull and unprofitable and on Saturday morning the people took down their booths and cleared off. Charges against Mr Hubbard were dropped and the Enfield fair faded quietly, never to be seen again, as did so many other local fairs in the age of Victorian respectability. Edmonton fair was killed off about the same time, but the Waltham Abbey fair survived, and as late as 1928 the market and the whole of the main street was given up for three days to roundabouts and swings.[10]

There were rural sports and games on Chase Green on Good Fridays and every May Day a maypole was set up at the back of Roof Pope's house, which had once been the Pest House where plague victims had been confined in the seventeenth century; it was demolished in 1910. A greasy pole was erected with a leg of mutton on top, near the forge, now Newsom's shop on Windmill Hill. Chimney-sweeps and their wives exchanged clothes for the day, decorated

165.   *Enfield Bonfire Boys procession 1896.*

themselves in garlands and made merry. A procession went round the Town and
the children finished for a treat in the grounds of Mrs Everett at Chase Side
House, now the Town Park.

The Enfield Bonfire Boys put on a display on 5 November each year when
thousands turned out to watch. About eighty of them took part in 1891. A
procession around the Town was led by Mr Shuter dressed as Lord Randolph
Churchill in South African costume. The Foresters brass band and the Enfield
Town brass band marched with them, followed by a cowboy wagon and wild west
riders. The Enfield fire brigade joined in on their steamer, and the 'Dark Town'

166. Over Whitsun 1905 some eight thousand Enfield people took the train to the seaside. This excursion from Ponders End station must have been packed.

fire brigade riding on the old manual engine 'which used to extinguish the burning homes of our ancestors a hundred years ago'. There was a huge fire on Chase Green and a display of fireworks. A collection was made on behalf of the Cottage Hospital, and afterwards everyone important gathered at the Rising Sun for a smoking concert.[11]

Four bank holidays were established by the Bank Holidays Act 1871; at Easter, Whitsun, August and Boxing Day. Enfield remained a highly popular venue for bank holiday trips; six thousand people were brought here by rail alone during the bank holiday in August 1884. 'The number of vehicles through the Town', said the *Observer* 'was something marvellous'. The Great Eastern Railway ran excursions to popular resorts throughout each summer, like the one advertised in August 1882 to Hunstanton for 4s return. Over the Whitsun week in June 1905 some eight thousand people took the train for a day out, and about the same number arrived in Enfield for a day in the country. Well over seven thousand day excursionists took the train, mostly to Southend, Clacton or Harwich over the Whitsun holiday in 1911. Six thousand Londoners arrived by the new railway at Cuffley on the Monday; one can only wonder what they did when they got there.[12]

'The beautiful scenery in and around Enfield', wrote the *Observer* in July 1896, 'has been the means of attracting numbers of holiday-makers'. The only drawback had been the difficulty in finding a pleasant spot for them 'to pitch their tent'. Wood's Retreat remedied all that; it stood off Chase Side on the north side of Holtwhites Hill 'commanding a view of beautiful forest scenery'. Thirty-five acres of meadow land had been set aside as a pleasure ground where parties could 'stroll about and take their ease in sequestered spots'. W.G. Wood, baker and confectioner of Chase Side, the proprietor, had erected pavilions

167. *Enfield Tradesmen's Association with their good wives resplendent in their most elegant hats, at Rye Park in 1907.*

168.   W. G. Wood, refreshment contractor, opened his 'retreat' off Chase Side Enfield in 1896. On thirty five acres of meadow land, Mr Wood erected pavilions where six hundred visitors could sit down for dinners or tea parties. He provided cloakrooms and lavatories, swings and excursions to places of interest.

W. G. WOOD,

BAKER AND CONFECTIONER,

Chase Side, Enfield,

Begs to inform the Public that he makes the

WHOLEMEAL   BREAD   DAILY.

wherein, wet or fine, six hundred people could sit down for dinner, breakfast, tea parties, or school treats. The preparation and cooking of food was done on site, cloakrooms and lavatories were provided, there were swings and high-flyers and donkeys to ride on. The proprietor, for a small fee, would make arrangements to take visitors to local places of interest, Waltham Abbey, Rye House, Temple Bar or Theobalds Park.[13]

The retreat prospered. Nearly one thousand people visited there on two occasions in early June 1897, including parties from the Ringsdale mission hall in Wood Green and from Gifford Hall by Caledonian Road. The ponies and the donkeys were in great demand, as were the two Victorias (low four-wheeled carriages). The week ending 18 July 1902 saw the visit of a large party from Wood Green, two hundred from Stratford Wesleyan Sunday School on Wednesday, and three hundred 'little cripples' on Saturday.[14]

Preparations were made in 1887 for the celebration of the Queen's jubilee.

169.   Chase Side Gardens was laid out to mark the occasion of Queen Victoria's jubilee in 1897. The bust is of Dr J. J. Ridge. The photograph must have been taken in the 1920s.

170.   The Holly Bush celebrates the coronation of King Edward VII

It was proposed that there should be a dinner given at the Riding House for those of sixty-eight (the Queen's age) and over. There would be an entertainment for the children and a new wing would be added to the Cottage Hospital, to be known as the Victoria wing. To the delight of the parish clerk, Charles

Boswell, a new flag was purchased for St Andrew's Church. For the Diamond Jubilee of 1897 the vestry clerk proposed that a portion of Chase Green abutting on the New River be laid out as a Queen's memorial, to make it 'a thing of beauty'. The work was begun. 'Very soon now', said the *Observer* (7 September 1900) 'the newly planted gardens in Chase Green, which have done credit to the gardener, will be ready'. In 1897, also to mark the jubilee, the parish church clock, first placed in the tower in 1764, was cleaned and decorated; it was finally replaced in 1910. The coronation of Edward VII aroused less enthusiasm. It was planned that it should be celebrated with a tea party for all the children, but the subscription proved not to be in accordance with expectations and coronation medals were proposed as a less expensive option, but even this plan had to be abandoned.[15] However money was eventually raised to erect a market house, in 1904, to replace the market cross which found its final resting place in the garden at Myddelton House.

The turf on Chase Green was repeatedly cut up by tradesmen and carriers who drove their carts across the grass. Complaints were so frequent that the matter was taken up by the churchwardens, who set to work to raise a fund to enclose the Green 'with neat open and cheerful painted railings' extending along Chase Side towards the Lecture Hall. After this was done the ground was levelled and the turf relaid so that it could again be used for cricket. The management, in March 1879, was placed in the hands of the local cricket clubs.

Ebenezer Marshall was prominent in 1886 in raising a subscription among his well-to-do neighbours in Bycullah Park to plant trees and place seats on Chase Green; £70 was collected. Few districts, declared the *Observer* (17 December 1886) are favoured with the advantage of so large a green so near the Town. Some portion of it, the report went on, is used for cricket, and the whole of it for grazing hungry-looking horses. But despite the efforts of the well affected, milk dealers, butchers and drivers of coal carts continued to cross the Green near Conical Corner, where the ground was cut up and reduced to a sad state. The *Observer*, by 1894, described the Green as little better than a nuisance; the grass was disappearing, the fence put up to divert the footpath away from the cricket pitch was torn down, ruts, holes and broken bottles appeared everywhere. 'Except for carpet-beating...' it was said, 'it might as well be done away with' (18 May 1894). A remedy was sought in an ancient, almost forgotten body; the state of the Green was presented in the manor court where Henry C. Weld, the steward, was instructed to ensure that the land was placed under some public authority. In consequence the Local Board enquired of the churchwardens whether they would be willing to hand it over. The churchwardens had only £9 a year available for maintenance. It was offered to the District Council in 1897.

The activities of the regular Army and the Volunteers were always a source of entertainment for the public. The first battalion of the Royal Dragoons, and the Middlesex Rifles, were billeted in Enfield around the time of the Crimean War. Alec Woodfield remembered the riflemen drawn up on pay parade in the Town to collect their shilling a day. As soon as they were dismissed, they were in and out of the shops buying food. The regiments drilled on Chase Green. When the Dragoons left, at least two Enfield men went with them as recruits and fought through the whole of the Crimean campaign. Soldiers were often billeted in Enfield in the days before they built depots. This was probably the origin of the oddly named Barracks at Clay Hill.[17]

171.   Enfield Volunteer Rifles band photographed at a garden party on the lawn at Claysmore in the summer 1865.
Left to right. Front row:
Sgt A. Woodfield (baritone) S. Lane (bass) R. Barnes (bass) M. Kaye (2nd cornet) D. Barclay (soprano) G. Hall (1st cornet) E. Woodman (bandmaster) C. Mathews (solo cornet) G. Horlock (drummer) J. Newman (side-drummer) W. Simms (3rd cornet) H. Biscoe (triangle)
Back row:
W. Wells (clarinet) C. Hall (euphonium) R. Ralph (1st cornet) G. Brown (1st cornet) M. Smith (bass) E. Gale (tenor horn) C. Gale (clarinet) Cpl W. Woodfield (solo tenor)

The Enfield Volunteers had been formed in 1803 (see Vol. 1, p324) in conjunction with Volunteers from Tottenham and Edmonton. More than £3,000 had been raised locally and each man, on joining, agreed to serve three years; he was paid a small sum of money. The 35th Middlesex Rifle Volunteers was formed in 1859 with Alfred Somerset as captain. It was attached with its band in 1861, as the Enfield Company, to the 40th Middlesex, known as the Central London Rifle Rangers of which Somerset was appointed colonel. The band became part of the regimental band. A year or so later the unit was transferred with Colonel Somerset to the 9th West Middlesex Rifle Volunteers and the band of the Enfield Company became the regimental band. It was then at the zenith of its glory and numbered about thirty players. All costs were defrayed by Colonel Somerset. The colonel however, in 1872, was transferred to the Kings Own Light Infantry Militia and both the band and the unit lost his financial support. The band deteriorated; it was short of funds and was forced to relinquish the services of Mr Woodman the bandmaster. Eventually it became the Enfield Town Brass Band and the Enfield Town Volunteers, until 1881, went out of existence. In January 1932 Alec Woodfield, aged ninety-two, died at Blagdon Villa in Gordon Hill. He was the last survivor of Colonel Somerset's Volunteers band and had been band sergeant and secretary; he also kept wicket for Enfield Cricket Club. He had been employed for eighteen years as a rifle borer at the RSAF and subsequently as a collector for the Enfield Gas Company.

The Enfield Foresters established a band in 1881. The Foresters had done so

172.   The new bandstand on Chase Green was built in August 1900. The new Court House was opened that same year in September, which is probably why the photographer aimed his camera at both. The young ladies, though charming, are merely there to take advantage of an opportunity to show off their new hats.

well in the two previous years that they were able to purchase ten instruments and two drums. C. Matthews, already bandmaster of the Enfield Town Brass Band, became bandmaster for both bands. The Foresters played once a week in the Town throughout the spring of 1895, despite the fact that there were no seats or shelter for the musicians. A bandstand was promised on Chase Green but it was not erected until August 1900. Bands remained highly popular in the early years of this century. Members of the Enfield Silver Prize Band, the Highway (North Middlesex) Silver Prize Band, the Royal Small Arms Institute Band, the Enfield Temperance Mission and the Ponders End Mission Bands gathered together for a concert in July 1905, 110 players in all. The Enfield Silver Prize Band was the direct descendant of the Foresters Band; it had twenty-four players by 1907, uniforms had cost £56 and instruments £280. Despite all their efforts they remained burdened with a debt of £150 in 1910. It was paid off by Colonel Somerset and other Enfield gentlemen. The bandstand in Durants Park was first brought into use in June 1913 with a performance by the Ponders End Silver Prize Band; a penny gained entrance into the enclosure, either to join the dance or to sit and watch.[18]

A new rifle corps was set up in the Town in September 1881, under Captain Renshawe, with 'forty respectable men'. They paraded on practice nights in the Market Place, in full uniform, and drew a crowd of sightseers. Unfortunately as well as 'the staid class of people who came to admire', there came the usual urchins and 'hobbledehoys, and others old enough to know better, who caused no little annoyance to the willing defenders of our country'. This rough element, by ridicule and by mimicking the commands of Sergeant Instructor

173.   The Ponders End Mission band about 1905.

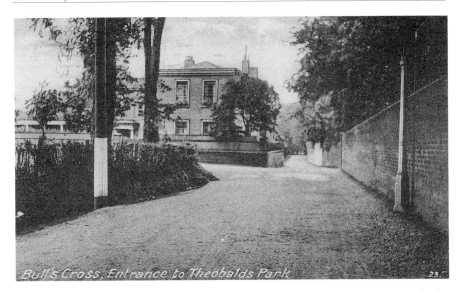

Bull's Cross, Entrance to Theobalds Park

174. Manor House, Bulls Cross, the home of Sir John French. A steep increase in rates following the 1929 revaluation made it difficult to find tenants for such large houses. Manor House among others had to be demolished.

Forbes, managed completely to disrupt the parade. A corps of Volunteers had been in existence at the Royal Small Arms Factory since 1860. It was known as the Enfield Lock Rifles, the forty-first corps to be raised in Middlesex. The funds were provided by local subscriptions, particularly from honorary members and officers, though the men, in addition to an entrance fee, paid the cost of their uniform and travel. They had the use of an armoury at the RSAF and of the government range and magazine. The uniform at that time was green with red facings, shako and pompon. The officers wore black with red facings and carried gilt-mounted swords. The corps (1863) had both a brass band and a drum and fife band, fifty-six members in all, but the expense of a second band proved too heavy and it was disbanded after a few years. The corps was at its highest strength, 753, in 1869, but with the run-down of the factory personnel in 1873 and the replacement of skilled men by machinery, many left the corps. The Enfield Lock Rifles lost both its separate identity and its close association with the Royal Small Arms Factory under Cardwell's army reforms in 1880.[19]

A drill hall was built in 1901 for the recently formed Enfield Town Company of the 1st Volunteer Battalion of the Middlesex Regiment. The Enfield rifle club was formed and flourished. Sir John French, who took the chair at their annual dinner in February 1908, described the club as a happy augury for the success of the new Territorial system. Members expressed their pleasure that he had decided to settle among them. He had taken the Manor House at Bulls Cross. Under recent changes the Volunteers were to become part of the new Territorial forces with enlistment for four years and pay at army rates while on a week's camp each year. A recruiting march with martial music was held in March 1908, but this was not a martial age and it was found difficult to keep the Territorial company in being. Only two years before the outbreak of the First World War, the *Observer* (19 January 1912) lamented that the movement could find so little

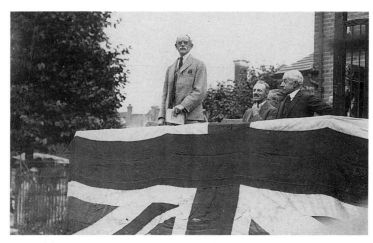

175.   Colonel Sir Henry Ferryman Bowles addresses a meeting. He became Member of Parliament for Enfield in 1889 and so remained for seventeen years until defeated by James Branch (Liberal) in 1906. Sir Henry was elected again for Enfield, for the last time in 1918.

support; out of a population of 56,000 there were only 168 Territorials, eighty in the Town and eighty-eight at Enfield Lock. A Voluntary Aid Detachment was forming throughout Middlesex to render help to the sick and wounded of the Territorial forces.[20]

The National Service League formed a branch at Enfield in August 1912 and at a meeting attended by J.R. Pretyman Newman, Lady Somerset, the Reverend Howel Brown, the Reverend A.E. Witham and Colonel Bowles, none of them potential front line troops, it was resolved that it was the duty of every able-bodied man to take part in the defence of his country.[21]

There were innumerable branches of the PSA (Pleasant Sunday Afternoon) which provided both slate clubs and entertainment. Many were associated with churches and chapels. At the flourishing Bush Hill Park PSA there was a large attendance on the first Sunday in February 1906 to hear the Hallelujah Chorus played by a band. George Spicer, the president, read a passage from scripture, and two solos were sung, *'Lead Kindly Light'* and *'Lord God of Abraham'*. It was announced that as several members were out of work, the PSA would be glad to hear of any vacancies. Finally there was an address by the Reverend G.W. White, who was minister at the Baptist church, on 'Indifference'.[22]

Saville Bros, in 1905, offered pianos at twenty-four guineas; in rosewood, black or walnut, they could be bought through hire-purchase at 10s 6d a month over four years. Pianos returned from hire were offered in 1910 for sale at eight guineas and upward. Nickold's of Palace Parade, before Christmas 1910, advertised a large stock of gramophones, talking machines and phonograph records 'at less than London prices'. Before the following Christmas they were calling them gramophone records, 'new twin double-sided' at 2s 6d each. Albert Chevalier appeared at the Athenaeum in January 1908.[23]

A proposal to hold a cinematograph show in Alma Road School hall in December 1901 caused a crisis. Plans had to be submitted to the county surveyor and the apparatus had to be set up by half-past four ready for his inspection. Dr

176.   A local PSA gathering in July 1911.

Seaton's Animated Picture Company put on a number of shows at the Athenaeum in 1908, 'hundreds of magnificent cinematograph films' were shown. Taylor's Cinematograph was attracting large and appreciative audiences each night at Lavender Hill. 'Both in their quality', said the *Observer* (29 May 1908) 'and in the manner of their manipulation these animated pictures are a long way in front of anything of a like nature on the road'. They were further described as being novel and up-to-date and 'quite free from the least suspicion of coarse humour'. Operatic and other selections by the 'chromomegaphone' were a special feature of the programme. 'The instrument', went on the *Observer*, 'has a very clear enunciation and the words are in perfect harmony with the lips and gestures of the singers'. Mr Taylor operated from a large caravan, twenty-seven feet long with two bedrooms separated by a dining-room. Dyke's Ensign Animated Pictures were shown at the Athenaeum in February 1909.[24]

January 1910 saw the opening of the first permanent cinema in the parish, the Enfield Empire, a newly built electric theatre in Silver Street adjoining the offices of the *Enfield Observer*. The proprietors, the London Bioscope Company, owned other theatres. The Empire could seat 300 to 400, admission was a shilling, sixpence or threepence (children, with adults, half-price) the seats could be booked at a number of shops around the Town. The theatre was comfortably warmed by eight large radiators installed by the Enfield Gas Company and was lit by electricity. The projection room was reassuringly cut off from the auditorium by a brick wall lined with iron sheeting. The floor was raked to give all seats a good view. Music was to be furnished by a 'capable orchestra', and by Miss Winifred Grey, a popular vocalist. After a week or two the proprietors declared themselves pleased with the patronage received. The films shown had been highly popular; *'The Bride and Bridegroom Visit the Zoo'*, *'The Uncontrolable Runaway Motorcycle'*, or *'The Recruiting of Muggins'*. There was

177.   The New Picturedrome opened in Chase Side in 1911 in the building later known as Suttons Warehouse.

178.   The Queens Hall in London Road opened in November 1911; it had seating for eight hundred. The building is now the Town House.

something for everybody, and patrons' cycles were stored free. The most expensive, up-to-date apparatus for showing singing pictures was installed in September.[25]

Twelve months after the opening of the Enfield Empire, the New Picture-

179.   The Ponders End Electric Theatre (now Howard Hall) opened in 1913; seats cost 3d and 6d (children 2d and 3d).

drome was pronounced open in Chase Side (in what was later known as Sutton's Warehouse) 'comfortably upholstered and well lighted', it could accommodate 260. Two programmes a week were presented, three performances daily which featured illustrated songs by professional vocalists. The most expensive seat was sixpence (ninepence reserved) and half-price for children. '*Semiramis Queen of Babylon*', 'coloured animated photography' was shown there in March 1911.[26]

The much larger Queens Hall cinema, to hold 800, opened in London Road on 11 November that year; the interior was lavishly furnished and finely decorated. January 1913 saw the first picture palace to be opened at Ponders End, the Ponders End Electric Theatre, on the corner of Derby Road; seats were 3d and 6d, children 2d and 3d. Cinema advertisements were beginning to take up more space in the local newspapers. The Empire in Silver Street was by this time feeling the effects of competition. It seems to have closed for a time from midsummer 1913, it reopened as the Grand Cinema and closed again the following July, then reopened after extensive renovations and under entirely new management in November 1914, as the Silver Kinema, showing that week '*Robin Hood and Maid Marion*'. There was now a Saturday matinee for children at one penny. Meanwhile negotiations were in progress for a cinema site at Enfield Wash where A. Linscott the vendor was insisting on a covenant forbidding Sunday opening. There were boxing promotions at the Alcazar Edmonton in 1914 where local lads could try their luck against the professionals.[27]

4. Sport

Cricket flourished throughout the 1860s. *Meyers's Observer* in June 1868 for instance, reported matches between Enfield Amateurs and the Forest School, Victoria Cricket Club versus Enfield New Town, and Enfield versus Edmonton which Enfield won by an innings and sixty-three runs. Enfield Amateurs played the Palace School, Forty Hill and Hill House School* played Enfield Amateurs. The Tradesmen of the Town played Chase Side House. August bank holiday Monday each year saw the commencement of a week of cricket in Major Bosanquet's beautiful grounds at Claysmore; his son was B.J.T. Bosanquet the well-known Middlesex and England cricketer, the inventor of the googly. The event attracted some of the leading figures in the game. In August 1885 for instance Viscount Folkestone and Lord Harris (who later became president of the MCC) were present. Enfield Cricket Club was playing at Lincoln Road; the ground was secured to the Club in 1910 by the then president H.L. Adams.[28]

The Palace School played rugby in the winter, the game was more popular in the parish than association football. The leading team in Enfield in the early seventies was the Pirates, though they seem to have started most of their games with less than a full side. Enfield Rovers took over from the Pirates in the late seventies; their home games were played on a field opposite the Enfield Town railway station. Spectators, it was said, (*Observer* 29 November 1879) would be welcome so long as they kept outside the touchline. The Enfield Football Club (association football) was recorded in January 1885; they played at Bush Hill Park where they drew two goals each with Remington FC. Away they met Bowes Park and Tottenham Hotspur, probably on Tottenham marshes. Enfield lost three nil and was decidedly overmatched.

At the beginning of the season 1893/4 the Enfield Football Club moved to one of the vicar's fields in Back Lane (later Cherry Orchard Lane, now Churchbury Lane). The team played in the North Middlesex League. Two years later the club amalgamated with the North Enfield Football Club and began the season with a match against a Spurs eleven (which Enfield won), the game was followed immediately afterward by another against Tollington, whom Enfield beat six-one, 'the three hours football was universally appreciated'. This Enfield club seems to have gone out of existence. The Enfield Football Club which celebrated its twenty-first anniversary in 1914 claimed to have begun life as the Enfield Spartans in 1893; at this time games were played on Bailey's fields in Baker Street. They adopted the title of the defunct Enfield Football Club in 1900 and became the tenants at Cherry Orchard Lane. The club won the championship of the North Middlesex League in 1901/2, also in 1902/3 and again in 1909/10. They were top of division one of the London League in 1911/12.[29]

Tottenham Hotspur became a professional team in December 1895. Their crowds were beginning to grow; in January Spurs played Millwall at Northumberland Park before a crowd of 4,000, a cup-tie against Luton in December 1898 drew a crowd of 10,000, in February 1899 they beat Sunderland in the Cup before a crowd of 13,000. In March 1901, 21,000 saw Tottenham beat Bury the Cup holders; receipts amounted to £1,330. They beat West Bromwich in the semi-final and went on to draw the final against Sheffield United before a crowd of 114,815 at Crystal Palace. In the replay at Bolton they won 3-1, and to

---

*at the north end of Baker Street

180.   *Cricket on Chase Green was taken very seriously in the early part of the nineteenth century and considerable bets were placed on the results of games and on individual performances. The beadle was in charge of mowing and rolling the pitch and the purchase of cricket balls, and he acted unofficially as the bookmaker. Drawing by Rutherford,* Enfield Gazette *July 1938. The house was rebuilt soon afterwards.*

celebrate the occasion Tottenham cake, made by local bakers, was given away to the children. The Spurs entered the second division of the Football League in 1908 and won promotion in their first season. The club began to modernise its ground at once with the erection of a new grandstand to accommodate 13,000 under cover, including 5,375 seated. The banks were terraced so that when it was all finished, at a cost of £8,000, the ground could hold 60,000 spectators. Thus Tottenham Hotspur was ready for first division football.[30]

The Enfield Football League was set up at the beginning of the season 1896/7, also the Enfield School Boys Sports Association. Within one month seven elementary schools had joined for football. The first Board school team was formed at Chesterfield; the headmaster appealed for money to purchase the kit.[31]

Prize fights took place occasionally, though they remained illegal. *The Times* (9 September 1882) reported a contest fought on a Thursday morning in a field near Enfield, between Cooke and Blackett for stakes of £25. Great care was taken to prevent the police from hearing of the encounter. There were many spectators. For three rounds in succession Cooke was knocked down, his injuries were so serious that at the end of the eleventh he was in a semi-conscious condition and unable to come up to time. Blackett therefore won. A prize fight on Hadley Common was broken up by police in December 1883. Another at Enfield was reported in certain London journals and in the *Observer* (20 September 1889) though the precise location is not stated. Harry King of Hackney fought Joe Simmonds of Wood Green for £30 a side, the ring was twenty-four feet square and the fight, over twenty-one rounds, lasted one hour

181. Members of the Enfield Tradesmen's Cycling Club outside Seamer Bros shop in Church Street. This was the first occasion on which motor cycles participated. On the left is Tom Seamer with a basket trailer behind his motor cycle, on the right is Sid Graham with the sidecar which was his invention.

182. *William Garrud, the newsagent on the corner of Southbury Road, advertised teas for cyclists. The* Daily Mirror *headlines read 'England's great victory in the first test match'. The shop sells almost everything from beach spades and fishing nets to coal, it is also a post office. It is June 1909 and the young lady is Ada Garrud.*

183.   1905 and the world still moved at the pace of the horse. Looking south from the Woolpack bridge, St Stephen's Road on the left, Albany Park in the distance, the signboard to the Prince of Wales on the left.

and a quarter. Simmonds was left with both eyes closed and several teeth knocked out. The principals, the backers, the referee and the seconds left the scene in a furniture van immediately afterwards. The police knew nothing of the matter until they read of it in the journals.

The early cycles in the 1870s were what are popularly known as penny-farthings (the ordinary), built for enthusiasts only. With the introduction of the low, chain driven, safety bicycle in the 1880s, and pneumatic tyres at the end of that decade, cycling became a mass activity. The roads could now be used for pleasure. The *Observer* (31 March 1883) announced a ride on Saturday afternoon to Hoddesdon, 'and probably thence to Ware' by members of the recently formed Enfield Cycling Club; members wore their new uniforms of reddish brown, with helmets of the same colour. The captain could be distinguished by a gold band on his helmet, the vice-captain by a silver. The following week their ride took them to London Colney and St Albans, by way of South Mimms. Another Saturday the Club rode to Hatfield returning at nine o'clock. Olley's, the cycle builders of Baker Street, advertised their models in the *Observer* in April 1894, Charles Coote of Church Street was the agent.

The increasing use of motor cars caused concern to the County Council and new rules were issued in November 1896. Speed was not to exceed twelve miles per hour and the vehicle must be capable of moving backwards. Like a harbinger of the twentieth century, a motor tricycle passed through Enfield in September 1897, along Baker Street to the Town, drawing large crowds and creating much excitement and curiosity. The machine, which was rather low, 'was ridden at a fairly rapid pace by two gentlemen one of whom steered while the other sat at ease ..., a novel, if not very attractive, means of locomotion', said our somewhat conservative local newspaper (24 September 1897). Even as late as 1904 the motor car was still regarded as the rich man's toy. Dr Ridge strongly

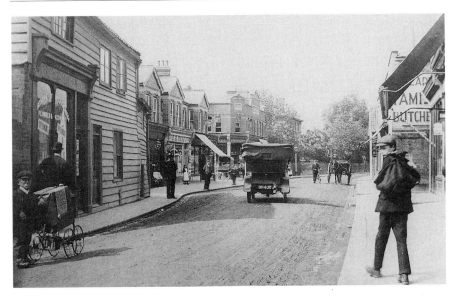

*184.   Heavy traffic in Baker Street before the First World War. The shops in the photograph were
G. R. Ward's dairy, Miss Clair's china and glass shop, Mason's tea rooms and, on the far corner
of Bell Road, the Co-op. Just beyond the old weatherboarded cottage was Andersons Lane, formerly
Andersons Yard.*

urged that Enfield impose a speed limit of ten miles an hour, as both Edmonton
and Southgate had done. His motion was carried on the Council by one vote.
The roads were becoming so heavily used by the summer of 1905 that the
County Council erected white iron posts, each surmounted by a red triangle, to
indicate to motorists the dangerous crossroads, corners and hills. They also
began to replace, with iron ones, the old wooden signposts, though many had
already disappeared through age and long neglect.[32]

Roads were now improved and the prosperity of many a wayside inn was
restored. Dust was the greatest problem created by the car; there were repeated
complaints from people living at Cockfosters. A tar surface was the remedy, but
only half a mile of the Cockfosters Road, the section through Potters Bar, had
been tarred. Restrictions bore heavily upon motor transport. William Billson
was prosecuted in July 1907 for driving along the Hertford Road 'at a speed
exceeding five miles an hour'; he was carrying coke in his lorry from the
Tottenham Gas Works in Dysons Road to the greenhouses.[33] Another ominous
precursor appeared in Enfield that year. A flying machine passed not over, but
through, Ponders End. 'The mammoth apparatus', said the *Observer* (13
September 1907) travelled on one of Pickford's road trolleys and was drawn by
a strong horse. By 1914 a Ford five-seater touring car could be purchased for
£135.

The *Observer* (5 August 1882) reported that a beautiful lawn tennis ground
had been opened, with three grass courts and one of gravel, at Bush Hill Park
by the side of the series of three lakes which extended from London Road to
Bush Hill. Enfield Bowling Club was founded 1903, its forty-two members had
the exclusive right to use the large green attached to the Crown and Horse-

185.   The bathing lake opened in the Town Park in the summer of 1905. It proved popular though the Medical Officer had to complain after a month because the water had never been changed.

shoes.[34]

People used the River Lea for swimming, particularly near the bridges at Enfield Lock where boys bathed naked. A lady would have to unfurl her parasol to hide her blushes. The Lea Conservancy complained in July 1889 of the 'outrages to property and decency' caused by the bathers, and it was demanded that police be stationed on the bridges on Sundays. The Victoria Swimming Club was set up in 1887 at the Greyhound (Ordnance Road) and every August it held a race along the Lea from Enfield Lock to Waltham Abbey. The Club by 1895 had taught hundreds of boys to swim.[35] The year 1889 had seen the birth of a scheme to provide a public baths at Enfield Lock. The campaign was launched by an entertainment in the Sheridan Theatre at the Royal Small Arms Factory. 'Cox and Box' were billed to appear, but had to withdraw because of the indisposition of Mr A. Bayfield. A committee was appointed, chaired by J. Rigby the superintendent at the factory, to raise funds. In 1890 the Local Board adopted the Baths and Wash-Houses Act, agreeing to erect the baths at Enfield Lock provided the committee contributed £900 towards the cost. The campaign by this time had raised £650 and Rigby appealed to the men for the outstanding £250; their earnings, he said, now amounted to a total of nearly £6,000 a week. Further swimming facilities were provided by the conversion of the lake in the Town Park. It was ready by the summer of 1905, the bottom having been concreted and dressing boxes erected. It opened with a gala in August and it proved very popular, though there were problems with children falling in. A month later the medical officer complained that it was in an insanitary condition, the water had not been changed since it opened.[36]

Steeplechase meetings were held at Bycullah Park from 1864 to 1879. Fine weather on Easter Monday 1870 drew 'hundreds, nay thousands, into the parish' for the event. The course extended from Windmill Hill to the Ridgeway,

and a grandstand had been erected. Subscribers of one guinea, it was announced, would be entitled to *free* admission to the reserved carriage ground.
The races began with the Bycullah Plate, run for fifty sovereigns. Fine weather
again the following year brought a stream of carriages to Bycullah Park,
thousands more arrived at the two railway stations. R.I. Riddell opened his
house to friends and favoured visitors. A whole menagerie of noblemen was
present. The development of the Bycullah estate for housing forced the
steeplechase meetings to move to Holly Hill Farm on The Ridgeway, but the
Observer reported (9 April 1879) that the races on the new site had not been a
success, for two or three years the venture had trembled in the balance, it had
received no support from the local gentry or tradesmen, only obstruction. A
liquor licence, which had been granted at Bycullah Park, was refused on the new
site. Each year the meeting brought two hundred extra vagrants into the
Guardians' casual ward at Edmonton and this created resentment in the
neighbourhood. Although on Whit Monday 1881 the races drew a crowd of
more than two thousand, by December that year the official liquidator had
taken possession of the assets of the Enfield Studfarm and Racecourse Company
and the races were over. The year 1899 saw the end, after fourteen years, of the
Enfield Chase stag hunt and Colonel Somerset disposed of his renowned pack
of staghounds.[37]

   Both the Enfield and the Bush Hill Park golf clubs had been opened by 1895.
The Bush Hill Park Club used land hired from two farmers who mowed and
rolled the course, but the club had to be wound up in 1902 when the area was
purchased for building. The £65 balance of their funds was applied, £6 for
gratuities to servants, and the remainder to local charities. The Enfield Golf
Club continued to prosper. 'In no portion of suburbia', boasted the *Observer* (5
June 1903) 'is golf more firmly established than in Enfield'. They had an
eighteen-hole course at Swannell's farm (ie Old Park Farm) 'where the Twenty-
five Club had started in 1893'; a lease of the farm had later been secured.
Membership was limited to two hundred gentlemen and a certain number of
ladies who were admitted at half the normal subscription. Golf was certainly
being played again at Bush Hill Park by 1907. This became painfully apparent
to one cyclist peddling contentedly along Village Road; 'I was struck on side by
a golf ball', he complained, 'which rebounded to the railway at the side of the
field. Surely a high wire netting ... ' The editor pointed out that he had received
previous complaints from cyclists (*Observer* 30 August 1907). Towards the end
of the year 1911 the club received notice to quit; the new tramway had increased
the potential of the land for development. It was reported in November that
year to be 'negotiating for a large estate' (Old Park) where they proposed to
establish an eighteen-hole golf course. This was opened in June 1913.[38]

5. Politics

Until the passage of the Reform Bill in 1832, Middlesex returned only six
members to Parliament. This was increased to twelve by the 1832 Act which gave
the vote to householders of houses of £10 annual value or more.[39] Although the
Reform Act of 1867 was not very effective as an instrument of change, it did add
to the electorate and it enfranchised people who had not voted previously; it

also increased the number of members returned in Middlesex to seventeen. The Conservative candidate for the Middlesex county constituency, Lord George Hamilton, attended a meeting at the Riding House, Enfield Court on 11 December 1868 and all the important local gentry were there. James Meyer took the chair. The meeting of the Liberal candidate two days later was less well supported. Radical Liberal Clubs were set up in the 1860s at Ponders End and at Enfield Highway, the members were mostly skilled artisans and a number of engineers from the Royal Small Arms Factory served on the committees. The Enfield and Edmonton Conservative Association was formed in January 1869; annual subscriptions were one shilling upward. In 1872 Gladstone introduced the secret ballot.

The Conservative Party organisation in Enfield for the election of 1874 was very strong. The chairman of the committee was James Meyer, his vice-chairmen were Colonel Somerset, H.C.B. Bowles, F.C. Adams of the Jute Mill and T. Negus. It is interesting to note that the chairman of the Edmonton committee was the Jewish schoolmaster Henry N. Solomon. Public opinion seemed to suggest that the Conservative candidates, Lord George Hamilton and Octavius Coope the brewer, would be elected. Since the Licensing Act 1872 the brewers had been strong supporters of the Conservative Party. Coope made an impassioned plea before a large and enthusiastic audience at the Riding House demanding revision and if possible the repeal of the income tax laws. He opposed any alteration to the Education Act of 1870 which might diminish support for religious teaching in voluntary schools or exclude the study of the Bible in Board schools. The Liberal meeting at the King's Head Assembly Rooms was, by contrast, according to *Meyers's Observer* (February 1874) neither large nor enthusiastic in character. The Reverend Henry Storer Toms, the Congregational minister, took the chair and introduced the candidates, Lord Enfield (Byng) and Mr Lehmann. The election nationally resulted in a great Conservative victory and Disraeli became Prime Minister. Both Conservative candidates were elected for Middlesex county constituency of which Enfield remained part until 1885.

Preparations for the 1880 general election began with the visit to Enfield on 30 March of the two members for the county, Lord George Hamilton and Octavius E. Coope. The gentrification of Enfield was proceeding apace as each new house on the Bycullah estate and in the New Town was occupied. Like a number of other London suburbs Enfield became progressively more Conservative. James Meyer, the chairman of the party committee, was widely respected. That week saw the funeral of his wife; shops in the Town and along the main thoroughfares closed, people drew their blinds as a mark of respect. The same week had seen the Liberals meet at the Lecture Hall in Chase Side. The large gathering included a knot of noisy Conservatives who kept up a barrage of uncomplimentary remarks about the speakers. The Reverend Toms in the chair could scarcely utter a sentence before he was reduced to silence by the uproar, and Herbert Gladstone (the son of William Gladstone) who was the candidate, was heckled throughout his speech. The *Observer* reported both this meeting and the Conservative Party meetings fully (20 March, 3 April 1880) emphasising the cheers for the Conservatives and the disruption faced by the Liberals. Once again the Middlesex county elected two Conservative members by a substantial majority, although nationally the election resulted in a Liberal victory. A Local Board of Health election followed in April, when the candidates elected were:

James Meyer, Forty Hall, Conservative 1,301
Bernard Tindall Bosanquet, Forty Hill, Conservative 848
Peter Rumney, Baker Street, Liberal 815
Robert Morley, Old Park Farm, Conservative 811

When a real challenge came in local elections, it came from further right, from the Ratepayers' Association. After the general election of 1880 a separate Conservative Association was established in Enfield and Conservative and Constitutional clubs were set up at Enfield Highway, Ponders End, Bush Hill Park (now the Oddfellows Hall) and in Enfield Town.

A widespread public interest in parliamentary democracy was reflected in the proliferation, during the late nineteenth century, of local 'houses of commons', each with its own government and opposition, with 'ministers' appointed, and following parliamentary rules. Such activities demonstrated the insatiable appetite of the middle classes for participation in party politics. A 'parliament' had long been in existence in Tottenham when, in October 1883, a meeting was called at the Duke of Lancaster Hall in Silver Street to set up a 'house of commons' in Enfield. Political, social and local topics would be discussed there, such as, it was suggested, the disestablishment of the church. Membership would cost 5s a year and would be open to all above the age of eighteen. Non-members might be admitted for 2d or 3d. The first parliament discussed a motion moved by the 'Conservative member for the City', played by J. Briggs, concerning Lord Salisbury's policy on the franchise question. W.H. Bull, 'Birmingham Liberal', the prime mover in the formation of the 'house of commons', was elected 'speaker', and J. Briggs became 'deputy speaker'. Henry Ferryman Bowles became 'prime minister'. In real life he was a barrister and had become chairman of the Enfield branch of the Conservative Association; he had been adopted as the (real) parliamentary candidate for the Borough of Wycombe. Later in January 1885 a 'Liberal ministry' was formed in the Enfield parliament.[40]

The Representation of the People Act 1884, extended the franchise to all male householders and all male lodgers occupying lodgings of £10 a year or more, unfurnished; this greatly increased the number entitled to vote in Enfield. A year's residence however was necessary to qualify for both house-holder and lodger votes. Thus, since the poor tended to move frequently in search of work, many of the working class who might have been included, were disenfranchised. Meanwhile, until it was abolished in 1948, plural voting gave the owners of business premises the right to additional votes in respect of those premises. Under the Redistribution of Seats Act 1885, constituencies like Middlesex, returning two members, were broken up into single member divisions. Thus the Enfield parliamentary division was created, incorporating the parishes of Enfield, Edmonton, Southgate, South Mimms and Friern Barnet.

There was a crowded meeting at the Athenaeum preceding the election of 1885; Lord Folkestone, the Conservative candidate, spoke there. Many of those in the audience were his supporters, but there was a strong element of disorder present, and placards supporting Kempster, the Liberal candidate, were held aloft. The chairman, H.C. Weld, was unable to obtain a hearing. He was met with shouting and whistling, and birds were released which flew panic-stricken about the noisy hall. A large caricature of Lord Folkestone was held up in front of the platform. Passions mounted, harsh words were exchanged and there was a general scrimmage in the body of the hall. The opposition threatened to take over the platform, and Conservative ladies were escorted discreetly into the safety of one of the anterooms. Captain Bowles stepped forward to urge upon those magistrates present that it was their duty forthwith to read the Riot Act. Messengers were despatched for the police. Mr Nye, a Liberal, called upon those of his party present to give the platform a hearing, and W.H. Bull, president of the Radical Association, in an endeavour to restore calm, called upon those in favour of order to hold up their hands, then those in favour of disorder. Few present were willing to be seen voting for disorder, but when Lord Folkestone rose to speak, pandemonium broke out once more. The cheers for him, and counter-cheers for Kempster, drowned his speech and fighting again ensued. Once more Mr Bull restored order at the back, but it did not last. Lord Folkestone had to declare the meeting closed, but he shook hands cordially with Mr Bull. It was said subsequently that the disruption had been caused by a gang of youths who did not belong to Enfield. Lord Folkestone got a better hearing at the Ordnance factory where he had two thousand in the audience. The workmen there, thought the *Observer* (7 November 1885) still considered a Conservative government necessary to ensure a brisk demand for guns. Opposition to the Conservatives in the factory was organised by J.H. Matthews who complained that he had been handed Conservative leaflets when he went into work, but Henry Barrass, another leading trade unionist there, maintained that no undue influence was brought to bear on the men; he had seen bills posted there for both candidates. A women's political meeting, very middle-class, was held in the Lecture Hall, Chase Side, in support of Kempster and the view was expressed that it was high time women had a voice — not all women of course, but the women taxpayers, why should not they have the vote as well as men? As usual, the Conservatives won locally; Folkestone 3,644, Kempster 2,684. Subsequently his lordship held a great open air meeting in front of the new drinking fountain in the Town to thank the artisans from the Royal Small Arms Factory for their support, and large numbers of the workmen came over in wagonettes. In May Lord Folkestone addressed a political demonstration in Ponders End (its organisers claimed that there were two thousand present) to protest against Gladstone's Home Rule Bill. Afterwards they held a procession through the streets led by the Ponders End drum and fife band.[41]

The election in the following July (1886) gave the Conservatives an overwhelming victory and when the result was announced Viscount Folkestone addressed the crowd from the top of a brake. *Rule Britannia* was sung, and the National Anthem, and coloured rockets lit up the sky to let supporters in eastern Enfield join in the triumph. That November Lord Folkestone spoke at the opening of the Ponders End Conservative Working Men's Club in South Street, but he had to relinquish his seat in March 1889 when he was elevated to the peerage on the death of his father, the Earl of Radnor (15 March 1889). Henry Ferryman Bowles won the resulting by-election defeating his Liberal opponent, W.H. Fairbairns, by 1,512 votes.[42]

Enfield, said the *Observer* in 1895 (although it was not an entirely unbiased observer) had always been regarded as a stronghold of conservatism and this apparently had not been weakened by the extension of the franchise, nor even by the influx into the parish of working-class residents. The register at that time listed nearly 15,000 voters, an increase of between 4,000 and 5,000 in nine years.

With the growth of the electorate, the Conservative majority had even increased. Bowles had a majority of 1,831 in 1892 and in 1895 he was returned unopposed.[43]

By the time the 1906 election was held, Colonel Bowles had represented Enfield for seventeen years. 'He stands', said the *Observer* (5 January 1906) 'for integrity of Empire now threatened by a Liberal declaration in favour of Home Rule'. Enfield was one of the largest constituencies in the Home Counties. The population was 125,291 and the number of electors had risen from 17,044 in 1900 to 23,368. The Liberal candidate was James Branch, a boot manufacturer with factories at Bethnal Green and Northampton; he was a member of the London County Council and of the Metropolitan Water Board. The *Observer* (19 January 1906) complained that a meeting addressed by Colonel Bowles in Edmonton Town Hall had been deliberately broken up, there had been disgraceful scenes of rowdyism, atrocious falsehoods had been voiced about Chinese 'slave labour' in South Africa, and the colonel's explanation had been howled down. It had been almost as bad at Chase Side, for although the hall was two-thirds filled with respectable citizens, a mob of men and boys ranged at the back, sang 'snatches of street melodies' and made 'personal remarks and foolish jokes'.[44]

James Branch and the Liberals this time emerged victorious with 9,790 votes against 7,674 for Bowles. A feature in the Enfield election was the high percentage of the lodger vote, especially in Edmonton and at Enfield Lock. Colonel Bowles retired as parliamentary candidate in October 1907. The Unionists had failed to retain the vote of the working class. 'Vast numbers of working men' said the *Observer* portentously (26 January 1906) 'will refuse in the future, as now, to associate themselves with either of the old parties'. The Enfield Lock branch of the Independent Labour party held a series of open air meetings at Albany Road in 1908.[45]

Empire day was celebrated at the Enfield Grammar School in May that year, but not at any of the council schools. The total electorate of the Enfield constituency was now 29,985. For parliamentary purposes it was 26,575, which number had grown to 28,574 by 1910. By 1914 the member for Enfield represented 32,980 electors while the member for Kilkenny represented 1,500 and for Durham 2,500. J.R. Pretyman Newman was appointed Unionist parliamentary candidate for Enfield.[46]

Miss Christabel Pankhurst and Miss Brackenbury, attempting to hold a meeting on women's suffrage at Wood Green in May 1908, faced a large audience of men ringing bells, bicycle bells and setting off alarm clocks. One 'gentleman' rendered *'Tell me the Old Old Story'* and *'My Darling Clementine'* with great gusto. The Enfield Constitutional Club was more civilised. In 1909 it held a debate on women's suffrage and invited Isabelle Seymour from the Women's Social and Political Union (militants). She presented her case, according to the very conservative *Observer* (12 March 1909) with unusual skill and persuasiveness and had 'very much the better of it'. A branch of the National Union of Women Suffrage Societies (suffragists, non-militant) was formed at Bush Hill Park in 1910. The militants in September 1912 cut the telegraph lines on the London road from Potters Bar; a railway guard reported seeing women up telegraph poles. There was such strong antipathy towards these suffragettes (militant) that it is difficult to be certain that a letter, received by the Council in July 1913, did in fact emanate from them, and I am inclined to think it was anti-suffragette propaganda.

'Sir' it said, 'The Enfield Urban District Council has offered a deliberate insult to the just aims of an indignant womanhood by its refusal to sanction the use of a public park for a perfectly legitimate expression of free speech. We must teach such arrogant assumption that the women of England are not to be trifled with. What more righteous retribution than a sharp swift reprisal in a public park in beautiful Enfield. We shall strike a blow through your horse show by not permitting it to commence. We can make ourselves felt even as our sisters have by potent agencies. We shall strike for Free Speech, for Liberty and for the Vote'.[47]

Enfield Public Welfare Association was set up in April 1909. It aimed to stimulate interest in local administration, to watch over public expenditure, and to provide candidates in the local elections. It was, it claimed, wholly free from party bias. The Association presented candidates in the local election. Henry Ferryman Bowles (Unionist) took the chair at their meeting in 1910 and George Spicer (Liberal) sat beside him on the platform. The two older parties appeared to be drawing together to face a threat from the Labour Party. Welfare candidates were elected in three wards at the local elections in 1910, but on a turn-out of less than fifty per cent. By contrast, in the fourth ward, Ordnance, there was a 69 per cent poll, many factory workers voting during their dinner break, and J. H. Matthews the Labour candidate, a worker at the RSAF, was elected by an overwhelming majority. The workers assembled to applaud the victory. There was at this time much dissatisfaction among the workforce, caused by the introduction of 'sweating methods' resulting in a heavy reduction of wages.

Parliament had been considering a redistribution of seats since 1905 but it was not until 1918 that Edmonton and Enfield became separate Parliamentary constituencies.

Notes to Chapter Eight

1. *Observer* J1 1860, Ja 1862, Mr 1862, 7J1 1893
2. *ibid* 25 Mr 1895
3. *ibid* 27N 1908, 29N 1907, 11N 1910, 25X 1912, 12 J1 1912, 13S 1913
4. *ibid* 8S 1922, Au 1863, Ja 1873
5. *ibid* 8D 1883, Enfield cuttings, 4 Je 1915
6. *Observer* 18 Ap 1885, 6 Mr 1886, 9 Ja, 16X 1891, 14S 1894, 3 Au 1900, 1 Ja 1909
7. *ibid* 2S 1892, 3J1 1891, 20D 1907
8. *ibid* S 1867, 20 Ja 1909
9. *Recollections* p20, 21
10. *Observer* X 1869, 13 Ap 1928
11. *ibid* 6N 1891
12. *ibid* 9 Au 1882, 16 Je 1905, 9 Je 1911
13. *ibid* 3 J1 1896
14. *ibid* 1 Je 1897, 18 J1 1902
15. *ibid* 5F 1897, 7 My 1897, 23, 30 My 1902
16. *ibid* 31 My 1895, 8 Je 1894, 27 Au,.1X 1897
17. *Recollections* p41, 42
18. *Observer* 31 J1 1886, 23 Au 1907, 18N 1910
19. *ibid* 17S 1881, Eddie Collins, *Enfield's Own*
20. *ibid* 18X 1901, 7F 1908, 27 Mr 1908, 11 Mr 1910
21. *ibid* 16 Au 1912
22. *ibid* 2F 1906
23. *ibid* 4 Au 1905, 17 Ja 1908
24. *ibid* 27 Mr 1908, 15F 1909
25. *ibid* 29J1, 9S 1910
26. *ibid* 17F 1911, 17 Mr 1911
27. *ibid* 3, 10, N1911, 17 J1 1914, 27F 1914
28. *ibid* 1 Au 1885, 18 Mr 1910
29. *ibid* 24 Mr 1914
30. *ibid* 29D 1895, 17 Ja 1896, 9D 1898, 18D 1908
31. *ibid* 18S 1896, 4D 1896, 1 Ja 1897, 18D 1896
32. *ibid* 12F 1904
33. *ibid* 9 J1 1907
34. *ibid* 23 My 1903
35. *ibid* 12 J1 1889, 7 J1 1895
36. *ibid* 8 F 1889, 12 J1 1889, 20S 1889, 16 Je, 11 Au 1905, 1S 1905
37. *ibid* 30 Ap, 11 Je, 17D 1881, 7 Ap 1899
38. *ibid* 22 Ap 1898, 25 Ap 1902, 5 Je 1903, 3N 1911
39. *ibid* 28 Ja 1910
40. *ibid* 13X 1883, Sylvia Collicott *Enfield School Board* EHHS 1985
41. *ibid* 28N 1885, 31X 1885, 5D 1885, 22 My 1886
42. *ibid* 10 J1, 19N 1886, 15 Mr 1889
43. *ibid* 12 J1 1895
44. *ibid* 14 J1 1905
45. *ibid* 26 Ja 1906, eg 8 My 1908
46. *ibid* 22 My 1908, 14 Ja 1910, 9X 1908
47. *ibid* 15 My 1908, 1 Ap 1910, 6S 1912, 8 J1 1913
48. *ibid* 30 Ap 1909, 8 Ap 1910

Subscribers' List

London Borough of Enfield
The Worshipful the Mayor of Enfield
Cllr. John Wyatt, BA, C.Eng., MIEE

Brimsdown Junior School
Brettenham Junior School
Bush Hill Park Junior School Library
Capel Manor Primary School
Carterhatch Junior School
Chace School
Chase Side Primary School
De Bohun Primary School
Eastfield Primary School
Edmonton School
Eldon Junior School
Enfield County School
Firs Farm Primary School
Galliard Primary School
George Spicer Primary School
Jane Addams School
Lavender Primary School
St Andrew's C.E. Primary School,
  Enfield
St Michael's C.E. Primary School
St Paul's C.E. School
Southbury Primary School
Southgate School
Wilbury Primary School
Worcesters Primary School

Hatfield Public Library

Adams, Mr Ronald
Addington, Mr and Mrs E.W.
Ainsworth-Smith, Mrs Charles
Alcock, Mrs June
Allan, Mrs Joyce
Allbutt, Patricia
Allen, Mrs Dorothy
Allen, Joan
Andrews, Geoffrey L.
Andrews, Mrs Vera
Appleby, Dr and Mrs E.C.
Archer, E.M.
Artiss, Mr & Mrs E.F.
Ashton, Mr Wm W.
Atkin, Alan Scott

Austin, Mrs Maureen
Austin, Michael, B.Sc., F.I.M.L.S.
Authers, Ellis W.
Bagley, Mrs K.
Baldock, Philip J.
Ball, Anne Elizabeth
Barber, Paul J.
Barbour, Margaret S.
Barker, Mr J.D.
Barker, Ray
Barkham, Rev. H.P.
Barnard, Joyce Eugene
Barnard, Richard A.C.
Barnes, L.T. & D.A.
Barton, Timothy H.
Baruch, Mrs P.
Bascombe, Dr K.N.
Battams, J.E.
Bayford, Mr Frank
Beadle, Mr Donald
Beale, Adrian H.
Beale, Edwin H.
Beale, Edwin T.
Bedford, Miss Mabel
Belcher, John and Pat
Bell, Rene
Benjamin, Jenny
Bennett, B.
Bennett, Herbert F.
Bennett, Mr T.R.
Berkeley, Mrs Sonja
Bevan, S.H. & G.B.
Biggs, Mr A. & Mrs M
Bignell, Victor & Janet
Blake, Mr J.H.
Blaskett, Sidney Robin John
Board, Mr & Mrs D.E.
Boardman, Mr F.T.
Bocock, Marian
Bolden, Keith F.
Bone, Mrs J.M.
Booker, Sylvia A.M.
Booth, Mr S.H.F.
Bougnague, Mr P.
Bourne, E.C.W.
Bouttell, Mr C.J.
Bowie, Val

Bowyer, Mrs Vera
Brewer, Ray
Brock, Mrs M.M.
Brockie, Allan G.
Brooker, Mr F.N.
Brown, Mrs Joan Lilla
Brown, Mrs Joyce
Brown, Terry
Browning, Miss Sheila
Bruce, Mr and Mrs J.
Bryant, V.O.E.
Budd, Miss Valerie
Bull, Graham & Lynn
Bull, Mr L.H. & Mrs D.M.
Bulling, Sarah Jane
Bullock, Alan
Burgess, Mr D.V.
Burke, Mrs Doreen M.
Burnby, Dr J.
Burrell, Mr & Mrs R.S.
Butler, Frank
Butler, Miss I.G.
Butler, Margaret
Butterworth, Dr Harry
Byron, Pat
Capp, Alan
Carr, Mr & Mrs K.T.
Carr, Ronald F.
Carter, Henry & Valerie
Castor, Mrs Joyce
Cattermole, Leonard
Cattermole, Shirley
Chamberlain, Marian & Neville
Chaplin, Edgar M.
Chapman, Mr E.S.
Chapman, Norma
Charge, S.P., M.A.
Charlton, Mrs C.E.
Chase, Mr R.
Chase, Mr Roland F.
Cherry, Mr & Mrs J.
Christen, Leta C.
Christmas, Frederick G.
Churchill, Ruth
Clark, Miss B.D.
Clark, D.
Clark, Mr V.E.
Clarke, Geoffrey T.
Clarke, Mrs L.E.
Clarke, Mr Roger
Clarke, Mr R.P.
Clarke, Dr W.E.
Clifton, James
Close, David M.
Cockle, Dave

Coles, Mr N.S.
Coleman, Mr & Mrs K.L.
Collie, Mrs Rita
Combe, Christine and Andrew
Combe, David and Stephen
Comyns, Mary C.
Conrich, Mrs Gilda
Convery, Christine
Cook, Mr & Mrs Russell
Cooper, David
Cooper, Mr K.A.
Coote, Major A.D.
Coote, Mr S.T.
Coote, Mr & Mrs W.R.
Corbett, Robin
Cordell, Mr J.R.
Cornock, M.
Cornwell, Mrs Jean L.
Cotton, Shirley & Albert
Course, Cllr. Richard
Couzens, Mr & Mrs A.E.
Cox, Helen May
Cracknell, Mr M.E.
Critchlow, Frances P.M.
Crofts, Ethel
Crutchley, George & Joyce & Michael
Cufley, Mr D.R.
Cufley, Mr R.R.
Curati, Mrs B.
Cutler, Mrs Elizabeth J.
Dabbs, Valerie
Dane, Peter D.L.
Daniels, Harry
Darling, Mrs N.W.
Davies, Mr W.R.
Davis, Derek C.W.
Dawe, Richard
Dawson, Mr C.
Day, Erik
Deacon, M. John
Deamer, J.R.
Deer, Mrs D.M.
Deering, Peter H., J.P.
Delvin, Stuart
de Warrenne, Anna
Dickson, Mr B.J.
Dixon, David A.
Dixon, John George
Dorrington, Albert & Beryl
Douglas, John
Doust, Mr P.
Draper, Mr R.J.
Dumayne, Alan
Ebbels, Mrs Daphne
Eddington, Mrs Enid

Eden, Joyce R.
Edwards Estates Ltd., The
Edwards, John E.
Egan, Mr C.J.
Elkin, Mr Roger
Ellis, Andrew
Ellis, Mrs J.M.
Ellwood, Mrs D.
Elmes, Sylvia
Everett, Arthur H.
Fairclough, K.R.
Fairhurst, David
Farquharson, Carole
Farrant, Frieda F.
Farthing, Mr & Mrs M.G.
Featherstone, Laurence
Featley, Mr Colin
Featley, Mr Kenneth
Fenn, Stephen R.
Fenton, Patricia
Ferguson, Mr R.J.
Finkel, Jeanette
Fish, Mrs Eileen
Fisher, Brian E., M.B.E.
Fisher, David and Paula
Fishpool, Claire
Fleming, Mrs Hazel
Fletcher, Mrs A.L.
Flecher, Mr & Mrs K.E.
Flitter, Miss J.R.
Ford, Mr B.
Ford, Miss Jane
Foret, Mr Raymond M.
Foster, Edna
Foster, Jeanne Odette
Frear, Brian
Freer, Mrs P.
French, Mr Sidney W.
Frost, Mrs M.E.
Gale, Paul
Ganderton, Mr Colin
Ganderton, Mrs Margaret C.
Gardner, Brenda
Gay, Ken
Gee, Miss G.
George, Leslie J.
Gibbons, Colin F.
Gibbs, John G.
Gibbs, Peggy
Gibbs, Mr & Mrs R.A.
Gilburt, Stephen
Gillam, Geoffrey
Gitter, Mrs A.J.
Godfrey, K.H.
Godwin, Mr K.W.

Gordon Road Bookshop
Gould, Mr & Mrs John
Goulding, Mr T.G.
Goward, Alan E.
Gower, Paul J.
Gowers, Mr R.
Gravell, Mrs & Mr T.J.
Gray, Mr William A.
Grayston, Cllrs. Brian & Sheila
Greenaway, Mr V. Hugh
Greening, Alan
Groom, Mrs Audrey E.
Guttridge, Mr N.V.
Hackney, Mrs V.L.
Haley, Mr & Mrs T.D.
Hall, Arthur
Hall, C.E.
Halsey, Wilfred & Betty
Halstead, Miss Margaret B.
Hamer, Miss Doris
Hammond, David H.
Hampton, Janet
Hancock, Jean & Frank
Handley, Graham and Barbara
Hannaford, David and Lynda
Hardy, Edward F.
Harper, J.W.
Harris, Mrs H.J.
Harrison, Ted & Doreen
Hartridge, R.J., M.A.,MSc.(Econ)
Harvey, Laurence C.E.
Hastings, Leonard Wm
Hawkes, Herbert G. (Hon. Member,
   E.H.H.S.)
Hawkins, Graham & Susan
Hayes, Miss J.
Head, Mr R.L.
Hearfield, Mrs K.M.
Henderson, Dr L.W.
Hicks, Mr A.T. & Miss L.R.
Hicks, Graham
Higgins, Mr D.J.
Hillsdon, D.J.
Hoare, Roger
Hobbs, Mrs M.J.
Hodge, Mr P.R.
Hogben, Mrs Grace
Holland, Mrs B.A.
Holtam, Mr S.R.
Honeyball, Mr & Mrs G.
Hopkins, Miss Joyce
Hornby, Mr B.F.
House, Mr Michael N.
Howard, Mrs L.
Hoy, Mr & Mrs D.L.

Hudson, David & Marlene
Hudson, Mr Norman G.
Hughes, Julia & Ken
Hulley, J.R.
Humphrey, Stephen C.
Humphries, Mr & Mrs J.
Hunt, Mrs Barbara M.
Hunt, Mr & Mrs W.C.
Hurry, Mr Alex
Hutchings, William N.
Huxley-Robinson, Kenneth,
  B.A.(Lond.)
Jachim, Mr & Mrs J.
Jackson, Cllr John, J.P.
Jacob, Mr & Mrs Arthur
Janes, M.J.
Jeeves, Mr David H.
Jenkins, Mrs G.
Jenkins, Mrs P.A.
Jephcott, Dr C.J.A.
Jerwood, Mr Arthur S.
Jewell, Martin F.
Johnson, John C.
Johnstone, Miss Kirsty
Jones, Arnold and Margaret
Jones, Mr D.S.
Jones, Mr E.E.
Jones, Geoffrey J.
Jones, Mr Ian K.
Jones, Ken
Jones, Mrs Maxie
Kearney, John
Keeble, Len
Kelly, Kay
Kennedy, Miss M.E.
Kerridge, Mr & Mrs J.F.
Kingdon, Mr Ronald P.
Knight, Arthur
Knowles, Dr Wendy A.
Lambe, Mrs Carol
Lambert, Joyce & Prue
Lambie, Brenda and John
Lambourn, Mr E.H.
Lancaster, Mr M.T.
Lancucki, Mrs J.M.
Lancucki, T.S.J.
Lane, Mrs Elsie
Lane, Margaret
Langridge, Mr L.W.
Langston, Mr & Mrs P.A.
Larrett, Mary W.
Law, Mr & Mrs C.
Lawrence, Mr William
Leftwich, Darren, B.A., F.R.G.S.
Leighton, M.B.E.

Lewis, Ewan
Lewis, Valerie
Lister, Mr Peter
Little, Mrs D.
Love, Mrs Geoff.
Love, Philip
Lowe, Bob
Lowe, Ms E.E.
Lowen, Mr & Mrs S.J.
Luker, Charles G.
Lunn, Colin A.
Luxton, Mr M.C.
Luxton, Richard J.
Macfarlane, Gordon
McEleney, J.
McLellan, Mr Kevin
Madge, Gladys E.
Malleson, Mr & Mrs R.P.
Malone, Mr C.N.
Manning, Allan
Manning, Eric Stanley
Mantell, Mr G.A. & Mrs A.C.
Marsh, E.W.
Martin, Bob
Martin, Mr R.W.
Mason, Mr H.S.
Matthews, Mr Paul R.
May, Mrs Margaret I.
Meeson, Edwin Laurence
Mellor, Mrs Joyce
Middleton, Mrs B.C.
Middleton, Pat
Miles, Ted & Mary
Miller, Mrs V.
Mills, Mrs E.E.
Mills, Stuart D.E. & Cope, Carol
Mooney, David, M.A.
Moore, Bryan
Moore, Mr & Mrs Fred
Moorhouse, Mrs D.J.
Morgan, Patricia
Morris, M.A.
Mortimer, Anthony
Mortimer, Owen D.
Morton, B.D. & L.M.W.
Moulden, Jack L.
Murdock, Miss
Mussett, Mrs Frances
Nafzger, Alan
Needham, Mr & Mrs D.P.
Newton, Mr & Mrs Brian
Niehorster, Mrs Audrey J.
Nix, Harold
Noble, Harold & Sheila
Nurse, Mr D.A.

Oakman, Miss Lily E.A.
Oakman, Mr Ray D.
O'Connolly, F.X.
Oliver, Barry M.
Orr, Phyllis
Othen-Price, Lawrence and Lindsey
Parker, Mrs Gwendoline Rose
Parker, M.A.
Pask, Mr Brian J.
Patrick, Anthony
Pattison, Miss Maggie
Pavey, Mr & Mrs D.R.
Peach, John Christopher
Pearce, Kathleen M.
Pearl, Mr & Mrs C.J.
Peck, J.N.
Peffer, Mr M.T.
Pennell, Mr T.R.
Pepper, Mrs L.S.
Perham, Heather J.
Perman, Mr David
Perrins, Terence
Perry, Mrs Frances, M.B.E., V.M.H.
Perryman, Cllr Peter
Pinkham, Miss M.J.
Pointer, Mr C.L.
Pond, Mrs J.M.
Pope, Dennis
Popham, Mrs F.
Porter, Valerie Jean
Prentice, Ron & Gladys
Price, John Rea
Pritchard, Mr & Mrs P.
Prudames, Anne
Purssell, Mr A.W.
Puttock, Kay
Ramsbotham, Leonard
Read, Marjorie B.
Read, Mrs Norah
Redford, Mr A.W.
Reed, Mr & Mrs H.J.
Reed, Mr Nick
Reeve, Mr Harry C.
Regester, Mrs Ruth M., J.P., LL.B.
Reid, Mr & Mrs A.G.
Richardson, Brian & Margot
Richardson, Mr & Mrs D.
Richardson, G. James
Richardson, S.I.
Ricketts, Betty
Ridge, Dr R.B.L.
Ridgewell, Mr W.L.C.
Robbins, Dr R.M., C.B.E., F.S.A.
Roberts, Mr P.H.
Roberts, Ronald D.

Robinson, Mr A.L.
Robinson, Audrey
Robinson, Miss J.O.
Robinson, Sid
Rolfe, Eric
Rolph, Fred
Rondeau, Stanley
Rooke, P.E.
Rowley, Mrs Joy
Rubenstein, Dr I.D.
Rudall, Rev M.E.
Rudland, Mrs Joan M.
Ruskin, Douglas
Rye, Mrs H.E.
Rye, Mr Michael J.
Sanders, Mr & Mrs C.C.
Sargent, A.E.
Sargent, Irene
Saunders, S.C.
Say, P.I.
Scarles, Thomas A.
Schofield, Miss Kathleen M.
Seaborne, Mrs F.D.
Seaman, Mr A.J.
Searle, Mr & Mrs P.
Sedgwick, Mrs Dilys
Seeley, Mr & Mrs R.H.
Seeley, Mr & Mrs V.F.
Sellers, Mrs Marion
Sellick, Olive
Sewell, Miss C.A.
Sewell-Alger, Mr P.A.
Sharkey, Justine
Sharman, Betty
Sheppard, Mr A.G.
Shotter, Mrs D.
Simons, Sally, Christopher, Thomas &
  Sarah
Simpkins, Mrs Gwyneth
Singleton, R.R. & J.S.
Skilton, Alan J.
Sluter, Mr F.A.
Smale, Mrs W.
Smart, Philip J.
Smith, A.F.P. (Peter)
Smith, Betty
Smith, Donald
Smith, Hildegard and Eric
Smith, Irene & Stanley
Smith, Mr & Mrs L.J.
Smith, Mark R.P.
Smith, Martyn and Valerie
Smith, Peter B.M.
Smith, Mr & Mrs R.L.
Smith, Mr & Mrs T.G.

Soma, Mr J.
Somerville, Stephen
Soutar, Mrs B.
South, Mr & Mrs N.
Southan, Mrs I.E.
Spiegel, Margaret
Spray, Zygmunt
Stamp, Mrs Doreen
Standbrook, Stanley & Audrey
Stanford, Eric F.C.
Stapleton, Mr A.C.
Staunton, Mr Lee
Steele, Audrey
Stewart, Mr R.F.
Stones, Richard & Liz
Surtees, Mr H.K., C.Eng.
Swain, Mrs D.
Symons, Ivan P.
Tait, W.J.
Tarrant, John
Taylor, Dr A.R.
Taylor, M.P.
Taylor, Michael A.P.
Temerlies, H.&E.
Tether, Pam
Thompson, Mr & Mrs E.G.A.
Thompson, Jacky
Thompson, Mr P.A.
Thomson, I.J.
Thorn, Ted & Betty
Tibbatts, Mr & Mrs K.L.
Tillbrook, Mr & Mrs C.J.C.
Tollady, Mr C.
Toms, Alan E.J.
Tott, Anne & Trevor
Toussaint, Howard J.
Trayhorn, Mr T.G.
Trew, Mr M.A.
Triggs, Sue
Trussell, D.G.
Turnbull, P.
Tuson, Jean & John
Tuttle, Albert John
Tyler, Mr & Mrs E.T.
Tyler, John
Tyrrell, Mr T.G.
Vacher, Robert & Alison
Valentine, Graham
Vaughan, Mr A.J.
Vick, Rex D.

Vickers, Mr D.T.
Villin, Mrs Dee Roberts
Voisey, Mr Roger J.
W, A.E.
Walby, Janet
Walker, Colin
Walker, Pat & Brian
Walters, Mr G.P. & Mrs L.P.
Warren, Mr B.
Warren, Mrs D.
Waters, Mr Terence H.
Watkins, Mr & Mrs R.W.
Watson, G.W.
Watson, L.M.
Watson, Vera
Wayland, Mrs J.D.
Webb, Patrick A.
Welsh, Sylvia B.
West, Mr Peter D. B.A.(Hons).
  L.R.A.M.,F.Coll.P.
Wetherall, Emma J.
Whatmore, Mr Rhys D.
Whitaker, Mr & Mrs J.
White, Mr David J.
White, Miss J.L.
White, Mrs J.M.B.
White, Peter & Irene
Wibberley, Mrs R.A.
Williams, John
Williams, Dr Molly T.
Williamson, Dr J.
Wilson, Alan G.
Wilson, Mr Frank
Wing, Cecilia
Wolfson, Leslie
Wolton, Joan & John
Wood, Gladys E.
Woodfield, Mr & Mrs W.T.
Woodroffe, Mr & Mrs S.E.
Woods, Brian & Gillian
Woods, H.G.
Woollett, Mr P.F.
Woolgar, Mrs Gwen
Woolveridge, H.T.
Worrall, Mr Edw S.
Wright, Miss Jean Annastasia
Wright, Mr & Mrs John H.
Wright, Mr & Mrs Lionel
Wright, Peter S.
Young, Mr M.R.

Index to Volume Two

Abbey Road 142
Abbiss, James 283, 303, 311
Abernethy, Dr John 88
Abingdon House 71
Acacia Road 33, 35, 53
Adams, Miss 304
Adams, F.C. 344
Adams, J. 122
Adelaide House 287
aeroplanes 141, 341
Agar, Dr Frederick 195
Albany Hall 118
Albany Park 84
Albany Road 347
Alcazar, Edmonton 335
Alexandra Palace 178, 179
Alfrey, Revd R. 298
Alma, the 192
Alma Road, plans for houses 12, 36
houses empty 54
overcrowding 131, 214
smallpox and typhoid 195, 207
condemned houses 131, 211
children not at school 270
Baptist chapel 298
Roman Catholics 274
Salvation Army 305
waterworks 190
Alma School 274, 277, 332
exhibition 134
Amalgamated Society of Carpenters and Joiners 138
Amalgamated Society of Engineers 112, 126
ambulance service 195, 237
Andersons Yard 212
Annis, Samuel 99
anti-semitism 178
arable farming 153
Archer, Henry 99
Archway Tavern 86

Arnold, Matthew 263
Asbury, Dr Jacob V. 162
association football 275, 336-337
Atkins, John 270

Babbage, Charles 88
Baker, Herbert 270
Baker, J.W.T. 152
Baker Street 12, 59, 88, 92, 185, 203
chapel 88, 284
infant school 260, 263, 270
Ball, Alan 101
Bampfield, Father George 298
Band of Hope 303
bands 328-329
see also Enfield Brass Band
Foresters Brass Band Volunteers
Ponders End Brass Band
bandstands
Durants Park 329
Chase Green 329
Bank Holidays Act 1871 323
Banks, C. 153
Banks, Lewis 296
banks 43
Bannerman, Sir Henry C. 118, 121
Baptist chapels 149, 296, 298
Barclay's Bank 228
Barker, William Nutter 201, 210, 295, 296
Barn Cottages 194
Barnard and Co. 143
Barnes, George 131
The Barracks, Clay Hill 211, 212, 327
Barrass, Henry 120, 121, 122, 124, 275, 346

Barratt's sweet factory 137
Barton, Rebecca 100
Bartlett's agency 79
basket factory, Enfield Lock 152
Batters, George 296
Baxters Yard 194
Bayfield, A. 342
Bayliss, John 97
Beaconsfield Road 57
Bean of South Square 101
Beardmore, Nathaniel 196
Bearman of Ponders End 99
Beauchamp House 88
Beavan, Silas 278
Beech Hill Park 28, 29
Bell 303
Bell Lane 114
Bell Road 12, 92
Benjafield, Dr William, B. 170
Bennett, John 149
Bethell, Frank 76
Betts, the baker 303
Bevan, David 47
Emma 47
Francis 47
Robert Cooper Lee 47, 188, 243, 286, 293
billeting 327
Billson, William 341
Birkbeck estate 33, 53
Birkbeck Freehold Land Soc. 33
Birkbeck Laundry 146
Birkbeck Road 33, 35, 53
birth control 223
birth rate 223, 239
Biscoe, James 29, 172
Bitterlich, C. 221
Blackford, Reuben 182
Blinko, Thomas 153
blood drying works 142
Blythe, Ann 259
Boddam, Rawson Hart 52

Boer War 122, 123
Bollaerts, Revd Charles W. 283
Bonnetts Yard 171
bookmakers 177
Boreham F. 300
Bosanquet, B.J.T. 336
Bosanquet, Captain (see Admiral Charles Bosanquet)
Bosanquet, Admiral Charles 290, 291, 292, 293
Bosanquet, James W. 266, 285, 290, 295, 303
Bostock and Wombwell's menagerie 318
Boswell, C.J. 15, 327
Botany Bay 234
Boultwood, Joseph 15
boundary ditch 187
Bowles, E.A. 51
Bowles, Henry, C.B.B. 50
  evangelical 293
  Conservative Party 344
Bowles, Sir Henry F. 50, 51, 295, 306
  RSAF 120, 121, 122, 124
  meals poor children 178
  Town Preservation Assn 228
  technical education 258, 259
  National Service League 332
  local house of commons 345
  parliamentary elections 346, 347
  Public Welfare Assn 348
bowls 341
Bowyer, Alfred 63, 81, 279
boxing 337
Boyd, Dr Catherine 281
Brace, George 249, 250
Bradford, Rosa 196
Brading, Thomas 246
Brailsford, Richard 13, 246
Branch, James 124, 347
bread club 172
Brecon House 87
brickmaking 20, 52, 154-155
Bridgenhall estate 26, 212
Bridport Hall 169
Brigadier Hill Mission 302

Brigadier House 33, 36, 52, 296
Briggs, J. 345
Brimsdown power station 69, 143
Brimsdown railway station 9
Britain, W. 141
British Land Co. 16, 37
British and Foreign School Soc. 259-260
British School, Chase Side 172, 260, 265, 267, 270, 273, 277, 311
The British Workman 303, 304
Broadlands 38
Broadwalk 79
Broadway, Winchmore Hill 78
Bronsgiest, Father 299
Brooks, J. 33
Broome, E.R. 253
Broomham, Henry 99
Brown, Charles 155
Brown, Revd R. Howel 279, 332
Browne, Dr C.H. 128, 170
Browning Road 35, 52
Brush Electrical Engineering Co. 71
Buckskin Hall see Dacre Lodge
Bugbird, Frederick 201
builders 13, 14
building societies 13
building trades strike 1914 139, 140
Bull, W.H. 345, 346
Burchall, John 120
Burial Board 198
Burleigh House 86
Burleigh Road 53
Burlington Road 35, 36
Burman and Sons 15
Burn, Colonel 109
Burns, Dr Foster 169
Bury Hall 78
buses, motor 51, 71
  horse 5, 7
Bush Hill 67
Bush Hill House 78
Bush Hill Park, the area 76-78, 173, 268
  the mansion 15

Bush Hill Park Club 76
Bush Hill Park Company 20
Bush Hill Park estate 12, 15-22, 76, 129
Bush Hill Park Farm 150
Bush Hill Park Golf Club 74
Bush Hill Park School 268, 273, 275, 278
Bush Hill Park station 5, 77
Busk, Edward 292, 293
Butterfield, William 26
By, Captain John 104
Bycullah Athenaeum 316, 317
  built 1883 28
  exhibition 1885 311, 313
  Bycullah Athenaeum Co 316
  cinematograph 333
Bycullah estate 12, 22, 24, 343
Bycullah Park 22, 342
by-laws 11
Byng, George H.C. 344

Camlet Way 235
Canning, Mrs Gordon 55
Canonbury Road 92
Canton Road 12, 34, 53
Capel Manor 51, 52
Cardigan estate 77
Carey, William 35
Carpenters and Joiners, Amalgamated Society of 138
Carrington of Goat Lane 98
Case, Charles 5
casual ward 179
Catisfield Road 57
cattle fair 153
Cave, Henry 284, 321
Cecil Avenue 53, 55
Cecil Road 42
Cedars estate 12, 33, 36, 52, 212
cemeteries, Lavender Hill 198, 302
  St James 198
cesspits 209, 223
Challis, Alderman Thomas 261

Challis, William 88
Chambers, Charles 243-248
Chambers, Edith and Louisa 257
Chandler, Arabella 54
chapel of rest see mortuary, fire station
Chaplin's nursery 151
Charity Commissioners 245, 246, 247, 248
Charles Buildings 194
Charles Street 77
Chase Court Gardens 69
Chase Farm Schools 164-168
band 258, 306
Chase Gardens see New River Gardens
Chase Green, GNR extension 63
preachings on 300
late 19th century 327
Chase Green Avenue 24, 63, 65
Chase Hill House 286
Chase Lodge 63, 201
Chase Park 63, 67, 153
Chase Side 12, 30
Chase Side chapel 284
Chase Side House 41, 42, 83, 230, 322
Chase Side School 166, 260, 277
Chaseville Park 214
Cheshunt College 284
Chesterfield Road 57
Chesterfield School 124, 274, 275, 337
Chevalier, Albert 332
Chine, The 68
'Chirgwin' 317
cholera 184, 192
Christ Church, Chase Side 300, 302
Christ Church, Cockfosters 47
Church, Jabez 128, 129
church rates 285, 296
Church Street, changes c.1900 40, 84
changes c.1912 86
paving and kerbing 203
Church Walk 40
Churchbury Farm 149

churchyards, St Andrew's 38, 197, 198
St James 198
Chase Side chapel 198
see also cemeteries
cinema 332-335
circus 318
Citizen's League 278
Clarke, Capt D.R. 132, 195
Clarke, Elizabeth 132
Clarke, F. 33
Clarke, T.C. 133
Clay, Sir Arthur 230
Claysmore 52, 258, 285, 290, 294, 336
Claysmore School 258
Clockhouse see Bush Hill Park
Clutten, Edith 254
coaches, horse 2
coal club 172
coal tickets 175
Cocker Lane see Browning Road
Cockfosters 47, 235
Cockfosters Road 341
Cole, Alfred 59
Cole, E.G. 170
College Road 54
Collins, Sir William J. 170
Congregational churches Ponders End 92, 299
infant school, Ponders End 259
Connop, Richard 293
Connop estates 37, 38
Connop Road 81
Conservative Assn and Party 344, 345
Conservative clubs 120, 345
Conservative Land Soc. 12
Constitutional clubs 40, 83, 347
Conyard of South Street 102
Conyard, David 100
Cook, Reuben 153
Coombes of Scotland Green 102
Coope, Octavius 344
Coote, Charles 340
Copeman, Dr S. Monkton 222

Cornish, William D. 155
coronation, Edward V11 327
Cortecine factory 133, 143
Cosmos 145
Cottage Hospital 198, 326
Cotton, Revd A.F. 132, 173, 174, 269, 270
Cotwells 71
council offices 42, 227, 228
Countess of Huntingdon's Connection 285
Court House, Windmill Hill 83
Cowden Clark schoolhouse 42
Crabb, John 35
Cracknell, John and Thomas 149
Crampin, the usher 244
Cranes Alley 103
crape 97, 98
Crape Factory see Grout, Baylis & Co.
Creake, Edward 34
creosote treatment 144
Cresswell, Dr Daniel 285
cricket 336
Croft, E. 140
Croft, Sarah 132
Crompton, R.E. and Co. 118
Crown and Horseshoes 341
Crown Brickworks 155
Crusha, Edward H. 169
cucumbers 151
Cuffley, A.T. 255
Cuffley 66, 323
Cumming, John 47
Cunard, Sir Samuel 78
Currie, Isaac 78
Cutaneous Institute 162
cycling 340

Dacre Lodge 51
dairy farming 153
Dalziell, 'Professor' 317
Davis, James 270
deaf children 278
Dean, W. 86
Dean and Pullen 219
Dearsley, Charles B. 155
death rates 207, 219, 221, 222, 223

dentists 30
Devine, Alexander 123, 258
Dick, Kerr & Co. 71
Dickens, Alfred 190, 191
Dillon, Mrs 255
Dillon, Thomas 255
diphtheria 221, 222, 237
disability benefit 182
Dixon, Col. Manly 112, 116, 260
domestic servants 79-80
Door, James 321
Dowty, Inspector John 305
Drage, H.J. 142
Drake, George and John 155
Drapers pond 92
Drapers Road 53
drill hall 331
drinking fountain 39, 42, 305
Drummond 290
drunkenness 303
Duck Lees Lane 132
Duke of Abercorn 226
Duke of Lancaster, Coffee Tavern 175, 304, 345
Dukes, Alfred and George 270
Dunraven 276
Durants Arbour nursery 147
Durants Nursery 147
Durants Park 84
Dyer, Major Henry C. 114
Dyke's Animated Pictures 333

Eagle House, Ponders End 92
Eagles, Edwin M. 253
East London Water Co. 233
East London waterworks cut 187, 191, 193
East View estate 69
Easter, John 144
Eastfield Road 12, 207
Eastfield School 255, 280
Ebben, William 174
Eden, Morton P. 201
Edenbridge Road 15
Edison, Thomas 133
Edison and Swan 133-137, 138, 143

Ediswan Institute see Technical Institute
Edmonton Empire 318
Edmonton fair 321
Edmonton Local Board of Health 191
Edmonton parish workhouse 160
Edmonton School Board 273
Edmonton Union 160, 171
   workhouse 160, 171, 305
   infirmary 139, 169-171, 215
   Enfield House see workhouse Chase Side
   see also Chase Farm Schools, North Middlesex Hospital, casual ward
Education Act 1870 263, 273
Education Act 1876 266
Education Act 1880 266
Education Act 1902 278
Education Act 1907 280
   See also Free Education Act 1891
education, elementary 259-281
   secondary 243-255
   technical 258-259
   see also under names of schools
Eeles's forge 318
elections, parliamentary 120, 344, 345, 346, 347
elections, local
   1881 345
   1882 210
   1883 215
   1885 220
   1894 231
electric lighting 130
Electrical Trades Union 138
electricity supply 59
   see also Brimsdown power station
Eley's Angel Road 139
Elliott, South Square 100
Ellis, James and William 100

Elm House, Gentleman's Row 192, 255
The Elms, Ponders End 134, 201
Elmscott 67
Ely, Albert 250
Emery, James 243
emigration 112, 164, 166, 179
Empire day 281, 347
Empire, Enfield 333, 335
employment exchanges 174, 177, 179, 181
Endowed Schools Commission 249
Enfield, Lord see Byng
Enfield Bonfire Boys 322
Enfield Camera Club 28
Enfield Chase Stag Hunt 343
Enfield Chase Works 142
Enfield Chemical Manure Co. 193
Enfield Church Schools Committee 270
Enfield Coffee Tavern Co. 303
Enfield County School 253, 255
Enfield Court, the Riding House 316, 344
Enfield Distressed Children's Fund 175, 181
Enfield Fair 318
Enfield Football Club 336
Enfield Gas Co. 128-130, 137, 139
Enfield Gazette see Enfield Observer
Enfield Grammar School 243-253, 255
Enfield Highway 190, 191
Enfield Highway Conservative Working Men's Club 118
Enfield Highway Co-operative Society 114, 115
Enfield Independent Building Society 13
Enfield Literary and Mutual Improvement Inst. 311
Enfield Loan Blanket Soc. 172

Enfield Local Board of
Health 184, 187, 201,
231
Enfield Lock Co-operative
Assn 114, 115
Enfield Lock Rifles see
Volunteers
Enfield Lying-in Charity
172
Enfield Magazine 311
Enfield Martini rifle 118,
119
Enfield New Town 16, 196
Enfield Observer 218,
221, 310, 311
Enfield parliamentary
division 345, 346, 347,
348
Enfield Parochial Chari-
ties 40
Enfield Permanent
Building Society 13
Enfield Permanent Relief
Council 179
Enfield Philanthropic
Inst. 171, 172
Enfield Public Welfare
Assn 348
Enfield Relief Council
178, 179, 181
Enfield Rifle 110
Enfield Rifle Club 123,
331
Enfield Savings Bank 43
Enfield School Board 166,
273-278
Enfield School Sports
Assn. 275
Enfield Silver Prize Band
329
Enfield Spade Husbandry
Soc. 161
Enfield Star Minstrels 304
Enfield Town brass band
317, 322, 328
Enfield Town Christian
Mission 306
Enfield Urban District
Council 185, 231
Enfield vestry 159, 160
England, of Raleigh's
Cottage 293
enteric fever see typhoid
enteritis 239
Estates Trust Ltd 77

evangelical deaconesses
198
Evans yard 194
Everett, Bert 176
excursions 323
exemption certificates
279-280

Factory Acts 138
Fagan, Maria 132
Fairbairns, W.H. 346
Fairhead, Allen 13, 17,
226
Farr, R.L. 28
Field, W.F. 71, 278
Fielding, Thomas 284
Fifth Avenue 12, 54, 77
Fincher of West Street 176
fire brigades, Town 133,
200, 223, 224, 226, 234
Ponders End 197, 224-
226
fire engines manual 323,
201, 226
steamer 322, 226
fire stations, Ponders End
313
churchyard 201, 226
Pepper's yard 226
Southbury Road 226
Fish's Field 88
Fitch, Frederick G. 272
Fleming, Prof. Ambrose 134
Flexible Metallic Tube
Co. 143
Folkestone, Viscount, ie
William Pleydell-
Bouverie 118, 119, 345,
346
Forbes, Sgt Instructor 331
Forbes, Nina 313
Ford, Edward 49, 63, 245,
246, 250, 260, 286, 292,
293, 295, 321
Ford, Elizabeth H.W. 250
Ford, John Walker 49, 63,
67, 69, 76, 83, 210, 306
Fords Grove estate 79
Fords Grove nursery 150
Foresters brass band 322,
328, 329
Fortescue Lodge 192
Fortescue Villas, Gentle-
man's Row 166, 192, 257
Forty Hall 50, 51

Forty Hill 185
Fotheringham Rev. D. 164
Fotheringham Road 53
Fowell, James 209, 210,
211, 212, 214, 217
Fowler, Martha 169
Fox, Edward 291, 295
Fox beerhouse, The 194
Fox Hall 88
franchise 201, 343
Fraser, James, John and
Joseph 101
Fraser, Jonathan 101
Free and Popular Educa-
tion League 272
Free Education Act 1891
271
free meals 181, 182
Freeman, Emma 101
Freeman, Revd Stephen 88
French, Sir John 52, 331
friendly societies 112
Fuller House 57

Gale and Plummer 142
Gammon, Walter 179
Gardener, Frank L. 49
Gardner and Nordenfeldt
machine gun 118
Garner, James 153
Garrard's day school 257
Garrard J. 15, 28
gas showroom 131
Gas Workers …Union
130, 138
gas works 128, 129, 143
general elections, see
elections, parliamentary
General Labourers Union
138
Gentleman's Row 83
George V reservoir 233
The George 42, 303
George Spicer School 280
Gibbons, E.S. 306
Gibbons, Ebenezer
(b.1796) 148
Gibbons, Ebenezer
(d.1911) 148, 149, 194,
209, 210, 214, 216, 218,
221, 272, 287, 302
Gilbert Road 12
Gilbert Terrace 207
Gilbert's, Enfield Highway
140

Gilsenan, Daniel 215, 217
Girls' School of Industry,
  C of E 259, 265
Gladstone, Herbert 344
glasshouse industry 95,
  146-152
Glebe Avenue 13, 221,
  256
glebe lands 26
Glover, William 2, 5
Goat, The, Ponders End
  92
Goat Lane well 213
Gobions 15
golf 343
Gordon estate 5, 30, 53
Gordon House 30, 92
Gordon Lane school see
  St Andrew's School,
  Gordon Lane
Gordon Lodge 255
Gordon Road 12, 15, 30,
  53, 209
Gore, Anne, Hannah and
  John 15
Gorst, Sir John 252
Gothic Hall 88, 255
Gough of Scotland Green
  102
Gough Park 88
governesses 29
Government Row 106
Graham, Sidney 140
gramophones 332
Grange Drive see Green
  Dragon Lane
Grange Park estate 67-69
Grange Park station 66,
  67
Grangeway 68
Graphotone printing 142
Gray, C.W. 143
Green, William 270
Green Dragon, The 78
Green Dragon Lane 67,
  68
Green Lanes 78
Green Street 185, 214
Greenwood Farm 28
Grey, Winifred 333
Greyhound, The, Market
  Place 42, 227
Greyhound, The, Ord-
  nance Road 121
Griffin, Police Sgt 305

Groom, James 145
Grout, Baylis and Co 94,
  95-104, 143
Grout, George and Joseph
  97
Grout's shop 42, 43, 86
Grove Road 178, 195
Grovelands Park 79
Guardians, Board of, see
  Edmonton Union
Guiver family 147
Gundry, William 234
gypsies 143

Hadley Green 185
Hadley Road pumping
  station 233
Hadley Wood 28, 235
Hadley Wood station 28
Halcyon House 311
Halifax Road 12, 30
Hall, Ellis 201
Halliwick see Bush Hill
  House
Halsey, George 142
Hamilton, Lord George
  113, 198, 344
Hammerson of South
  Square 101
Hannaford, Frederick 144
Hardman, H.S. 53
Hardman, Henry 100
Hardie, Kier 121
Harman, Edward 258, 285
Harman, Revd John 263
Harman Road 77
Harrison, C. Frederick
  313
Harrison, Daniel 187, 243,
  245, 246, 286, 288, 292
Harrison, James F. 193, 194
Hart, Betsey 101
Hart, Susan 98
Hart, William 51, 169
Hawkins, George 112
Hawthorne Road 33
Head, Insp. George 226
health insurance 182
Heath, Revd John M. and
  the Local Board 188
  and the Grammar
  School 243-248
  and the High Church
  controversy 285-294
Heene Road 54

Hertford Road 56, 57, 216
Hickford, Edward 252
High Street 71, 92
Highgate, smallpox
  hospital 215
Highlands Hospital 214
Hill, John Cathles 154
Hill Lodge, Clay Hill 202
Hill School, Baker Street
  255
Hilly Fields Park 84
The Hirondelle 316
Hitzell, Harry 270
Hodson, Prebendary
  George 169, 264, 265,
  294, 295, 302
  and the schools 166,
  264-279 *passim*
Hollingberry, G. 318
Holloway Empire 318
Holly Bush, The 303
Holly Bush School, The,
  see St Michael's School
Holly Hill Farm 343
Holmes Alley 103
Holmwood 88
Holtwhites Hill 63
Home Farm 153
hooliganism 305, 306
Hop Poles, The 86, 303
Hope House, Winchmore
  Hill Road 160
Hoppers Road 79
horticultural society 311
'house of commons' local
  345
  housing, see chapters I
  and II, 185
Housing League 54
Howard, George 35
Howat, J.B. 299
Hubbard, William 321
Hubbards pond 91
Hubbuck, George P. 100
Hunt, C.H. 275
Hunt, J.G. 278
Huntingdon, William 302
Hutchins, William 153

ILMH rifle 120
Imperial Lamp Works see
  Cosmos
incinerator 235
Independent chapels
  Highway 284

Ponders End 285
Sunday school 98
see also Chase Side
chapel and Zion
chapel
Independent Labour
Party 347
industrial disputes 137-
140, 146
infant mortality 238, 239
infectious diseases see
typhoid, typhus, scarlet
fever etc.
Ingersoll, R.T. 201
inspector of nuisances 3,
211
Ironside, Henry 148
Ironside, William 190,
192, 193
isolation hospital 139,
195, 209, 213, 214, 222,
235
Ivy House, Chase Side 86

Jack, Charles 28, 29
Jackson, Arthur 35
Jacobsen, C.H. 15, 53
James Street 77
Jammet's farm 12
Jasper Close 112
Jebb, Sir Richard 47
Jeffery, Walter J. 252
Jenkins, H.M. 311
Jesus Church 283
Jiggins of West Street 176
John Morley Club 119
John Street 77
Jones, George W. 270
jubilees 1887 325, 326,
327
1897 327
Judd, Caroline 103
Jute Works 95, 131-133,
201
Jute factory school 265,
267, 268, 269, 270

Kauffman, Solomon 272
Kelvin, Lord see
Thompson, William
Kemp, Alfred and Mary
M. 302
Kemp, Joseph 302
Kempe, Revd E.W. 174,
278

Kempster, John 345, 346
Kimberley Road 55
King, J. 35
King and Tinker 306
Kingdom Hall 141, 263
King's Head, The, Market
Place 40, 41, 176, 288,
303
King's Head, The,
Winchmore Hill 78
Kirk, Mary 101
Kitching, A.G. 271
Kitteringham, William 7,
202, 209, 212, 218, 220,
223
Knight, Ernest 252
Knight, Thomas 246
Knox Soutar, Dr 53
Kynaston Road 53

La Barte, Revd 291
Labour Party 306, 348
Labour Protection League
137
labour yard see stoneyard
Lady Huntingdon's
chapel 285, 299
but see also Chase Side
chapel
Ladysmith Road 55, 143
Lamb, Charles 309
Lancaster Hall see Duke
of Lancaster Coffee
Tavern
Lancaster Road 35
land companies 12, 13
Landseer Road 55
Langford of South Street
102
Langford Place, South
Street 102
Larsen, H. 151
Larsen, M. and
Douthwaite 152
Laseron, Dr Michael 198
Latham, M. 173
Latymer School 253, 255
Laurel Bank estate 13
Laurence, G.E.T. 275, 277
Lavender Hill 64
Lavender Road 33, 53
Lavender School 255, 280
Law, J.S. 303
Lawrence, Sir John 260
Lea Valley Road 3

Lecture Hall, Chase Side
271, 311
Lee Enfield Modified rifle
124
Lee Enfield rifle 122
Lee House see Gothic
Hall
Lee Metford rifle 121, 123
Lee Navigation 94
Letchworth, Sir Edward
228
Lewis, H.T., surveyor 202,
212
Lewis, Sir Duncan Orr 49
Sir Frederick Orr 49,
306
Lewis, H.T. 195
Lewis machine gun 126
Liberal Club 125
Liberal Party 344
Library Green 42, 230,
316
Lieden, Annie 132
Lincoln House 200
Lincoln Road
Recreation ground 84
isolation hospital 222
Linscott, A. 335
Linzell, Henry 34
Little Park (council
offices) 42, 227, 228
Littler, Sir Ralph 118
Lloyd, Revd F.C. 173
Lloyd's Bank 43
Local Government Board
216, 219
Lock, William 81
lock-up, Enfield Highway
57
Lodge, The, High Street
71
lodging houses 194, 195
Logsden, coach builder
195
Logsden's yard, chapel
302
London and Provincial
Bank 43, 228
London Bioscope Co. 333
London Brick Co. 155
London Cocoa-nut Fibre
Co. 142
London Jute Works Co. 131
London Road 12, 17, 20,
38, 59, 72, 73

Lovell, George 106-109
Loves Row 54, 185, 192
  meeting house and
  school 263
Low, Stuart Henry 148
Lucas of South Square 100
Lushington, Sir Henry 47

McAlpine, contractor 66
Macdonald, Mary 132
Macdonald, William 249
McGee, manager RSAF
  122
Mackmurdo, Arthur 311
MacLagan, Revd William D.
  38, 249, 266, 294, 295
McSorley, Revd Hugh 305
Macy, Revd V. Travers 84,
  177, 296
Mafeking 122
Mandeville Crescent 55
Mandeville Road 12, 37,
  55, 114, 203
Mann, Tom 121
Manning, Thomas 181
manor court 40, 327
Manor House, Bulls Cross
  52, 331
Manor House, Chase Side
  53, 92
Manor House, Church
  Street 39, 40, 45, 83
  see also Palace School
Manor House estate 92
Manor Road 92, 181
Margetsons pond 87, 92
market 1840-1870 38
  1893-1895 40
market cross 38, 42, 327
market gardens see
  glasshouse industry
market house 42, 327
Market Place 38, 153
Marryat, Capt Frederick 88
Marshall, Ebenezer 148,
  174, 212, 213, 214, 215,
  216, 218, 219
Martini Henry rifle 112,
  115, 116, 119
Matthews, Amos 152, 147
Matthews C. 329
Matthews, J.H. 119, 121,
  124, 126, 275, 279, 346,
  348
Matthews, Joseph 147

Mauser rifle 123
May Day 321, 322
Maypole Dairy 154
Mead, William Smith 290
Mead's Cottages 214
measles 162, 235
mechanics institutes,
  Ponders End 284, 311
  RSAF 313
Medcalf, Sydney 52
Medcalf Road 36
medical officer of health
  195, 207, 211
Meeting House Yard 88,
  185, 207, 211
Mellish, Joseph 15
Mellish, William (m. Ann
  Gore 1762) 15
  William (d. 1838) 15
Merchant and Elston 150
Merton Road 35
Metherell, Richard and
  W.R. 66, 67, 69
Metivier, Edgar E. 168,
  170, 182
Methodist churches see
  Wesleyan Methodist
Metropolitan Electric
  Tramways Co. 69, 76
Metropolitan Freehold
  Land Co. 13
Metropolitan Police 45
Metropolitan Turnpike
  Roads 2
Metropolitan Water
  Board 233
Meux, Sir Hedworth 51
Meux, Lady Valerie 49, 51
Meyer family 230
Meyer, James d. 1894 50
  death 231
  and the Local Board
    187, 188, 193, 210,
    215, 217, 218
  portrait 230
  and the Grammar
    School 243, 245
  and John Moore Heath
    286, 287, 293, 295
  and W.D. MacLagan
    294, 295
  and George Hodson
    295
  Conservative Party 344
Meyer, Paul C. 283

Meyers, James H. 311
Meyers, Milton 200
Meyers's subscription
  library 311
Middlesex County
  Council 71
  secondary education
    252, 253
  technical education 258
Middlesex Parliamentary
  Constituency 343
Middlesex Regt 328
Middleton, H.W. 153
Miles and Fortescue 142
Mill Corner, Hadley 195
Mill Marsh bridge 57
mill, Ponders End see
  Ponders End mill
Millar, Dr John 187
Millfield House 47
Milner Sons and White 79
miners' strike 1912 139
Mitchell, Bernard and
  William 155
Mitchell family, market
  gardeners 147
Mitchell, John and
  William 201
Mitchell, W. 38
Moggs, William 145
Monk, A.E. 55
Monro, Mordaunt M. 214,
  303
Moorat, John 20, 298
Morley, Robert 345
Morley Hill 33
Morrison, R.C. 160
Morson, T.D., chemical
  manufacturer 144
Mort, Dr Spencer 170
mortuary 226
motor transport 151, 341
motoring 340, 341
Mountjoy Cycle Works
  140
Moxam, J. 122
Murray committee 126
music halls 317, 318
Myddelton House 51, 327
Myrtle Grove 33

Nags Head, The 42, 303
Nags Head Lane see
  Southbury Road
Napier Road 36, 270

National Freehold Land
Soc. 16
National Schools
Bush Hill Park 268
Cecil Road 266, 270,
272
Forty Hill 263
London Road 261
Trent 263
see also St Andrew's, St
George's etc
National Service League
332
National Society 259-260
National Union of
Gasworkers 130
navvies 63, 66
Navvies, Bricklayers,
Labourers and General
Labourers Union 138
navvy mission 63
Negus, T. 344
Neilson, James 52, 81
Nepean, E.C. 303
New Lane see Lancaster
Road
New Lane estate 35
New Picturedrome 334
New River 187
New River bridge, Church
Street 39, 86
New River Co. 12, 190,
232, 233
New River, Enfield loop
204
New River Gardens 327
New Town estate
see Enfield New Town
Newman, Edward 154
Newman, J. Pretyman 332,
347
Newman, William 154
Nicholls, Betsey 98
Nickolds Bros 332
Nightingale Hall Farm
147, 151, 193, 234
nitrogen factory 145
North Lodge Farm 153
North London Estates Co.
20, 30, 155
North Metropolitan
Power Co. 69, 143
North Middlesex High
School for Girls 257
Northampton Road 270

Northcourt 71
Northern Hospital see
Highlands
Notts Farm 153
nurse children 239
Nursery and Market
Garden Development
Society 152
nursery industry see
glasshouse industry
Nye, Richard 33, 153, 346

Oakhurst Road 55
Oakman, David 302
Oatlands Nursery 150
old age pensions 181
Old Coffee House 252,
259
'Old Curiosity Shop' 226
Old Nursery 147
Old Park 49, 50, 63, 69
Old Park estate 26
Old Park farm see
Swannell's farm
Old Park Grange see
Pikes Farm
Old Park Ridings 67, 68,
69
Old Road 38, 190, 191,
194
Oldbury 53
Olley, Albert 140, 340
omnibus, motor see buses
motor
Operative Bricklayers 138
Orchard brickfield 155
Orchard estate, Lancaster
Road 277
Ordnance Road 12
Orme, Henry and
Thomas 99, 100
out-door relief 176-7

P.S.A. 176, 178, 332
'Palace', The, see Manor
House, Church Street
Palace Gardens 40
Palace Parade 40, 83
Palace School 39
Pankhurst, Christabel 347
Paris, Thomas 28
Parish, Michael 290
Park Avenue 72, 76
Park Farm 84
Park Terrace 77

Parker, Henry E. 161, 164
Parkside Farm 154
Parry, H. 201
Parsonage Lane 87, 185
Parson's Nursery 152
Parson's report 204
Pascoe, Josiah 197
Patman, the builder 12,
50, 86, 226
Pattensweir 88
paving and kerbing 221
Pearson's Bros 81
penny bank 172
penny readings 311
Peploe, Charles 178
Pepper, Alfred 29
Pepper, Joseph 223, 226
percussion musket 107
Percy House 84, 257
Perry, Amos 151
Perry, Charles 152
Pest House 99, 321
Pestalozzi, George John
28
Peters, James 102
petty sessions 45, 83
Pharoah, Mrs 102
philharmonic societies 311
Phillips, J. 153
photographers 28
pianos 332
pigs 194
Pike, George, the
turncock 226
Pike, R.F. 215, 216
Pike's Farm 67, 68
Pinckney, D.G. 28
Pinnocks pond 92
Pipers Yard see the
Barracks
The Plough, Hertford
Road 219
Plume, Charles 128
plural voting 345
police courts 46
police stations 45, 46
Ponders End 192, 178,
219, 311
Ponders End Brass Band
132
Ponders End Conservative
Working Men's Club
346
Ponders End Electric
Theatre 335

Ponders End Gas Co 128
Ponders End mill 36, 57, 143
Ponsbourne tunnel 67
population 185
Portcullis Lodge 303
post offices 43, 71, 84, 92
Potter, Archdeacon 84
Powys, Henry P. 160
Poynettes Farm 252
Poyser, Eliza and Mary 102
Prickett, G. 152
Primitive Methodists 200, 300
Primrose Avenue 33, 53
  see also Canton Road
prize fighting 337, 340
Protestant Assn 289, 290
Protestant church, Flash Lane 283
Protestant school, Flash Lane 263, 265, 290
Providence Chapel, Winchmore Hill 302
provision tickets 175
public baths 342
public conveniences 40
public libraries 313
pupil teacher centre 254
Purdey, John 174
Pursel of South Square 100
Putney Lodge estate 37
Putney Road 12, 37, 55, 203, 298
Pyne, Miss L. 316

Quakers Walk waterworks 20
Queen Annes Gardens 76
Queen Annes Grove 76
Queen Annes Place 76
Queens Hall 335
quoits 318

Radical Liberal clubs 276, 344
ragged school 171
Railway Hotel, the 317
railway excursions see excursions
railway lines Lea Valley 4, 9, 94
  Angel Road to Enfield 4, 5

Liverpool Street to Enfield 5, 21, 22, 76, 77
  Wood Green to Enfield 5, 6, 7
  Cheshunt loop 7, 9, 11, 71
  Enfield to Stevenage 63-67
Rainer, James F. 155
Raleigh Road 16, 17
Raleigh's Cottage 33, 300
Ranger, William 185
Raphael, Lewis 16, 20
Ratepayers Assn 209, 210, 212, 215, 220, 221, 345
rates 1881 210
  1884 217
  1898/9 176
Rawlins, Benjamin, Fred and Harry 270
Rayment, Lydia 102
Raynton Road 12, 203
Rectory 88
Rectory Farm 153
Red Ridge estate 72
Redburn, Thomas 71
Redistribution of Seats Act 1885 345
Redlingtons, Silver Street 227
Reform Acts 1832 343
  1867 343
refuse disposal 193, 209, 223, 235
religious census 1851 283
religious census 1903 306
Rendlesham viaduct 65
Reorganised Church of Jesus Christ 302, 303
Representation of the People Act 1884 345
reservoirs, Holtwhites Hill 190
  Southbury Road 197
  George V 179, 233
Reynolds, Walter 313
Richards, J. 33
Richards, W. 272
Riddell, H.J. 22
Riddell, R.I. 343
Ridewood, Dr W.S. 249, 250, 253, 305, 306
Ridge, Dr J. J. on housing 35, 54
  biographical 53, 181,

228
  as MOH 142, 211, 213, 214, 219, 223
  on milk sterilization 237
  on a school board 273
  Citizen's League 278
  on temperance 54, 181, 303, 304
Ridge Avenue 71
Ridgeway 26
Ridgeway farm 153
Ridgeway Oaks estate 26
Ridgeway Park estate 24
The Riding House see Enfield Court
Ridler Road 92
Ridley Whitley 146
Rignall, John Riley 245, 290, 292, 293
Riley Road 12
Rising Sun, The, Church Street 296, 318
River Lee Conservancy Act 192, 193
River View 88
road signs 341
road surveyor 3
Robbins and Lawrence, Utah 109
Robinson, Benjamin and Isaac 81
Robinson, Edward 300
Rochford, John 152
Roman archaeology 53
Roman Catholic Church London Road 298-9
  Ponders End 299
  school Alma Road 274, 275, 299
  Cecil Road 278
  St George's 279
Roof Pope's house see Pest House
Rose House 255
Roselands 52
Rosemary Avenue 33, 35
Rowan, Culloden 22, 28, 164, 215, 218
Rowland, James, MP 137
Royal Chase Building Society 13, 148
Royal Enfield bicycle 142
Royal Gunpowder Factory 105, 122, 126

Royal Nurseries 148
Royal Small Arms Factory
  before 1914 94, 103-
    128, 130, 348
  trade unions 137
  apprentices 258
  church 283
  school 109, 263, 265,
    269, 273
  Volunteers 331
  public baths 342
  provident society 120
  pension scheme 137
Ruberoid 145
rugby football 336
Rummer 42
Rumney, Peter 215, 217
Russell, John F. 98, 288
Ruth Elliott Home 53

Saddlers Mill stream 187,
  190, 191
Sage, Harold 250
Sainsbury's, Church
  Street 83
St Andrew's Church
  lit by gas 245
  galleries 295
  religious census 1851
    283
  pews 286-288, 295, 296
  burials in church 197
  restoration 1866-7 294
  clock 327
  Lovell monument 294
  pulpit and lectern 294
  restoration 1908 307
St Andrew's School, Cecil
  Road 254, 270
St Andrew's School,
  Gordon Road 265, 270,
  277
St Andrew's Upper Grade
  255
St Aubyn, John P. 286,
  290
St George's Church 296
St George's R.C. School
  279
St James Church 283
St James Road 38
St James School 177, 260,
  266, 268, 269, 270, 273
St John's Church 290,
  292, 294

St John's School 263, 266
St Luke's Church 35, 296
St Luke's vicarage 177, 178
St Mark's Church 21, 178,
  296
St Mark's Institute 77
St Mary Magdalene
  Church 26
St Matthew's Church 173,
  296
St Matthew's School 177,
  260, 270
St Michael's Church 30,
  296
St Michael's Hospital see
  workhouse, Chase Side
St Michael's School 263,
  265, 266, 268, 277
St Patricks Terrace 185,
  219
St Paul's Church 86, 307
St Stephen's Church 76,
  296
Salmons brook 68
Salvation Army 304, 305
Sambrooke, Sir Jeremy 15
  Sir Jeremy V. 15
Sanders, Revd E.A.B. 178
Sanders, Thomas 155
Sandringham Motor
  Works 145
Sanger's circus 318
Sarnesfield Road 42
Sassoon, Sir Edward 47
  Sir Philip 47, 48, 49
Saunders, J.H. 55
Saville Bros 332
Sawyer, Arthur 191
Sawyer, H. 15
Sawyer, John 189, 190,
  226, 243, 245
scarlet fever 213, 214
school attendance
  committee 266
school attendance officers
  271, 279
school fees 271
school health service 280-
  281
school strike 139
Schools Canteen Fund 182
schools medical service
  280, 281
Scotland Green Road 54
Scott, John W. 169

Scott, W. Gilbee 43, 228
Scott, Walter 194
Seal, H. 151
Seamer Bros 140, 142
Seamer, R.M. 141
Searle, F. 303
Seaton's Animated
  Picture Co. 333
sewerage 1849 187, 190
  1867 192
  sewage farm 143, 193,
    194
  Parson's report 204,
    205, 207
  Copeman's report 223
  1894 234
  1906 234
  1911 235
Seymour, Isabelle 347
Shaw, Horace 139
Shepherd, John 305
Sheppard, William 302
Sheridan Theatre 342
Shirley Lodge 257
shop assistants 138
shops 85-86, 138
Shoreditch workhouse 88
Shrubbery, The 63
sickness benefit 182
signposts 341
Silver Street 84, 201, 203
Sixth Avenue 77
Sketty Road 55
Skirrow report 248
slate clubs 176
Slaughter House Lane see
  Sydney Road
Small Arms Union 126
Small Dwellings Acquisi-
  tion Co. 55
small holdings 154
smallpox 194, 195, 214,
  215, 237
Smith, Alfred 152
Smith, Charles 201
Smith, Harold 250
Smith, M. 255
Smith, Capt S.W. 89
Smith, Samuel J. 216, 284
Smith, Tayler 130
Snider breech loader 112
Social Democratic
  Federation 138, 305
Solomon, Henry N. 344
Somerset, Col. Sir Alfred

P. 33, 253, 293, 294, 306, 328, 343, 344
Somerset, Gwendoline 259
Soper's farm viaduct 65
soup kitchens 172, 173, 175, 177
South Lodge 303
South Place 192
South Square 99
South Street 12, 55, 185, 195, 203, 213
South Street chapel 300
Southbury Road 12, 42, 54, 76, 215, 216
Southbury School 139
clinic 280, 281
Southgate County School 253, 255
Southside Labour Union 137
Spark of South Square 101
Spicer, George the School Board 166, 273, 275, 276
the education committee 278, 279
PSA 332
Public Welfare Assn 348
'Spike Island' 131
Spotted Cow, The 176
Spreckley, T. 200
Springcroft estate 24, 164
Spurs see Tottenham Hotspur
Stamford Hill Green Lanes Turnpike Trust 2
Standard Freehold Land Soc. 219
Standard Road 219
Stanley Street 299
steeplechase 342, 343
Stephenson, Sir Roland M. 184, 202, 210, 214, 216, 217
Sterling Road 35
stoneyard 171, 173, 174, 181
Stotter, Charles 154
street lighting 38, 39
street names 39
street numbering 59
Stribling, John 284, 300
Stribling, John, grocer 321
Strict Baptist chapels 300

strikes 137-140
Stuart Low nursery 148
student teachers see pupil teacher centre
Sturgis, Revd F.G. 185
Suez Road 270
suffragettes and suffragists 347, 348
Summerfield Works 144
Sunday school, Ponders End 98
Sutton's warehouse 335
Swan, Joseph 133
Swan and Pike, The 106
Swannell's Farm 343
swimming 342
Sydney Road 185, 226
Sykes, H. Dugdale 42, 83, 306

Tait, Archibald C. 290, 294
Taylor Sons and Santo Crimp 232
Taylor's Cinematograph 333
Technical Institute, Ponders End 92, 134, 258
Holly Walk 259
telegraph service 43
telephone service 46, 59
temperance movement 303
tennis 341
Territorials 331, 332
theatre, Enfield Town 317
Theobalds Park 51
Thirgood, Joseph and John and Henry 147
Thompson, William, Lord Kelvin 134
Tibbs, John 192
Tindall, Rear Admiral L.S. 201
Tisdall, Col. Arthur L. 128
tomatoes 151
Toms, Revd Henry S. 6, 267, 278, 300, 344
Tottenham and District Gas Co. 86, 130
Tottenham Grammar School 253
Tottenham Hotspur 336, 337

Tottenham Local Board of Health 192
Totteridge Road 12, 37, 55, 203
chapel 278
school 265, 267
The Town, 1890s 40
paving and kerbing 203
tree planting 218, 219
town hall 226, 227, 228, 230, 316
Town Parade 84
Town Park 83, 342
Town Preservation Soc. 228
trade unionism 137-140
trades and labour council 139
trams, electric 69-76
horse 7, 9
steam 8, 9
Tree, Lady 52
tree planting 218, 219
Trenchard, Hugh 51, 314
Trent Girls and Infants School 263
Trent Park 47, 48, 49
Trinity Street 277
tuberculosis 237, 238
Tuckers field 84
Tuff, John 246, 247
Tully, J. 152
Turkey Street 56
Turkey Street station 11
turnpike gates 2
Twells, Philip 270, 295
Two Brewers, The 57
typhoid 196, 207, 209, 222
typhus 207

Uff, John 15
unemployed marches 175, 176, 179
unemployment insurance 182
United Government Workers Assn 124, 126
Uvedale House 306

Varden of South Square 100
varnish factory 144, 145
Vestry House 45, 228
Victoria Swimming Club 342

Village Road 72
Vincent, John 148
Vine, The 40
Violet Avenue 33
Voluntary Aid Detach-
   ment 332
Volunteers 122, 327, 328,
   329, 331
   bands 328, 331

Waddington, David 4,
   287, 288
Wade, Dr 144
Walker, J.H. 255
Waltham Abbey fair 321
Warlow, Lt 109
Warren, James 52, 303
Warren, Dr W.P. 238
Warwick Road 36, 214
water closets 223
water supply
   1849 187
   1856 196
   1867 193, 197
   1881-2 204, 205, 212
   1894 232
   see also Metropolitan
      Water Board
water towers
   Bush Hill Park 20
   Botany Bay 234
   Holtwhites Hill 212,
      216, 219
waterworks Alma Road
   190, 212, 232
   Bush Hill Park 20
   Bycullah Park 22
Watts, J.C. 118
Watts, Reading 190
Waverley Road 257
Webb, Joseph 270
Welch, Revd A.W. 278
Welch, William 7, 29
Weld, H.C. 327
wells 187
   Goat Lane 213
   Eagle House 232, 197
   Bycullah Park 232
   Alma Road 204, 205,
      212, 232

Hadley Road 233
Wesleyan Methodists
   Church Street 300
   Ordnance Road 300
   Ponders End 283, 300
   Sydney Road 284
   Fighting Cocks Lane
      284
West Enfield High School
   for Girls 256
Weston, David 55, 71, 76,
   125
Whitaker, Joseph and
   Cuthbert 295, 306
Whitbread, C.S. 221
White, Revd G.W. 170,
   179, 332
White, Henry 302
white lead factory,
   Ponders End 142
white lead factory,
   Brimsdown 144, 145
White Lodge 295
Whitewebbs, estate 49,
   306
   hamlet 195
   farm 49
Whitewebbs Lane 185
Whitley, J.T. 92
Widdowes, F.G. 294
Wigston, John 47
Wildwoods 290
Wilkinson, Dr Abraham
   49
Wilkinson, George 284
Wilkinson, Henry Cox 49
Williams, A.T. 178
Williams, W.E. 306
Wilsden, South Street 102
Wilson family, market
   gardeners 147, 148
Wilson, John J. 54, 215,
   231
Wimpey and Co. 74
Winchmore Hill 78-79
Winchmore Hill Green 78
Winchmore Hill Hardy
   Plant Farm 151
windmill 81, 82

Windmill Hill 26, 63, 65,
   185, 203
Wing, William 270
Winterburn, Charles and
   Joseph 148
Winterburn, William 38
Wisbeys pond 91
Witham of South Street
   103
Witham, Revd A.E. 332
women's franchise, 346,
   347
Wolverton 51
Wood, W.G. 323
Wood House, Chase Side
   86
Woodbine Grove 33
Woodfield, Alec 260, 328
Woodfield, Baker Street
   261
Woodlands 53
Woodlands estate 35, 212
Woodman, E. 328
Wood's retreat 323, 325
Woolley, Miss 257
Woolven, Edward 15
workhouse, Chase Side
   161
   privileged paupers 168
   the building 161
   the school 161-164
workhouse, Edmonton
   see Edmonton Union
workmen's trains 21, 22
workmen's train mission
   306
Worlds End Farm 222
Wrampling, A.J. 42, 176
Wright, Charles,
   almshouses 158
Wright, William 270
Wright's mill see Ponders
   End mill

Yarra House 142
Yeeda Grange 51

Zion chapel 284, 300